PEACE, WAR, AND NUMBERS

Peace, War, and Numbers

Edited by

BRUCE M. RUSSETT

 SAGE PUBLICATIONS / *Beverly Hills London*

For information address:

SAGE PUBLICATIONS, INC.
275 South Beverly Drive
Beverly Hills, California 90212

SAGE PUBLICATIONS LTD
St George's House / 44 Hatton Garden
London E C 1

Printed in the United States of America

International Standard Book Number 0-8039-0164-X

Library of Congress Catalog Card No. 72-77769

FIRST PRINTING

CONTENTS

Introduction   9
    Betty Crump Hanson and Bruce M. Russett

1. Capability Distribution, Uncertainty, and Major Power War, 1820-1965   19
    J. David Singer, Stuart Bremer, and John Stuckey

2. Status, Formal Organization, and Arms Levels as Factors Leading to the Onset of War, 1820-1964   49
    Michael D. Wallace

3. U.S. Foreign Relations: Conflict, Cooperation, and Attribute Distances   71
    R. J. Rummel

4. Cooperating to Conflict: Sources of Informal Alignments   115
    John D. Sullivan

5. American and Soviet Influence, Balance of Power, and Arab-Israeli Violence   139
    Jeffrey S. Milstein

6. War Power and the Willingness to Suffer   167
    Steven Rosen

7. Symbolic Involvement as a Correlate of Escalation: The Vietnam Case   185
    Michael P. Sullivan
    with the assistance of William Thomas

8. Internal and External Influences on Bargaining in Arms Control Negotiations: The Partial Test Ban   213
    P. Terrence Hopmann

9. In Search of Peace Systems: Scandinavia and the Netherlands,
    1870-1970   239

    Nazli Choucri
    with the collaboration of Robert C. North

10. Models for the Analysis of Foreign Conflict Behavior of States   275
    Jonathan Wilkenfeld

11. The Revolt of the Masses: Public Opinion on Military Expenditures   299
    Bruce M. Russett

    Bibliography   321
    Name Index   337
    Subject Index   343
    Contributors   351

PEACE, WAR, AND NUMBERS

BETTY CRUMP HANSON and BRUCE M. RUSSETT

Introduction

SCIENTIFIC RESEARCH ON WAR AND PEACE

Students of war are under a special injunction to "publish or perish." War is one of the most intractable human problems. The fear of war, and the threat of global cataclysm, is always with us. Perhaps many people would name some other horseman—hunger, or disease—as the most fearsome; each of us has different private fears. Others would place the quest for human dignity and equality above that for peace. But the danger of war is so great, and so immediate, that without reliable peace it hardly seems possible to pursue other goals effectively. Contemporary wars, military preparations, and continued payment of the cost of past wars amount, in the United States, to more than all public expenditure for health and education combined. True, war has been so universally part of the human condition that the prospects for understanding how to avoid it, especially under the pressures modern technology puts upon us, do not seem very good. But the need to try is certainly there.

An effort to understand such a complex problem should make use of the tools of modern social science. Science may not save us, but we are unlikely to be saved without it. And in fact a good deal of social science research on war has been accomplished in the last few years. Although, of course, far more is required, it seemed to Bruce Russett in the spring of 1969 that enough had been done to try to present a reasonable sampling at a forthcoming annual meeting of the American Political Science Association. Thus he solicited papers from a number of scholars he knew to be working on these problems. Virtually all who were approached agreed to take part in the enterprise, and another, at first overlooked, volunteered. After an exchange of drafts or outlines with the organizer, the papers were presented at the September 1970 annual meeting in Los Angeles. For the panels, Ralph Goldman, D. Bruce Marshall, and Russett served as chairmen, and William Caspary, Roy Licklider, Manus Midlarsky, and James Stegenga were discussants. The authors rewrote the papers on the basis of

Editor's Note: Preparation of this volume was significantly aided by Contract No. N0014-67-A-0097-0007 from ARPA Behavioral Sciences, monitored by the Office of Naval Research. Of course no agency is responsible for any statements of fact or opinion.

comments at the meeting and later, and with the exception of Charles McClelland all eventually submitted versions for publication. Those papers, plus one by Russett not prepared for the meeting, make up this volume.

The theme of the panels at the meeting, and hence of this volume, was to show the increasing relevance of much of the work that has been done under the rubric "peace research." The terms of reference indicated to the panelists were that all papers should: (1) Develop specific hypotheses about the causes or conduct of international violence, (2) Test those hypotheses with actual data about international behavior (hence simulations were excluded.) The emphasis on empirical work meant that mere prospectuses were ruled out. (3) Indicate the broader relevance of the findings for theory and for policy. Thus we intended to show that "peace research" had come far enough to make some—very modest to be sure—statements about actions that might diminish the probability of international violence. We shall bring together in this introduction some of the implications from that work.

This set of papers indicates the degree to which peace and conflict research is becoming a cumulative, ongoing endeavor. In every case the work included in this volume represents only a part of a substantially larger study. Every paper builds upon and extends the author's earlier analyses. The papers by Rummel and by Singer and his colleagues each draw on a major research project now almost a decade old. Most of the other papers are written by relatively junior scholars who are developing their own projects. Some sense of the cumulative character of the enterprise can be gained by examining the combined references at the end of the book; quite a number of materials are cited in three or four different papers here. In addition, many contributors use data compiled originally by other contributors, illustrating the richness of possibilities for secondary analysis of existing materials. Wilkenfeld and John Sullivan use data from Rummel's project, Sullivan also uses material from Russett's studies, and Rosen and Wallace, as well as Singer and his colleagues, use data from Singer's Correlates of War project.

The papers also share a common general perspective that, while certainly not representative of all peace and conflict research, does characterize a large portion of the field. That perspective can be identified as aggregate or macroscopic; in the majority of cases the unit of analysis is some collectivity rather than the individual. Analysis is concerned with the characteristics of nations; the differences and similarities of a pair of nations; a sub-system of the global system, defined regionally or by power capabilities; or even the entire international system.

One possible exception is the contribution by Hopmann, which contrasts the behavior of nations in two different spheres—within the negotiating arena and their interactions outside that arena—and one might contend that two different decision-making subsystems within a national government are responsible for behavior in the two different arenas. But that is not a very convincing argument, and basically the behavior can still be understood as that finally expressed by a single state as actor, however complex the bureaucratic conditions under which the behavior is decided upon. Michael Sullivan does address himself to "symbolic commitment as expressed by the President of the United States, and compares this with escalatory and de-escalatory military acts. Even there, the emphasis is upon the interrelationship of these two kinds of acts, not on the relationship between two different actors within a government. Russett is concerned with popular approval or disapproval of military expenditures, but more with general trends in the proportion of the populace sharing a particular attitude than with identifying the correlates or causes of various shades of opinion within segments of the populace. And in virtually every case the emphasis is on the context or environment in which international behavior occurs. Hopmann's paper, for instance, even though focusing to some extent on nations' negotiating behavior, relates that behavior to those nations' other actions in the entire arena of international politics.

There are, however, difficulties with a macroscopic view. Often the number of cases available for analysis is small. The pieces by Singer, Rosen, and Wallace, for example, are concerned with all international wars since 1815, but those wars actually number hardly more than 40. Choucri examines long-term changes in but four countries. Most of the interesting theories about the causes of war specify several interacting variables rather than just one causal factor. Very quickly the model becomes too complex given the small number of cases. Once a relationship is found in the data, if someone comes up with a plausible hypothesis about the effect of yet another variable it may be difficult or impossible to test that hypothesis. Both Singer and Wallace suggest that relationships in the international system of the 19th century may have been very different from those of the 20th. But one could just as easily hypothesize that relationships changed even more in the nuclear post-1945 world than they did at the turn of the century, hence the contemporary relevance of any generalizations from the pre-1945 period would be suspect. Yet there are too few cases from the post-1945 period to test such a hypothesis. One is therefore thrown back on the need for very careful hypothesis-construction, and a demand that all generalizations of this sort be scrupulously grounded in theory as well as in the empirical patterns emerging inductively from the data. With such a demand, of course, we still are not handicapped in the fashion of a traditional analyst of diplomacy trying to generalize from a microscopically detailed scrutiny of a single case. Whatever the difficulties with systematic macroscopic analysis there are powerful reasons for prefering it, under many circumstances, to the available methodological alternatives.

SOME QUESTIONS

Let us at this point summarize the various investigations and some of their interrelations. The first two papers focus upon the structural characteristics of the international system as a source of violence. Singer, Bremer, and Stuckey in their paper attempt to ascertain the relationship between the distribution of power and the incidence of war. Looking at the relevative capabilities and behavior of the major powers since 1815, they investigate the role of uncertainty about nations' relative power in promoting peace or provoking war. In doing so they contrast theories stressing the specific influences of power parity among leading nations with those that predict stable peace only where one nation or coalition is clearly preponderant over its rivals. Wallace is concerned with essentially the same time period and set of wars (although he looks at many small and middle-level powers in addition to the major ones) but looks at the distribution of national prestige or recognition as well as at the distribution of power in the system. Specifically, he asks what is the causal sequence whereby status inconsistency (that is, a major difference between a nation's rank in military power and the diplomatic recognition accorded it by other states) leads to aggressive behavior against other nations. Citing earlier findings linking status inconsistency and war, he seeks to strengthen evidence for the relationship and to discover how it operates through such other factors as alliance formation and military preparations.

Rummel links together, by ideas of attribute and behavior "distance" (the degree to which nations are alike or unlike in various cultural, political or economic characteristics and internal behavior) six sets of hypotheses into a framework called field theory. These hypotheses are then developed and tested for their ability to predict and explain the behavior of the United States toward other nations. Rummel's hypotheses explicitly include power and status distribution perspectives similar to those employed in the first two papers, and so provide an additional test with quite a different data base. Addressed only to the behavior of the United States vis-a-vis one or another specific other nation, his level of analysis is thus the nation-pair or dyad. While this differs from the first two papers' system-level focus, the propositions tested about behavior are very similar.

John Sullivan also takes the dyad as his unit of analysis, but instead of asking whether there are particular characteristics of the pair leading them to conflict with each other, he asks what causes them to cooperate, through informal alignments, in conflict with third parties. He seeks to explain alignment by examining a variety of bonds and the experience of past alignment. And Milstein looks at a situation of continuing conflict—between Israel and the Arab states—seeking to discover how the behavior of the conflicting states can be understood both in terms of the opponents' actions and reactions and of inputs from each of the opponents' major power ally. Thus he considers the extent to which one nation's violent actions can be explained by some form of response to the other's violence, and also considers the influence of economic aid, military aid, and trade from the United States and Soviet Union on the Arab-Israeli struggle.

Another paper taking a dyadic focus is that by Rosen, who wants to explain the reasons why one nation rather than the other should win a war. He thus develops a theory of "war power" built on two concepts of strength (the ability to inflict damage on the opponent) and cost-tolerance (the willingness to absorb damage and still keep fighting). He suggests that if an adequate theory of war power existed, and both the prospective winner and especially the prospective loser could predict the outcome, then many wars might be avoided. He tests conflicting hypotheses on the same basic set of wars as was analyzed by Singer (and also used by Wallace) in the Correlates of War project.

Two other papers examine the dynamics of conflict interactions. Michael Sullivan is interested in the possibility of finding systematic patterns in the escalation of international conflicts. Focusing upon the Vietnam War, he seeks to ascertain what changes actually occured in the symbolic involvement of the United States and how those changes were related to changes in that country's physical involvement as measured by troop commitments and casualties. Hopmann, like Michael Sullivan, uses content analysis in his case to discover the extent to which behavior within negotiations is influenced by the cooperative and conflictful actions of the participating states both within and outside of the negotiating arena. Focusing on the negotiations leading up to the Partial Test Ban Treaty, he attempts to weigh the relative importance of exogenous and endogenous variables and to determine the nature and direction of influence exerted by the conflictual as compared with cooperative actions of the participants. Specifically, are the parties more ready to reach agreement as a result of promises and rewards, or of threats and punishment? Although his method is quite different, in this respect the questions he asks are closely related to some of those Milstein poses about Arab-Israeli conflict interactions.

Choucri poses some specific questions about the ways in which various relations between economic and demographic pressures within a nation affect the nation's external behavior; for example, its relative attention to foreign trade or military preparations. She differentiates between conflict systems and peace systems both by the severity of those pressures and the way in which the pressures express themselves in foreign policy. She attempts to delineate national profiles of smaller, pacific nations that are empirically distinguishable from those of conflict-prone major powers. Wilkenfeld also is concerned with the degree to which particular national attributes affect nations' readiness to engage in foreign conflict. He is dissatisfied with earlier research apparently demonstrating no general linkage between the level of domestic conflict and a nation's propensity to external conflict, and hypothesizes that interesting relationships will emerge when he controls for (1) the type of state under consideration, (2) the type of conflict behavior involved, and (3) the temporal relationship between domestic and foreign conflict.

Finally, Russett inquires about the role of public opinion in encouraging or supporting heavy military expenditures in the United States. Insofar as high military spending may make war more, rather than less, likely (a question on which several other papers in the volume bear), and insofar as arms race interactions with other powers do not by themselves offer a fully satisfactory explanation of a nation's military spending, various domestic influences demand attention. He thus tries both to map changes in popular attitudes toward military spending, as those attitudes are expressed in public opinion surveys, and to explain major changes in those attitudes over the past 35 years.

SOME
ANSWERS

In spite of diversity in the specific problems to which the authors address themselves, the investigations supplement and even reinforce each other to a considerable extent.

Several of the papers provide new evidence and refine existing hypotheses regarding war causation. Three papers devote major attention to the relative distribution of power, and relative rates of change of nations' capabilities, as a cause of war. Singer, Bremer, and Stuckey, for example, identify two classic perspectives; one stressing "peace through preponderance" and the other, somewhat close to the traditional balance of power model, stressing the likelihood of "peace through parity." Their results are mixed. For the international system of the 19th century, peace is generally associated with power parity, but the 20th century peace generally has been maintained when the leading power or coalition had a clear preponderance of power over the challengers.

Other papers suggest that neither theory has very general predictive power. Milstein found that neither differences in military capabilities between Israel and her Arab neighbors, nor differences in rates of change in the antagonists' capabilities, showed strong or consistent relationships to the initiation of violence. Rummel, taking off from the power parity vs. predominance perspective, asked whether the United States was more likely to direct conflict actions toward much weaker states. He too failed to find important consistent relationships. Similarly, while Wallace found that differential changes in nations' capabilities did lead to war, that happened essentially only through the intermediary of differential changes in nations' status (to be discussed below). He found little or no *direct* link between capability changes and war. Together, these studies suggest that all in all there can be no general expectations that strong states will tend to fight weak ones more than near-equals, or vice versa. Nor empirically is there good evidence that states are particularly likely to fight either when a challenger is catching up in basic power to a leader or when the leader begins to pull away. To say that there is no general relationship of course does not rule out the possibility that specific conditions, interacting with levels or changes in relative capabilities, may not lead to violent conflict. Further research, on appreciably more refined hypotheses, will be required.

Rosen found that while superior power was a good predictor to winning a war, there were enough exceptions that one power's knowledge of its opponent's superior strength often would not alone be enough to prevent the weaker side from resisting anyway—and sometimes winning. One of the principal arguments of the preponderance model's proponents is that clear asymmetries are preferable to the uncertainties of a balanced equilibrium, in that there is less temptation to close any gap and less opportunity for misperceived estimates of opponents' capabilities. Rosen's study clearly indicates that accurate estimates of strength alone will not suffice.

Another perspective, related to that stressing power differences but drawing more on the sociological literature about status, proved more productive. By using controls which eliminated a number of possibilities that the correlations were spurious, Wallace strengthened the evidence previously existing about the effects of status. In his data the relationship between status inconsistency and the outbreak of war was strong. Wallace's attention to status centered on the difference between a nation's power base (achieved status) and the prestige or recognition (ascribed status) accorded the nation. In a variation of this perspective Rummel investigated the effect of discrepancy on two measures of achieved status, power and economic development, and found some evidence that discrepancy was associated with conflict.

Similarly, Choucri found that high rates of population growth are related to expansion and military preparation, but that high rates of technological development tend to be negatively related to military preparation. Thus if a nation's rate of growth on one status dimension—technology—is at least as fast (and preferably faster) than its growth in population, war would seem less likely. This inference may be further strengthened by Wallace's very important finding of a direct strong link between military preparation and the actual onset of war. His specific causal analysis indicated that this last link was truly a causal one and not a spurious relationship. In this context, Russett's finding of a dramatic rise in popular opposition to military spending in the United States is highly relevant. Russett's effort to explain that shift in popular opinion, however, was only partially successful, so it is difficult to generalize from it to statements as to how the military preparation link can be weakened.

Another thread running through more than one paper is the attention to the effect of different attributes of nations in producing different foreign policy. Rummel and Wilkenfeld consider this most extensively. Rummel found that differences in the economic development, size, and political orientation of object nations explained much of the differences in United States conflict and cooperative behavior toward those nations. Wilkenfeld found that differences in the political systems of nations (separating them into polyarchic, centrist, and personalist states) accounted for substantial variation in their foreign conflict behavior. With these controls he found several types of instances where domestic conflict was related to foreign conflict, and in so doing modified Rummel's earlier finding that for all types of nations, taken together, foreign and domestic conflict were unrelated. Both these findings support James Rosenau's earlier "pre-theory" orientation to foreign policy. Other papers in this volume which find major differences in foreign behavior dependent upon different attributes of nations are Choucri's, on what kinds of nations develop peace systems, Hopmann's, on the greater impact of external constraints on the United Kingdom's negotiating behavior than on that of the United States and Russia, and Rosen's, on the great variation in nations' willingness to suffer heavy battle casualties and still carry on a war.

Rummel's field theory exemplifies a broad perspective which stresses the role not of nations' attributes per se, but of the differences and similarities in those attributes for any particular pair of nations. The appreciable number of positive results obtained when he tested various propositions employing this perspective testifies to its power. John Sullivan, however, did not find it so valuable in predicting nations' alignment patterns. In his results, by far the most important predictor to current alignment patterns was the presence or absence of past alignment. Other dyadic characteristics with some power were trade between the two states, shared membership in a formal military alliance, and geographic proximity. But such other characteristics as similar levels of economic development, socio-political similarity, and shared membership in many international organizations proved unimportant.

In the analysis of the dynamics of international conflict, the point is repeatedly made—most strongly perhaps by Rummel and Choucri—that conflict and cooperation are not opposite ends of a spectrum but rather are present in varying degrees in all international contacts. Peace is considered not the absence of conflict, but a particular relationship between conflict and cooperation where conflict is channeled into non-violent outlets. Furthermore, a very important common theme of the majority of the papers is the great stability in patterns of conflict and cooperation over time. For example, we already mentioned John Sullivan's finding that the most important indicator of current alignment was past alignment. Wilkenfeld found that the tendency of most states is to maintain existing levels of foreign conflict. Particularly among the polyarchic states he found an overriding tendency to pursue a policy of foreign conflict behavior that matched the previous level of foreign conflict.

Russett also found great stability in popular attitudes toward military spending over a twenty-year period and then, after a sharp shift, a new stability at a different level. And Michael Sullivan suggests on the basis of his Vietnam case that an increase in the level of foreign conflict is likely to require a rise in symbolic commitment by the nation's leaders, thus greatly hampering subsequent efforts to extricate the nation from the conflict. Very possibly, as Wilkenfeld indicates, this is a general problem faced in most democracies or polyarchies, and one therefore would urge special caution by polyarchic governments before entering into foreign conflict—they especially may find it hard to stop.

Two papers considering specific instances of conflict interaction reach similar conclusions. Milstein, concentrating on Arab-Israeli violence, found the violent actions of each side to be primarily dependent upon the violent actions of the other side. Each side reacted, more or less in kind, much more to the other side's actions than to changes in the other's power base, and the immediate effects of outside powers' actions—for instance, trade with or military and economic assistance to Middle Eastern nations—were generally slight. From this Milstein drew the conclusion that the major powers should be very wary of becoming involved in a pattern of Middle Eastern hostility that they could not effectively control but that might well draw them into the fray. In a different arena Hopmann found a substantial symmetry in the negotiating behavior of Britain, the United States, and the Soviet Union over the Test Ban. Also, he found that the degree of conflict or cooperation in the external interactions among the negotiating parties was positively related to the parties' behavior within the negotiations. That is, increased conflict outside was followed by less cooperative action within the negotiations. In combination, all these papers stress the degree to which international conflicts have a momentum which, apart from the issues involved, operates against their solution and makes it difficult for the parties to extricate themselves. There also is some lesser but still important support for propositions about the degree to which such conflicts, once begun, have a tendancy not only to continue but to escalate. Milstein, for instance, finds some evidence for retaliatory behavior on the order of "an eye for a tooth."

Together, all the papers do produce an image of heavy environmental constraint on nations' behavior, of the serious degree to which nations' leaders are prisoners of the situations in which they find themselves, and especially of their past policies. This emphasis on the structural properties of national systems, the global international system, and of conflict sub-systems should sober us. The search for peace, for a systematic change in behavior away from the old patterns that have led to conflict, will indeed be hard. It will be hard not only for policy makers to take new actions, but also for peace researchers to identify those variables which are in fact fairly manipulable and thus make possible choices which will break the chain to violence. Research attention to the personality and behavioral idiosyncracies of particular leaders may not be very fruitful; on the other hand, attention to bureaucratic constraints—a theme not pursued here—might be quite productive.

At the same time, the conclusion we draw need not be one of despair about a deterministic world. Old patterns can be changed—the Test Ban Treaty was signed, and the Scandinavian states and the Netherlands did evolve from conflict to peace systems. But efforts to break the chain must be based on careful research. We must identify the restraints on nations' actions if we are to illuminate those areas where choice is possible and so broaden the area of effective choice.

J. DAVID SINGER, STUART BREMER, and JOHN STUCKEY

1. Capability Distribution, Uncertainty, and Major Power War, 1820-1965

ABSTRACT

We have synthesized from the literature two distinct and incompatible views of the way in which the distribution and redistribution of capabilities affects the incidence of major power war. One predicts that there will be less war when there is approximate *parity* (and change toward it) among the nations and a relatively *fluid* power hierarchy. The other predicts that there will be less war when there is a *preponderance* (or change toward it) of power concentrated in the hands of a very few nations, and a relatively *stable* rank order among the major powers. While both schools agree that parity and fluidity increase decisional uncertainty, only the first would hold that such uncertainty makes for peace; the preponderance and stability school sees uncertainty as leading to war.

These two viewpoints were consolidated into a single basic model incorporating the three predictor variables (capability concentration, rate and direction of change in concentration, and the movement of capability shares among the powers) and the outcome variable (amount of inter-state war involving major powers). Since the classical theorizers say little regarding the sequence in which the variables should exercise their effects, or the way in which those effects might combine, we articulated and tested four versions: an additive and a multiplicative form with the measurement of concentration *prior* to the measurement of its change and movement, and an additive and multiplicative one with concentration measured *after* change and movement.

For the 19th century, the additive version of the parity-fluidity model produces a close fit to historical reality (R^2 = .73), while the multiplicative preponderance-stability model matches the 20th century, but not nearly as well (R^2 = .46). When capabilities are highly concentrated and there is little

Authors' Note: Comments on an earlier version of this paper by Karl Deutsch, Melvin Small, Michael Wallace, and James Ray were particularly helpful. We would also like to thank Dorothy LaBarr for her patience and thoroughness in preparing the tables and text, and to acknowledge the support of the National Science Foundation under Grant number 010058.

movement ir their distribution, then, one finds more war in the 19th century and less in the 20th.   ■

INTRODUCTION

In any systematic effort to identify the immediate or remote sources of international war, one has a variety of more or less equally reasonable options. First of all, one can focus either on the behavior of the relevant governments, or on the background conditions within which such behavior occurs. And if one leans toward ecologically oriented models—as we do—the choice is between the attributes of the nations themselves and the attributes of the system or sub-system within which the nations are located. Further, one may choose to focus on the structural attributes of the nations or the system or on their cultural or physical attributes.

In the Correlates of War project, we have recently begun to examine the behavioral patterns of nations in conflict, in order to ascertain whether there are recurrent patterns which consistently distinguish between those conflicts which eventuate in war and those which do not (Leng and Singer, 1970). But even though we contend that no model is adequate unless it includes such behavioral and interactional phenomena, we also believe that behavior cannot be understood adequately except in its ecological context.

Hence, the first two phases of the project have been restricted to the attributes of the system and those of the nations and pairs of nations that comprise the system. In the process, we have found it necessary to allocate more energy to data generation and acquisition (not to mention data management) than to data analysis, and in addition to making these data sets available via the International Relations Archive of the Inter-University Consortium for Political Research, we have published a fair number of them (Singer and Small, 1966a, 1966b; Russett, Singer, and Small, 1968; Small and Singer, 1969 and 1970; Wallace and Singer, 1970). In due course three handbooks will be published, embracing respectively the fluctuating and cumulative incidence of war (Singer and Small, 1972), the changing structure of the international system since the Congress of Vienna (Singer, Wallace, and Bremer, 1973), and the capabilities of the states which constitute that system (Singer and Small, 1973). We prepare these volumes not only to make our data as widely available as possible, but also in order to explain why and how we construct our most important measures. That is, unlike some other social science sectors, the international politics field finds very little data of a ready-made nature, requiring those of us in that particular vineyard to first convert our concepts into operational indicators, prior to any analysis. And even though we still have some major index construction and data generation tasks before us, we have not been completely inattentive to the possibilities of some modest theoretical analyses (Singer and Small, 1966c and 1968; Singer and Wallace, 1970; Wallace, 1971; Bremer, Singer, and Luterbacher, 1972; Gleditsch and Singer, 1972; and Skjelsbaek,

1971). These partial and tentative analyses are, of course, essentially of a brush-clearing nature, preliminary to the testing of more complex and complete models.

The report at hand falls into that same brush-clearing category, designed to help us sort out some of the dominant regularities in the international system, and to aid in evaluating a number of equally plausible, but logically incompatible, theoretical formulations. To be quite explicit about it, we suspect that anyone who takes a given model of war (or most other international phenomena) very seriously at this stage of the game has just not looked at the referent world very carefully. Just as our colleagues in the physical and biological sciences have found that nature is full of apparent inconsistencies and paradoxes, requiring a constant interplay between theoretical schemes and empirical investigations, we believe that the complexities of war and global politics will require more than mathematical rigor and elegant logical exercises. So much, then, for the epistemological case on which we rest our research strategy. In the Conclusion, we will address ourselves to the equally important normative case, but let us turn now to the investigation at hand.

THE QUERY AND ITS RATIONALE

Our concern here is to ascertain the extent to which the war-proneness of the major powers, from 1820 through 1965, can be attributed to certain structural properties of the sub-system which they constitute. The first of these properties is the distribution of national capabilities within it at given points in time, and the second is the direction and rate of change in that distribution between any two of those points in time.

Before presenting our measures and analyses, however, it is pertinent to ask why one might expect to find any relationship between the distribution of "power" on the one hand, and the incidence of war, on the other. Without either tracing the discussion as it has unfolded in the literature of diplomatic history and international poltiics, or developing a full articulation of our own line of reasoning, we may nevertheless summarize what looks to us like a fairly plausible set of considerations.

The Major Powers' Preoccupation with Relative Capability

We begin with the assumption that the foreign policy elites of all national states are, at one time or another, concerned with their nation's standing in the power and/or prestige pecking order.[1] For any given nation at any given time,

1. While power and prestige are far from identical, and nations may well have statuses on these two dimensions that are quite inconsistent with each other, there is usually a high correlation between the two. In this paper, we focus only on power, but will deal with prestige (or attributed diplomatic importance) in a later one; for some tentative analyses, see Midlarsky (1969), East (1969), Wallace (1971), and Wallace in this volume. For more detail on the composition of the international system and its sub-systems, see Singer and Small (1966a) and Russett, Singer, and Small (1968).

certain ranking scales will be of considerably greater salience than others, as will the relative position of one or another of their neighbors. Normally, we would not expect the decision makers of Burma to worry very much about their nation's military-industrial capability vis-a-vis that of Bolivia, or find the Swedish foreign office attending to the rise in Afghanistan's diplomatic prestige. Nor would it be particularly salient to the Mexican defense ministry that Australia's preparedness level had risen sharply over the previous half-decade. That is, the salience of a given nation's rank position on a given power or prestige dimension will only be high for the foreign policy elites of those other nations that are relatively interdependent with the first, and are "in the same league."

But we are talking here only about major powers, which—almost by definition—are highly interdependent one with the other, and clearly in the same upper strata on most of the recognized power or prestige dimensions. This becomes more evident if we indicate which states comprise the major power sub-system during the different periods of the century and a half which concerns us here. While the data introduced in a later report will indicate how valid the classification is, we emphasize that our criteria—quite intentionally—are less than operational. That is, rather than define the major power sub-system over time in terms of certain objective power and/or prestige indicators, we adhere to the rather intuitive criteria of the diplomatic historians. On the other hand, the consensus among those who have specialized in the various regions and epochs is remarkably high (especially from 1816 through 1945), and it leads to the following.

As the post-Congress period opens, we find Austria-Hungary, Prussia, Russia, France, and Britain constituting this select sub-system. Italy joins the group after unification in 1860, as does Germany as the successor state to Prussia in 1870. The two non-European newcomers are Japan in 1895, following its victory over China, and the United States, after defeating Spain in 1898. These eight continue as the sole major powers until World War I, which sees the dismemberment of the Austro-Hungarian empire, and the temporary loss of position for Germany (from 1918 to 1924) and Russia (from 1917 to 1921). World War II leads to the temporary elimination of France (from 1940 to 1944) and the permanent (i.e. at least through 1965) elimination of the Axis powers of Italy, Germany, and Japan. As the victors in that war, Britain, Russia, and the United States continue as members of the major power category; France regains membership in 1945, and China qualifies as of 1950.

It should not be difficult to argue that these states become major powers by dint of close attention to relative capability, and remain so in the same way. Of course, mere allocation of attention to their power and prestige vis-a-vis others will not suffice. They must begin with a solid territorial and demographic base, build upon that a superior industrial and/or military capability, and utilize those resources with a modicum of political competence.[2] Nor would it be difficult

2. If one accepts the propositions that successful war experience usually leads to increases in national power, and that the more powerful nations usually "win" their wars,

to argue that all of the major powers are sufficiently interdependent, directly or indirectly, to warrant treatment as a discernible sub-system. To a very considerable extent, during the epoch at hand, the policies of each impinge on the fate of the others; and as Campbell (1958) has urged in another context, this condition, plus a similarity of attributes, permits us to think of them as a single social system. We could, of course, go on to construct and apply a number of indices which might reflect the similarities and the interdependence of the major powers, but such an exercise is probably not necessary here.

If, then, we can assume that the states which constitute this oligarchy (Schwarzenberger, 1951) do indeed represent the most powerful members of the international system and that they are in relatively frequent interaction with one another, the next question is the extent to which they all collaborate to preserve the status quo, or conversely, vie with one another for supremacy. Our view is that neither extreme holds very often, and that the cooperative and competitive interactions among them fluctuate markedly over time. Further, as Langer (1931), Gulick (1955), Kissinger (1957), and others have demonstrated, even when they work together to impose a common peace, they keep a sharp eye on their relative capabilities. Each major foreign office is, at a given point in time, deeply concerned with the growth of some of their neighbors' strength and the decline of others'. Moreover, yesterday's allies are often tomorrow's rivals or enemies. Even as domestic political power has passed from the hands of the kings, kaisers, czars, and emperors to party bureaucrats and elected bourgeois rulers, the instability of coalitions has abated but slightly. Despite the inhibitory effects of articulated ideologies, competition for public office, and all the demagoguery which comes in the train of popular diplomacy, major power relationships continue to shift, albeit more slowly.

The Role of Uncertainty

It is, however, one thing to argue that the distribution and redistribution of relative capability will turn out to be a major factor in the behavior of national states, and quite another to predict the strength—and direction—of its relationship with war. As a matter of fact, we contend that a rather strong case can be made for two alternative, but incompatible, models. In each of these models, capability configurations represent the predictor or independent variables, and decision makers' uncertainty serves as the (unmeasured) intervening variable. By uncertainty we mean nothing more than the difficulty which foreign policy elites experience in discerning the stratifications and clusters in the system, and predicting the behavior of the other members of that system.

How does uncertainty link up with capability patterns on the one hand and with war or peace, on the other? Considering the latter connection first, those who believe that it is *un*certainty which usually makes for war will argue that most war is the result of misjudgment, erroneous perception, and poor predictions. The opposing view is that high levels of *certainty* are, on the

---

the high war involvement and win-lose scores of the major powers offer some evidence that the majors are not only attentive to, but high on relative capabilities (Small and Singer, 1970).

contrary, often at the root of war, and that the major inhibitor to war is a *lack* of clarity, order, and predictability. When relative capabilities are difficult to appraise, and when coalition bonds are ambiguous, outcomes are more in doubt, and it is that very uncertainty which helps governments to draw back from the brink of war (Haas and Whiting, 1956, p. 50).

Shifting from the possible link between uncertainty and war to that between capability distributions and such uncertainty, both schools of thought tend to converge. Here, the assumption is that three different variables will affect uncertainty in the system: the extent to which capabilities are highly concentrated in the hands of a very few nations, whether the distribution is changing toward higher or lower concentration, and the rate at which relative capabilities are moving. The model, as we see it, holds that uncertainty levels will rise when: (a) capabilities are more equally distributed and not concentrated; (b) the direction of change is toward such equal distribution and away from high concentrations; and (c) when there is high fluidity, rather than stability, in capability distributions.

To summarize, we find two contending models of more or less equal plausibility. One, which we might call the "preponderance and stability" model, holds that war will *in*crease as the system moves away from a high and stable concentration of capabilities. The other, which might be called the "parity and fluidity" model, holds that war will *de*crease as the system moves away from such a high and stable concentration and toward a more ambiguous state of approximate parity, coupled with a relatively fluid movement of the nations up and down the power hierarchy.

For the moment, we will leave these models in their pre-operational and verbal form. Then, after describing the measures and the resulting data in some detail, we can return to their formal articulation and to an examination of the extent to which each fits the empirical world of the past century and a half. It should, of course, be emphasized that even if our design were flawless, our measures impeccable, and our analyses beyond reproach, the findings would nevertheless be far from conclusive. First of all, there is Popper's dictum (1965a) regarding the disconfirmability, as opposed to the confirmability of empirical generalizations. Second, we must stress that the generalizations being tested here are very gross and undifferentiated. This, we believe, is as it should be in the early stages of a particular line of theoretical investigation, but we recognize at the same time that a more refined set of tests, with attention to additional variables and tighter analytical controls, is ultimately required.

THE VARIABLES AND
THEIR MEASUREMENT

Space limitations and the conventions of scientific reporting usually preclude a fully detailed description of the precise operations by which one's verbalized constructs are converted into machine-readable data. This is especially unfortunate when most of these constructs or variables are not found in ready-made operational form (such as votes) and have not yet achieved even partial acceptance as reliable and valid indices (such as gross national product). But as we noted at the outset, we have been neither bashful nor niggardly in publishing our data, and we can therefore refer to those separate studies in which our rationale, procedures, and results are presented in greater detail. Thus, we will describe and justify our measures in only the briefest fashion here, beginning with the outcome variable (war) and then moving on to our predictor variables: concentration, change in concentration, and movement

The Incidence of War

We begin by distinguishing among inter-state, extra-systemic, and civil wars; the latter two are of no concern here, and we deal only with those of the first type in which at least one major power was an active participant and in which each side sustained at least 1,000 battle-connected fatalities. The particular index used in the analysis at hand is a reflection of the magnitude of war underway, as measured in nation months of such major power inter-state war. And since our time unit is the half-decade, we measure the warlikeness of each such period as the average annual amount of war underway during that period. The war data for each of the 29 periods from 1820 to 1965 are shown in Table 1, at the end of this section.[3]

National Capabilities

To this juncture, we have alluded to power, strength, and capability, but have side-stepped any definitions; that delicate chore can no longer be avoided. As one of us (Singer, 1963) emphasized some years ago, power is to political science what wealth is to economics, but not nearly as measureable. The focus there was on the influence *process,* and the range of strategies appropriate to each basic type of inter-nation influence situation; relative capabilities, or the bases of power, were by and large ignored.

Recently, several serious efforts to convert the intuitive notions of national capability or power base have appeared (German, 1970; Fucks, 1965), but rather than examine them or compare our approach to theirs, we will merely summarize our measures here. In a later volume we plan to discuss the several existing efforts, indicate the theoretical reasoning behind our own measures, and present our data in considerable detail.

We begin with six separate indicators, combine them into three, and then combine those into a single power base or war potential (Knorr, 1956) score for

3. Despite the modest fluctuations in the size of the major power subsystem, we do not normalize the war measure. Full details of our data generation and index construction procedures, and the considerations of validity and reliability upon which the indices rest, along with extensive tabular materials, are found in our forthcoming *Wages of War* (Singer and Small, 1972).

each nation every half decade. The six fall into three groupings of two dimensions each. The *demographic* dimension includes, first, the nation's total population, and second, the number of people living in cities of 20,000 or larger. The *industrial* dimension embraces both energy consumption (from 1885 on) and iron or steel production. The energy may come from many sources, but is converted into coal ton equivalents, and the iron/steel production is based on the former only until 1895, at which time we shift to steel alone. The third pair of measures are *military* expenditures and armed forces size, excluding reserves.

As to the more obvious validity questions, we carefully considered the need for separate indicators of social organization, national unity and motivation, and technical skills, but concluded that each of those was adequately reflected in one or more of the six specific indices. Closely related to the choice of indices and sub-indices is the matter of their relative contributions to a nation's power base. And while we are still experimenting with a number of weighting and interaction effect schemes, our tendency is to treat them as equally important, and additive in their effect. In line with these tentative assumptions, we first compute the total score (in people, tons, dollars, etc.) for the system, and then ascertain each nation's percentage share. This has the virtue of normalizing all of our data, reduces the computational problems associated with fluctuating currency conversion rates, avoids that of changes in purchasing power, and puts the figures into ideal form for the computation of our concentration-distribution scores, to which we will turn in a moment.

In addition, since the validity of the composite six-dimensional score is a long way from being demonstrated, we computed these percentage share scores not only for all six dimensions combined, but for the three two-dimensional indices of demographic, industrial, and military capability, and then for each of the six separately. There are, thus, ten power indices for each nation every half-decade, but only the *composite* scores are utilized in our analyses here.

The Distribution of Capabilities

In our discussion of the impact of certainty and uncertainty on the incidence of major power war, we indicated that capability distributions should exercise a strong effect on these certainty levels. How do we measure CON, or the extent to which these capabilities are concentrated or diffused among the nations which comprise the major power sub-system?

Once more, the measurement problem is sufficiently complex to warrant reference to a fuller statement elsewhere (Singer and Ray, 1972). To summarize here, we have been struck with the empirical inadequacy of several measures of inequality which have been rather widely used, and have thus devised our own.[4] To operationally measure the concentration of capabilities (within the

---

4. For example, the Gini is often as sensitive to a changing N as to the allocation of shares, when the N is low. And the Schutz index, because it sums the ratios of advantage of those above the equal share point, is sensitive only to their shares *as a group* and is not sensitive to the distributions *within* that group. Thus, the index would be the same (.5) for

grouping of from five to eight major powers) we proceed as follows. First, we compute the standard deviation of the *observed* percentage shares. Second, we divide that figure by the *maximum* standard deviation of the percentage shares that is possible for a given N; that maximum would occur if one nation held 100 percent of the shares, and the others had none at all. The resulting index ranges from zero (reflecting perfect equality in the distribution) to 1.0 (in which case one nation holds 100 percent of that capability), and—if our interpretation of the relevant data is correct—should turn out to be high in face validity. The concentration scores are listed in Table 1, along with the war data and the change and movement measures, to which we now turn.[5]

Movement and Change of Capability Distributions

Having dealt with the measurement of our outcome variable and the key predictor variable, we can now shift to the indices which reflect change across time in the latter. As the scores in Table 1 make clear, the distribution of power in the major power sub-system is by no means a static thing. How do we measure such shifts?

Two rather distinct indices are employed. The first is a straightforward reflection of the extent to which the concentration index has gone up or down during the period (usually five years) between any two observations. We call it simply change in concentration, or ΔCON. The second is a bit more complex, and it reflects the number of percentage shares which have been exchanged between and among the major powers during each period, whether or not that redistribution leads to a change in the rank ordering.

We begin by comparing the percentage of capability shares held by each of the nations at the beginning and the end of the half-decade. If, for example, the top ranked nation held 30 percent of the composite capability shares at the beginning of a half-decade, and the other four held, respectively, 25, 20, 15, and 10 percent, and the distribution at the end of the period were 35, 25, 15, 15, and 10, there would have been a movement of 10 percentage shares. That is, the top nation picked up 5 percentage shares, number three lost 5, and the remaining three scores remained constant. But in order to make the movement

---

each of the following percentage distributions; 70-20-10-0-0; 70-7.5-7.5-7.5-7.5; and 70-15-15-0-0. The same holds if the index is computed on the basis of those below the equal share point. An alternative approach is that of Brams (1968), and a useful discussion is in Alker and Russett (1964).

5. The formula for computing concentration is as follows:

$$CON = \sqrt{\frac{\sum\limits_{i=1}^{n} (Si)^2 - \frac{1}{n}}{1 - \frac{1}{n}}}$$

where n = number of nations in system, and Si = nation i's share (from .00 to 1.00) of the system's capabilities.

index (called MOVE) comparable across all 30 periods in our 150 years, with the size (and composition) of the sub-system changing from time to time, it must be normalized. That normalization is achieved by dividing by the *maximum possible* amount of movement or redistribution. That maximum, in turn, would occur if the lowest ranked nation picked up all the shares between the two observations, and ended up with 100 percent of them. Thus, our denominator is computed by subtracting the lowest nation's score from 100 percent and multiplying that difference by 2, since whatever it gained will have been lost by the others.[6]

It is now time to mention two irregularities that must be dealt with in computing our capability distribution and war measures. First, as already noted, the major power sub-system (as we define it) gains and loses members at several points during the century and a half under study. This not only requires us to normalize for its size when measuring capability distributions, but also to eliminate the distortions that could arise in measuring change or movement between two observations that are based on dissimilar sub-system membership. We do this by counting only the movement of shares between and among nations which were members at both observation points, and thus avoid any artifact which could arise merely because the 100 percent is divided among a smaller or larger population at the separate data points.

The second irregularity stems from the fact that we would get rather distorted indices of relative capability if we measured the military, industrial, and demographic strengths during the two world wars. Thus, in place of the 1915, 1940, and 1945 observation years, we use 1913, 1938, and 1946, respectively. But this makes several of our inter-observation intervals longer or shorter than five years. For the war measure, as mentioned earlier, we solve that problem by converting each period's total nation months of inter-state war underway into an *average annual* index. For the change in concentration and the movement measures—which are essentially rate of change measures—we merely divide all the inter-observation scores by the number of years which have elapsed between them; this again produces an average annual index.

Having now summarized, albeit briefly, the ways in which we convert our separate war and capability concepts into operational indices, we can present the resulting figures. In Table 1, then, we list the CON, ΔCON, MOVE, and WAR indices for each of the 29 observation points embraced in the study. Bear in mind that CON is the only one of our indices which is measured at a *single* point

6. The formula for computing movement is as follows:

$$MOVE = \frac{\sum\limits_{i=1}^{n} \left| Si_{t-1} - Si_t \right|}{2(1 - Sm_t)}$$

where n = number of nations in system, Si = nation i's share of the system's capabilities, m = nation with lowest share of capabilities, and t, t−1 = observation points.

in time; the change and movement indices reflect the average annual magnitudes during the period immediately following the CON observation, and the amount of war is also that underway during the years immediately following that observation. However, a variety of time lags and leads will be introduced when we turn to our analyses, resulting in re-alignments across the rows as we move the various columns upward and downward.

Table 1. Capability and War Indices

Period Beginning (T0)	CON (T0)	Average Annual ΔCON (T0→T1)	Average Annual MOVE (T0→T1)	Average Annual Nation-Months of WAR Underway (T0→T1)
1820	0.241	−0.15	0.40	(2.92)
1825	0.233	0.17	0.47	6.68
1830	0.242	0.02	0.41	0.00
1835	0.243	−0.22	0.88	0.00
1840	0.232	0.50	0.60	0.00
1845	0.257	0.06	0.28	6.40
1850	0.260	0.34	0.67	9.36
1855	0.276	0.07	0.38	17.24
1860	0.280	−0.49	0.82	16.82
1865	0.255	−0.45	1.23	12.98
1870	0.233	−0.15	0.46	5.44
1875	0.225	0.02	0.34	3.52
1880	0.226	−0.36	0.53	2.64
1885	0.208	−0.10	0.65	2.12
1890	0.203	0.39	0.55	0.00
1895	0.223	−0.41	0.67	0.00
1900	0.202	0.09	0.93	4.32
1905	0.207	0.10	0.37	3.40
1910	0.212	−0.14	0.74	8.47
1913	0.208	2.34	1.69	87.06
1920	0.371	−2.49	1.26	0.00
1925	0.247	−0.13	0.80	0.00
1930	0.241	−0.25	2.57	6.68
1935	0.228	−0.37	2.23	8.73
1938	0.217	2.50	2.82	123.97
1946	0.417	−3.10	1.88	0.00
1950	0.293	0.76	0.99	103.34
1955	0.331	−0.56	1.36	0.52
1960	(0.303)	(0.09)	(1.21)	0.44

Note: For display convenience the values of ΔCON and MOVE have been multiplied by 100. The original values were used in all computations. Figures shown in parenthese ( ) are shown for information only; they are not used in the univariate statistics of Table 2 or in the CON LEADS models.

Examining the Data

Before we get to our analyses and the testing of the contending models, certain characteristics of the several data sets merit a brief discussion. Our motives are two-fold. The careful examination of one's data series, time plots, and scatter plots is, in our judgment, an important prerequisite to the conduct of statistical analyses. In addition, there are the well-known constraints which one's data distributions can impose in the selection and interpretation of the statistical analyses employed. The relevant summary statistics for our four variables are shown in Table 2.[7]

Looking at the measures of central tendency, we note that the differences between the means and medians for our three predictor variables are quite small in all three time spans. This suggests that these variables do not have seriously skewed distributions. The same cannot be said for the war variable, however. The mean nation-months of war figure for the 20th century is 24.78, while the median value is only 3.86, indicating that the distribution is positively skewed. This condition is no doubt due to the extreme values associated with World War I, World War II, and the Korean war.

Examining the measures of dispersion (range and standard deviation), we find that, as one might expect, all of our measures vary less in the 19th century than in the 20th. With one exception these differences are not serious, and that exception is the war variable. Again we find the three large wars in our series exerting a disproportionate influence on the distributional properties of the war variable. The standard deviation of war in the 19th century is 6.08, while the comparable figure for the 20th century is 44.07. Although Chauvenet's criterion (Young, 1962) might cast some doubt on the analyses associated with such outliers, we feel that the brush-clearing nature of this work suggests neither the transformation nor the elimination of these data points. We realize, however, that these values may weaken the predictive power of our models, particularly in the 20th century.

Two additional descriptors will also be important when we turn to our analyses. One of these is the *auto-correlation* coefficient, reflecting the extent to which each successive value of a given variable is independent of, or highly correlated with, the prior value of that same variable. For the entire time span, several of our indices show rather high auto-correlations, with ΔCON at $-.58$ and MOVE at .63. These turn out, however, to be quite different when we examine the centuries separately, suggesting further that these epochs are divided by more than a change in digits. Now we find that CON shows a .62 auto-correlation in the earlier epoch but only .13 in the present. The two indices of redistribution are negligibly auto-correlated in the 19th, but discernibly so

7. As we move into the examination and analysis of our data, we want to acknowledge our debt to Dan Fox of The University of Michigan Statistical Research Laboratory, for the creation of a set of programs particularly suited to time series data management and analysis in the social sciences.

Table 2. Descriptive Statistics

	CON	ΔCON	MOVE	WAR
Entire Span (N=28)				
Mean	.250	−.0007	.0096	15.36
Median	.237	−.0012	.0071	3.92
Maximum	.417	.0250	.0282	123.97
Minimum	.202	−.0310	.0028	0.0
Standard Deviation	.0504	.0105	.0069	32.33
Range	.215	.0560	.0254	123.97
Auto-correlation	.21	−.58	.63	−.15
Secular trend (beta)	.30	−.09	.66	.32
(b)	.0004	−.00002	.0001	.2501
19th Century (N=14)				
Mean	.244	−.0005	.0058	5.94
Median	.242	−.0004	.0050	4.48
Maximum	.280	.0050	.0123	17.24
Minimum	.208	−.0049	.0028	0.0
Standard Deviation	.0201	.0028	.0026	6.08
Range	.072	.0099	.0095	17.24
Auto-correlation	.62	.18	.01	.72
Secular trend (beta)	−.24	−.37	.17	−.01
(b)	−.0002	−.0005	.00002	−.0042
20th Century (N=14)				
Mean	.257	−.0009	.0315	24.78
Median	.226	−.0014	.0113	3.86
Maximum	.417	.0250	.0282	123.97
Minimum	.202	−.0310	.0037	0.0
Standard Deviation	.0692	.0149	.0078	44.07
Range	.215	.0560	.0245	123.97
Auto-correlation	.13	−.60	.50	−.32
Secular trend (beta)	.61	−.14	.56	.18
(b)	.0020	−.0001	.0002	.3849

Note: The auto-correlation coefficient shown is first-order only. For the separate century series, each variable was divided according to its lag-lead relationship in the ADD/CON LEADS model. Thus, the statistics shown above for the 19th century include the CON observation at 1885, ΔCON and MOVE 1885-1890, and WAR 1890-1894. The 20th century series begins with the following observation on each variable.

(−.60 and .50) in the 20th. As to the amount of war underway in each half decade, there is a high .72 correlation between successive periods in the earlier century, but a low −.32 in this century. We will return to the implications of these in the context of our multivariate analyses, but we should point out here that the important consideration is not so much that of auto-correlation of the indices, but of the auto-correlations of the differences between the predicted and observed values (i.e., residuals) of the outcome variable.

Then there is the closely related problem of secular trends. If one's variables are steadily rising or falling during the period under study, they can produce statistical associations that are largely a consequence of such trends. Hence the widespread use of "first differences" and other techniques for de-trending in the analysis of time series data. How serious is the problem in the study at hand? If we standardize each variable and regress the resulting series on the year of observation, also standardized, we can then estimate the trend of our various series by comparing the resulting slopes (or beta weights, which of course are equal to the product-moment correlation coefficients).

For the entire time span, MOVE shows the steepest slope, with a standardized regression coefficient of .66; CON and WAR are moderately steep with coefficients of .30 and .32 respectively. In the 19th century, ΔCON ($-.37$) and CON ($-.24$) show downward slopes, MOVE is slightly positive (.17), and WAR ($-.01$) shows virtually no trend whatever. CON develops a sharp positive trend (.61) in the 20th century, as does MOVE (.56). The other variables show weak 20th century trends, $-.14$ for ΔCON and .18 for WAR.

Before turning to our analyses, one additional data problem requires brief attention. Important, from both the substantive and methodological viewpoints, is the extent to which the predictor variables covary with each other, and these coefficients are shown under the correlation matrices in Tables 4, 5, and 6. For the entire span, the product-moment correlation between CON in one period and ΔCON in the next is $-.71$; that between CON and ΔCON during the preceding half-decade is .47. When CON is correlated with the amount of movement in the subsequent half-decade, we find a coefficient of .21, and it is .50 when correlated with the half decade preceding it. As to the top indices which reflect the durability of capability distribution, any suspicion that they might be tapping the same phenomenon is quickly dispelled; the correlation between ΔCON and MOVE is a negligible .08. When we turn to our multivariate analyses and discuss the problem of multi-collinearity, these correlations as well as those that obtain within the separate centuries will be examined further.

THE BIVARIATE ANALYSES

With our theoretical rationale, index construction, and data summaries behind us, we can return to the query which led to the investigation in the first place: what are the effects of capability distribution and redistribution on the incidence of war involving the members of the major power sub-system? We approach the question in two stages, the first of which is a series of bivariate analyses. These are employed not only because it seems useful to know as much as possible about such relationships prior to the examination of more complex models, but also because the theoretical argument suggests that CON, ΔCON, and MOVE should exercise independent—as well as combined—effects on decision maker uncertainty and on war. From there, we will move on to a number of multivariate analyses, in which we compare the war fluctuation patterns *predicted* by several additive and multiplicative models against the patterns which were actually *observed*.

We begin in a direct fashion and ask whether there is any discernible association between our several measures of capability distribution on the one hand, and fluctuations in the incidence of war, on the other. Bear in mind that: (a) CON is measured as of the first day (more or less) of every fifth year (except for the 1913, 1938, and 1946 substitutions noted earlier); (b) ΔCON and MOVE are measured between two successive readings of CON; and (c) WAR is measured during the period immediately following either the observation of CON or the second of the two observations on which ΔCON and MOVE are based. (A typical set of observations would be: ΔCON and MOVE from 1 January 1840 to 1 January 1845; CON at 1 January 1840; and WAR from 1 January 1845 through 31 December 1849.) The working assumption here is that whatever independent effects each of the predictor variables will have upon the incidence of war will be felt within the subsequent half-decade. In the multivariate analyses, we will experiment with these time lags and leads, and in a follow-up study (when our annual data are in) we will further explore the effects of different, and more precisely measured, time lags and leads.

Turning, then, to the product-moment correlations between these predictor variables and major power inter-state war, we examine the coefficients reported in Table 3. If those who view high concentration, upward change in concentration, and low movement as conducive to decisional certainty (and thus to low levels of war) are correct, we should find negative correlations for the CON-WAR and ΔCON-WAR association and positive ones for the MOVE-WAR association. Conversely, if the world is closer to the model articulated by those who see low concentration, downward change in concentration, and high movement as conducive to uncertainty (and thus to low levels of war), the signs would be just the opposite. What do we find?

Examining the total century and a half first, it looks as if the preponderance and stability school has the better of the predictive models. While correlation

Table 3. Bivariate Correlation Coefficients (r) and Coefficients of Determination Between Capability Indices and WAR in Succeeding Time Period

$$\textit{AVERAGE ANNUAL NATION-MONTHS OF}$$
$$\textit{WAR UNDERWAY}_{t_1 \to t_2}$$

	Total Span (N=28)		19th Century (N=14)		20th Century (N=14)	
	r	r^2	r	r^2	r	r^2
CON_{t_0}	$-.10$	$.01$	$.81$	$.66$	$-.23$	$.05$
$\Delta CON_{t_0 \to t_1}$	$-.38$	$.14$	$.19$	$.04$	$-.41$	$.17$
$MOVE_{t_0 \to t_1}$	$.34$	$.12$	$-.01$	$.00$	$.24$	$.06$

coefficients of −.10, −.38, and .34 are not impressively high, all three are in the direction predicted by that particular model.[8] But as we have already intimated, there seem to be intuitive as well as empirical grounds for treating the centuries separately. Not only have many historians noted the transitional role of the 1890's, but several of our own analyses to date (Singer and Small, 1966c, 1968, and 1969) reinforce that impression.[9] Our suspicions are further reinforced when we compute the correlations for the centuries separately. We now find that those who recommend high concentration and low movement in order to reduce the incidence of war do not do quite so well. In the 20th century, the signs are all in the direction predicted by their model, while for the 19th century (or more precisely, the period ending with the 1890-1895 observations), the signs are reversed.[10]

Before leaving the bivariate analyses, however, a brief digression is in order that we might check for the presence and effect of cross-lag correlations. Here the search is not for the impact of the predictor variable on the outcome at subsequent observations, but for the impact of the "outcome" variable on chronologically subsequent values of the putative "predictor" variable. In the case at hand, we expected to find a number of cross-correlations, and some did indeed turn up. That is, when we correlated the amount of war underway in any period against the concentration measure in the subsequent period, we found a coefficient of .80 for the full 150 years, .52 for the 19th century, and .81 for the 20th. Similarly, for the impact of prior war on ΔCON, the coefficients were −.66, −.51, and −.68; and for its effect on MOVE, they were .30, .46, and .17. Most of these are sufficiently strong to suggest the need for re-examining the extent to which our capability indices predict to subsequent war when the effects of *prior* war have been removed. Hence, we predicted the CON, ΔCON, and MOVE measures from preceding levels of war; the variance in those measures which could *not* be so explained (i.e. residual variance) was then used as a relatively less biased predictor of war in the following half-decade.

For the entire period, the residual correlation between CON and WAR is a negligible .01, the effect on the 19th century coefficient is to reduce it from .81 to .65, and for the 20th, the association drops from −.23 to −.03. As to the

8. Throughout this paper we employ standardized measures of association (correlation coefficients and standardized regression coefficients). Our objective is to evaluate the relative contribution of variables rather than to establish empirical laws, and in this regard we have adopted what Blalock (1961) has called the "quantitative" criterion for evaluating the importance of variables.

9. In this and prior studies we have examined the effects of dividing the 150 years into three or more periods, or of using such salient years as 1871 or 1914 as our cutting point, but the clearest distinctions tend to be found when the 1890-1900 decade is used as our inter-epoch division.

10. The scatter plots, while not reproduced here, reveal the stronger linear relationships quite clearly, and in the case of the 20th century CON-WAR association, suggest a possible curvilinear pattern; the conversion to logarithmic plots does not, however, produce a linear association. On the other hand, a rank order (rho) correlation of −.53 also suggests that the CON-WAR association in the 20th century is far from negligible.

relationship between the residuals of ΔCON and WAR, the coefficients drop from −.29 to −.01, from .18 to −.03, and −.34 to −.06, for the full and the separate epochs respectively. The impact on the predictive power of MOVE, however, is to strengthen rather than reduce it. The full span's coefficient rises from .34 to .45, and those for the 19th century rise from −.01 to −.17, and from .23 to .41, respectively.[11]

Having emphasized the importance of such a cross-lag correlation check, however, we would now back off and argue that residuals should *not* be used in either the bivariate analyses at hand or in the multivariate ones which follow in the next section. That is, our theoretical concern here is exclusively with the effect of the concentration and redistribution of capabilities upon the incidence of war in the following period, regardless of what produced those capability configurations. Thus, while the war-to-capability association must be kept in mind, it is of minor consequence in the analyses at hand. We will, however, return to it in later reports, in which a number of feedback models will be put to the test.

Thus we conclude this section on the associations between capability concentrations and major power inter-state war by noting that the evidence is, for the moment, quite divided. While high concentration and changes toward it do—as the preponderance and stability school suggests—tend to reduce the incidence of war in the current century, such is clearly not the case in the previous century. Those patterns are much closer to what is predicted by the peace-through-parity-and-fluidity model. Let us turn, then, to a more detailed and complex scrutiny of the question.

THE MULTIVARIATE ANALYSES

With the bivariate analyses and some very tentative conclusions behind us, we can now turn to the multivariate models and consider the possible *joint* effects of capability configurations on the incidence of major power war. We do this via the consideration of four different versions of our model, reflecting those of an additive and those of a multiplicative type, and distinguishing between those in which we measure CON before ΔCON or MOVE and those in which CON follows ΔCON and MOVE chronologically. Before examining the several models and the extent to which they match the historical realities, we consider the rationale behind each type.

Looking at the additive-multiplicative distinctions first, let us think of our

11. Given the fact that most of the changes in the size of the major power sub-system occur as the result of high magnitude wars, we also examined the extent to which such changes themselves might be affecting the value of CON. It turns out—not surprisingly—that whatever decrease is found in the predictive power of CON vis-a-vis subsequent war is already accounted for by prior war; thus there is no need to control for the effects of both prior war *and* change in system size.

three predictor variables as if they were merely binary in nature, with 1 reflecting a high value of each and 0 reflecting a low value. Let us assume, further, that war will result if the variables, singly or in combination, reach a threshold of 1 or more. If their effects are additive, it is clear that we will have wars as long as *any one* of them is equal to 1. On the other hand, if their effects are *multiplicative, all* of them must equal 1, since a 0 value on any one of them will give us a product of 0. Another way to look at this distinction is to think of the road to war as having either fixed or flexible exits. In the multiplicative case, there are several exits, since we only need to have a low value (i.e., 0, for *any* one of them to avoid war; hence the flexibility of exits from the road to war. In the additive case, however, the exits are quite fixed; unless *every* one of the predictors is low (i.e. 0), war will result. We might also think of the additive version as a "marginal" one, in that the magnitude of each variable can only exercise a marginal effect on the probability of war, whereas the magnitude of each in the multiplicative case can be determining, at least in the negative sense.[12]

In addition to considering additive and multiplicative versions of the basic model, we need to consider the chronological sequence in which the variables are combined in accounting for the incidence of war. In the bivariate analyses, since the effects of each predictor variable upon war were measured separately, this was no problem. But here, especially since we already know that there is some interdependence among the three predictors, that sequence becomes critical. Unless we want to assume that the capability configurations could exercise their impact later than five years after being observed—which we do not—there are two major options. In one, we measure CON at 1870 (for example), ΔCON and MOVE between 1870 and 1875, and WAR from 1875 through 1879; we call this the CON LEADS version. In the other, we measure CON at 1875, with ΔCON and MOVE observed between 1870 and 1875, and WAR again measured during the 1875-1879 period; this is the CON LAGS version.

Thus, the basic model can be represented in four different forms:

ADD/CON LEADS: $WAR_{t_1 \to 2} = \alpha + \beta_1(CON_{t_0}) + \beta_2(\Delta CON_{t_0 \to 1}) + \beta_3(MOVE_{t_0 \to 1}) + \epsilon$

ADD/CON LAGS: $WAR_{t_1 \to 2} = \alpha + \beta_1(\Delta CON_{t_0 \to 1}) + \beta_2(MOVE_{t_0 \to 1}) + \beta_3(CON_{t_1}) + \epsilon$

MULT/CON LEADS: $WAR_{t_1 \to 2} = \alpha \times (CON_{t_0}^{\beta_1}) \times (\Delta CON_{t_0 \to 1}^{\beta_2}) \times (MOVE_{t_0 \to 1}^{\beta_3}) \times \epsilon$

MULT/CON LAGS: $WAR_{t_1 \to 2} = \alpha \times (\Delta CON_{t_0 \to 1}^{\beta_1}) \times (MOVE_{t_0 \to 1}^{\beta_2}) \times (CON_{t_1}^{\beta_3}) \times \epsilon$

where α = estimated constant term, or intercept; β = estimated regression coefficient, and ϵ = error term, or unexplained variance. How well do the several versions predict to the actual historical pattern of major power inter-state war? In Table 4 we show the following for each version of the model: the multiple regression coefficient (R), the multiple coefficient of determination (R^2), and the corrected multiple coefficient of determination ($\bar{R}^2$), as well as the beta

12. For an illuminating discussion of the statistical treatment of multiplicative and other interactive models, see Blalock (1965).

weights, or standardized regression coefficients (b), and the squared partial correlation coefficients (r^2) between each of the separate predictor variables and war, controlling for the other two.[13]

Table 4. Predictive Power of Four Versions of the Capability-War Model, ENTIRE SPAN (N=28)

Version	MULTIPLES			CON		ΔCON		MOVE	
	R	R^2	$\bar{R}^2$	b	r^2	b	r^2	b	r^2
ADD/CON LEADS	.56	.31	.23	−.28	.04	−.61	.20	.45	.20
ADD/CON LAGS	.55	.30	.22	−.18	.02	−.33	.11	.46	.18
MULT/CON LEADS	.43	.19	.09	−.27	.04	−.57	.15	.21	.04
MULT/CON LAGS	.43	.18	.08	−.22	.03	−.28	.07	.24	.05

R = Multiple correlation coefficient
R^2 = Coefficient of multiple determination
$\bar{R}^2$ = Corrected coefficient of multiple determination
b = Standardized regression coefficient
r^2 = Squared partial correlation coefficient

Correlations among the predictor variables:

$\Delta CON_{t_0 \to t_1}$	1.00	−.71	.47
$MOVE_{t_0 \to t_1}$	.08	.21	.50
	$\Delta CON_{t_0 \to t_1}$	CON_{t_0}	CON_{t_1}

The overall impression is that all four versions of the preponderance and stability model do moderately well in predicting to the incidence of war. Every one of the signs is in the direction predicted by that model, with high CON and

13. $\bar{R}^2$ is the coefficient of multiple determination, corrected for degrees of freedom in the following way:

$$\bar{R}^2 = 1 - \left[\frac{(1 - R^2)\,(N - 1)}{N - k - 1} \right]$$

where N = number of observations, and k = number of predictor variables. This index thus conservatively adjusts the goodness-of-fit estimate, penalizing the researcher for a large number of predictor variables and a small number of observations. This rewards parsimony and high N/k ratios; see Ezekiel and Fox (1959, Chap. 17) and Deutsch, Singer, and Smith (1965).

The regression coefficients of the multiplicative models were estimated by means of a $\log_e (X + C)$ transformation on all the variables, where $C = 1.0$ minus the minimum value of variable X. As Russett et al. explain (1964, pp. 311-313), *addition* of these transformed series is equivalent to the *multiplication* of their original values, and permits the researcher to isolate a unique coefficient for each variable's contribution to the combined multiplicative term. Without this transformation, only a gross coefficient for the interactive effect of the three variables could be estimated.

upward ΔCON preceding low levels of war (i.e. negative correlations with war) and high movement predicting to high levels of war. But the direction of the signs is a relatively crude index; how close is the fit between predicted and observed war levels?

Here we see that the two additive versions of the model, accounting as they do for 31 and 30 percent of the variance, do fairly well, whereas the multiplicative versions do not do as well. But this is only true before we correct for the degrees of freedom lost or gained by the number of observations and the number of predictor variables. When we introduce those corrections, none of the versions turns out to be particularly powerful in accounting for the observed levels of war. We also note that it makes little difference whether we observe CON before or after the two redistribution indices (ΔCON and MOVE). As to the predictive power of the separate indices, the impact of CON in the additive versions is consistently less than that of ΔCON and MOVE; in the multiplicative versions, this pattern is less clear. In sum, however, it is noteworthy that a model could predict as well as this one does, given the already apparent differences between the 19th and 20th century systems. One indication of its overall predictive power is revealed in Figure 1; the observed war values are shown as o's and those predicted by the ADD/CON LEADS version are shown as plus signs. What we see, in the distance between each pair of half-decade points, is that our fit is considerably better for the earlier than for the later epoch. More specifically, while it seems to predict fairly well to the occurrence and non-occurrence of war, it seriously underestimates the war levels generated by the two World Wars and the Korean War, for example.

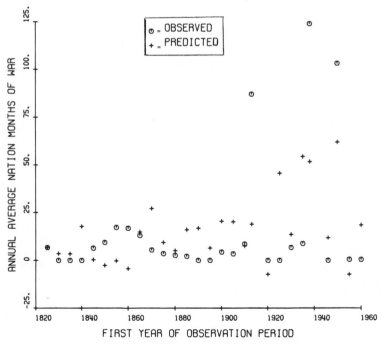

Figure 1. ADD/CON LEADS Model, Full Span

Do the several versions of our model do better when we examine the two centuries separately? As Tables 5 and 6 indicate, their predictive power is impressively high for the 19th century and rather low for the 20th; this disparity would account for the mixed results in the overall time span. In Table 5, reflecting the earlier epoch, we find that the additive versions are once again considerably more powerful than the multiplicative ones. More important, however, are the differences among the corrected coefficients of determination. This very conservative index shows that the additive versions account for at least 65 percent of the variance in our outcome variable (WAR) in the first of our two epochs.

Table 5. Predictive Power of Four Versions of the Capability-War Model, 19TH CENTURY (N=14)

Version	MULTIPLES			CON		ΔCON		MOVE	
	R	R^2	$\bar{R}^2$	b	r^2	b	r^2	b	r^2
ADD/CON LEADS	.85	.73	.65	.85	.72	.29	.19	−.38	.00
ADD/CON LAGS	.85	.73	.65	.96	.71	−.31	.17	−.39	.00
MULT/CON LEADS	.72	.52	.38	.73	.52	.16	.04	−.08	.01
MULT/CON LAGS	.72	.52	.38	.83	.50	−.35	.13	−.08	.01

Correlations among the predictor variables:

$\Delta CON_{t_0 \to t_1}$ 1.00   −.14   .49

$MOVE_{t_0 \to t_1}$ −.46   .19   −.12

$\Delta CON_{t_0 \to t_1}$ CON_{t_0} CON_{t_1}

Table 6. Predictive Power of Four Versions of the Capability-War Model, 20TH CENTURY (N=14)

Version	MULTIPLES			CON		ΔCON		MOVE	
	R	R^2	$\bar{R}^2$	b	r^2	b	r^2	b	r^2
ADD/CON LEADS	.59	.35	.15	−.50	.12	−.85	.29	.44	.19
ADD/CON LAGS	.56	.31	.10	−.31	.07	−.32	.10	.45	.17
MULT/CON LEADS	.68	.46	.30	−.81	.31	−1.11	.46	.37	.18
MULT/CON LAGS	.64	.41	.23	−.58	.24	−.24	.07	.42	.18

Correlations among the predictor variables:

$\Delta CON_{t_0 \to t_1}$ 1.00   −.75   .49

$MOVE_{t_0 \to t_1}$ .14   .16   .51

$\Delta CON_{t_0 \to t_1}$ CON_{t_0} CON_{t_1}

R = Multiple correlation coefficient
R^2 = Coefficient of multiple determination
$\bar{R}^2$ = Corrected coefficient of multiple determination
b = Standardized regression coefficient
r^2 = Squared partial correlation coefficient

As to the 20th century, the multiple coefficients of determination (R^2) are far from negligible, but unlike the findings for the entire period and the 19th century, here we find the multiplicative version to be more powerful than the additive one. This is not only quite consistent with our bivariate results, but is understandable in the context of our interpretation of multiplicative models. That is, the −.23 correlation between CON and WAR in the 20th century suggests that there is *some* association between the two, and an examination of our scatter plots showed that while most war did occur when CON was low, there were several periods in which CON was low, but *no* war occurred. To put it another way, low CON was *necessary* in order for large wars to occur, but it was far from sufficient. The multiple exit interpretation would suggest, then, that the absence of a downward change in CON (i.e. −ΔCON), a high MOVE, or the effect of some unmeasured intervening variables(s) nevertheless permitted the low CON state of affairs to remain a peaceful one.

Looking at the beta weights, we find that all the signs but one are in the directions predicted by the parity-fluidity school's version of the model in the 19th century, and by the preponderance-stability version in the 20th. That exception occurs in the 19th century ADD and MULT models, when we observe CON after ΔCON and MOVE in the unfolding of events. Whereas a change toward higher concentration makes for more war when CON itself leads, it makes for less war (as the preponderance-stability school would predict) when CON follows behind ΔCON and MOVE. This result is a consequence of the high auto-correlation (.62) in CON in the 19th century.[14]

Returning to the other beta weights, we ask which of the separate indicators

---

14. The explanation for this phenomenon is somewhat lengthy and several discussions of it may be found in Harris (ed., 1963). To put the matter briefly, suppose that the true CON measures at t_0 and t_1 were equal. ΔCON would then be positively related to the errors in CON at t_1 and negatively related to the errors in CON at t_0, since ΔCON would under these circumstances be equal to the difference between these error terms. If the simple correlation between WAR and ΔCON were positive, as we have found, then the partial relationship between WAR and ΔCON controlling for CON at t_0 would also be positive. This necessarily follows since by controlling for CON at t_0 we are controlling for its error as well; thus the partial association between WAR and ΔCON is the equivalent of the relationship between WAR and the error in CON at t_1, controlling for the error in CON at t_0. As the error in CON at t_1 increases, ΔCON will also increase, and since the relationship between ΔCON and WAR is positive, so also must the relationship between WAR and the error in CON at t_1 be positive.

However, when we control for CON at t_1, rather than at t_0, and investigate the relationship between ΔCON and WAR, we are analyzing the relationship between WAR and the error in CON at t_0, controlling for the error in CON at t_1. As the error in CON at t_0 increases, ΔCON will decrease, and since the relationship between ΔCON and WAR is positive, the relationship between WAR and the error in CON at t_0 must be negative.

Even though our ΔCON measure is not, as assumed above, simply a function of error, the error components are present and apparently responsible for the observed sign reversal. This reversal supports the positive effect of ΔCON on WAR in the 20th century, but it also points up some of the problems which may be encountered when both a variable and its first-difference derivation are used in a regression equation.

exercises the strongest impact. In the 19th century, CON is by far the most potent variable in the regression equation, with all r^2 values greater than .50. This is, of course, fully consonant with the bivariate findings, as is the negligible strength of the movement index. And, as noted above, the effect of ΔCON (when we control for CON and MOVE) is a moderately strong and positive one when CON leads the redistribution measures, and almost as strong but negative when CON follows in the chronological sequence. In the 20th century, on the other hand, we find that all three predictor variables exercise approximately the same impact.[15] And whereas the additive versions give the better fit in the earlier epoch, the multiplicative ones do better in the current century. As a matter of fact, the MULT/CON LEADS version shows fairly strong predictive power, with an R^2 of .46 and partial r^2s of .31 and .46 for CON and ΔCON, respectively. Again the bivariate and multivariate analyses point quite consistently in the same direction.[16]

An examination of Figures 2 and 3 will not only reaffirm, but strengthen, the above statistical results. Plotted on the same scale as Figure 1, these indicate the discrepancy between the levels of war predicted by the ADD/CON LEADS model and the amounts that actually occurred in each half-decade. The deviations (i.e. the distances between 0 and + for each half-decade) are remarkably small in the 19th century, but much less consistent in the 20th century plot. The parity-fluidity school is thus strongly vindicated in the earlier

15. Parenthetically, for those who suspect that the definition of war used here may be too broad in that it embraces *all* inter-state war involving major powers, we mention a relevant finding. That is, if we look only at those eight wars in which there is a major power on *each* side, we find that there was a decline in CON during the half decade preceding all but one of those wars. Since these are almost equally divided between the centuries, they lend some support to the peace through preponderance doctrine.

16. We mentioned earlier the problems of multi-collinearity (high correlations among the predictor variables) and auto-correlated error terms. Because our predictor variables are highly correlated in several cases, we omitted one of them at a time and computed the predictions each of our models would have made from each pair of predictor variables, to see the effect of deleting a variable which was highly correlated with another in the equation. The coefficients from those equations were, predictably, similar in sign and strength to the predictions made from our three-variable models, although they naturally produced somewhat poorer overall results. Had we been interested in finding the "perfect" model we would not have included all three variables each time, but for the purposes of this paper, we considered it useful to present the results for each of the variables in all four variations of the multivariate model. As noted earlier, the correlations between the various predictor variables for each time period are shown beneath Tables 4, 5, and 6, respectively.

As to the auto-correlation problem, Table 2 shows that several of our variables do exhibit noticeable first-order auto-correlation r's: −.13 for the 150 year WAR series, and .73 and −.29 for the separate centuries. The predictions of our four models do a fair job of explaining, where it exists, the auto-correlation in the war variable. The most highly auto-correlated residual terms result from our 19th century predictions; in the case of the ADD/CON LEADS model, the coefficient of that residual series is .47, which, although sizeable, is considerably lower than the amount of auto-correlation in the original series. The coefficients for the residuals of its predictions are .27 for the 150 year span, .47 for the 19th century, and −.13 for the 20th.

epoch, while those who look to peace-through-preponderance-and-stability have the better of the argument in the later one.

A close look at Table 7 permits us to see more specifically wherein the amount of war predicted by the models deviates from that which actually occurred. Note, by way of introduction, that even though the same basic model is employed (i.e. ADD/CON LEADS, reflected in the first line in Tables 4, 5, and 6), the difference in the predictions made by the full span model and those for the separate centuries is a result of the difference in signs, as already mentioned. That is, since the best-fitting equation for the entire span has the same signs as that which is nearly the best for the 20th century, it therefore imposes *its* predictions on the 19th century.[17]

Shifting to the columns for the war levels predicted by the parity-fluidity (19th century) and preponderance-stability (20th century) models, a number of specific discrepancies merit explicit comment. Working our way down, we first note that the model underestimates—or more accurately, lags in predicting—the amount of war in the 1820-1840 period. From there on to the end of the 19th century, the fit is fairly good, giving us our estimated standard error of 3.60, which is a function of the actual discrepancy between the predicted and the observed values.

Moving into the later of our two eras, the 20th century model tends to overestimate the levels for 1925-29 and 1935-37, to underestimate the magnitudes of World War I, World War II and the Korean War, and to overestimate the final decade's warlikeness. This latter discrepancy may well be accounted for by the coding rules used for this particular study, excluding as they do the appreciable levels of *extra*-systemic war which marked that period. In general, the 20th century model spreads out the total amount of war more evenly, rather than predicting the radical fluctuations which do in fact occur; the standard error of the prediction is 40.48. For both centuries, of course, the inclusion of additional variables would have given us a better fit, but our objective was not so much to create or discover a best-fitting model as it was to *test* an *a priori* one.

CONCLUSION

Before we summarize the results of these analyses, it is important to make very explicit the tentative nature of our findings. Nor is this a mere genuflection in the direction of scientific custom. The study is preliminary in several fundamental meanings of the word.

First, there are the standard problems associated with any "first cut" investigation. Among these are: (a) the absence of any prior analyses of the same type; (b) the possibility of inaccuracies in our data, and as Morgenstern (1963) reminds us, the soures of error may indeed be considerable; and (c) the lack of

17. We say "nearly," because we actually get the best fit in the 20th century with the multiplicative version.

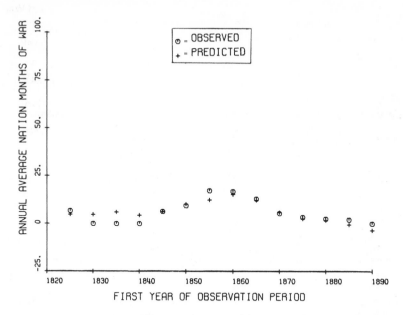

Figure 2. ADD/CON LEADS Model, 19th Century

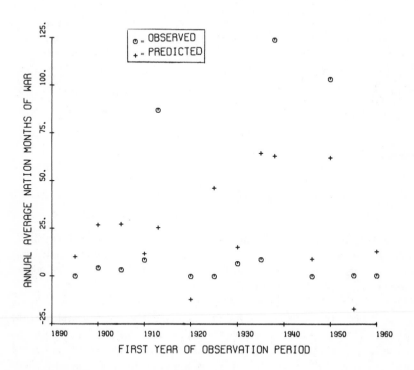

Figure 3. ADD/CON LEADS Model, 20th Century

Table 7. Observed Levels of War and Levels Predicted by ADD/CON LEADS Model:
Entire Time Span and Separate Centuries

AVERAGE ANNUAL NUMBER OF NATION-MONTHS UNDERWAY

Period Beginning	Observed	Full-Span Model Predictions	19th Century Model Predictions	20th Century Model Predictions
1825	6.68	6.72	4.80	
1830	0.0	3.51	4.78	
1835	0.0	3.44	6.06	
1840	0.0	17.79	4.39	
1845	6.40	0.36	6.32	
1850	9.36	−2.54	10.23	
1855	17.24	−0.20	12.41	
1860	16.82	−4.35	15.33	
1865	12.98	14.87	12.32	
1870	5.44	27.10	5.92	
1875	3.52	9.31	2.69	
1880	2.64	5.06	1.89	
1885	2.12	16.03	−0.43	
1890	0.0	16.84	−3.51	
1895	0.0	6.35		10.16
1900	4.32	20.44		26.92
1905	3.40	20.15		27.39
1910	8.47	7.47		11.91
1913	87.06	18.96		25.62
1920	0.0	−7.29		−11.95
1925	0.0	45.64		46.28
1930	6.68	13.56		15.36
1935	8.73	54.36		64.54
1938	123.97	51.70		63.13
1946	0.0	11.83		9.12
1950	103.34	61.94		62.24
1955	0.52	−7.36		−16.90
1960	0.44	18.45		13.12

any hard evidence against which the validity of our predictor variables might be measured. In this vein, our use of the composite index of capability may possibly conceal certain important differences that could be revealed by each of the separate (demographic, industrial, and military) indices.

Secondly, the reliance on quinquennial observations might well account for an untoward portion of the results, in both the positive and negative sense of the word. The cutting points between the half-decades can so distribute the capability and war scores that, by accident alone, they may fall into either the "right" or "wrong" time period. Had we used a measure of the amount of war *begun* in a given period, that problem would have been even more accentuated; by measuring war underway, we minimize but do not eliminate the dangers of such an artifact. And any *annual* fluctuation in the predictor variables is concealed. In addition, the fixed interval between observations forecloses the use of briefer or longer spans in experimenting with various lag and lead relationships. In a follow-up study, when our annual capability data are available, we will have much more flexibility in our design, and will be able to ascertain whether the quinquennial time units do indeed represent a source of distortion in the results.

Third, our use of the single nation as our object of analysis may not only be an inaccurate reflection of who the "real" actors are, but produce distorted measures of capability and its distribution. Fourth, as we noted, our decision to defer the analysis of the feedback loops which connect *prior war to concentration* as well as *concentration to subsequent war* leaves our analysis of the problem far from complete. Fifth, it may well be that these findings will continue to hold as we re-examine our model's applicability to the major sub-system, but turn out to be quite inapplicable to the power and war dynamics of other sub-systems or the international system as a whole. Finally, it should be emphasized that this investigation is at the systemic level only and that no inferences can be made as to which particular nations, blocs, or dyads become involved in war resulting from the distribution or redistribution of capabilities.

With these caveats in mind, let us summarize what we have done in the investigation at hand, and what we think has been discovered. To recapitulate the theoretical argument, we have synthesized from the literature two distinct and incompatible models of the way in which the distribution and redistribution of capabilities affects the incidence of major power war. One, which we see as a formal and integrated version of the classical balance of power viewpoint (Haas, 1953) predicts that there will be less war when there is: (a) approximate parity among the major nations; (b) change toward parity rather than away from it; and (c) a relatively fluid power hierarchy. The other, reflecting the hegemony view, predicts that there will be less war when there is: (a) a preponderance of power concentrated in the hands of a very few nations; (b) change, if any, toward greater concentration; and (c) a relatively stable rank order among, and intervals between, the major powers. Even though a variety of intervening variables may be introduced as the link between such capability configurations and the preservation of peace, we suggest that decisional uncertainty is a parsimonious and appropriate one, and is implied in many of the traditional analyses. While both schools agree that parity and fluidity increase that uncertainty, only the first would hold that such uncertainty makes for peace; the preponderance and stability school sees uncertainty as leading to war.

These two sets of predictions have been consolidated into a single basic model incorporating the three predictor variables (capability concentration, rate and direction of change in concentration, and the movement of capability shares among the powers) and the outcome variable (amount of inter-state war involving major powers). But the classical theorizers were less than precise in their formulations, and said little in regard either to the sequence in which the variables should exercise their effects, or the way in which those effects might combine, making it necessary to construct alternative representations. Since an examination of only the most obvious version would be less than a fair test, we articulated and tested four versions: an additive and a multiplicative form with the measurement of concentration prior to the measurement of its change and movement, and an additive and multiplicative one with concentration measured after change and movement.

The first test of all four versions was for the entire century and a half since the Congress of Vienna, and it showed the preponderance and stability school's predictions to be closer to historical reality than those of the parity and fluidity school. But even though the correlations were all in the direction predicted by the preponderance school, their goodness of fit was not very impressive. Then, on the basis of prior findings, as well as a number of visual and statistical examinations of the data, we divided the century and a half into two separate eras of equal length, and re-tested the models.

This time, the predictions of the *parity and fluidity* school turned out to be correct in the direction of their associations and strong in their fit with 19th century reality. Particularly powerful was the additive form of the model with concentration measured prior to its redistribution. And, not surprisingly, given the results of the full 150 year analyses, the *20th* century findings matched the predictions of the *preponderance and stability* school. But whereas the corrected coefficient of determination ($\bar{R}^2$) for the parity model in the earlier era was .65, the best of those for the preponderance model in the contemporary era was .31.

Bearing in mind the opening paragraphs in this section, as well as the relatively clear empirical results, we conclude that the concentration of major power capabilities does indeed exercise an impact on the incidence of war and that its impact has been a radically different one in the past and present centuries. As to possible explanations for these radical differences, space limitations preclude any lengthy consideration. For the moment, though, we might speculate that uncertainty—our unmeasured intervening variable—plays a different role in the two centuries. When diplomacy was still largely in the hands of small elite groups, the uncertainty factor (allegedly resulting from an equal distribution of power, and fluidity in the rank orderings) may have been modest in both its magnitude and its effects. Schooled in the accepted norms of the game, these professionals might be uncertain as to exactly who ranked where, but nevertheless fairly confident as to general behavior patterns. The shared culture made it relatively clear what each would do in given—and familiar—situations of conflict or crisis, and their relative freedom of action made it easier to conform to such regularized expectations.

By the turn of the century, however, industrialization, urbanization, and the democratization of diplomacy may have begun to erode the rules of the game. Conventional definitons of the national interest were no longer widely accepted at home, and political oppositions and interest groups could make certain foreign policy moves difficult and costly to a regime. The increasing need to mobilize popular support as well as material resources meant that the vagaries of domestic politics would intrude more fully into a nation's diplomacy. And a grasp of other nations' domestic politics has never been a strong point in the foreign offices of the world. Hence, the normal uncertainties of the "balance of power" system were aggravated by these additional uncertainties, meaning that the probability of war could only be kept within bounds when power configurations were exceptionally clear and the pecking order was quite unambiguous. This is, of course, only one of several possible interpretations, and a highly speculative one at that.[18] In due course, then, we hope to bring more solid evidence to bear on the power-war relationships which are reported here; in that context, a number of technological, sociological, and political hypotheses will receive due consideration.

Given our findings and the associated caveats, are any policy implications worth noting? On the one hand—as our critics continue to remind us—such macro-level phenomena as the distribution of military-industrial capabilities are not exactly susceptible to short run policy control. In this, as in other of our analyses to date, the independent variables are indeed "independent" as far as immediate human intervention is concerned. They change rather slowly, and worse yet, they seldom seem to change in response to conscious and intelligent planning.

On the other hand, a fuller understanding of these structural conditions is much to be valued. Not only do they appear to exercise a powerful impact on the peacefulness of the international system, but they also constitute some of the major constraints within which men and groups act and interact. Despite the views of Rapoport (1970) and others that "there is no lack of knowledge about 'what men could do' to insure peace," we are struck with the evidence to the contrary.

Closely related is the familiar issue of how similar the world of the 1970's and 1980's is to that of the 1816-1895 or 1900-1965 periods. If the system has changed drastically on one or more occasions in this century, or is likely to do so in the near future, how relevant are the results of historical analyses? Our findings in the Correlates of War project to date suggest rather strongly that: (a) today's world *is* different from that of the 19th century, but (b) the most discernible changes occurred around the turn of the century and not with the first or second World War or with the advent of nuclear weapons and ballistic missiles. For the moment, then, all we can say is that it behooves us to treat all such alleged transformations as empirical questions, and to ascertain the extent

18. It has been alleged (e.g. Bleicher, 1971) that one abuses the scientific method by advancing alternative interpretations without supporting data. Our view is that such a practice not only enhances the quality and cumulativeness of science by suggesting possible follow-up investigations, but helps keep our discipline relevant to the real problems of war and peace in the immediate future.

to which such changes have affected the probability of war. We suspect, as noted above, that the 20th century system *is* a less stable and less easily understood one than the 19th, and that we *are* experiencing different types of war brought on by differing conditions. But it may also have given us the knowledge and skills that make it more tractable to us than the 19th century was for those who sought to understand and control the international politics of that era.

In saying this, however, we have no illusions that social scientific discoveries related to war (or other problems of social justice) will inevitably be utilized to better the lot of humanity (Singer, 1970). Knowledge can not only remain *un*applied; it can also be *mis*applied. But that is no justification for eschewing knowledge. Rather, our job is to ask the most important questions, seek the answers in the most efficient and rigorous fashion, publish our findings and interpretations in an expeditious fashion—and act on them in a forthright manner. As we see it, peace research—especially on the structural conditions that make for war—*is* peace action of a critical sort. Thus, as we continue to press for the policy changes that we *suspect* may improve man's chances for survival and dignity, we nevertheless continue that research which will permit us to replace mere suspicion with relatively hard knowledge.

MICHAEL D. WALLACE

2. Status, Formal Organization, and Arms Levels as Factors Leading to the Onset of War, 1820-1964

ABSTRACT

Recent theoretical and empirical literature in international politics contains many references to the effect of status inconsistency on national behavior. It has been found that if there are wide discrepancies between a nation's ranking on two or more dimensions of a nation's status set, the nation concerned has a tendency to manifest aggressive behavior and internal instability. In this paper, an attempt is made to determine, (a) the causal sequence linking status inconsistency with the outbreak of conflict, and (b) whether the observed effect of status inconsistency is merely an artifact of the action of some other status variable.

Using dependence analysis on data for the international system from 1820 to 1964, four main discoveries were made. First, although status inconsistency was strongly related to the degree of national mobility on the capability and attributed dimensions of status, status inconsistency was not an artifact of the relationship between national mobility and war but rather a crucial intervening variable between the two. Second, the degree of formal alliance commitment in the international system was an important factor linking status inconsistency with the onset of war. Third, inconsistency and conflict were linked to an extent by the rate of generation of international organization in the system, but this variable played an important role only during the latter part of the period under study. Finally, and most important of all, the tensions generated by these structural variables were translated into actual armed conflict primarily via increases in the size of armed forces.

These findings seemed to imply that the preservation of peace in the international system may depend on two main factors: (a) the ability to reduce either the amount or the salience of status inconsistency in the international system, and (b) the ability to prevent or control arms races. ∎

Author's Note: I wish to thank J. David Singer for his generous provision of the data used in this study, and Russell Uhler, Director of the Statistical Center at the University of British Columbia, for his assistance with the mathematics.

49

INTRODUCTION

A significant focus of attention in recent peace research literature has been the relationship between the international "pecking order" of power and status, and the frequency, magnitude, and severity of international war. Long a matter for speculation and discussion among practitioners and "power theorists" (Organski, 1968: ch. 9; Morgenthau, 1967: chs. 9 & 10), this relationship has, within the past few years, come within the purview of rigorous data-based analysis. In the process, it has drawn heavily upon insights from the other social sciences where theory and evidence linking individual status and behavior are comparatively well-developed.

One such insight is the well-tested proposition that individual behavior is affected not only by overall position on the social hierarchy, but also by the degree to which an individual's rankings on the "achieved" and "ascribed" dimensions of his status set correspond. If, for example, an individual's salary and job status do not match up to his education and skills, he will experience frustration in social situations which emphasize this "status inconsistency." Such frustration will manifest itself as psychological stress, attitude change, and, occasionally, as aggressive or hostile behavior.

A number of theoretical and empirical studies suggest that an analogous relationship between status inconsistency and conflict may exist in the international system. In a pioneering work, Galtung (1964b) noted that many aggressive nations in the modern period seem to have been status inconsistent, typically higher on "achieved" status dimensions such as military-industrial capability than on "ascribed" dimensions such as recognition and prestige.[1] The most often-cited example is in Germany, prior to World War I, which did not achieve a "place in the sun" comparable to that enjoyed by Britain and France despite her first rank military-industrial capability.

But support for this hypothesis is not confined to anecdotal evidence. Fossum (1967) discovered a relationship between status inconsistency and the likelihood of military coups d'état amongst Latin American nations. Midlarsky (1969) found a moderately strong association between long term upward tendencies in status inconsistency and the amount of international war experienced by nations between 1870 and 1945, and East (1971) found an equally strong relationship between status inconsistency and war at the level of the system as a whole for the period 1948 to 1964. Finally, the present author found that with a time lag of 15 years, status inconsistency explained as much as 71 percent of the variance in nation-months of war begun in the system during certain periods between 1820 and 1964 (Wallace, (1971). Collectively, these results provide good evidence that status inconsistency is associated with

1. In what follows, the distinction between the "high achieved-low ascribed" and "high ascribed-low achieved" configurations of status will not be emphasized, as no predictions concerning their relative importance can be tested with the present research design (Section 9 below). For a discussion of the implications of this distinction, see Galtung (1966).

international conflict, especially considering the magnitude of the reported relationship and the consistency of the findings despite wide variations in domain, indicators, and techniques. Nonetheless, they leave important gaps in our knowledge which reduce the practical usefulness of the results and which must be filled before it can be claimed that status inconsistency has been established as a cause of international war.

First, these studies report that the highest level of association is observed only when a substantial time lag has been introduced, sometimes as long as 15 years. This could mean that the tensions and stress produced by status inconsistency require a long time to build up to levels which noticeably increase the probability of violence, or it might be that status inconsistency is a very indirect cause of war, setting in motion a sequence of change in the characteristics of the system which terminates in war only much later. But none of these studies adduce any evidence about the causal sequence, and it will not do to assume by analogy with the individual that status inconsistency leads to national "frustration" which in turn results in aggression. While it has been said often, it bears repeating that analogies between nations and individuals are on very uncertain ground when they involve the projection of internal psychological states into a collectivity. If we are to speak properly òf a causal sequence, it must be specified empirically.

That this has not been done is a double liability. For one thing, the purpose of studying international violence is presumably to facilitate its control, and this will not readily be achieved if only the background conditions of war are known, since control over these may prove possible only in the very long run. In the case at issue, obviously the manipulation of national status to increase consistency would require much greater control over the processes of the international system than is likely to be achieved for some time. A far more promising approach would be to control or neutralize the changes which result, i.e., manipulate the intervening variables.

In addition, long time lags inevitably raise the suspicion that the observed relationship results from some artifact in the data, particularly when the number of observations is quite small.[2] For example, if the actual causal sequence was reversed (i.e., the disruptions of war generated status inconsistency, not an unlikely state of affairs) and if the dependent variable was serially correlated (and the suggestion that war is cyclical is as old as Socrates[3]), then the observed associations could have been produced even though no causal relationship existed.[4] Thus, definitive confirmation of the hypothesis requires some empirical verification of the causal sequence.

2. The East and Wallace studies which observed a time lag effect were based on 17 and 29 observations respectively.

3. A somewhat more contemporary version of this hypothesis, along with some supporting evidence, may be found in Wright (1965a, ch. 9), and in Singer and Small (1972, ch. 9).

4. The relationship between time lags and reciprocal causation is explored in Wold (1960) and in Wright (1960).

The possibility that the relationship is a statistical artifact leads to a consideration of the second major gap in our knowledge, the connection which may exist between status inconsistency and other background variables associated with war. Because all previous studies report only bivariate relationships, it is possible that some third variable, closely associated with status inconsistency, is responsible for the observable results. This possibility is very important in the present case, since theoretical considerations allow us to identify several variables which might play such a role. Status inconsistency is defined in terms of two or more status hierarchies in the international system, and so presumably will be statistically associated with other variables defined with reference to hierarchy. It could therefore be argued quite plausibly that they, and not status inconsistency, are causally related to war.[5] A list of the possibilities would include such "theory-rich" variables as the rates of upward and downward mobility in military capability, level of economic development and prestige status, and the size of gaps or differentials between nations on these basic status measures. It would therefore be foolhardy to rule out the possibility of spuriousness a priori.

The task of this paper, then, is to incorporate the observed strong bivariate relationship between status inconsistency and war into a multivariate explanatory model by introducing into the analysis both variables which are logically prior in the causal order as well as those which theory indicates are likely intervening links in the hypothesized relationship. The correct causal inferences can then be ascertained using multivariate analysis.

THE BACKGROUND VARIABLES—
DIFFERENTIAL RATES OF CHANGE

We now take up the question of which additional variables should be included in the analysis, beginning with those which might have caused us to observe a spurious relationship between status inconsistency and war.

Of course, since the many possible relationships between international hierarchy and national behavior have scarcely begun to be explored, it is hardly feasible to examine all such variables. However, there is one set which is of particular importance to the present effort. Galtung (1964b) has suggested that among the most likely causes of status inconsistency are differences in national rates of growth on the demographic, economic, and military dimensions of power capability. If a nation experiences rapid growth relative to that of other nations on one or more of these attributes and thereby acquires a higher achieved status, it is unlikely that a corresponding rise in ascribed status will occur immediately, creating a discrepancy in the nation's status set. Moreover, the more rapid the growth, the larger this gap is likely to become.

---

5. Blalock has pointed out that this fact represents a virtually insurmountable difficulty at the level of the individual social actor, since the effects of status inconsistency cannot be mathematically distinguished from those produced by position on the two hierarchies (Blalock, 1966).

We would therefore expect such differences in rates of growth to be closely associated with status inconsistency. But it is quite plausible that differential rates of capability change will lead to conflict in quite other ways. For one thing, many theorists believe that widening capability gaps between nations play an important role in the generation of conflict either by threatening an existing distribution of power (Morgenthau, 1967), or rendering defenseless those who are (relatively) downwardly mobile (Lagos, 1963). It has also been suggested that under some circumstances different national rates of change on these dimensions lead to the narrowing of capability differentials, and that among the larger powers this results in challenges to the international status quo and increased conflict (Organski, 1968). In either case, it would be differential changes in capability and not status inconsistency that were causally connected with war.

A similar line of reasoning may be offered with regard to rates of change on the ascribed status dimension. Here too differential change is likely to be associated with status inconsistency—negatively insofar as this change occurs in respond to change in capability, positively if induced by exogenous factors. Once again we may hypothesize a direct causal connection between such differential change and conflict without reference to status inconsistency. As with any constant-sum attribute, upward mobility for some implies downward mobility for others, and there is little evidence that most nations readily acquiesce in obtaining a declining share of recognition, prestige, or other benefits they have acquired as a result of their importance in the eyes of their national coevals.

Having introduced two additional background variables—differential rates of change on both achieved and ascribed status dimensions—let us now turn to consider some possible causal sequences connecting status inconsistency and war.

THE INTERVENING VARIABLES—ALLIANCES, INTERNATIONAL ORGANIZATIONS, AND ARMED FORCES

There are many possible causal sequences which could be responsible for the observed association between status inconsistency and war. The simplest of these is the direct connection which some writers have assumed by analogy from social psychological theory (Kimberley, 1966; Adams, 1965). According to this line of reasoning, a nation (or, more accurately, national decision-makers and their attentive publics) will adjust its status expectations to the higher of its two rank-positions. In interaction situations which emphasize its lower status it will presumably obtain outcomes less favorable than would have been expected had its higher status governed the situation, and this will be perceived as unjust and inequitable. In short, status inconsistency creates dissatisfaction within a nation because, from its point of view, it violates the crucial system norm that nations receive rewards in proportion to their position on the pecking order. Galtung argues that the frustration thus engendered, coupled with the leverage possessed by such a nation in having at least one high status, create both the motive and the opportunity for increasingly aggressive international behavior, resulting in war if the discrepancy remains uncorrected (Galtung, 1964b).

However, one can hypothesize many alternative ways in which status inconsistency might increase the probability of conflict. For example, an important effect of status discrepancies may be to blur national perceptions about the status hierarchy. In particular, if a nation's ascribed status ranking is different from its capability status, it is not too far-fetched to suppose that other nations will be less likely to evaluate its capability correctly than they would if its statuses were consistent. This would lead us to expect an increased likelihood of conflict since one of the main prerequisites for a successful functioning of a balance of power system (supposed to exist for most of the period under study here) is thought to be the ability to evaluate national capability accurately; if mistaken evaluations are made, the "balance" of the system may become too seriously disturbed before the danger is perceived (Gulick, 1955).

Moreover, the "frustration-aggression" version of the status inconsistency-war relationship is not really in accord with most common beliefs about the structure and functioning of the international system. It is quite plausible that status inconsistency does indeed put discomforting pressures on a nation, leading it to seek changes in at least that aspect of the international status quo which is understood to be at the root of the discrepancy. But it is very doubtful indeed that unilateral action of an aggressive nature would always be the first method employed to achieve the necessary changes, except perhaps in the case of international "pariahs" which do not have the normal opportunities for relationships with other nations. In most cases, a better strategy will be to attempt such changes by acting in concert with other nations:

> "States [struggle] for what they regard as appropriate places in the distribution of power . . . [by the] "artificial" method of linking themselves to the strength of other states. Indeed, this is the only method available to the bulk of states in the actual circumstances of modern history." (Claude, 1962: 89)

In other words, we might suppose that a high level of status inconsistency in the international system will result in an increased level of alliance activity directed towards altering the status quo.[6] Another line of reasoning leading us to the same hypothesis is suggested by the theory of coalition formation. Since the problem facing a status inconsistent nation may be viewed as that of obtaining certain types of outcomes which are consistent with its capabilities, one would expect national decision-makers to seek new interaction opportunities which produce such outcomes. Russett (1968a) has suggested, as a working

6. Liska has proposed the reverse relationship, namely that status inconsistency leads to the disintegration of alliances. However, his argument seems to be relevant primarily to tightly-interdependent postwar alliance systems; here, most changes in the status quo occur within an alliance (see Liska, 1962: 107).

hypothesis, that it is not unreasonable to assume that the distribution of payoffs within an aliance will be some function of the capabilities of the partners. If so, it might be supposed that another attraction of alliances for status inconsistent nations would be that the alliance bond would result in an upgrading of ascribed status within the framework of the alliance, as well as assisting the nation in achieving a higher status in the system as a whole. One might expect further that such coalitions would stimulate the formation of defensive pacts or agreements on the part of those whose interests are threatened by such activity. The combination of these two mutually-reinforcing tendencies should result in an increase in the proportion of nations entering into alliance bonds.

The reader has no doubt anticipated that this causal chain may readily be extended directly to the onset of war. International relations scholars are by no means in agreement over whether alliance bonds are negatively associated with war in that they reduce the temptations for potential aggressors, or positively in that they polarize conflict in the system, but the empirical evidence indicates that the relationship is positive, though weak and varying with the time period examined (Singer and Small, 1968). This suggests the possibility of a two-stage causal link between status inconsistency and war via alliance aggregation.

Another possible link between status inconsistency and war may result from effects on the formation of intergovermental organizations. If the reasoning set forth thus far is correct, status inconsistency will both increase tensions and result in a greater degree of stress being placed on the competitive aspects of the relationships between nations. In such an atmosphere, major initiatives of a cooperative nature between nations will be relatively less frequent. One would expect this to be especially true of those acts of cooperation which imply formal, long-term commitments at a time when the status quo is under attack. Indeed, a continuing theme in the history of many international organizations has been the assaults made upon them by "revisionist" nations. In other words, status inconsistency is likely to have a strong negative impact on the creation, development, and functioning of international organizations, regardless of whether they are oriented towards political objectives or are designed to fulfill a purely technical role.[7] And if, as most of us believe, the existence of such organizations does in some way help to reduce the likelihood of international war (Singer and Wallace, 1970), we may hypothesize the existence of a causal link based on the tendency of status inconsistency to inhibit the growth or organizations which serve to promote cooperation and reduce tension in the international system.

A fourth possibility is that status inconsistency increases the probability of war by stimulating increases in armed forces levels. Since the early work of Richardson (1960b)—if not before—we have been aware that the self-feeding spiral of military might has explosive properties if carried forward for any length

7. The argument that international organizations cannot escape the impact of international tensions solely because their function is technical is made convincingly by Haas (1964).

of time, and anything that contributes to the initiation of such a spiral will be an indirect cause of violence. Of course, one of the most obvious contributors to arms increases is a high level of tension in the system, and for this reason we would suppose that not only status inconsistency, but also the other variables which have been introduced into the analysis thus far will be related to changes in military capacity. Moreover, it is possible that status discrepancies may affect armaments levels in another way. If a nation's military capability should drop below the other dimensions in its status set, and if it has the industrial and demographic capability to rectify the situation, the inconsistent nation may embark upon a rapid military build-up to balance its rankings. In either case, if other nations have reason to feel threatened by such an expansion, an arms race is not an improbable outcome.

Having introduced the variables to be used in this study and specified the hypotheses and theoretical assumptions underlying the model to be constructed, we shall now turn to a specification of the empirical domain and operational procedures employed to produce the indicators.

THE DOMAIN AND
LEVEL OF ANALYSIS

The temporal domain of this study comprises the period from 1820 to 1964. With the exception of 1945,[8] data on each of the variables was collected at intervals of five years beginning with 1820. The purpose of examining such a lengthy time period is to increase the generality of the result; synchronic studies or those based on short intervals run the risk of producing findings which are merely a reflection of short-run idiosyncrasies in the period under consideration. In order to determine whether the relationships between and among the variables underwent any substantial changes during the 145 years from Vienna to Vietnam, the hypotheses were tested for two shorter periods as well, 1820-1944 and 1850-1964.

The choice of a spatial domain is somewhat more complex. To include all state-members of the system would not only create severe data collection problems, but would violate a crucial limiting condition of the hypothesis; for status inconsistency to affect national behavior the nations concerned must be in fairly constant interaction in order that they perceive their own status and that of others as relevant to their goal structure.[9] Hence the test population included only the members of the Singer-Small "central system" (Singer and Small, 1966a) from 1820 to 1919, and from 1920 onwards only those nations receiving diplomatic representation from at least 30 percent of the other system members.

Finally, I decided to test the hypotheses of this study at the level of the international system (Singer, 1961), that is, to examine the relationships

8. Data for most nations could not be obtained immediately after World War II, and for this reason the 1945-1949 period was omitted.

9. For a discussion of this point in a sociological context, see Wesolowski (1966).

between the variables measured over the entire test population of nations. Of course, this procedure has the important disadvantage that it precludes generalizing directly to national behavior on the basis of the results obtained here. However, this decision was made necessary by the previously cited difficulty in separating out the effects of status inconsistency when tests are made at the national level,[10] and the fact that the data on some of the present variables are not easily adaptable to such tests.

OPERATIONALIZING THE VARIABLES

The raw data for this study are taken from the compilations produced by the Correlates of War project under J. David Singer. Detailed descriptions of the operational procedures are available elsewhere (Singer and Small, 1966b; Small and Singer, 1969; Wallace and Singer, 1970; Singer and Small, 1972; Singer, et al., 1973), so only brief sketches will be given here.

The dependent variable, international war, includes all violent conflicts in which over 1,000 battle-related fatalities occurred and in which at least one participant was a state member of the international system; colonial and imperial as well as interstate wars were included, but civil wars were not. The index of war used is the number of fatalities among military personnel eventuating as a result of war involvement begun in each five-year period commencing in 1820. This index was chosen for two reasons: it has proven the most sensitive index of war involvement (Wallace, 1970) and it is the measure of war which touches directly on the central ethical theme of peace research, concern over the enormous loss of life in war. It is therefore appropriate as our index since the ultimate purpose of our endeavor is to reduce the probability that men should die violently.[11]

Status inconsistency, differential change in capability and ascribed status, and rate of change in military capability are all computed from the raw data on three national attribute variables: total population and size of regular armed forces, both of which are indicators of national capability; and the number of diplomatic missions received as a percentage of the number of nations in the system, an indicator of ascribed status. A possible objection to calculating so many indicators in this way is that it puts a great deal of weight on three measures whose validity will not go unchallenged. Total population cannot, in the contemporary world, be considered an indicator of capability, and armed forces size is little better since it "overestimates" nations with large ill-equipped armies.[12] In reply it can be pointed out that for much of the earlier part of

10. See note 5. A complete discussion of the difficulty is to be found in Wallace (1970).

11. This issue is well treated in Singer and Winston (1969).

12. On the thorny question of the measurement of capability, see German (1960), Knorr (1956), and Russett (1965). The difficulties involved in relying on military indicators alone are pointed out in Russett (1968a) and Organski (1968).

the temporal domain under study, indicators of gross magnitude such as population and number of effectives may actually reflect national capability better than those based on industrial development or sophisticated hardware. As regards diplomatic importance, this index is in fact a combined one, since diplomatic representation "is a reflection of a wide range of internal and external considerations affecting those responsible for deciding upon each such assignment" (Singer and Small, 1966a: 247). Given that the relatively underdeveloped state of our discipline precludes more definitive pronouncements about index validity, it is reasonable to employ these simple indicators until further investigation demonstrates the need for, and assists us in constructing, more complex ones.

Status inconsistency is calculated first at the national level; the two indicators are computed by ranking the nations on all three attributes, then taking the absolute difference between the diplomatic importance and each of the capability rankings. The national indices are summed over the test population and normalized [13] to produce indices of the level of status inconsistency in the system.

Differential change in capability and ascribed status are measured by first determining the time rates of change (deltas) for all nations between adjacent five-year periods on each of the three status variables taken separately. To measure the differential rate of change in the system as a whole, the standard deviation of the national rates within the test population was computed for each index. Increases in armaments levels as well were measured with reference to the deltas for all nations on the military personnel variable. This time, however, we take the mean rate of change for all nations in the test population, as we are interested in the overall trend in military might in the system.

The prevalence of formal alliance bonds among members of the system, or "alliance aggregation," is measured with reference to three forms of alliances: defense pacts, neutrality pacts, and ententes signed between two or more members of the system. From these data on alliance involvement an index is calculated, using the number of national alliance commitments normalized by the number of nations in the system.

Finally, intergovernmental organizations include those international bodies set up by the signature of two or more members of the system possessing a permement secretariat and holding regular plenary meetings. The index of intergovernmental organization used here is computed by determining the number of national members in organizations in the system for each period, weighting each membership by the respective nation's diplomatic status score, and summing to produce a score for the system. Because of the strong upward secular trend in intergovernmental organization, our final index is based on the time rate of change of the raw index.

13. The raw scores were normalized by $n^2 + n$ where n is the size of the test population.

TECHNIQUES OF ANALYSIS

The product-moment correlation coefficients between the independent and dependent variables for the three time periods are shown in Tables 1-3. By inspection, it would seem that the relationships between the independent variables and the amount of war begun are, by and large, strong and in the expected directions. However, there are intercorrelations between the independent variables themselves, and so it is quite likely either that (a) some of the observed relationships are spurious, or (b) the five independent variables do not exert separate influences on the severity of war, but constitute one or more developmental sequences. Therefore, as expected, we cannot give any definitive causal interpretation to these correlations without further analysis.

To examine the causal relationships, the method of dependence analysis developed by Boudon (1968) was employed to decompose the correlation coefficients into dependence coefficients, another name for the standardized partial regression coefficients of all independent variables on each dependent variable. These may be interpreted as "the fraction of the standard deviation of the dependent variable ... for which the designated factor is responsible" (Wright, 1934: 162). This technique offers three advantages over the Simon-Blalock methods of causal modeling.

First, it allows us to determine precisely the direct effect of each independent variable on the current dependent variable. This makes it possible to detect not only spurious relationships, but also to determine the relative importance of the independent variables. Second, where there are indirect as well as direct causal connections between variables, dependence analysis allows us to determine the relative importance of each causal pathway. A final advantage is that it allows us to depart somewhat from normal causal modeling usage in that we need make no a priori assumptions as to which independent variables do, and which do not, affect the variables below them in the causal hierarchy. Such a procedure is permissible using dependence analysis, and is more suited to the present exploratory state of the analysis than is the testing of specific predicitve models. [14]

Now, based on the earlier theoretical discussion, we can write, in a normal regression form:

(i) $x_3 = a_{13}x_1 + a_{23}x_2 + e_3$
(ii) $x_4 = a_{14}x_1 + a_{24}x_2 + a_{34}x_3 + e_4$
(iii) $x_5 = a_{15}x_1 + a_{25}x_2 + a_{35}x_3 + a_{45}x_4 + e_5$
(iv) $x_6 = a_{16}x_1 + a_{26}x_2 + a_{36}x_3 + a_{46}x_4 + a_{56}x_5 + e_6$
(v) $x_7 = a_{17}x_1 + a_{27}x_2 + a_{37}x_3 + a_{47}x_4 + a_{57}x_5 + a_{67}x_6 + e_7$

where

x_1 = differential change in capability

14. A similar procedure was employed by Choucri and North (1969).

Status, Formal Organization, and Arms Levels

Table 1. Correlations for the 1820-1964 Period

		a	b	c	d	e	f	g	h	i
(a)	Differential change: total population (ΔCAP)	1.00								
(b)	Differential change: military personnel (ΔCAP)	.05	1.00							
(c)	Differential change: diplomatic status (ΔDIP)	.59	.21	1.00						
(d)	Status inconsistency: total population (STATIN)	.30	.37	.16	1.00					
(e)	Status inconsistency: military personnel (STATIN)	.16	.41	.10	.86	1.00				
(f)	Alliance Aggregation (ALL)	.13	.33	.19	.45	.57	1.00			
(g)	Intergovernmental organization growth (ΔIGO)	-.20	-.07	.30	-.37	-.33	-.26	1.00		
(h)	Armed forces expansion (ΔARMS)	.03	.02	.07	.39	.38	.50	-.49	1.00	
(i)	Battle fatalities (WAR)	.11	.16	.09	.47	.45	.32	-.41	.68	1.00

Table 2. Correlations for the 1820-1944 Period

		a	b	c	d	e	f	g	h	i
(a)	Differential change: total population (ΔCAP)	1.00								
(b)	Differential change: military personnel (ΔCAP)	.05	1.00							
(c)	Differential change: diplomatic status (ΔDIP)	.60	.12	1.00						
(d)	Status inconsistency: total population (STATIN)	.33	.30	.11	1.00					
(e)	Status inconsistency: military personnel (STATIN)	.19	.27	.01	.87	1.00				
(f)	Alliance aggregation (ALL)	.26	.07	.09	.38	.38	1.00			
(g)	Intergovernmental organization growth (ΔIGO)	.22	-.03	.31	-.39	-.36	-.45	1.00		
(h)	Armed forces expansion (ΔARMS)	.03	-.10	.03	.38	.38	.70	-.49	1.00	
(I)	Battle fatalities (WAR)	.10	.16	.09	.50	.53	.60	-.40	.69	1.00

Table 3. Correlations for the 1850-1964 Period

	a	b	c	d	e	f	g	h	i
(a) Differential change: total population (ΔCAP)	1.00								
(b) Differential change: military personnel (ΔCAP)	.59	1.00							
(c) Differential change: diplomatic status (ΔDIP)	.40	.72	1.00						
(d) Status inconsistency: total population (STATIN)	.58	.53	.45	1.00					
(e) Status inconsistency: military personnel (STATIN)	.55	.57	.56	.90	1.00				
(f) Alliance aggregation (ALL)	.24	.38	.35	.47	.66	1.00			
(g) Intergovernmental organization growth (ΔIGO)	-.15	-.05	-.04	-.48	-.52	-.31	1.00		
(h) Armed forces expansion (ΔARMS)	.14	.12	.16	.37	.38	.53	-.57	1.00	
(i) Battle fatalities (WAR)	.34	.18	.29	.47	.47	.34	-.56	.72	1.00

x_2 = differential change in diplomatic status

x_3 = status inconsistency

x_4 = alliance aggregation

x_5 = growth in intergovernmental organization memberships

x_6 = mean rate of change in armed forces size

x_7 = battle-related fatalities.

The a's are the unstandardized regression coefficients, and the e's are the error terms.[15]

Boudon shows that if we substitute the standardized regression coefficients or dependence coefficients (b's) for the unstandardized coefficients by dividing by the ratio of the appropriate standard deviations, and then multiply through by each of the independent variables in the equation, we obtain a system of equations which permits us to solve for the b's in terms of the correlation coefficients (r's), since there are as many equations as there are unknowns. By way of illustration, the first two sets of derived equations for the present model are given in Table 4. To solve for the b's, it remains only to substitute the correlation coefficients from Tables 1-3 into these derived equations.

Table 4. Dependence Equations

(i.a) $b_{13} + b_{23}r_{12} = r_{13}$

(i.b) $b_{13}r_{12} + b_{23} = r_{23}$

(ii.a) $b_{14} + b_{24}r_{12} + b_{34}r_{13} = r_{14}$

(ii.b) $b_{14}r_{12} + b_{24} + b_{34}r_{23} = r_{24}$

(ii.c) $b_{14}r_{13} + b_{24}r_{23} + b_{34} = r_{34}$

THE RESULTS

Since there are two indicators of differential change in capability and two of status inconsistency, there are two different solutions to the above equations. The calculated values of the more important dependence coefficients[16] obtained in each of the solutions are diagrammed in Figures 1-3.

The most obvious result to emerge is that our fears regarding the possible spuriousness of the status inconsistency-war relationship appear to have been groundless, at least as far as the variables employed in this analysis are

15. The variables are assumed to have zero means, to remove the constant term.

16. The problem of determining the statistical significance of dependence coefficients is extremely complex, and often exact confidence limits cannot be obtained. Rather than attempting such a trying task for the sake of a peripheral aspect of the analysis, I decided to employ a cutoff threshold of .20 in diagramming the relationships. For a discussion of the problems of obtaining confidence levels in dependence analysis, see Turner and Stevens (1959).

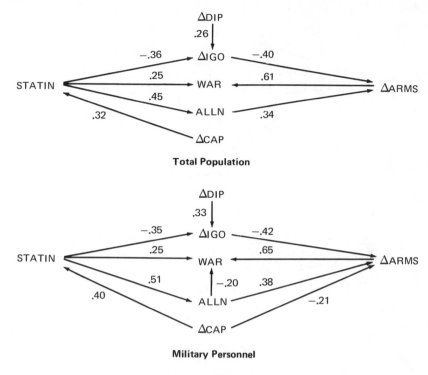

Total Population

Military Personnel

Figure 1. 1820-1964

concerned. Regardless of which indicators we use, the effects of status inconsistency on both the dependent and intervening variables remain strong, even controlling for differential changes in capability and diplomatic status. Moreover, in four of the six solutions differential change in capability affects war only through status inconsistency, and in the other two chiefly in this way. While differential change in diplomatic status has relatively little effect on the other variables in the analysis, in the 1850-1964 sub-period its principal influence is through its effects on status inconsistency. These findings would appear to confirm the importance of this latter variable as a cause of war. Combined with the fact that differential change in both status variables together explains as much as 30 percent of the variance in status inconsistency, they would also appear to confirm Johan Galtung's hypothesis (Galtung, 1964b: 113) linking such differential changes in rank-position to conflict via their tendency to produce status discrepancies.

A second important feature of the results is the existence of a weak but noticeable direct link between status inconsistency and war in all but one of the six solutions. Of course, this link is a rather weak one, explaining no more than 9 percent of the variance, and we would be wise to use caution in interpreting it, since we cannot be sure we have specified all relevant intervening variables.

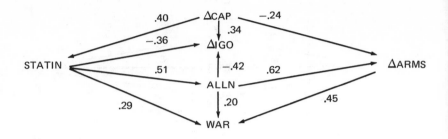

Total Population

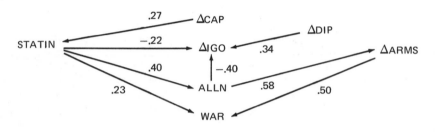

Military Personnel

Figure 2. 1820-1944

However, even if this link is eventually found to be indirect, it is interesting of itself that status inconsistency affects war in other ways than by stimulating increases in armed force levels; all other variables act only in this way.

Another hypothesis largely verified is that which posits the existence of a link between status inconsistency and alliance aggregation. Regardless of which index of capability is used, and regardless of the time period we choose to examine, status inconsistency explains over 20 percent of the variance in the alliance index. Moreover, it is the only variable included in the model to do so; conspicuous by its absence is differential capability change. The fact that neither differential change in armed forces levels nor differential rates of growth in the demographic determinants of capability appear to exert any direct influence on alliance aggregation appears, indeed, to run rather contrary to expectation. If, as many have hypothesized, the international system were organized along "balance-of-power" lines, such differential changes should stimulate alliance formation (Gulick, 1955).

Following this causal chain a step further, one hypothesized link not found was the one presumed to connect alliances and war directly. Although there is some direct effect, it is neither strong nor consistent in direction, and in not one of the three time periods is it observed with both indices of differential

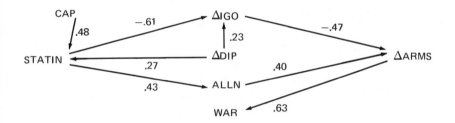

Total Population

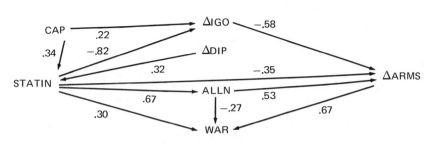

Military Personnel

Figure 3. 1850-1964

capability change and status inconsistency. It seems, rather, that the chief effect of alliance aggregation is indirect; alliances act to increase armed forces levels in the system, and these increases then act on war. This indirect effect is quite strong, the two-step path coefficient [17] varying from .23 to .36. The existence of this path seems to support those who believe that alliances polarize the system and so create tensions. Apparently this only occurs when the polarization is severe enough to trigger an arms race. Moreover, the fact that the alliance-war path is a two-stage one means that the status inconsistency-war path via alliances is three steps long, and hence does not explain much of the variance; the coefficient is not larger than .24 in any of the six solutions, and in all cases but one is less than the magnitude of the direct link. However, the existence of such a path may explain why a relationship was found between status inconsistency and war when a long time lag was used (Wallace, 1970).

While alliance aggregation has a consistent, albeit indirect, effect on war, the establishment of intergovernmental organizations appears to have a more restricted impact; for the 1820-1944 period, the negative bivariate relationship between intergovernmental organization and war appears to be entirely spurious.

17. Note that a two-step coefficient is the product of the coefficients of the single paths.

However, for the 145-year period as a whole, there does appear to be a fairly strong relationship, and for the 1850-1964 period it is even more evident that intergovernmental organization has a strong negative impact on the severity of war. This strengthening of the link over time accords well with our theoretical expectations. More surprising, perhaps, is that the effect is entirely indirect, intergovernmental organization apparently acting to reduce war by lowering arms levels in the system. Even so, its magnitude is quite strong; the two-step coefficient is as high as .39, indicating that at least during the latter part of the period under study, intergovernmental organization plays an important role in damping the effects of the forces which lead to war.

Regardless of the period we examine, status inconsistency has a strong negative effect on the rate of growth of intergovernmental organization membership. In one case the direct path linking these variables is an extremely high −.82, which relationship explains about 65 percent of the variance. This in turn implies the existence of a fairly important three-step path linking status inconsistency and war via intergovernmental organization and arms levels. For the 1850-1964 period, the coefficient for this link is .32, larger than either the direct link connecting status inconsistency and war or the three-step path via alliances and arms levels. Thus, the hypothesis which posits intergovernmental organization as an intervening variable appears to be confirmed as regards the latter part of the temporal domain, but does not hold in the earlier years.

Turning to changes in armed forces levels, we find they have a direct—and very powerful—effect on international war. In one case, this factor accounts for almost 40 percent of the variance. While its effects are not always so large, the only variable besides status inconsistency to have a direct effect on war was the mean rate of increase in armed forces. All other variables—including, to some degree, status inconsistency itself—affect war only indirectly through arms levels. This very important result strongly underlines what Singer has termed "the perils of para bellum" (Singer, 1958): increases in arms levels would appear to be the key factor in transforming the tensions generated by the structure of the international system into a tendency toward open belligerency. This would appear to discredit the widely-held theory that armaments are not of themselves a cause of war, but only reflect the tensions generated by other factors which are the true causes. If this were the correct explanation, the relationship between armaments and war would have turned out to be spurious, an artifact of the relationships between the other explanatory variables and war. Such is very far from the case.

INTERPRETING THE RESULTS—SOME CAVEATS AND QUALIFICATIONS

Before entering into a discussion regarding the implications of the findings, it would be well to issue a few warnings regarding both the inferences we may draw from them and the degree of certainty we can attach to these inferences.

First, with regard to the reliability of the findings, it must be remembered that they are based on an N of 28 and that the observations are taken five years apart. While the magnitude of the reported relationships is such that they are very unlikely to have been caused by random fluctuations, the interrelationships between the variables are so strong that a systematic error on only one of the variables for even a few observations could produce important changes in the relationships observed in the model. This sensitivity was demonstrated in the differences in the observed relationships produced by using alternate indicators. In short, without further tests these relationships can only be considered tentative.

Second, the validity of these results is critically dependent upon the assumption that there are no other variables not specified in the model which act directly on more than one of the variables in the analysis at once.[18] Since data-based studies about the origins of international war have left many variables still unexamined, obviously no research design can exclude this possibility with any degree of certainty. The point is that the values of the coefficients derived by the analysis depend not only on the correlations calculated from the data, but also upon the theoretical assumptions which governed the choice of variables. Causal modeling techniques cannot endow our inferences with certainty, but only render them rather less uncertain than had they been made from measures of bivariate association.

Third, the present analysis examines only some of the relationships between the variables, since it specifically excludes the possibility of reciprocal causation and feedback loops. It would be very interesting to see, for example, if war had the effect of reducing or increasing status inconsistency, or if armed forces levels produce any effects in the patterns of alliance aggregation. However, the fact that our measurement intervals are five years apart, coupled with the difficulties of identification and estimation inevitable in non-recursive or feedback models,[19] renders such a task beyond the scope of the present study.

Finally, the fact that the present analysis is undertaken at the system level means that the interpretation we can give our findings is somewhat restricted. For example, the present design does not allow us to choose between competing interpretations of the direct link between status inconsistency and war. Whether it is due to a direct connection between discrepancy-induced frustration and conflict behavior which holds for all nations of the system, whether such a relationship exists only in the case of pariah nations which have few alternatives

18. Technically, that the e's in the prediction equations are not correlated with each other or with any of the independent variables (see Blalock, 1967).

19. Note that the possibility that alternative causal paths could account for the observed results or that the coefficients could be biased as the result of reciprocal interaction is ruled out by the time lags built into the measurement process; for example, the "observation set" for 1850 would include the differential rates of change in capability from 1845 to 1850, the amount of status inconsistency in the system in 1850, and the amount of war begun from 1850 to 1854. For a general discussion of the above problems as they apply to recursive models, see Forbes and Tufte (1968) and Johnston (1963, ch. 9).

to aggression as a means of goal attainment, or whether it exists as the result of status inconsistency-engendered errors in the evaluation of national capability remains unclear. Note also that it is impossible to determine which inconsistent configuration (high achieved-low ascribed or high ascribed-low achieved) explains most of the variance, since in the system as a whole the same amount of each must exist by definition.

SOME IMPLICATIONS
OF THE FINDINGS

Given the note of caution sounded above, what follows may well be an overinterpretation of what are essentially tentative findings. Nonetheless, so scarce are data-based propositions about international war that it is well to extract the most from what we have.

To begin with, the results suggest that the wide discrepancies which exist between national rates of economic development and population growth have the effect of sharply intensifying international violence by increasing the level of status inconsistency in the international system and perhaps by directly inducing the polarization of international alignments as well. This should give us pause, since the differences in rates of growth—and hence of capability—seem by most accounts to be increasing rather than decreasing.[20] Just as the model predicts dire consequences if present tendencies continue, it also offers a number of possible strategies to cope with the situation.

The most obvious, but least plausible, strategy would be to attempt to reduce the differences between rates of change in capability to a level the system can accommodate. But given the vast disparities that exist in absolute terms between nations in levels of economic development, and the pressures which exist to "close the gap" in one fashion or another, this strategy of gradualism is almost certain to fail; nor is it without ethical drawbacks. In essence it implies that the best method to reduce conflict that creates wars is to allow the status quo to change only very slowly. If this is offered as the price of peace, few buyers are likely to be found. At the present state of development of the international system, it would seem that differing rates of capability change must be accepted as a given, and the causal chain broken at another link.

Following the chain downwards, another possible strategy would be to control the level of status inconsistency in the system directly, since this variable apparently plays so crucial a role in the genesis of conflict. This would involve a more expeditious procedure for adjusting national ascribed status so that it

20. This is not to imply, of course, that there is necessarily a tendency observable between blocs of nations taken as a whole, i.e., that "the rich are getting richer and the poor poorer." However, it is obvious that differences in rates of growth between nations both at similar and at dissimilar levels of development do exist. Moreover, these may become accentuated as the nations at the bottom of the economic ladder reach the phase of rapidly-accelerating growth while the nations near the top level off. See Russett (1965) and Russett, et al. (1964, Part B, Section 6).

responds more rapidly to changes in achieved status; in terms of our model, we need to increase the negative value of b_{23}. But, as mentioned earlier, since ascribed status is inevitably a constant-sum attribute, there can be little doubt that any attempt at "re-apportionment" will meet with tremendous resistance on the part of those on the losing side of the equation. Such a redistribution could still take place if the superpowers, secure in their status and aware of the dangers of inconsistency, were to act so as to promote status equilibration. Unfortunately, in view of the attitudes which both have displayed towards that most prominent of status inconsistent nations, China, it would seem unlikely that they can be relied upon to play this role.

If it is improbable that status inconsistency can be reduced very readily, it is not at all unlikely that its salience for national behavior can be lowered. The author has argued elsewhere (Wallace, 1971) that the present upsurge in domestic unrest in many countries of the world may actually help lower the likelihood of international war by distracting policy-making elites during a time of high inconsistency. This may prove to be a particularly important means of moderating international tensions if coping with the unrest requires the diversion of national resources from armaments to domestic uses, given the strong observed connection between changes in armed forces levels and war.

This leads to another major consideration: the direct link between arms levels and war and its implications for the resolution of the "armament-tension dilemma." It is evident that the "tensions-first" approach to peace has validity to this extent: both the factors which are presumed to increase tensions such as alliance aggregation, and those which presumably reduce tensions such as intergovernmental organizations, explain a good portion of the variance in armed forces increases, and therefore it is true that if tensions are reduced, armaments will in part take care of themselves. But it is also true that since most other factors act on war not directly but via changes in arms levels, a signfiicant reduction in the level of war could be obtained by reducing armed forces even if tensions are not reduced. It is not merely that the existence of weapons increases the probability of their use; rather, their rate of accumulation constitutes one of the major reasons for their use.

This must surely lead us to reflect that the "utopian" advocates of arms control and disarmament may be more hardheaded than they know. If the control of armaments is problematic, it could not possibly be more so than an attempt to alter the background conditions of development and status which initiate the drive to war. The relationship between intergovernmental organization and arms levels—while disappointing to those who would wish its magnitude to be larger—is perhaps important simply owing to its negative sign and the upward secular trend of the relationship. This signifies that the imposition of international control over the multiplying weight of military might is at least not outside the bounds of possibility. Combined with Russett's finding elsewhere in this volume of an almost unprecedented popular revolt in the United States against the burden of defense expenditures, it offers us at least a ray of hope and a clear direction for further effort in the cause of peace.

R. J. RUMMEL

3. U.S. Foreign Relations: Conflict, Cooperation, and Attribute Distances

"... of all forms of mental activity, the most difficult to induce even in the minds of the young, who may be presumed not to have lost their flexibility, is the art of handling the same bundle of data as before, but placing them in a new system of relations with one another by giving them a different framework, all of which virtually means putting on a different kind of thinking-cap for the moment." (Butterfield, 1959: 1)

ABSTRACT

The foreign relations of the United States are considered in terms of 6 hypotheses based on (1) the linkage "pre-theory" of James Rosenau, (2) the social status theory of Johan Galtung, (3) the distance theory of Quincy Wright, (4) the power transition theory of A. F. K. Organski, (5) the integration-regional findings of Bruce Russett, and (6) propositions about geographic distance. These hypotheses are linked together by the notion of attribute and behavior "distance" and developed within a geometric framework called field theory.

Data on 19 foreign relations and actions of the United States, ranging from tourists and treaties to negative communications and sanctions, toward 81 object nations were correlated with the distances between the United States and other nations on economic development, size or power bases, political orientation, socio-cultural dimensions, and geographic distance. The general results support the "pre-theory" of Rosenau, the status theory of Galtung, and an emphasis on homogeneity in integration theory. This suggests that these theories can be synthesized in a larger framework such as field theory. The specific results are:

(1) American behavior toward other nations consists of 6 independent patterns: Western-European Cooperation, Anglo-American Cooperation, Aid, Cold War behavior, deterrence, and Negative Sanctions.

Author's Note: My thanks to Warren Phillips for carefully reading and commenting on a previous draft of this paper. This is a revised version of "Dimensionality of Nations Project Research Report" No. 41; Honolulu: University Of Hawaii, July, 1970. Prepared in connection with research supported by the Advanced Research Projects Agency, ARPA Order No. 1063, and monitored by the Office of Naval Research, Contract No. N 000 14-67-A-0387-0003.

(2) Joint Western-European Cooperation (such as treaties, military aid, students, and conferences) and Deterrent action of the United States toward another nation are a function of the power parity of the object nation (with a multiple correlation of .94).

(3) Western-European Cooperative behavior relative to deterrent behavior of the United States toward another nation is dependent on the similarity in political orientation of the two and the degree to which the other nation has a Catholic culture (with a multiple correlation of .78).

(4) Differences in economic development, size (or power bases), and political orientation from the object nation jointly explain about 27 percent of the variation in American behavior.

(5) Overall American differences on attributes from the object nation explain about 47 percent of the variation in United States behavior.   ∎

In any one day, the foreign relations of the United States consist of a multitude of distinct actions. Some of them are consciously a part of the government's foreign policy, such as warning the Soviet Union on her overt military involvement in the Middle East prior to publicly announced discussions with Israel's foreign minister on the Israeli request for U.S. jet fighters. Other actions are separate from immediate foreign policy considerations and distinct from each other, such as a shipment of American automobiles to Denmark and 25 American students entering India for a year of foreign study. And still other actions are of such importance and consequence as to immediately affect most U.S. international relations, such as the sudden American attack on Viet Cong and North Vietnamese sanctuaries in Cambodia.

Obviously, the international relations of any one country, especially one as economically developed and powerful as the United States, will be diverse and multidimensional. How are we to make sense out of all these actions, for both the scholar and practitioner of international relations?

Traditionally, the scholar refines a conceptual framework of international relations which places these actions in relation to each other, orders them in a cause-effect hierarchy, and weights them in their prominence for practicing and understanding international politics. He divides a nation's actions into public and private; relates them to immediate, short, and long run foreign policy goals; imbues them with consequences for the power and national interest of a nation; and categorizes them into causes, effects, conditions, or processes. The practitioner, less self-consciously theoretical and abstract, generally deals with international relations on a day by day basis, responding to actions of other nations when necessary to satisfy bureaucratic and political demands, innovating and initiating actions to meet contingencies, and restraining or channeling other actions as events require.

The conceptual world of the practitioner consists of individuals—decision makers, elites, and influentials. The structure of a nation in its economic development, political system, culture, and history are givens. International law and organizations, the number and variety of nations and their geographic separation, and the configuration of power and alliances are the context within which human beings barter, exchange, fight, negotiate, and cooperate. If the practitioner, as he does often, says that the United States has done such, or that the United States desires . . ., he knows this is a semantic convenience—an accepted and understood reification—and in effect he means that Dr. Henry Kissinger has influenced President Nixon to say . . ., or that Secretary Rogers initiated those diplomatic moves to placate Senator Fulbright. The practitioner's questions are generally not those of the scholar's. He is not, except in perhaps an intellectual sense, concerned with how the size of nations affects their trade, or even the relationship between economic development and foreign conflict behavior. He would prefer to know such things as the likely successor to Mao and his past attitudes toward the United States and the Soviet Union, and the changes he is likely to make in China's foreign behavior.

In short, the practitioner conceptualizes and understands the diverse international relations at the individual level—as the daily interaction of human beings. Scholars, on the other hand, often are interested in the theoretical understanding of such actions at the aggregate level. They wish to theorize about these actions in the aggregate and relate them to the practitioners' givens. They wish to isolate the forces and indicators, to delineate the patterns and trends in aggregate actions, and to stipulate or discover the social and political laws of international relations.

While the individual-aggregate distinction does not sharply differentiate scholars and practitioners, since many scholars are concerned with developing theoretical and empirical knowledge at the individual level[1] it does distinguish levels of understanding and conceptualization of a nation's actions and focuses on a source of misunderstanding between practitioners[2] and scholars themselves. At the individual level, actions often appear random, caused by idiosyncracies of the personality involved, specific circumstances, or never repeated occurrences. Actions can seem triggered by unique events, such as an assassination, or to be the plaything of chance. The behavior of nations, which consist of the actions of human beings, often appears unpredictable, unlawful,

1. By aggregate level, I mean that (1) the fundamental unit dealt with is a collective, whether a nation, system, organization, or group, (2) the theoretical or empirical focus is on relations, regularities, patterns, or correlations for all the units of the type being considered, such as nations. In other words, the aggregate level for nations concentrates on the comparative variation of nations. The individual level is concerned with (1) the decision maker, the statesman, or diplomat; (2) the activities of nations, not in the aggregate—but descriptively or discretely from the point of view of contemporary history; (3) the forces of international relations as they serve as motivational elements for policy makers. The distinction I make is analogous to that between physics and chemistry, between multivariate and clinical psychology, and between macro and micro economics.

2. For enlightening views of the U.S. practitioner's world, see Ogburn and Haviland (1960), Haar (1969, 1970), and Scott (1969, 1970). See Platig (1967), for a scholar-turned-practitioner's informed but individually oriented view of international relations research.

and irrational.[3] At the aggregate level, however, many actions are structured; they are highly correlated, ordered, and patterned.[4] They seem to be lawful and subject to scientific study and prediction. On the whole, aggregate international relations appear more regular then random, more to be explained by deterministic equations than probabilistic statistics.

This transformation in perspective which takes place as one shifts his vision from an individual to an aggregate level might be best illustrated by an example from physics. Gas molecules seem to move in an unordered, random fashion, as capricious as human behavior in international relations. At an aggregate level, however, the random molecular motions are patterned, ordered in their totality, enabling us to assert Boyle's law that gas pressure on a container times the volume equals a constant (at constant temperature).

The shift in appearance of international relations between the individual and aggregate perspectives causes difficulty in communication. A practitioner or scholar whose paradigm is individual-centered often neither appreciates nor understands the scholar's emphasis on scientific theory and laws.[5] Predict international relations? Absurd.[6] Who could have predicted Sukarno's erratic and highly personal actions? Who could have forecast the rise of a Hitler, Stalin, Mao, or Castro? On the other hand, the scholar summing across a number of actions, standardizing them, and comparing across countries and years knows he

3. This is not to imply that all scholars working at the individual level see actions this way. Many see and are seeking regularities, patterns, and predictability. This characterization, however, does generally apply to practitioners and laymen.

4. What is structure depends on our methods, our units of analysis, and the actions which are aggregated. For example, the number of wars of nations at one time period may have a high correlation with the number they are involved in during a previous time period, as found in Rummel (1963a, Table 2) for wars 1955-1957 and wars 1825-1945. However, if one looks at the number of wars of varying intensity in the international system at different time points, then war may be considered to be a random phenomena described by a Poisson distribution (Richardson, 1960a).

For the social scientist, no less than the natural scientist, our view of reality is given us through our instruments—through our methods. This is most obvious when the same aggregate data will yield different and sometimes contradictory results, depending only on slight changes in technique, as for example, using different communality estimates in common factor analysis or different rotation criteria. For this reason, among others (Popper, 1961), application of methods and choice of units should be dictated by clear hypotheses and theories.

5. "To concentrate attention on matters we can predict is to give less attention to matters we can effect" (Fisher, 1969: 2).

6. "The political behaviorists are wrong in their belief that a knowledge about political processes as gleaned from case studies and refinements in theory will enable us to predict policy outcomes (e.g., Richard Snyder's study 'The U.S. Decision to Resist Aggression in Korea'). The fallacy in their position is that it does not take sufficient cognizance of the degree to which decisions are based on contingent factors that vary from one case to another. 'Discretion is an ineradicable element of decision-making, and the limits set to reducing it are narrow' " (Hula, 1959: 158).

has strong relationships.[7] His correlations often exceed in magnitude those of the other social sciences and lead him to be impatient with the belief in the unpredictability of human behavior.

Certainly both the individual and aggregate perspectives can complement and supplement each other. Aggregate-level research contributes a conceptual framework and an understanding of the context within which individual actions take place. It can define the direction of aggregate behavior, the range of alternative directions (alternative worlds), and the crucial variables (such as energy consumption or national income) whose shift in values might provide calmer waters for the ship of state.

For the scholar, the practitioner's world should be the testing ground of aggregate research and theory. While study can proceed at the aggregate level, international relations, after all, consist of the actions and problems of people. It is at the practitioner's level that the crucial tests of the aggregate perspective must be applied. For of what use are concepts of integration and social distance, correlations between trade and economic development, dimensions of size and foreign conflict behavior, and nearly perfect multiple correlations if they give no guidance to human affairs, solve no problems, provide no solutions?

This long introduction is to set the stage for the field theory of U.S. conflict and cooperation to be presented and tested here. For this will use an aggregate level perspective with which most will be unfamiliar. It will treat international relations as a deterministic system and pose within the representation to be developed a fundamental proposition on foreign relations. As applied above, while the discussion from this point on will develop an aggregate theory, it is recognized that an individual world of everyday actions and decisions exists and that ultimately the ability to solve some of the problems of this world will be the final test by fire.[8]

Most attempts to develop aggregate theories of nations' actions have worked at a conceptual level not far removed from that of diplomats, politicians, and journalists. Power, national interest, nationalism, conflict, cooperation, integration, international law, international organization, politics, geographic distance, regionalism, threats, war, etc., are usually the major ingredients of aggregate theories. International relations has been gifted with men like Karl Deutsch,

7. One example of this regularity relevant to the aggregate-individual distinction has been reported by Russett (1967a: 92) for UN voting. "On these major issues in the United Nations, the importance of idiosyncratic and role variables is slight—changes in the person or even party of the major decision-makers made little difference in nations' alignments."

8. This paper represents part of a long range research project. The eventual aim is to develop the ability to forecast the areas and intensity of conflict and cooperation and the nations involved. The "test by fire," then, will be the ability to make accurate forecasts to practitioners and policy makers in international relations. If aggregate work in international relations can be likened to theoretical meteorology, then, as the meterologist must use his knowledge of gross weather patterns to say something about rain or snow over Detroit, if this theory and methodology are to be tested in practice, those of us at the aggregate level should also eventually say something specific about future—not past nor present—behavior.

Ernest Haas, Morton Kaplan, Charles McClelland, Lewis Fry Richardson, Bruce Russett, J. David Singer, and Quincy Wright, who with great insight wove such concepts into theories. It is to their credit that their insights have expanded our understanding and research in international relations. It does not detract from their contribution if we now build on their efforts by shifting our conceptual framework to a new plane further removed from daily affairs, and one that introduces constructs and imbeds traditional concepts like power within an explicit logical framework allowing deduction and falsification by observation.

Decades ago, Arthur Bentley (1954) observed that the study of human affairs could benefit from thinking in terms of a social space—like physical space with dimensions, movements, locations, and spatial relationships.[9] Social space, however, would define man's social world not in terms of physical location but in terms of his characteristics and behavior. Others, such as Sorokin (1943), have since employed the concept of social space. Tolman (1951) has proposed a behavior space comprising individuals, their behavior and perceptions. Parsons' theory of action explicitly conceives of a social space, with his pattern variables being the dimensions of this space. Lewin (1964) has in his field theory proposed a life space of social behavior—a topological space which defines the context of behavior. And Dodd (1947) has built a complex notation describing "societal phenomena" in a social space.

Influenced by the theoretical works of the sociologist Parsons and psychologist Thurstone (1935), Quincy Wright was the first to represent international relations as a social space in Bentley's sense, which Wright calls an analytic field.

> "The analytic field approach to the study of international relations ... implies that each international organization, national government, association, individual or other 'system of action,' or 'decision maker' may be located in a multidimensional field. Such a field may be defined by co-ordinates, each of which measures a political economic, psychological, sociological, ethical, or other continuum influencing choices, decisions, and actions important for international relations." (1955: 543)

Wright went on to specify what these coordinates might be and to locate nations in the resulting space on the basis of subjective estimates. Much of the factor analytic work in international relations,[10] as Wright suggested could be done,[11] has been implicitly filling in Wright's analytic field with coordinates (dimensions) based on aggregate data.[12]

9. It is important to point out that space is not a concept that one comes to by "unbiased" observation or by abstraction. "None of our sensations, if isolated, could have brought us to a concept of space. . . ." (Poincare, 1952: 58) We posit space as a construct. It is an imaginative construction that helps us order observations. (Margenau, 1950: 127-128)

10. For a bibliography of such work, see Rummel (1970a).

11. "What continua can most usefully be employed as co-ordinates for defining this analytic field? The problem is similar to that of determining the factors which account for a mental performance, studied by psychologists. E. E. Spearman assumed a single factor, E. L. Thorndike assumed a great number of independent factors, and L. L. Thurstone devised methods for determining the minimum number of factors necessary to account for the results of numerous tests of mental ability." (Wright, 1955: 545)

12. Surely, international relations or any other social behavior involves the complex

The representation of international relations as a social space is powerful. It enables the systematization of observations, the development of mathematical theory tied to methods for testing, and the picturing of the relationships involved. A social space of international relations will be the first aggregate construct I will use in representing U.S. foreign actions.[13]

In developing this social space notion, one metasociological assumption is relevant. Let us assume that in explaining the behavior of nations the "principle of relative values operates": the behavior and attributes of nations are relative. It is not the absolute economic development or power of a nation which should be taken into consideration (most nations today are more developed than any one nation two hundred years ago), for example, but its relative power vis-à-vis some explicit other nation.[14] And the action of one nation to another should be considered in relation to its other actions, as well as in relation to the object's behavior and that of all other nations.[15] As we shall see, the notion of social space allows the principle of relative values to be simply incorporated.

First, consider that the foreign actions and attributes of the United States are part of the social space of nations. The United States then is located in this space in terms of its actions toward other nations and its relative attributes. Second, conceptually divide the social space into behavior and attribute subspaces.[16]

---

interworking of a large number of variables in a social situation. Wright, however, just posited the field (space) and the elements within it. He did not indicate how they are functionally related. "The problem of combining factors is not automatically solved by formulating the combination in terms of a field theory. We do not obtain such a theory by merely recognizing a multiplicity of factors and treating them as constituting a phase space. . . . How the factors combine in their working must still be specified." (Kaplan, 1964: 325-6)

13. This is not a static space, but is considered to be made up of social-time dimensions. Time is considered relative from the point of view of the nation involved and to be multidimensional. Since the tests to be developed here are for one period, however, the social time aspect will be ignored. Data collection is now underway for a number of time periods and when completed will enable the social-time nature of this space to be made explicit. Those interested in the philosophical and mathematical aspects of time in this context, see Rummel (1970c).

14. There is some disagreement whether power is a relation or a property of an actor. I obviously define power as a relationship, as have Lasswell and Kaplan (1950: 65): "Power is here defined relationally . . .;" According to Easton (1953: 143-6), power is a relational phenomena "based on the ability to influence the actions of others," and for Morgenthau (1967: 142) the first error that nations can commit in evaluating power is to disregard "the relativity of power by erecting the power of one particular nation into an absolute."

15. The point of view developed here and given mathematical structure later is simply that the behavior of one nation toward another takes place in a context (or field) which includes the actions and attributes of other nations. This view is close to the "situational perspective" of Strausz-Hupé and Possony who, in their general theory of foreign policy, assert that "the analysis of the relationships between 10 to 20 nations is the absolute minimum for the adequate description of the international situation." (1954: 41, italics omitted)

16. These are not linearly independent subspaces. As we will see later, the behavior subspace is contained in the attribute subspace.

The attribute subspace, which will henceforth be called attribute space, defines the location of the United States (and other nations) in terms of her relative values on all her attributes and the intercorrelation between these attributes for all nations. The origin of the space lies at the average values for the attributes. Thus, the GNP, area, population, defense budget, censorship, number of political parties, number of riots, number of Roman Catholics, etc.,[17] of the United States will locate her in this space relative to the values that other nations, the potential objects of her actions, have on these attributes.

As in a physical space in which all the motions and spatial relationship are defined by three physical dimensions (ignoring time), the relationship between attributes and relative location of nations in attribute space is defined by a number of dimensions.[18] Figure 1 shows the United States and five potential objects of her actions located in attribute space on two dimension,[19] called economic development and power bases. These two dimensions have repeatedly been delineated in attempts to define the attribute space of nations as the comparison of a number of studies has shown (Russett, 1967a; Rummel, 1969c). Attributes most highly correlated with the economic development dimension are energy consumption per capita, telephones per capita, and gross national product per capita. Those elements most correlated with the power bases dimension are national income, population, area, men under arms, and size of the defense budget. Not shown in Figure 1, but a third major dimension found to define attribute space is political orientation, which is highly correlated with censorship, freedom to oppose the government, and proportion of communist party members. The three dimensions together—economic development, power bases, and political orientation—typically subsume over 40 percent of the variation of nations on their attributes.

Keeping attribute space in mind, for the moment, let us move to a second basic construct (where the first is social space), that of dyad. A dyad is a coupling of two nations together in terms of the actions of one to the other.[20] It is an actor-object pair of nations. In terms of U.S. actions, U.S.→

17. Note that I am dealing with aggregate attributes, that is, characteristics on which nations can be scaled, observations summed, or statistics collected. This would also include survey or polling data, were they available for a number of nations. Thus, to reiterate, the theory being developed is at the aggregate level and not to be confused with conceptual frameworks at the individual level.

18. "It is common for sociologists to say that society is a many-dimensioned field. What the social dimensions are, or more properly what the most important social dimensions are for any specialized line of investigation, is our sociological problem in general. The search for precision in their analysis and use is the sociological space problem." (Bentley, 1954: 94)

19. Attribute space appears to be at least ten dimensional (Rummel, 1969c), but for pictorial simplicity only two are shown.

20. Much of the aggregate analysis, theory, and research in international relations is on the characteristics and behavior of the nation itself and not on the nation in relation to some particular other one. The concern is with the policy of the nation, the development of the nation, the conflict behavior of the nation, the relationship between the nation's trade

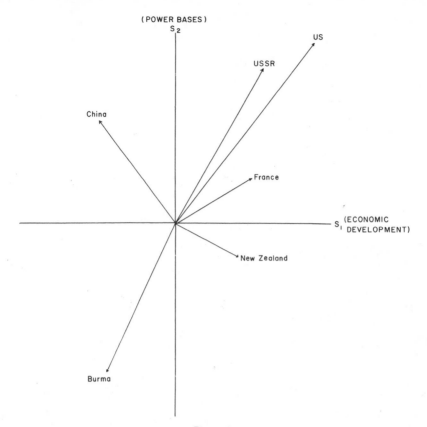

Figure 1.

China, U.S.→ USSR, U.S.→Greece, are such dyads, where each object is coupled separately with the United States by U.S. actions toward it.

The concept of dyad now allows the behavior of nation's subspace, henceforth to be called behavior space, to be defined. Behavior space locates all

---

and development, or internal unrest and foreign conflict, or power capability and foreign policy. Yet, we know that a nation's policies and behavior shift depending on the object nation, and whether development, power, or any other variables are relevant will also shift by object. For example, economic development is a more important aspect of the United States in relation to India, while with China power is the most salient.

Students of international relations share with their fellow social scientists this monadic lock-in—this over-emphasis on the individual, group, or nation. Kaplan (1964: 323) has commented on this bias. "I believe that one of the sources of this tendency is the image of the self as monadic. The principle of local determination may appear to us to be naturally and necessarily true of our own behavior, as a reflection of our sense of individuality and freedom. It is easier for us to accept a theory of behavior with complex predicates than one which introduces complex subjects for its propositions. The subject of a theory of behavior may be complicated, but not complex—it is just 'me,' a unitary self," On the disposition of social-psychologists to think monadically, see Sears (1951: 469)

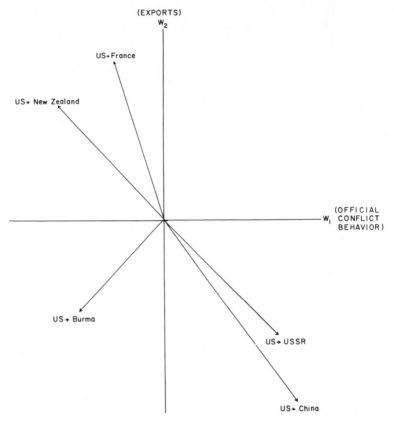

Figure 2.

dyads relative to each other in terms of their [21] behavior actions. The principle of relative values is involved here also, where the origin of behavior space lies at the average values for each behavior (such as threats). Figure 2 shows the relative position of five dyads involving the United States as actor on two behavior-space dimensions, exports, and official conflict behavior. [22]

So far, I have proposed an aggregate level representation of U.S. actions and attributes as existing in a social space, conceptually divisible into attribute and behavior spaces, and embodying the principle of relative values and the concept of dyads. This representation can now be used to tie together six hypotheses about a nation's international relations.

21. Since a dyad, say US→China, is considered a unit, it can be treated as a point or vector in behavior space and manipulated mathematically as any single unit. To speak of the behavior of dyads, therefore, is to mean elliptically the behavior of specific actors to certain objects.

22. See Rummel (1969c) for a discussion of how such dimensions were derived and the other dimensions delineated. Behavior space also appears to be at least ten dimensional.

The first hypothesis is that a nation's foreign behavior is linked to certain of its characteristics, specifically its economic development, size, and political system (whether the polity is open or closed). This hypothesis is from Rosenau's (1966) building block, which he calls "pre-theory," approach[23] to tying together international relations and comparative politics. For Rosenau, the three characteristics are basic for understanding the outputs of a nation. In particular, the profile a nation has on these characteristics will determine the ranking of idiosyncratic, role, governmental, societal, and systemic variables in explaining the outputs.[24] Rosenau does not specify the manner of this linkage, for clearly he is trying to present concepts and considerations that a theory can incorporate and not a theory itself, nor does he consider how such a linkage might be tested. In other words, the hypothesis is open for considerable interpretation, and this we will do later.

The second hypothesis has to do with the concept of distance as it has been applied in the social sciences to explain behavior.[25] The basic idea is that the similarity between people in socio-economic and cultural activities determine behavior; that prejudice is a function of dissimilarities in characteristics and that interaction is the greater the more homologous the people.[26]

23. "The same bricks and lumber can be used to build houses or factories, large structures or small ones, modern buildings or traditional ones. So it is with the construction and use of social theories. There must be, as it were, pre-theory which renders the raw materials comparable and ready for theorizing. The materials may serve as the basis for all kinds of theories—abstract or empirical, single or multi-country, pure or applied—but until they have been similarly processed, theorizing is not likely to occur, or, if it does, the results are not likely to be very useful." (Rosenau, 1966: 40)

24. "Suffice it to note that the potency of a systemic variable is considered to vary inversely with the size of a country (there being greater resources available to larger countries and thus lesser dependence on the international system than is the case with smaller countries), that the potency of an idiosyncratic factor is assumed to be greater in less developed economies (there being fewer of the restraints which bureaucracy and large-scale organization impose in more developed economies), that for the same reason a role variable is accorded greater potency in more developed economies, that a societal variable is considered to be more potent in open polities than in closed ones (there being a lesser need for officials in the latter to heed nongovernmental demands than in the former), and that for the same reason governmental variables are more potent than societal variables in closed polities than in open ones." (Rosenau, 1966: 45)

25. For a review and bibliography of social science research and theories using distance as a concept, see Olsson (1965). Geographical distance is the main focus of Olsson's review and his primary scientific concern is regional economics.

26. Distance in the work of Bogardus (1925, 1933) and his followers (Landis, et al., 1966; Von Den Berghe, 1960) is an attitudinal distance—called social distance—and the distance is measured by the degree to which one is willing to enter into a variety of relations with and be spatially close to another person. Social distance defined in this way has mainly been employed to study racial prejudice. In much of the sociological research on marriage, however, social distance has a different meaning: the dissimilarity in the characteristics of two people (Parkman and Sawyer, 1967; Marsh, 1967: 93-4). It is in this sense that I have used the concept of social distance in the past (Rummel, 1969b). Unfortunately, the concept of social distance is confusing in two ways. One, as suggested above, it is not often clear whether the desirability of social relations or dissimilarity in characteristics is being

The concept of distance has been employed by Quincy Wright to define the relationships between nations (1955: 127), and particularly to develop a model of the probability of war. He proposes that the relations between two nations are a function of eight distances: Technological, Strategic, Psychological, Political, Social, Intellectual, Legal, and Expectancy (1965a: 1241). He combined these distances in a differential equation, subjectively estimated the eight distances between the great powers in July 1939, and found that the "relative probability of war at that date was highest for Japan-USSR (.96), Germany-USSR (.86), and Germany-France (.82)" (1965a: 1280). This work of Wright and the general connections between behavior and such distances suggest the hypothesis that the actions of nations are a function of a variety of distances between them.

The third hypothesis concerns social stratification. Following the work on class and stratification in sociology,[27] Johan Galtung (1964b) and colleagues (Galtung, Araujo, and Schwartzman, 1966; Schwartzman, 1966; Gleditsch, 1969) have defined the international system as a status system in which nations are located on status dimensions. They then propose that the behavior of nations toward each other is a function of their relative status positions. For example, if wealth, power, and prestige are status dimensions of international relations, as proposed by Lagos (1963), then the behavior of the United States to the USSR will be a consequence of the relative profiles of the United States and USSR across these three status dimensions. The third hypothesis is then that the actions of one state to another is a function of their relative statuses.[28]

The fourth hypothesis has to do with the central thesis of international relations: that the configuration of power among nations determines their policy and behavior. That power considerations structure international politics has been attested to by scholars and practitioners alike. That power is basic is a fact of practical experience and scholarly study. That power is measurable, constrain-

---

referred to. Second, in any case, social distance seems to restrict the concern to purely social characteristics or behavior, when what is meant is the distance on all characteristics, political, cultural, military, economic, psychological, as well as social. Therefore, to avoid this confusion in the future, I will use the term "attribute distance" to refer to the dissimilarity of two nations in their characteristics.

27. For example, see the work of Lenski (1966), Merton (1957) and Homans (1961). Homans (1961: 150) is the clearest in defining status. It "is a matter of perception, and of perception that puts stimuli in rank order." He points out (1961: 149) that the "stimuli that make up a man's status include the kinds of reward he receives—among them his esteem itself—the kinds of activity he emits, and anything else about him, like the kind of clothes he wears or the kind of house he lives in, provided that these stimuli are recognized and discriminated by other men. To serve, moreover, as the sorts of stimuli that determine a man's status, people must be able to rank them, in comparison with the stimuli presented by other men, as relatively 'better' or 'worse', 'higher' or 'lower'."

28. The hypotheses being discussed here overlap considerably. For example, in Rosenau's "pre-theory," he proposes (1966: pp. 82-3, 97-88) that four major issue-areas vertically divide interest and activities within nations and from the nation to the international system. One of these issue-areas is status.

able in equations, and a concept leading to testable predictions of nation behavior, however, has not at all been established.

One of the more explicit theories of power has been offered by A.F.K. Organski (1968). He argues that nations are ranked in a power pyramid and that the international order is largely shaped by those at the top of the pyramid. International conflict then comes about when a nation lower down in the pyramid is changing in its power in a way to threaten to displace the more dominant nation and when there are few bonds to tie the two nations together. For Organski, international politics is shaped by the relative (and changing) power between nations and the bonds that bind them.[29] This theory, then, suggests the fourth hypothesis: a nation's conflict and cooperation with another nation are results of their relative power and cooperative ties.

The next hypothesis embodies the general orientation of those working on international and regional integration (Russett, 1963a, 1967a; Deutsch, et al., 1957; Jacob and Teune, 1964). The fundamental notion is that the interaction and cooperation leading to political integration result from, among other things, a high level of social and cultural homogeneity, similarity in political attitudes and values, and geographical proximity. Metaphorically, like marry like. Based on this perspective, the fifth hypothesis is that the relative cooperation between nations is related to the degree of similarity between them, and their geographical distance.

To assert that geographical distance conditions international relations is trite. To specify how it does so is no easy matter (Wohlstetter, 1968). Does geographical distance influence the relations between nations as astronomical distance between planets in conjunction with their mutual gravity influences the relative motion of plans?[30] Does geographical distance only set up boundaries of behavior (Sprout and Sprout, 1962)? Or does distance provide a gradient of behavior (Boulding, 1962)? Rather than adopt any of these alternative functions at this point, I will make explicit the general hypothesis: the relations between nations are conditioned by the geographical distance between them.

To recapitulate, the six relevant hypotheses of international relations are:

(1) foreign policy behavior is a function of economic development, size, and political system.

(2) the behavior of one nation to another is a function of distances.

(3) the behavior of the one nation to another is a function of relative status.

29. In general terms, Organski's position is not much different from other scholars. Although few would accept Morgenthau's (1967: 25) blanket "International politics . . . is a struggle for power," many would agree with Liska (1956) that international politics is reducible to an interplay between politics and norm. By norm is meant in part the values associated with cooperative bonds. In specifics, Organski disagrees with much of the literature. He casts out the sacred balance of power theory and argues that a large power imbalance promotes peace; power parity promotes war; the dominant nation is a secure and peace-loving nation.

30. See Catton (1965) for a discussion of social "gravity."

(4) a nation's conflict and cooperation with another nation are results of their relative power and cooperative ties.

(5) the relative cooperation between nations is related to their homogeneity and geographical distance.

(6) the relations between nations are conditioned by the geographical distance between them.

To connect these hypotheses using the social space representation, I propose the following law-like field theory proposition: the relative behavior of one nation to another is a linear function of the distance vectors between them on the dimensions of attribute space.[31] This law in conjunction with the social space representation and the principal of relative values discussed above is what I call a field theory of social action. The axioms and mathematics of the theory have been developed elsewhere.[32] The interest in this paper is to apply it to U.S. conflict and cooperation.

How can the field theory propositon subsume the six aggregate level hypothesis of linkage, status, distance, power, integration, and geographical distance? First, the proposition links the dyadic behavior (the actions of one nation to another) to their attributes. Applying this law to the United States, the equation expressing this linkage is

$$w_{US \to j,k} = \sum_{l=1}^{p} \alpha_{US,l} \, \alpha_{l,US-j}, \tag{1}$$

where $w_{US \to j,k}$ is the projection of the behavior of the United States toward nation j on the kth dimension of behavior space, $\alpha_{l,US-j}$ is the distance (difference) vector between the United States and nation j on the lth attribute dimension of attribute space, and $\alpha_{US,l}$ is a U.S. specific parameter weighting the distances.

Second, the proposition asserts that relative dyadic behavior is a resolution of

31. Such a law-like statement of international relations may seem presumptuous, and perhaps arrogant, and certainly without empirical foundation. Since no such law has been established yet (this is why it is called "law-like"), I could avoid this impression by speaking of "generalization," or at a more acceptable level, "hypothesis." But, this would not communicate the explanatory strength I am according the statement, unqualified as to nation, time, or place. I am not implying that it is based on invariant research results, but rather am proposing it as a law yet to be largely tested and as one upon which effort should be focused. To publicly state this as law-like is to invite criticism and a great deal of effort to disprove the assertion. But this is what I seek, for science advances by making our assertions definite and public and by the subsequent attempts to qualify and to falsify them.

32. See Rummel (1965). For a more recent and somewhat revised exposition with tests, see Rummel (1969b). The mathematical relationship between what I call attribute theory—the attempt to relate the total behavior of a nation to its attributes—and field theory is discussed in Rummel (1969a). For an application of field theory to a study of Asian conflict and cooperation, see Park (1969). For an application of field theory to the regional economics of India, see Berry (1966). For a theory of behavior using a behavior space conception and overlapping in axioms with field theory, see Phillips (1969).

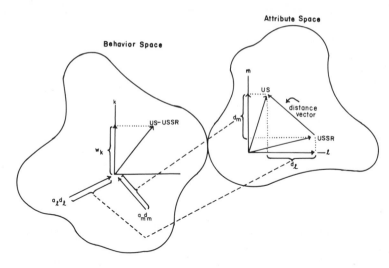

Figure 3.

the weighted attribute distance vectors; that distances are forces determining the behavior of nations toward each other. Figure 3 may help to make this linkage clear. These distances operationalize the notion of relative values and of differences and similarities between nations that is at least implicit in the hypotheses mentioned. To show how equation (1) can link the hypotheses, each of the six will now be made more explicit.

With regard to the linkage hypothesis, Rosenau specifies economic development, size, and political system (open or closed) as important characteristics in understanding the foreign behavior of a nation. As mentioned above, in research done to date to identify the dimensions of the attribute space of nations, economic development, power bases or size, and political orientation have consistently emerged. The political orientation dimension is very close in content (censorship, freedom of groups to oppose the government) to Rosenau's open-closed distinction.

A problem is defining how these three dimensions relate to behavior. If we take an attribute theory approach (Rummel, 1969a)[33] we would say that U.S. values on those three dimensions influence its conflict and cooperation. A careful reading of Rosenau, especially how he makes decision making dependent on the profile of nations on these dimensions and relates this to "issue areas", implies that the behavior of the United States toward other nations will vary depending on the differences between them on these dimensions.

33. An attribute theory is defined as one which tries to explain the variation in behavior of a nation in terms of its characteristics, without reference to other nations. For example, the theory that the involvement in foreign conflict of a nation depends on its internal stability is one. Attribute theory is in contrast to field theory which states that the relative differences and similarities between two nations affect the behavior of one to the other.

Finally, Rosenau's stimulating concept of issue area implies that actions of nations culster around certain issues (such as the cold war). That is, that there are distinct dimensions of nation behavior along which nations vary in their relations with each other, and, tying in the previous paragraph, they will vary in their behavior toward each other depending on their differences in economic development, size, and political system. Since differences between nations are defined by distance vectors, this suggests the following.

Linkage proposition: Distance vectors on the dimensions of attribute space which define economic development, size, and political orientation will contribute the most in accounting for the relative actions of the United States toward other nations on the dimensions of behavior space.

Looking now at the status hypothesis, I have stated that among the major dimensions of attribute space are economic development and power bases.[34] These are consistently the largest dimensions found to define the space and can be considered the two status dimensions of wealth and power.[35] Prestige, a third status dimension, can be assumed dependent on the other two, as has been argued by Lagos (1963) and Lenski (1966)[36] and shown by Schwartzman and Araujo (1966) and Shimbori, et al. (1963) (This is, of course, a different perspective on status theory than is taken by Wallace in this volume.)

Now, the United States has high status on both dimensions of economic development and power. Following status theory,[37] we would therefore expect the United States to direct more cooperative actions toward other high status nations than toward nations that are of low status. That is, cooperative actions directed toward other nations should be inversely proportional to the distances from them on the two status dimensions.[38] Let CO denote the

34. Power bases and size are alternative labels for the same dimension of attribute space. These labels are possible by virtue of the high relationship of measures of power capability to the dimension on the one hand and the high relationship of measures of size, such as area and population, on the other.

35. According to Williams (1947: 55), the main classes of scarce divisible values are: wealth, power, and prestige within a given culture." Specifically with regard to nations, Lagos (1963: 9) says that "economic stature, power, and prestige . . . constitute the status of a nation."

36. "With respect to individual prestige, the evidence suggests . . .prestige seems largely a function of power and privilege" (Lenski, 1966: 431). Privilege for Lenski is often measured by income.

37. According to status theory, the higher the total status of two nations the more "associative" their interactions should be (Galtung, 1966).

38. It is possible to operationalize status difference in this way because the United States is high on both status dimensions. As long as we do not calculate distance on both dimensions, but treat distance on each dimension as a separate variable, then (1) if the distance of the United States from object nation is near zero on both dimensions, they both have high status; (2) if distance on one dimension is low and on the other high, then they have one status in common; (3) if both distances are high, then they have different status. In

cooperative acts of the United States toward an object nation, ED denote distance (difference) between the United States and object nation on economic development, and PB distance on power bases. Then, this part of status theory states that

$$aCO = -ED - PB + b, \qquad (2)$$

where a and b are constants, a is positive, and ED and PB are presumed to have equal weight. In words, the more similar the United States and object are in economic development and power bases, the more cooperative the actions the United States directs toward the object.

There is another, perhaps more exciting, part of status theory, to wit, that the conflict between two nations will be a consequence of status disequilibrium.[39] Relations between them will be most cooperative if they both have balanced profiles on their status, say both high, both low, or one nation high across the status dimensions and the other consistently low. If, however, one or both of the nations are unbalanced on different status dimensions, then the tendency is toward conflict as one or both try to balance their status upward and thus threaten the dominance of the other.[40]

Since the United States is high on both status dimensions, imbalance will exist when another nation is close to the United States on one and far on another, such as China, which is much closer to the United States on the power

---

this paper, status is treated as a matter of degree since its measure—distance—is a continuous variable.

Also, distance is a vector here and not simply a magnitude. However, since the United States has top values on economic development and power bases, the results (correlations) for the United States are invariant of whether distances on these dimensions are treated as a magnitude or vector.

39. The concept of status disequilibrium, or imbalance, inconsistency, or crystallization has provoked considerable research in sociology. See, for example, Lenski (1966), Segal (1969), Mitchell (1964), and Homans (1961). The basic idea is that a person unbalanced in his status will be under stress, inducing him to act in a way to balance his status. For example, he may, as Lenski believes (1966: 88), be more likely to "support liberal or radical movements designed to alter the political status quo than are persons of consistent status." Not all the evidence on the political consequences of unbalance was consistent until Segal (1969) showed that the relevance of particular status under certain political circumstances has to be taken into account. Most of this work has been done treating the status of an individual and his overall behavior. Little work, with the exception of Homans (1961: 248) who defines status congruence in terms of two individuals, has been specifically concerned with the behavior between two persons in terms of their relative ranks. One of the contributions of Galtung is combining a number of ideas and results from the status literature to discuss dyadic relationships.

40. As Galtung (1964b) points out, his theory of status disequilibrium contradicts the criss-cross theory of conflict: nations that have no status in common should have more conflict than those that have one status alike, since the one status provides a cross-pressure—a bridge between them—that dampens conflict. Singer and Small (1968) have applied this theory to international relations with results supporting it. The empirical results to be described here also bear on this theory.

dimension than on economic development. It seems most likely that conflict will result when both the United States and object nation are jointly high on power—have power parity, so to speak—and far apart in economic development.[41] Power, then, provides the resources for conflict; differences in economic development supply many of the issues for conflict;[42] and the threat to the dominance of the United States is implicit in the greater power the other nation will have if it narrows the economic development gap and balances itself on these two status dimensions. This aspect of status theory can be put into an equation, denoting conflict by CF,

$$dCF = ED - PB + e, \qquad\qquad (3)$$

where d and e are constants, d is positive, and ED and PB are assumed to have equal weight. In words, the more the United States and object nation are dissimilar in economic development and similar in power, the more conflict actions the United States will direct toward the object.

We now have two equations, one for the conflict actions and one for the cooperative behavior of the United States. The international relations of the United States, however, are not neatly partitioned this way. Mixed actions are simultaneously directed at the same actor, some conflictful, some cooperative.[43] What then will be the relationship between these actions? Since equations (2) and (3) share some of the same variables, we can determine the relationship between them by adding dCF to both sides of equation (2) and using (3)

41. If economic development is considered an achieved dimension—one on which nations can be high by virtue of elements they have little control over today, such as area, population size, resources—then the imbalance on the achieved dimension could be especially conducive to conflict. It is along this dimension that evaluation of the ability of a nation is likely to take place and the dimension on which the nation can most mobilize its resources to move upward.

42. The gap between rich and poor nations has come to be the most important issue of international relations (Patel, 1964). Aside from being an issue, however, whether a nation is rich or poor affects the way it makes foreign policy. The process becomes "bureaucratized," with loss of control by the cabinet and growth in administrative politics (Morse, 1970). Aside from other considerations, this helps explain why U.S. actions should differ depending on how economically distant the other nation is, since economic distance will measure the level of modernization of the foreign policy process of the other nation.

43. This is consonant with Rosenau's (1966) issue area vertical division of a nation's outputs and Lerche's (1956: 147) "single objective conflict." The United States, for example, in the same day may be in conference with the USSR talking about strategic arms limitation, allowing U.S. tourists to visit the USSR and students to study there, exporting machinery there, and warning its leaders that the United States cannot stand by and let the Soviet Union unbalance the balance of power between Israel and her neighbors in the Middle East.

I might also point out that conflict and cooperation have a logical and sociological relationship to each other. Logically, many kinds of conflict behavior cannot occur unless

$$aCO + dCF = -ED - PB + b + dCF$$
$$= -ED - PB + b + ED - PB + e$$
$$= -2PB + (b + e)$$
$$(a/2)CO + (d/2)CF = -PB + (b + e)/2$$
$$gCO + hCF = -PB + k \qquad (4)$$

where the new constants in (4) are functions of those in the previous equation and g and h are positive. Equation (4) indicates that the joint amount of conflict and cooperative actions toward an object should depend on the power parity of the two nations.

The three equations developed above from status theory can be put into three status propositons.

Status Propositions:

A. The distances of object nation from the United States on economic development and power bases dimensions of attribute space will contribute negatively to the relative cooperative actions of the United States toward that nation.

B. The distance of the object nation from the United States on economic development will contribute positively and the distance on power bases will contribute negatively to the relative conflict actions of the United States toward that nation.

C. The distance of the object nation from the United States on power will contribute negatively to the joint cooperative and conflictful actions of the United States toward that nation.

To move on to the third hypothesis previously posed, Wright suggests a number of distances which affect the probability of war between two nations. Some, such as Psychic and Expectancy distances, may be considered as resultants of distances on attributes and not attribute distances themselves. Most of the others, Social (S), Technological (T), Political (P), Strategic (G), Intellectual (I), and Legal (L) can be related to the dimensions of attribute space. Following the spirit (and not the letter, since we will not use a differential equation and some of his distance relationships are being altered) of Wright's

---

there is cooperation to begin with. For example, boycotts cannot occur if there is no trade or transaction; diplomatic relations cannot be severed if there are no such relations; and a state visit cannot be cancelled if not visit had been planned to begin with. The sociological relationship is expressed by Coser (1963: 85): "The absence of conflict cannot be taken as an index of the strength and stability of a relationship. Stable relationships may be characterized by conflicting behavior. Closeness gives rise to frequent occasions for conflict, but if the participants feel that their relationships are tenuous, they will avoid conflict, fearing that it might endanger the continuance of the relation. When close relationships are characterized by frequent conflicts rather than by the accumulation of hostile and ambivalent feelings, we may be justified, given that such conflicts are not likely to concern basic consensus, in taking these frequent conflicts as an index of the stability of these relationships."

analysis of distances, assume that Psychic and Expectancy distances are subsumed by the others and that his "the probability of war" can be replaced by the level of conflict behavior (CF). Then we can render his distance theory by

$$CF = -aT + bS + eP + dI + fL - dG + g, \qquad (5)$$

where all the constants are positive. The equation states that the conflict actions between two nations are consequences of the positive distances of the United States on S, P, I, and L and the technological[44] and strategic similarity of the two.

How can we define the dimensions on which the distance should be measured and imbedded in attribute space? First, by technological distance, Wright means communication and transportation between two nations. That is, T is part of behavior space. It is defined by those behavior dimensions delineating communications and transactions between two nations as measured by their trade.[45] Second, the Social distances can be tapped by those attribute dimensions defining the socio-cultural characteristics of nations, such as Catholic Culture, Equality, Oriental Culture, and Diversity.[46] Third, Strategic distance, which is defined by Wright as the vulnerability of attack of one nation by another, can be partially measured by geographic distance.[47] Fourth, Political and Legal distances can be defined by the political orientation dimension of attribute space. Finally, intellectual distance can be indexed by economic development, since measures of education and of scientific (versus legal and religious) interests (such as proportion of science titles published) are highly related to the dimension (Rummel, forthcoming).

Putting the above correspondences together, remembering that T is now behavior on the communication-transaction dimensions, and letting SO stand for (a linear combination of) distances on the socio-cultural dimensions, we get the revised equation

$$CF = aT + bED + cP + dSO - eG + g, \qquad (6)$$

44. "If states are technologically near to one another, disputes will be frequent and dilatory tactics are likely to lead to an accumulation of disputes and an increasing aggravation of relations. Each incident comes to be considered in relation to its bargaining value in a general settlement, and it becomes progressively more difficult to settle any issue on its merits" (Wright, 1965a: 1256n. 45).

45. "The technological distances separating pairs of similar countries may be compared over short periods of time by comparison of trade statistics" (Wright, 1965a: 1244).

46. These are dimensions of attribute space reported in Rummel (1969b), and listed with indicators in Table 3.

47. Geographic location is theoretically a part of attribute space. In the latest unreported analyses of national attributes directed at delineating the dimensions of this space for 1963, three variables were included in order to define the location of a nation's capital. The resulting attribute dimensions captured this variance associated with location; national distances computed on these dimensions would then subsume geographic distance. For the 1955 results to be used here, however, geographic distance would have to be computed separately from distances on attribute space dimensions.

where a, b, c, d, e, and g are constants and all except g are necessarily positive. Now placing behavior on the same side,

$$CF - aT = bED + cP + dSO - eG + g. \qquad (7)$$

That is to say, from Wright we have developed another equation showing the relationship between conflict and cooperation. This time, rather than dealing with joint behavior we have the difference between conflict and cooperation: conflict relative to cooperation will be greater as the indicated attribute distances are greater and geographic distance less. This can be put into the following proposition.

Distance Proposition: The distance vectors[48] of the United States from object nation on the social, political orientation, and economic development dimensions contribute positively and the distances on geographic distance contribute negatively to the magnitude of conflict actions of the United States toward an object nation relative to its communications and transactions with that nation.

The fourth hypothesis is that conflict and cooperation between nations result from their relative power and the ties that bind them. The direction of influence here should be clear. The closer two nations are in their power, holding cooperative ties constant, conflict is more likely. To put this differently, for

48. No other nation is higher than the United States on economic development and on the ordinal rating for freedom of group opposition. Thus, distance vectors and distance magnitudes on each of these two dimensions would be equivalent. However, on Catholic culture and the other socio-cultural dimensions, the United States is neither the highest nor lowest. Consequently, if the other nation is higher on the Catholic Culture dimension, then the distance vector will have a negative magnitude and a positive magnitude if the other nation is lower. For distance magnitudes (Euclidean distance), however, both values would be positive.

Why deal with vectors rather than magnitudes? For two reasons. First, vectors allow a simpler representation of field theory and easier mathematical manipulation. They are more pleasing aesthetically and intellectually. Second, vectors are a more intuitively satisfying representation than Euclidean distance. It is sensible to say that if a nation is in the middle of a dimension, such as economic development or power, it acts differently to the higher nation than it does to the ones beneath it. To use Euclidean distances is to say that the nation's behavior will be the same to those at the top and botton, since both are equidistant from him.

The use of distance vectors creates a problem of its own. Theory based on distance vectors cannot be distinguished in the empirical tests to be used here from theory based on the characteristics of the object nation. A proposition that U.S. behavior is a consequence of distance vectors on the power bases dimension will have the same test reuslts as a proposition that U.S. behavior is a consequence of the power bases of the object nation. At some future time a crucial test between the two theories will have to be developed. I am indebted to Nils Petter Gleditsch for pointing out this problem to me.

peace to obtain between two nations, there should be a disparity in power between them.[49]

What is meant by binding or cooperative ties? Often this refers to alliances, treaties, trade, and the like.[50] These, however, constitute the cooperative behavior that is part of our behavior space—part of the dependent variable, to speak loosely. Therefore, we might say that the difference between these two kinds of behavior—cooperation and conflict—is a linear function of power parity. In symbols

$$CO - CF = +aP + b, \qquad (8)$$

where CO is understood to be cooperation on dimensions measuring such cooperative ties as alliances and treaties and a is a positive constant.

> *Power Proposition*: The distance between the United States and the object nation on power contributes positively to the magnitude of cooperative actions (such as alliances and treaties of the United States toward the object nation relative to the conflict with that nation).

The homogeneity hypothesis is that the more similar two nations are, the more likely they are to cooperate and enter into binding arrangements—the more integrative their behavior.[51] Russett (1967a) has systematically investigated this hypothesis by computing Euclidean distances between nations in the space of four attribute space dimensions (similar to my economic development, political orientation, Catholic culture, and density dimensions) and analyzing the

49. My interpretation of Organski's power transition theory will do some violence to it, since he is proposing that power change is the crucial variable. However, to enable analysis at this stage in the data collection, I am treating the hypothesis as a static one and not without justification. A power gap alone creates fear (Berkowitz, 1962: 43); the dominant power gets what it wants by the implicit threat of its power and the weaker submits—often unconsciously—to aovid the use of such power. Without a clear gap, however, there is an ambiguity (since statesmen have no precise measure of power). In Coser's terms (1963. 247), "when contenders feel that their power is more or less evenly matched, given their common inability to gauge their relative strength more precisely, then the temptation is strong to engage in trial through battle." See also Easton (1953: 303).

The theory that power parity makes conflict more likely contradicts the traditional balance of power theory, as expressed by Wright (1955: 143): "The greater the number of states and the more nearly equal their power, the more stable is the equilibrium." See also Wright (1965a: 755).

50. A case could be made that the bonds between nations are reducible to their relative homogeneity, which has been asserted by Kant and others to be a necessary condition for the successful operation of a balance of power. Homogeneity could mean easier diplomatic exchange and power calculations. On this, see Gulick (1955). This interpretation of "bond," while more consonant with the theory being developed here, would violate its meaning for contemporary writers.

51. "The most important analytical property for the study of the prerequisites of unification seems to be the degree of heterogeneity of the member units" (Etzioni, 1965: 19).

distances. The grouping of nations on these distances corresponded well with our intuitive regional grouping of nations[52] and accounted, to a considerable extent, for groupings of nations on trade, UN voting, and organization co-memberships. Russett also grouped nations on geographic distance and found some correspondence between such distance and the behavior groupings.

Building on Russett's work, and that of Jacob and Teune (1964) and Deutsch, et al. (1957)[53] who argue the need for similarity in values for integrative behavior, I will propose that cooperative (integrative) behavior of nations is a function of (1) the socio-cultural dimensions which index a nation's values, (2) the political orientation and economic development dimensions, and (3) geographic distance.[54] As a proposition for the United States, it becomes the following.

Homogeneity Proposition: Distance vectors between the United States and an object nation on economic development, political orientation, and socio-cultural dimensions will contribute negatively to the cooperative behavior of the United States to the object nation.

The final hypothesis is the geographic one. It states simply that the farther away nations are, the less they interact either cooperatively or conflictfully. This hypothesis may be more salient for Burma, say, than the United States with its technological ability to span the globe and its "world policeman" policy. Yet, would Soviet missiles in 1962 have caused the same crisis were Cuba located in East Africa or South East Asia? It is difficult to accept that the same U.S.

52. One impressive grouping comprised the Soviet bloc, then within it Albania and China as a subgroup (Russett, 1967a: 55). It should be remembered that this was on attribute distances alone!

53. Quincy Wright says (1955: 542) of Deutsch that he "uses the terms 'political integration and amalgamation; psychological identification and assimilation; mutual responsiveness and simple pacification; and mutual interdependence and interaction' to describe typical processes which if in proper relation to one another may develop a security community in an area. These appear to be similar, respectively, to the processes which I have described, from the point of view of increasing closeness of groups, as organization, standardization, co-operation, and communication . . ., and, from the point of view of increasing separation of groups, as social and political, psychic and expectancy, legal and intellectual, and technological and strategic distances. . . ." Wright's comment is pertinent to my attempt here to explicitly subsume both Wright's theory and some of Russett's and Deutsch's hypotheses within a common frame and to tie them together using the concept of distance vector.

54. Russett omitted the size dimension from his analysis, arguing that it is not a relevant criteria for cooperation leading to integration (Russett, 1967a: 21). I will do likewise. I will go beyond the four dimensions Russett used (Communism, Economic Development, Catholic Culture, and Intensive Agriculture), however, and include ten as socio-cultural dimensions in addition to economic development and political orientation. These are indicated in Table 3. Russett's four dimensions are based on an analysis of 54 variables; mine are based on 236. The additional dimensions I am including may therefore be considered a more comprehensive and refined delineation of socio-cultural patterns.

conflict and cooperation would be directed at a nation regardless of geographic distance. More likely, geographic distance acts as a moderator variable, dampening cooperation at a great distance or accentuating the conflict for close nations.

> *Geographic Proposition*: The geographic distance of the United States from the object nation contributes negatively to the cooperative and conflictful actions of the United States toward that nation.

Six aggregate level hypotheses about nation behavior have now been interrelated using the constructs of attribute and behavior space, dyad, and distance vector. Several propositions about the behavior of a particular set of dyads, all those involving the United States as actor, have been derived from these hypotheses. It may be helpful at this point to summarize the discussion by systematically placing the propositions in a table with the proposed relationships (Table 1). As seen from the Table, there is a consistency in the proposed

Table 1. Propositions About U.S. Aggregate Behavior

		ATTRIBUTE SPACE DIMENSIONS				
Proposition	*Behavior*	*Econ. Dev. Distance*	*Power Bases Distance*	*Pol. Orient. Distance*	*Geographic Distance*	*Socio-Cultural Distance*
Linkage	all	±	±	±		
Status A	cooperative	−	−			
Status B	conflictful	+	−			
Status C	coop. + conflict			−		
Distance [a]	coop. − conflict	−		−	+	−
Power	coop. − conflict		+			
Homogeneity	cooperative	−		−	−	−
Geographic	coop. or conflict				−	

a. The signs on this relationship have all been reversed from Equation (7) to conform with the direction of the other relationships expressed in the Table.

direction of relationships of distances to either cooperative or conflictful actions or their combination, as expected given the overlapping nature of the hypotheses, the consistency in the scholarly literature, and the common framework (e.g., distance vectors) within which the hypotheses were interpreted. The important thing, however, is not this consistency, but whether the common thread—the theoretical proposition that distance vectors explain nation behavior—and equation (1) giving specificity to this relationship are consistent with observation. For an answer, we must leave our armchair and confront the aggregate phenomenon.

Space and prudence do not permit a thorough discussion of the methods used in testing the above propositions—since this has been done elsewhere (Rummel, 1969b). It suffices to say that treating behavior and attributes within a linear space enables the product moment coefficient, and the multiple regression, component factor analysis, and canonical analysis models to be part of the theoretical structure of field theory. They then become the techniques for operationalizing and testing derivations from the theory and propositions imbedded in it.

In a previous study (Rummel, 1969b) the location of 13 dyads involving the United States as actor (objects were Brazil, Burma, China, Cuba, Egypt, India, Indonesia, Israel, Jordan, Netherlands, Poland, USSR, and U.K.) in 1955 behavior space was related (using canonical analysis) to 1955 distances (differences) between the United States and the 13 object nations. The distances were on economic development (indexed by energy consumption per capita), power bases (indexed by national income),[55] freedom of group opposition, and geographic distance. Because of the small number of cases (13), not all dimensions of behavior or attribute spaces could be used. Attribute space therefore was defined in terms of the dimensions mentioned: economic development, power bases (size), and political orientation. Geographic distance was also included.

The behavior space dimensions were summed into three statistically independent (orthogonal) dimensions of conflict behavior, administrative behavior, and private international relations.[56] For this sample on these three dimensions, 55 percent of the variation in overall U.S. actions were accounted for by the distances. Specifically, 90 percent of the variation in U.S. conflict behavior toward the 13 nations was accounted for by power and political orientation distance vectors. The function is

$$.87CF \doteq -.65PB + .57PO, \tag{9}$$

55. Organski (1968) recommends national income as the best measure of power. The reason national income was selected here was primarily because of its very high correlation with the power bases dimension (Rummel, 1969c) for all nations and secondarily because of Organski's suggestion and use of the indicator. As Lasswell and Kaplan say (1950: 147), it "is power potential, rather than power position directly, which is crucial in the political process. The players do not always pay to see the winning hand," see also Lasswell and Kaplan (1950: 83). Quincy Wright (1955) recommends energy production times population as an indicator of the power of a nation. This indicator, however, is also very highly correlated with national income in tapping almost the same variances that would be included were I to use Wright's indicator (or, for that matter, defense expenditures, men under arms, GNP, population, or energy production).

56. There were originally 11 behavior space dimensions for 182 dyads. "By studying the content of eleven dimensions, three kinds of substantive classifications emerge: dimensions manifesting private international relations, those comprising administrative behavior, and those involving conflict behavior" (Rummel, 1969b: 34). Private international relations consist of salience (e.g. translations, tourists, treaties), communications, exports, students and migrants dimensions; administrative behavior consists of diplomatic and international organization dimensions; conflict behavior consists of U.N. voting, self-determination voting, negative sanctions. and deterrence dimensions. See Rummel (1969b: Table 1) for the behavior variables related to these dimensions.

where CF denotes conflict behavior, PB denotes power bases distance, PO distance on political orientation, and $\doteq$ means approximately. The coefficients are for standardized data. With regard to U.S. private international relations (tourists, students, exports, immigrants, etc.), 70 percent of the variation in this behavior is accounted for by economic development

$$.99CO \doteq -.85ED, \tag{10}$$

where CO denotes cooperation (since private international relations encompass a cooperative range of actions) and ED denotes economic development.

Both equations (9) and (10) express empirical relations that overlap with the propositions of Table 1. Equation (9) relates to the status B proposition, but while power bases is included and in the right direction, economic development is not. In its place is political orientation distance. Equation (10) is similar to the status A proposition, except that while economic development is in the hypothesized direction, the power bases dimension is not included.

Overall, attribute distances accounted for 55 percent of the variance in the behavior of the United States toward the 13 object nations. This is consistent with the theoretical proposition that behavior is linearly dependent on distance vectors. The difficulty with generalizing the above results is the small sample, however. Accordingly, data have been collected for the behavior of the United States toward 81 other nations in 1955 and the results of analyzing these data will be reported here.

The choice of dyadic variables on which to collect U.S. behavior data was guided by the results of the analysis of 50 variables for 182 dyads (including the above-mentioned dyads with United States as actor) for 1955. Variables were included to index the behavior space dimensions[57] for the 182 dyads, to be as diverse as possible so as to capture a wide range of variation in U.S. foreign behavior, to exploit the greater availability of data in the United States for some variables (such as foreign investments), and to take account of the type of analysis to be done. On the last criterion, there was no reason to include, say, export US$\rightarrow$j/total U.S. trade, since the denominator will be constant for all U.S. dyads, and accordingly the variables will have a perfect correlation with exports US$\rightarrow$j alone. Thus, no variable normed by U.S. totals is included in the analysis. The list of variables for which data were collected is shown in Table 2.

Attribute space for 1955 has already been analyzed for all nations (Rummel, 1968) and all that is needed here is that distance vectors between the United States and object nations be computed on the dimensions of this space. Table 2 gives the attribute space dimensions and the indicator of that dimension on

---

57. These dimensions are shown in Rummel (1969b: Table 1). The difference between this set of dimensions for 1955 and those shown in Rummel (1969c) is that the latter are computed across missing data while the former are computed on a matrix with missing data filled in, using a regression estimation technique described elsewhere (Wall and Rummel, 1969).

Table 2. U.S. Behavior Space

Variable No.	Variable Code	Variable	Missing Data
1	BOOKS	exports of books and periodicals,	0
2	TOURIS	tourists, US→j	17
3	TREATY	treaties, US→j	0
4	EXPORTS	exports, US→j	0
5	STUDENT	students, US→j	24
6	EMIGRA	emigrants, US→j	11
7	EMBLEG	embassy or legation, US→j = 1; none = 0	0
8	IGO	intergovernmental organizations of which United States and j are comembers	0
9	D-UN	agreement US—j on major 1955 dimensions of U.N. voting	18
10	NEGSAN	negative sanctions factor scores,	0
11	MILVIO	military violence factor scores,	0
12	NEGCOM	negative communication factor scores, US→j	0
13	ECOAID	economic aid, US→j	0
14	INVEST	private investment, US→j	8
15	MILAID	military aid, US→j	0
16	COMMIT	military commitment, US→j	0
17	VISITS	official visits, US→j	0
18	MILPER	military personnel stationed in, US→j	0
19	CONFER	conferences, US→j	0

which distance vectors between the United States and object were computed.

The results to be presented are divided into three parts. First, the patterns among the dyadic behavior of the United States will be considered. Second, the findings relevant to the fundamental field theory proposition will be weighed. And finally, the results bearing on the six propositions discussed above will be measured.

The 19 actions of the United States toward 81 nations in 1955 range from tourists, through exports and treaties, to conflict behavior. How are these actions patterned? This is an interesting and important question in itself, but unfortunately, one on which we cannot dwell with great detail here. Nonetheless, in order to make the U.S. behavior suitable for subsequent canonical analysis, a preliminary factor analysis was necessary to reduce U.S. dyadic behavior to their independent patterns (or dimensions, as they are more technically known).[58]

58. My preference is to do a canonical analysis on the raw data. The relationship among the two sets of variables is given directly, then. However, because the correlation matrix of U.S. behavior was virtually singular (determinant = 0.5×10^{-5}), the data had to be first reduced to a set of independent dimensions.

The factor analysis results are given in Appendix II. The 19 U.S. dyadic actions were found to cluster into six distinct and independent patterns. The first pattern[59] comprises the movement of American students and emigrants to other nations, treaties with those nations, military aid to them and high level conferences involving them. At first, this appears to be a cooperation dimension, but if so, how does one explain that these kinds of actions are independent of exports, tourists, economic aid, etc.? A look at the values of U.S. dyads on this pattern[60] shows that the highest scoring object nations are Belgium, France, West Germany, Italy, Netherlands, Switzerland, and the United Kingdom. Lowest are Burma, Cambodia, El Salvadore, Guatamala, Laos, and South Vietnam. Obviously, this pattern is a cluster of U.S. actions peculiarly directed to Western European nations and will be named Western European Cooperation.

A second cluster of U.S. actions, independent of and larger than the above, also is cooperative in nature. This consists of U.S. exports of books, exports in general, U.S. tourists, U.S. private investments, and U.S. emigrants. Only two nations are the major recipients of this behavior: Canada and the U.K. Perhaps most would agree in calling this an Anglo-American Cooperation pattern. The nations with lowest values on this dimension are Venezuela and Mexico. This disparity in behavior to Canada and Mexico, especially since both are large nations contiguous to the United States, underscores the effects that socio-economic and cultural differences can have in foreign behavior. We will examine this more precisely later.

The Western European and Anglo-American patterns were cooperative. The third pattern delineated is of conflict. Specifically, a cluster of military violence and negative communications actions,[61] and only these actions, are involved in this pattern. The United States, as a major world power with global political interests and concerns employs negative communications, military warnings, and violence as ways of communicating its national interests and expectations—as ways of drawing the lines other nations cross at their own risk. Consonant with this point, the two major objects of this behavior are the USSR and China. I will call this behavior a Deterrence pattern.

Deterrence is independent of the other cooperative dimensions, meaning that sometimes the United States directs deterrent behavior at its Western European and Anglo-American friends, and sometimes the Unites States is cooperative with the major objects of U.S. deterrent behavior. This independence of conflict

59. From this point on, I will be interpreting the rotated dimensions in the order they are shown in Appendix II.

60. The values of U.S. dyads (factor scores) on these patterns are listed in Appendix III of "Dimensionality of Nations Project Research Report" No. 41; Honolulu: University of Hawaii, July, 1970. Due to space limitations, they could not be included here.

61. As can be seen from Appendix I which defines the military violence and negative communication variables, these variables themselves measure separate clusters of conflict actions found in conflict data for 340 dyads. Consequently, more is involved in the cluster than two variables; rather a whole spectrum of military activities and negative communications is defined by this pattern.

and cooperative type behavior has been consistently found in a number of studies. The foreign conflict behavior of 82 nations in 1955 was found independent of other kinds of foreign behavior (Rummel, 1966b). For about 340 dyads in 1955 conflict behavior was found independent of other kinds of dyadic behavior (Rummel, 1969b), and in 1963 the same independence was found for the same number of dyads (Rummel, 1970b) The evidence for the belief that conflict and cooperation are not antipodes—opposite ends of a continuum—but are statistically independent dimensions of international relations is mounting.

The fourth cluster of U.S. dyadic actions is diplomatic, administrative, and military in nature. These comprise the existence of a U.S. embassy or legation in the other nation, common intergovernmental organization memberships, U.S. voting agreement, and military defense commitments. Among nations high on this pattern are Australia, Belgium, Taiwan, Thailand, Union of South AFrica, and most central and South American Counties; lowest are Albania, Bulgaria, China, East Germany, North Korea, Outer Mongolia, and North Vietnam. This is a purely Cold War pattern.[62] (Remember, this is 1955 behavior.)

The fact that Anglo-American and Western European nations do not have high scores on this dimension (and the USSR has a low one) implies that although there are cold war elements in U.S. behavior to these nations, there are other ingredients as well, as we well know. The finding of a cluster of conflict actions called Deterrence apart from Cold War behavior is also understandable. The United States must constantly communicate intent to friend, foe, and neutrals alike. Military alerts, warnings, threats, and diplomatic protests are devices for signaling Egypt, France, Peru, Panama, and Israel, as well as obvious U.S. enemies, and they are so used. Thus, the Cold War pattern is a delineation of those actions with which U.S. behavior uniquely defines the Cold War.

The fifth pattern of U.S. behavior consists mainly of negative sanctions and, to a lesser extent, the stationing of U.S. military personnel in the country. In 1955, the United States directed some negative actions toward West Germany and Japan (as well as toward Burma, China, and Czechoslovakia). West Germany had, then, the largest contingent of American military personnel abroad, and Japan ran a close third to South Korea in U.S. troops stationed in the country. Thus, the relationship between negative sanctions and U.S. military personnel follows. This pattern will be called Negative Sanctions.

Finally, the sixth cluster of actions almost wholly involves economic aid. To a much lesser extent, military aid is also a part of the pattern. Aid is therefore a

---

62. This pattern conforms with the findings of Teune and Synnestredt (1965). Using bivariate statistics on 119 nations and alignment data on 70 variables for 1953 and 1963, they found that the best objective measures of U.S.-USSR alignments (as judged by comparison with expert ratings) are military commitments, U.N. votes, diplomatic recognition, and official visits. These four variables (official visits has a loading of −.48 in the Cold War pattern), in addition to international organizations, define our Cold War pattern for the United States.

specific kind of U.S. behavior, apparently independent of uniquely Cold War actions (which would be true if aid is given for a combination of reasons, including political and altruistic) as well as other kinds of cooperative activity. This will be called an Aid pattern.

These six patterns of U.S. dyadic behavior—Western European, Anglo-American, Deterrence, Cold War, Negative Sanctions, and Aid—should, if field theory is correct, be dependent on the attribute distances of other nations from the United States.[63] As listed in Table 3, below, 13 indicators of the dimensions of attribute space can be used to determine these distance vectors.

Appendix III contains the canonical analysis of U.S. dyadic behavior and attribute distances. The results show how well the variation of U.S. dyadic behavior on the six independent patterns can be explained by the attribute vector distances plus geographic distance. At the moment, our interest is in the overall relationship between U.S. behavior and U.S. attribute distances, for this would be high if results accord with the field theory axiom that distance vectors are forces determining behavior.

Specifically, we are concerned with how dependent the behavior space is on attribute space. When we ask about the relationship between spaces, we are

63. These six patterns that have been found in U.S. actions could be considered as operationalizing Rosenau's "issue area" concept. For Rosenau, an issue area comprises a distinct "interaction pattern" and mobilizes different interests (1966: 71) within a nation. Each of the six patterns, whether Aid, Deterrence, or Anglo-American, does involve different interest groups within the United States and, as I have shown, does involve distinct U.S. behavior. If this point is granted, then in effect this whole paper could be considered a definition of U.S. issue areas and a linking of these to "the variables defining the external behavior" of the United States within Rosenau's framework.

The possibility that Rosenau's "pre-theory" could be rigorously developed within a field theory context has been pointed out by others. At a 1966 conference on the Interdependencies of National and International Political Systems reported in Rosenau (1967b), one speaker (identified only as "First Speaker") said that: "When I think of a field that might present some analogies, some models for emulation, for studying national-international linkages, the field that comes most prominently to mind is Psychology, particularly certain schools of psychology. Among the schools of psychology, the one that seems to provide the most fruitful grounds for emulation is, of course, field theory. It is a natural area of psychology in which to look for analogies because it is specifically concerned with the linkages between the personality and its various environments or fields. Field theory is not concerned with personality per se—the needs, drives, and reflexes of human beings. It is not concerned with particular external objects or stimuli acting upon the personality. It is concerned with the characteristics of social fields in which and on which individuals operate (Rosenau, 1967b: 31)." The same speaker also pointed out later: "Another typological problem that has cropped up again and again in our discussions was also confronted by the field theories in psychology. It is the problem of how one constructs a differential spatial geometry for the various fields in which the unit acts and which act upon the unit. The (Rosenau) linkage paper we have discussed tackles the problem as one always does at the outset, in an offhand way. It breaks down the international environment of a national system by distinguishing among their contiguous environment, the rational environment, the cold-war environment, and so on. Some of the field theorists in psychology have tackled the problem in an extremely rigorous way (Rosenau, 1967b: 32)."

Table 3

Dimension	Indicator
1. Economic Development	energy consumption per capita
2. Power Bases	national income
3. Political Orientation	freedom of group opposition [a]
4. Foreign Conflict Behavior	number of threats
5. Density	population/national land area
6. Catholic Culture	Roman Catholics/population
7. Domestic Conflict	number of domestic killed
8. Oriental Culture	number of religious groups
9. (unnamed)	foreign college students/college students
10. Traders	exports/GNP
11. Equality	government education expenditure/ government expenditures
12. Diversity	number of language groups
13. Sufficiency	proteins/calories

a. Measured as: 0 = political opposition not permitted; 1 = restricted opposition permitted, but cannot campaign for control of government; 2 = unrestricted.

being severe in our test (as we should be), for we are asking how dependent all the infinite linear combinations of the six behavior patterns are on all the infinite linear combinations of attribute distances.[64] The actual result is that the (trace) correlation between two spaces is .68, which means that almost 50 percent of the variation of U.S. dyads in behavior space can be explained by distance vectors.

This result is well within the ball park. Social scientists point with pride to correlations of .4 and .5, and the behavior being explained here ranges from private international relations to public, and from cooperative to conflictful. And considering that such behavior to all nations is being explained, whether Yemen, Cuba, Haiti, U.K., France, or China and the USSR, then to account for almost fifty percent of the behavior on the six U.S. dyadic patterns or their linear combinations is positive evidence for the theory.

Our final concern is with the six propositions—the linkage, status, distance, power, homogeneity, and geographic propositions—tied together within field theory by the distance vector construct. How do the canonical results in Appendix III bear on these propositions?

64. This mathematical concept of "all possible linear combinations" may need clarification. Consider three variables, such as X_1, X_2, and X_3. A linear combination would be $X_1 + 3X_2$. Another would be $X_1 + X_2 + X_3$. A third would be $5X_2 - 16X_3$. In general, any combination Y where $Y = aX_1 + bX_2 + cX_3$ and a, b, and c are any real numbers, is a linear combination. In effect, Y is a scale derived from the three variables and an infinitude of such scales can be formed linearly from any set of variables. All these scales, including each variable itself, constitute a space in mathematical terms. Now, to consider the behavior space of the United States is to consider the infinitude of behavior scales that could be linearly formed from the six patterns.

Our first relevant finding is that U.S. Western European behavior and deterrence are explained by power parity, to the amount of 88 percent of the variance (.94 correlation). The equation for this is

$$.81(WE) + .66(DE) \doteq -.81(PO),$$

where WE means Western European behavior, DE stands for the deterrence pattern, and PO is the power distance vector as before.[65]

This is strong confirmation for status proposition C, which was derived from the theories that equal status leads to high cooperation and status disequilibrium causes conflict. This finding confirms both status notions and suggests how power alone can explain U.S. behavior; economic development as a status cancels out through having opposite effects.[66]

The above equation provides a set of estimates of behavior, the combination of WE and DE, from power distance (difference). Figure 4 plots the estimates of this behavior combination from power parity. The dyads fairly well align themselves along the perfect prediciton line, as to be expected from a correlation of .94. As shown, U.S. actions to France on this joint behavior (Western European plus deterrence) could be almost perfectly predicted from power distance, while U.S. to India is poorly predicted, U.S. behavior to India is relatively undercooperative or deterrent, given Indian power relative to the United States. This may be explained by a Western-oriented perception of the United States which tends to underrate non-European nations. Consider that those to whom the U.S. underbehaves in the Figure are Egypt, Japan, India, and China (excluding the U.K., which is a special case and which the U.S. much takes for granted), while those to whom the U.S. overbehaves are USSR, West Germany, Canada, Italy, and Israel (perceived in many ways as really a European-style nation). This suggests that a future test include an attribute that measures the Europeaness of a nation. Distance from the United States on this attribute should then account for these deviations from prediction of power distance.

The second relevant finding is that 68 percent of the variation in U.S. dyadic behavior on the Cold War pattern is explained by distance (difference) in political orientation and Catholic culture. The equation is

$$.79(CW) \doteq .56 (PS) + .48 (CC),$$

where CW is the cold war pattern, PS is political distance, and CC is Catholic

65. The scores for WE, DE, and PO are assumed standardized and this assumption will hold for all subsequent relationships to be discussed.

66. Since many papers of this type are written after the results are in, I should remark that this one was written (up to the discussions of the results) before completion of the computer analyses. Thus, in the true sense of the word, these results confirm an a priori hypothesis.

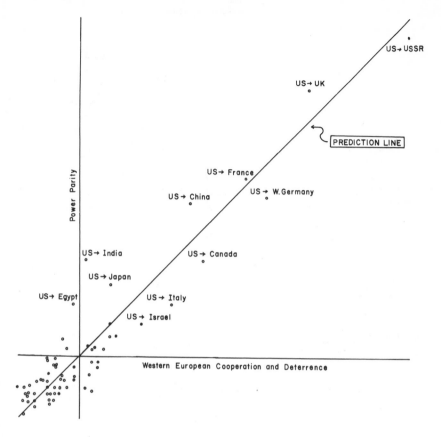

Figure 4.

culture.[67] The equation says that Cold War behavior increases, the more politically distance the object nation is and the less is its Catholic culture.[68] The plot of the behavior predictions from these two attribute distance vectors is shown in Figure 5. Given their distances from the United States, we overact toward Venezuela, Ireland, Outer Mongolia, China, and the USSR on the Cold War pattern and underact toward the U.K.

67. The coefficients for the second canonical variates have all been reversed in sign for simplicity.
68. The United States is near the mean in Catholic culture. Thus, when differences are taken, some U.S. dyads will be high positive, some high negative. Those at the high positive end will be those that are lowest on Catholic Culture; those that are high negative will be highest on Catholic Culture. Thus, the positive coefficient on CC is to be read as indicating that Cold War behavior increases the more non-Catholic the object. If CC were a distance magnitude, then the coefficient would simply mean that the more unlike the United States in CC, the more Cold War behavior.

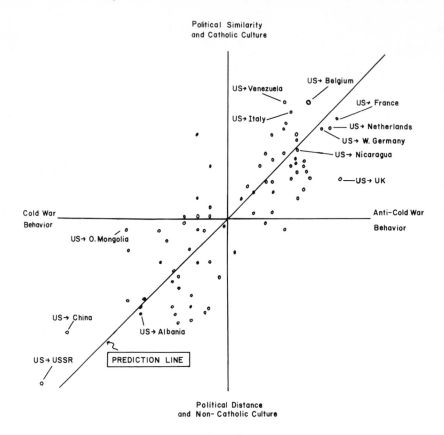

Figure 5.

The finding expressed by the equation indicates that Power Bases is irrelevant for explaining U.S. cold war behavior (when such behavior is understood to consist of those behaviors found to cluster together into the pattern I am calling Cold War). Rather, such behavior is mainly a function of political and religious distance—that is, ideology. The previous finding in conjunction with this one means that there are two overlapping spheres of U.S. action. Nations in one sphere consist of those which have relative power parity with the United States and toward which the United States directs Western European behavior or deterrence. In the other sphere are those which are far from the United States in political system and non-Catholic; to them we direct Cold War behavior. The USSR and China are in both spheres, which means that power parity and ideological distance are forces influencing U.S. behavior toward these two nations.

The Cold War pattern is almost a cooperative-conflict continuum, except at the Cold War end there is not conflict behavior, necessarily,[69] but rather a

69. Note that the conflict behavior is uncorrelated with this dimension.

lack of behavior. Nations high on this pattern are being systematically ignored—a conflict situation exists between them and the United States. At the other end of the continuum are a number of cooperative actions, such as U.N. voting agreement and military commitments. If this end of the Cold War continuum, or pattern, is taken as a type of cooperation, then how does the above finding relate to the six propositions of concern to us? The finding that about 2/3 of the variation in Cold War behavior can be accounted for by political and Catholic Culture distances partially confirms the homogeneity proposition. This proposition asserted that the more similar in economic development, political system, socio-cultural distance, and closer geographically, the more cooperative (or integrative) the two nations. We find that only political and socio-cultural distances are salient, but that economic and geographic distances are not. We will return to this point after some other results are considered.

The third relevant finding is that 53 percent of the variation in the volume of Western European behavior over deterrent behavior is explained by geographic distance and difference in density. That is, the United States is more inclined to de-emphasize Western European behavior and de-emphasize deterrence if the other nation is far away and densely populated; if close geographically and sparsely populated, then deterrence is emphasized over Western European behavior.[70] The equation is

$$.54WE - .52DE \doteq -.60DS + .61GD,$$

where DS is density[71] and GD geographic distance. The subtraction of deterrence from Western European behavior produces a scale, with U.S. object nations receiving high European behavior from the United States and no deterrence at one end and nations receiving high deterrent behavior and no Western European behavior at the other. Considering that the density dimension of attribute space has not been found to involve much more than the number of people per square mile and railroad and road lengths (Russett, 1967a; Rummel, 1972), why density should be relevant to this behavior is not clear.

The fourth finding is that about 1/3 of the variation in U.S. Anglo-American behavior can be accounted for by similarity in economic development, dissimilarity in foreign conflict behavior, the Catholic nature of the object, and geographic closeness. The equation is[72]

$$.82AA \doteq -.75ED + .80FC + .64CC - .46GD,$$

70. This is not a clean relationship between variables mentioned, for from the canonical coefficients for the third variate we can see that Anglo-American, Cold War behavior, and Economic Aid enter into a smaller degree, as do some of the attribute distances.

71. The high values on DS are nations of low density.

72. All signs on the coefficients for the fourth canonical variates have been reversed.

where ED is economic development, FC is foreign conflict, and AA is Anglo-American behavior.

The final relationship found in the canonical analysis is that almost 1/3 of the variation in aid given by the United States can be explained by similarity in political system and the degree of oriental culture. The equation is[73]

$$.78(AID) \doteq -.53(PS) - .84(OC),$$

where OC means oriental culture. If a country has religious diversity and many nationalities, a relatively high proportion of Buddhist and orientals, and has had former membership in the British Commonwealth,[74] then they are most likely to receive U.S. aid.

Five separate findings have been presented. Before these are pulled together with regard to the six propositions, the overall findings should be considered for the moment wholly in terms of the importance of economic development, power bases, and political orientation.

From the results in Appendix III it can be seen that economic development, power bases, and political orientation (as indexed by energy consumption per capita, national income, and freedom of group opposition) have good ability to explain behavior. Economic development distance alone explains 7.5 percent of the variation[75] in U.S. dyads in behavior space; the percentages for power bases and political orientation distances are 13.9 and 5.8 respectively. The average variance accounted for by all the remaining distances is 3.7. These three distances together have a higher ability to explain behavior than any three other distances among those involved in the analysis. The probability of this occurring by chance if each of the 14 dimensions has equal possibility to affect behavior is .0031, or odds of about 322 to 1.[76] This is strong evidence for the linkage proposition based on Rosenau's "pre-theory."

All the above results can now be organized into a table comparing them with the propositions, as shown in Table 4. First, the table shows that the field theory

73. All signs are reversed for the coefficients of the fifth canonical variates.

74. These attributes were those found to be part of the Oriental culture dimension (Rummel, forthcoming).

75. This variance and the following ones are the same as the trace correlation squared, but in this case it gives the variance in behavior space explained by the single distance. The variance is derived by summing the squared correlations (not shown in the Appendix) of the distance with the six patterns and dividing by six. Because the patterns are orthogonal (slightly correlated basic indicators were used to generate the distance vectors), these variance figures would all sum to the squared trace.

76. This is taking into account that three distances outside the economic development and size have a better ability to account for U.S. behavior than political orientation, and that one distance (Catholic culture) accounts for more variance than economic development. This means that there are six permutations of the fourteen distances, taken three at a time, that would have an average ability to account for U.S. behavior at a level greater than the three distances. When these three distances are counted in as a permutation, then the formula for the probability is 7/14 x 13 x 12.

Table 4. Actual and Predicted U.S. Behavior

ATTRIBUTE SPACE DIMENSIONS

Propositions	U.S. Dyadic Behavior[a]	Variance Explained %	Econ. Dev. Dist.	Power Bases Dist.	Pol. Orient. Dist.	Geog. Dist.	Socio-Cultural Dist.[e]
Field Theory	Predicted: Behavior Space	100.0[f]					
	Actual:	47.0[g]					
Linkage	Predicted: Behavior Patterns	27.2[c]	7.5[b]	13.9[b]	5.8[b]		
	Actual:						
Status A	Predicted: Cooperation		—	—			
Similarity	Predicted: Cooperation		—			—	*
	Actual: Anglo-American Cooperation	33.8	—			—	*
	Actual: Aid	31.8			—		*
Status B	Predicted: Conflict		+	—			
	Actual: Cold War	67.7			+		*
Status C	Predicted: Cooperation + Conflict			—			
	Actual: W. European + Deterrence	88.0		—			
Distance	Predicted: Cooperation − Conflict		—		—	+	*
Power	Predicted: Cooperation − Conflict			+			
	Actual: W. European − Deterrence	52.9				+	*
Geographic	Predicted: Cooperation or Conflict Behavior						
	Actual: Behavior Patterns	6.0[b]				6.0[b]	

a. Actual results are derived from the canonical analysis in Appendix III.

b. This percentage is the amount of variance in behavior space explained by the distance. See note 75 in text for discussion.

c. This is the total variance in behavior space explained by the three distances. See note 75 in text for discussion.

d. This is the total variance in behavior patterns explained by geographic distance. See note 75 in text for discussion.

e. The direction of socio-cultural distances were not predicted. All that was predicted was a relationship to behavior for at least one of these vectors, which is indicated by an asterisk. The finding of such a relationship is also shown by an asterisk.

f. Field theory predicts that 100 percent of the variance in behavior will be accounted for by attribute distances.

g. This is the trace correlation squared, which gives the total-variance in U.S. behavior space accounted for by all the attribute distances.

proposition is substantiated, as previously discussed. Second, the linkage proposition of Rosenau is shown to have much empirical value when interpreted in terms of distance.

Third, the status A and B propositions are not supported. For status A proposition, the actual results for economic development distance are in the wrong direction and power bases does not contribute much explanation to behavior. For the status B proposition (the disequilibrium one), the relationship is between dimensions other than those predicted.[77] These findings for status A and B propositions do not necessarily falsify status theory, however, since it was shown (Equation 4) that status A and B propositions in conjunction cause economic development distance to drop out (the United States is cross-pressured on this dimension) and leaves power, the status C proposition. This proposition, as mentioned and shown in Table 4, is strongly verified.

The evidence for the similarity proposition comes out slightly mixed, but on balance very favorably. Two kinds of cooperative type behavior are found related alone to the distances. One is Anglo-American Cooperation, which is most dependent on economic similarity, geographic closeness, and similarity in Catholic Culture. The second behavior is Aid, which is most dependent on similarity in political system and dissimilarity in Oriental Culture. Were we to define cooperation in terms of the sum of Aid and Anglo-American Cooperation, then the proper distances would be in the predicted direction, with the exception of Oriental culture. This also holds true if we consider cooperation the opposite of Cold War (classified in the Table for the status C proposition). Then we would find that the anti Cold War behavior of the United States is predicted by political similarity and Catholic culture.

The distance (from Wright) and power propositions do not seem applicable. The only part which holds up is that geographic and socio-cultural distances help to explain cooperation minus conflict, when such comprises Western European cooperation[78] minus deterrence.

Finally, the geographic proposition does have some validity. Of the 14 distances, 9 have less effect on behavior than geography and geographic distance explains more variance in U.S. dyadic behavior than political distance. Consequently, although the total contribution of geography in accounting for U.S. behavior is small (5 percent) relatively, geography plays a role in U.S. behavior.[79]

77. Note that the status B proposition is the only one defining conflict behavior alone. Our results on this tend to be in line with Russett (1967a: 199), who after relating U.N. voting patterns, proximity, economic interdependence, common institutional membership, and socio-cultural similarity to occurrence of war between nations, concluded that "we can rule out the possibility that similarity, by itself, is a cause of war."

78. For Wright's proposition, even the wrong kind of cooperation is involved here. Given his emphasis on technological distance being defined by communication and transactions as measured by trade, the Anglo-American pattern is more appropriate since exports load most highly on it.

79. This is consistent with Russett's finding that while geographic distance does explain some of the variance, it "explains less of international relations than does social space (Russett, 1967a: 214)."

In summary, field theory has been found to explain a considerable portion of U.S. dyadic behavior.[80] When status theory is subsumed by field theory and status differences are interpreted as vector distances, relative status on dimensions of economic development and power explain most of the Western European plus deterrent behavior of the U.S. Status and homogeneity appear at the aggregate level as more important concepts in explaining U.S. behavior than power or Wright's distance concepts.

U.S. dyadic behavior is patterned at the aggregate level, and a good proportion of this behavior is the consequence of attribute distances from other nations, particularly on economic development, power bases, political orientation, and geographical distance. The direction of the effect of power distance on U.S. behavior is better explained by status considerations than by traditional emphasis on power alone.

Were we to consider the hypotheses (1) U.S. conflict behavior is a result of power parity, (2) Cold War behavior or deterrent behavior is a consequence of the closeness in power of the object, (3) U.S. conflict is dependent on power, or similar hypotheses, then they also find little confirmation in the results.[81]

Why should this be so? The results suggest a misemphasis on power at the aggregate level, perhaps due to the individual-level traditions of theory and research in international relations. At the individual level, the effect of power on international behavior is clear. International relations appear to be shaped by power, as does the political world to the young radical who, disequilibrated on dimensions of wealth, power, and prestige, is trying to fight the establishment. The relevance of status dimensions cannot be seen at the individual level, for they are comparative and aggregate concepts. Status is a construct; power is an abstraction derived from observation of relative influence.[82] Similarly in international relations, power is obvious and status is something that has to be pointed out. The findings here and in the works of Galtung, Araujo, and Schwartzman (1966), Gleditsch (1969), Schwartzman (1966), Heintz (1969),

80. For contrast, the canonical analysis was rerun using distance magnitudes instead of vectors. This would be more consonant with the concept of distance employed by Wright and Russett. The trace correlation for magnitudes is .63, as contrasted with .68 for vectors, the first two canonical correlations for magnitudes are .94 and .80—exactly the same as the correlations for vectors. Moreover, the results relating Western European Cooperation plus Deterrence to power parity and Cold War behavior to political distance are the same in both cases. Thus, the choice between vectors and magnitudes must be made on the grounds other than the ability to explain variance. In this case, the elegance and ease of mathematical deduction of vectors clearly places the weight on their side.

81. See also J. Sullivan's contribution to this volume, where power parity was found to have no appreciable correlation with conflict. Only when conflict is considered relative to cooperation does power come in, and then as predicted by status theory.

82. To borrow a distinction from Etzioni (1965: 19), I am thinking of status as an "analytical property" of nations. "Analytical properties are not properties of any single unit but are derived from a study of the distribution of unit-attributes. Unlike unit-properties or relational properties [like power], analytical properties cannot be observed. They are 'second order' abstractions."

and Wallace in this volume suggest that in dealing with power in international relations we might put on a different thinking cap.

APPENDIX I:
DATA SOURCES AND DEFINITIONS FOR TABLE 2

1. Exports of books and periodicals US→j: "Commodity Trade Statistics." U.N. Statistical Papers, Series D, Vol. 5, No. 4: 573-576.

2. Tourists, US→j: "Statistical Yearbook" (1957, 1963). United Nations; International Travel Statistics (1955, 1963) Worldmark Encyclopedia of Nations.

3. Treaties, US→j: Includes all bilateral and multilateral treaties and agreements signed during 1954-1956 and filed with the Secretary-General of the United Nations during the years 1955-1961. Accessions, supplementary agreements, and exchanges of notes were counted; along with formal treaties and agreements. Source: "Statements of Treaties and International Agreements." (January, 1954 to January, 1961) U.N. monthly publications.

4. Exports, US→j: Includes re-exports. Source: *Statesman's Yearbook 1958*: 620-622.

5. Students, US→ j: U.S. college students studying abroad during 1955-1956 and includes students from U.S. territories. Source: "Study Abroad," (1956-58) UNESCO: 64-65.

6. Emigrants, US→j: "Demographic Yearbook 1957." United Nations: 618-28, 629-39.

7. Embassy or legation, US→j: *Statesman's Yearbook 1955*: 625-627. Data as of March 1, 1954.

8. Intergovernmental Organizations of which the United States and nation j are co-members: *Yearbook of International Organizations 1954-55*: 27-227.

9. Agreement US→ j on Major 1955 Dimensions of U.N. Voting: The agreement (or similarity) measure of UN voting between the United States and nation j is the reciprocal Euclidean distance [actually, the similarity equals $1 - (d_{i-j}/max\ d$ for all dyads in the U.N.), where d_{i-j} is the Euclidean distance between nations on the 7 major dimensions of U.N. voting and max d is the largest distance for all the dyads] between the two nations on the seven major independent dimensions of U.N. voting (roll calls in the Plenary Sessions and Committees). Each dimension was given equal weight in determining the distance. In effect, the agreement measure indexes how close the United States and object are on the issues to come before the U.N.

10. Negative Sanctions Factor Scores, US→j: See variable 12.

11. Military Violence Factor Scores, US→j: See variable 12.

12. Negative Communication Factor Scores, US→ j: Variables 10-12 are (orthogonally rotated) factor scores resulting from a previous component factor analysis (Rummel, 1967) of all nation dyads (340) manifesting foreign conflict behavior on any one of sixteen variables: violent acts, planned violent acts, incidences of violence, discrete military acts or clashes, days of violence, negative acts, diplomatic rebuffs, negative communications, written or oral negative communications, unclassified negative communications, accusations, representations or protests, warnings, and anti-foreign demonstrations.

For the negative sanctions factor, the major loadings involved diplomatic rebuff (.71) and incidence of violence (−.60). In 1955, the United States rebuffed diplomatically (once each) Burma, China, Czechoslovakia, and Japan.

For the military violence factor, the major loadings are number of violent acts (.97), planned violent acts (.97), discrete military actions (.97), days of violence (.97), and written or oral negative communications (.65). In 1955, the United States had violent military actions with China, USSR, and North Korea; planned violent acts and discrete military actions with the same nations; and in total two days of violence with China and the USSR and one day with North Korea. The United States expressed written or oral negative communications to China, Egypt, France, Peru, and Rumania once, South Korea twice, and the USSR six times.

For the negative communications factor, the major loadings involved number of negative communications (.95), accusations (.94), written negative communications (.92), oral negative communications (.89), negative acts (.77), warnings (.69), representations (.63).

13. Economic Aid, US→ j: Data are for loans and grants. Includes AID predecessors, Social Progress Trust Fund, Food for Peace, and Import-Export Bank. The data for 1955 are the annual average, 1953-1957. Source: "U.S. Overseas Loans and Grants and Assistance from International Organizations, 1946-1966" (March 17, 1967) Special Report for the House Foreign Affairs Committee.

14. Private Investment, US→ j: Total direct investment (in material productive or distributive items) as of 1955. Sources: Economic Almanac 1960, Newsweek Edition: 470; U.S. Production Abroad and the Balance of Payments, 1966, Polk, Meister, and Veit; U.S. Private and Government Investments Abroad, R. F. Mikesell; "Survey of Current Business" (various issues); Worldmark Encyclopedia of Nations.

15. Military Aid, US→ j: Data are for loans and grants and includes Military Assistance Program grants and credits and addition from excess stocks. The data for 1955 are the annual average, 1953-1957. Source same as variable 13.

16. Military Committment, US→ j: 1 = at least one such commitment exists in 1955; 0 = no such commitment. A military commitment is defined as a bilateral or multilateral collective defense treaty between the United States and nation j. Source: "Collective Defense Treaties . . ." 91st Congress, First Session (April 21, 1969): 1-14.

17. Official Visits, US→ j: Comprises state, official, or personal visits by the President, Vice-President, or Cabinet member to nation j and not involving participation in an international conference in j by three or more nations. Source: *The New York Times Index, Information Please Almanac.*

18. Military Personnel Stationed in, US→ j: Military personnel comprise Army officers and enlisted men serving in nation j. Source: "Strength of the Army" (June 30, 1955) Unclassified CSGPA-332, Department of the Army.

19. Conferences, US→ j: Number of international conferences the United States and nation j co-participated in during 1955. Such conferences include the U.N. General Assembly and all Security Council meetings. To be a conference it must be attended by at least three nations. Source: "U.S. Department of State Bulletin" (1955).

APPENDIX II:
FACTOR ANALYSIS

The following table gives the results of a component factor analysis of 19 foreign relations for the United States. Data are for 81 objects of U.S. behavior for 1955. The sample comprises all nations that had been independent for at least two years and had a population greater than 750,000. Correlations for the component analysis were product moment. Data were not transformed and missing data were estimated using a regression estimation technique (Wall and Rummel, 1969). The component analysis was done using the principal axis technique. All factors with eigenvalues greater than .90 were rotated. The number of factors criteria was lowered slightly below 1.00 to include a specific factor for economic aid and rotation was to the varimax criterion. Rotated loadings $\geq |.50|$ are underlined.

ROTATED FACTOR MATRIX

Factor Number		1	2	3	4	5	6
Sum Squares Over Variables		3.469	4.245	1.879	2.793	1.269	1.200
Percent of Total Variance		18.257	22.343	9.889	14.699	6.678	6.318

Variable No. Name	Communality 6 Factors						
1 EXPBOOKS	0.980	0.050	−0.986	−0.013	−0.074	−0.015	0.006
2 TOURISTS	0.944	0.000	−0.971	−0.013	−0.030	−0.004	0.006
3 TREATIES	0.754	0.628	−0.255	0.002	−0.466	0.206	−0.188
4 EXPORTS	0.967	0.257	−0.925	0.024	−0.195	0.083	0.002
5 STUDENTS	0.757	0.836	−0.071	0.046	−0.159	0.162	0.005
6 EMIGRANT	0.852	0.709	−0.548	−0.027	−0.202	0.072	−0.042
7 EMBLEGAT	0.550	−0.058	0.007	−0.108	−0.690	0.172	−0.169
8 COM IGOS	0.870	0.334	−0.142	0.114	−0.844	−0.012	0.117
9 UN VOTE	0.609	0.372	−0.240	0.189	−0.592	−0.133	−0.093
10 NEG SANC	0.669	−0.121	−0.032	0.062	−0.049	0.805	0.004
11 MIL VIOL	0.898	0.017	−0.031	−0.942	0.011	−0.071	0.068
12 NEG COMM	0.837	0.036	0.022	−0.898	0.168	0.017	−0.000
13 ECON AID	0.885	0.217	0.034	0.050	−0.076	0.082	−0.907
14 MILI AID	0.685	0.664	0.078	0.103	−0.203	−0.044	−0.429
15 INVESTMN	0.938	0.065	−0.956	0.000	−0.130	−0.033	0.029
16 MILCOMIT	0.707	0.287	−0.091	0.184	−0.761	−0.048	0.035
17 ARMYPERS	0.633	0.432	0.018	−0.022	−0.001	0.658	−0.117
18 CONFEREN	0.759	0.747	−0.192	−0.264	−0.135	−0.208	−0.182
19 OFFVISIT	0.562	−0.466	−0.242	0.018	−0.483	−0.002	−0.229

APPENDIX III:
CANONICAL ANALYSIS

The first table gives the canonical correlations, significance levels, and trace canonical correlation (the correlation between the two spaces). The formula for lambda, Λ, is

$$\Lambda = \prod_{k=1}^{q} (1 - r_k^2)$$

where q is the number of canonical correlations and k is the kth canonical correlation r. The chi-square equals $-[n - 0.5(p + q + 1)] \log_e \Lambda$, where n = the number of dyads (81), q = the number of behavioral dimensions (6), and p = the number of distances (14). The degrees of freedom equal $[p - (k - 1)] [q - (k - 1)]$ and the Z transformation is for reference to corresponding areas under the normal curve. The trace correlation is,

$$\text{trace} = (\sum_{k=1}^{q} r_k^2 / q)^{1/2}$$

The second table gives the canonical coefficients, which are equivalent to regression coefficients.

In evaluating the direction of relationship between distances and the patterns of behavior, careful attention must be given to the direction of loadings on the pattern in the factor loading matrix of Appendix II. For example, the high loadings on the Anglo-American pattern are negative. This means that dyads with Anglo-American behavior will have large negative factor scores. Thus, in evaluating the canonical coefficients for Anglo-American behavior, their signs should be reversed to get the proper direction of relationship of distances to high magnitudes of this behavior.

Canonical Analysis [a]

Number of Eigenvalues Removed	Eigenvalue	Corresponding Canonical Correlation	Lambda	Chi-Square	Degrees of Freedom	Z-Transformation for D.F. ⩾ 30
1	0.88011	0.93814	0.00771	343.00195	84	13.26882
2	0.67730	0.82298	0.06431	193.45963	65	8.31244
3	0.52868	0.72711	0.19927	113.72200	48	5.33445
4	0.33840	0.58172	0.42280	60.69034	33	2.95503
5	0.31786	0.56379	0.63906	31.56720	20	1.70072
6	0.06316	0.25131	0.93684	4.59953	9	−1.09011

Trace correlation = 0.68380

a. The determinant for the correlation matrix of distance variables is .035; that for the correlation matrix of behavior variables (factor scores) is 1.00.

Canonical Coefficients

Distance Variables	CANONICAL VARIATES 1	2	3	4	5	6
1 Energy/CAP	−0.111	−0.196	0.225	**−0.745**	−0.385	0.276
2 Nat. Income	**−0.805**	−0.062	**−0.362**	0.019	0.101	−0.174
3 Free Oppose	0.014	**−0.556**	0.007	0.288	**0.526**	0.234
4 Threats	−0.230	0.139	**0.398**	**0.801**	−0.296	0.191
5 Density	−0.032	−0.100	**−0.594**	0.318	0.102	−0.057
6 Catholic/CAP	0.063	**−0.479**	−0.065	**0.644**	−0.102	0.243
7 Dom. Conflict	−0.065	0.018	0.094	0.162	−0.191	**−0.500**
8 Religions	0.052	0.289	**0.385**	−0.244	**0.843**	−0.262
9 Foreign Students	−0.097	0.137	−0.090	−0.127	−0.349	−0.471
10 Educat. Expense	−0.054	0.052	0.129	−0.032	−0.096	−0.308
11 Exports/GNP	0.013	−0.131	0.063	0.069	−0.290	**−0.439**
12 Language Group	−0.038	0.033	0.122	−0.174	−0.112	0.303
13 Proteins/Cal.	0.043	0.002	−0.134	−0.005	0.187	−0.379
14 Geographic	−0.039	−0.035	**0.607**	**−0.464**	0.364	−0.143

Behavior Variables	1	2	3	4	5	6
1 Western European	**0.709**	0.358	**0.540**	0.028	0.235	−0.147
2 Anglo-American	−0.231	−0.110	0.361	**−0.819**	0.279	0.235
3 Deterrence	**−0.660**	0.384	**0.523**	0.317	0.035	−0.207
4 Cold War	0.011	**−0.795**	0.354	0.372	0.322	0.009
5 Neg Sanction	0.061	0.066	0.269	0.202	−0.394	**0.851**
6 Economic Aid	−0.076	0.276	−0.327	0.219	**0.779**	0.395

JOHN D. SULLIVAN

4. Cooperating to Conflict: Sources of Informal Alignments

ABSTRACT

This paper presents an analysis of the sources of informal alignments. The concept of an informal alignment is defined as the tendency for two nations to share a common conflict object, and two types of such cooperation, the scope of alignment and the intensity of alignment, are discussed. Measures for these two types of alignment are developed. The paper develops a set of hypothesis in which various national characteristics as well as bonds between nations are linked to the scope and intensity of informal alignments. Shared membership in formal alliances, shared geographical region, similar levels of economic development, intra-dyadic trade, and past levels of alignment are all hypothesized to have an effect on informal alliances.

Two types of dyads were identified for the purposes of the analyses. Great power dyads consisted of dyads in which the United States, Russia, and Communist China were joined with a set of nations exhibiting relatively high amounts of behavioral activity. The second type was a sample of most active nation dyads. The analyses indicated that, for both types of dyads, the most important was the past level of alignment. For the great power dyads, trade and shared membership in a formal alliance were also related to informal alignments. For the most active nation dyads, shared geographical region was related to informal alignments. An exploration of more complex models indicated that none of these variables explained very much more in combination than past levels of alignment did alone. ∎

Author's Note: This research has been supported by the World Data Analysis Program of Yale University Under grant No. GS614 from the National Science Foundation and contract No. N-0014-67-A-0097 from ARPA, Behavioral Sciences, monitored by the Office of Naval Research. Jeffrey Milstein, Al Schainblat, Ted Rubin, Roy Licklider, Bruce Marshall, and Chongwook Chung offered advice at various stages of this Research. The author is, however, responsible for this paper. Robin Nadel provided research assistance and Caroline Stancliff performed programming tasks.

INTRODUCTION

As they seek to achieve their foreign policy goals, nation-states engage in behaviors which range from the intensely conflictual to the optimistically cooperative. Such interactions take a variety of forms. Nations engage in wars, exchange trade, sign diplomatic agreements, establish scientific cooperative efforts, and organize formal military alliances. The range of conflictual behavior is generally intended to deter or stop other nations' actions that are considered by the nation engaging in conflict to be injurious to its goals and interests. The range of cooperative behaviors is generally intended to increase the probability that national goals will be achieved, or to increase a nation's resource base. The focus of this paper will be a specific type of cooperative event, namely, cooperative acts which involve conflict with third parties. In order to put such cooperative endeavors in a proper perspective, it will be useful to discuss briefly formal military alliances.

Cooperative endeavors often take the form of a formal military alliance in which, by means of a treaty and any organizational suprastructure created by that treaty, nations agree on common or complementary goals and specify the kinds of assistance they will provide for each other. In addition to providing for coordinating joint efforts, formal military alliances also permit nations to reduce uncertainty about each other's behavior with respect to shared problems. Put another way, a formal military alliance transforms an "inchoate" relationship into one in which rights, duties, and expectations are made explicit (Morgenthau, 1967; Liska, 1962). The treaty defining the scope of the alliance generally specifies the rights and obligations of treaty members and becomes a guide for their behavior in situations covered by the treaty.

The coordination of nation-state behavior is not limited to actions specified in a formal treaty. As they respond to problems and events within the international system, nations frequently react in a similar way and often appear to coordinate their behaviors. Such coordinated behaviors may be elicited because of some formal commitment or because the nations involved have explicitly agreed to act in concert with respect to a specific issue or problem. Such coordinated behaviors, however, have an ad hoc character, and it is this attribute which permits a distinction between formal commitments and informal or behavioral alignments.

Alignments, as conceptualized in this paper, in no way share the permanency of formal alliances nor are they as broad in scope geographically. Alignments refer to specific behaviors by groups of nations which are directed toward a common set of objects. Such alignments may, or may not, involve agreement and overt coordination. As will be indicated below, the behaviors referred to here are the daily words and deeds which nations direct at other nations in attempts to influence their behavior. Nations are said to be aligned when they direct their actions toward the same object or set of objects.

This focused, behavioral characteristic of alignments distinguishes them from formal military alliances. Alliances, as discussed above, involve the specification of shared goals and the identification of preferred actions and sharing of resources. In one sense, they provide the background conditions for much of the behavior of nation-states. Informal alignments on the other hand are specific, day-to-day cooperative behaviors in which nations engage in an attempt to achieve foreign policy goals. While alignments might result from membership in a formal alliance, they can be analyzed in a manner distinct from such phenomena.

This paper will report findings from research designed to investigate factors hypothesized to be related to informal alignments. Before proceeding to a discussion of these findings, a brief discussion of the measures employed in this study and of the general theoretical orientation which guided the research will be given.

MEASURING ALIGNMENTS

Assuming that aligning is conceptualized as acting in concert with regard to a specific problem, it would seem necessary to measure this concept by having access to an actual mutual agreement to coordinate behaviors. For two obvious reasons, it is not possible to generate such a measure. Such explicit agreements are never made in many instances, and when they are, access to them is usually very limited. In this study an attempt has been made to develop a measure of alignments by employing the behaviors of nation-states. The measure is the following: when two nations share the same object as the target of similar actions, they will be said to be aligned with respect to that object. For instance, if, in a specified time period, the United States and France engaged in similar behaviors towards Cuba, we would say that these two countries were aligned with regard to Cuba.

In operationalizing such a measure it was necessary to obtain data which contained information on the day-to-day behaviors of nations. The foreign conflict behavior data collected by R. Rummel in his Dimensionality of Nations project were employed for this purpose (Rummel 1966a). These data are daily events coded into conflict categories. Each act contains a number of types of information. The actor, the target, and the type of actions, such as warning or a defensive troop movement, are recorded from the primary data source, The New York Times. In coding these data, a distinction was made between *official* acts made by a recognized member of a country's government and *unofficial,* engaged in by citizens in the acting country. In developing an appropriate measure, only official acts of nations were employed. The general categories into which Rummel coded his data are the following:

Official Acts
A. Warning or defensive
B. Violence
   1. Planned Violence

        2. Unplanned violence
        3. Unclassified violence
     C. Negative behavior
     D. Negative communications
        1. Written communication
        2. Oral communication
        3. Written or oral communication

Thus, the operational measure employed in this phase of the research was the tendency for pairs of nations to have as the same nation as conflict object.[1]

   There are two ways in which the sharing of foreign conflict objects may be viewed. First, the "scope" of such sharing of common objects by pairs or nations may be measured. Here, the focus is on the number of separate nations a dyad had as common objects, regardless of the number of actions each nation directed towards each object. The second aspect of sharing of common conflict objects has to do with the amount or "intensity" of sharing of such objects for each dyad. Here, the number of actions directed by each nation toward their shared objects is counted regardless of the number of such shared objects. This research employed, then, two dependent variables: (1) the number of Separate Shared Conflict Objects (SSCO) for each dyad; and (2) the Total Shared Conflict Actions (TSCA) for each dyad.

   The procedures employed to compute these two measures are presented in Table 1.[2] As can be seen, these formulas are identical to a correlation coefficient except that the values employed are not deviations from the mean. Since for most of the nations in this study the mean number of foreign conflict behaviors is very near zero, it was possible to drop the mean from the calculation. The measure, however, is comparable to a correlation coefficient and varies between zero and one. For purposes of illustration, an example of the Separate Shared Conflict Object score for a dyda will be computed.[3] Consider the following dyad:

Targets

		A	B	C	D	D		
	X	0	1	1	0	1	...	$X_i = 3$
Actors	Y	1	1	0	0	1	...	$Y_i = 3$
	$X_i \cdot Y_i$	0	1	0	0	1	$X_i \cdot Y_i$	...

   1. The research design will be discussed at greater length below.
   2. These measures were suggested and partially developed by Al Schainblatt.
   3. The entries in each cell are zero or one depending on whether or not the actor had that nation as a target. The amount of activity directed at the target is ignored by the Separate Shared Conflict Object measure.

$$\text{Separate Shared} = \frac{\sum\limits_{i=i}^{n} X_i \cdot Y_i}{\sum\limits_{i=1}^{n} X_i \cdot \sum\limits_{i=1} Y} = \frac{2}{3} = .666$$

Thus nations X and Y had a Separate Shared Conflict Object score of .666. That is to say, their scope of alignment, as measured in terms of number of shared objects regardless of the total number of actions emitted, was .666 out of a possible score of 1.0. The same procedure is employed for generating a score for Total Shared Conflict Objects except that the actual number of actions directed by each nation to each target is entered into the formula. In sum, then, the measure employed for alignment in this study is the extent to which nations share the same conflict objects.

Table 1. Dependent Variables

Concept	Indicator	Operational Measure
Separate shared conflict objects	Rummel FCB data (official acts only, Rummel, 1963)	$$\dfrac{\sum\limits_{i=1}^{N} x_i \cdot y_i}{\sqrt{\sum\limits_{i=1}^{N} x_i \cdot \sum\limits_{i=1}^{N} y_i}}$$ where n = number of objects; $x_i, y_i = 0$ if no act directed to nth object; $x_i, y_i = 1$ if 1 or more acts directed to nth object.
Total shared conflict objects	Rummel FCB data (official acts only, Rummel, 1963)	$$\dfrac{\sum\limits_{i=1}^{N} \sqrt{x_i} \cdot \sqrt{y_i}}{\sqrt{\sum\limits_{i=1}^{N} x_i^1 \cdot \sum\limits_{i=1}^{N} y_i^1}}$$ where x_i, y_i = actual number of FCB's directed toward nth object; x_i^1, y_i^1 = total number of FCB's x and y *minus* those directed at each other.

Before proceeding further, it is important to consider briefly two problems with this measure. As the Foreign Conflict Behavior data are presently coded, it is not possible to determine whether nations which share the same conflict object are acting towards that object with respect to the same issue or set of issues. Thus, while they may share the same object, it is not possible to determine if their actions are in fact related to the same problem and if it makes sense to assume that some form of explicit or implicit coordination of behavior has occurred. The goal of this research is to discover factors, which lead to informal alignments, that is, attempts at coordinating day-to-day behaviors of nation-states. A refinement of the measure to include information about the similarity of dissimilarity of issues involved would be valuable.

The second problem concerns the use of conflictual alignments. As conceptualized in this paper, there is no theoretical reason why the term alignments should be limited to conflictual alignments. It can be hypothesized that the factors which give rise to conflictual alignments are the same as those which give rise to cooperative alignments, that is, alignments in which the actors direct positive and cooperative acts to the target. Alternatively, it might be hypothesized that cooperative acts are caused by factors other than those which cause conflictual acts. Unfortunately the only data presently available over a long enough time-span were those from the Dimensionality of Nations project, which are exclusively conflictual in nature. Thus, this study had to be limited to conflictual alignments.

EXPLAINING
INFORMAL ALIGNMENTS

The process of aligning in the international system is not considered to be a random process. Characteristics of the aligning nations and their targets as well as aspects of the problems they face have been felt to be crucial to international coalition formation. This section will present a set of factors hypothesized to be related to informal alignments. The concepts to be discussed (their appropriate measures are presented in Table 2) are the following: formal military commitment; system maintenance; political-social similarity; similar economic capabilities; intradyadic conflict; past alignment patterns; and geographical proximity. It is hypothesized that these predictors of alignments are related similarly to both dependent variables, that is, to both the Separate Shared Conflict Objects and to Total Shared Conflict Actions.

Formal alliances are devices whereby nations make explicit their relationships and mutual expectations. Part of such formalization might involve specifying the conditions under which the alliance partner would become aligned, that is, share a conflict or cooperative object. Alternatively, commitment to a formal alliance might not involve the specification of conditions for aligning but rather indicate that the nations in the alliance shared similar world views and anticipated that

Table 2. Independent Variables

Concept	Indicator	Operational Measure
Formal military commitment to cooperate	Dyadic membership in formal military alliance	Treaty forming a military alliance
Political-social similarity	Similarity of pairs in each dyad on Type of Political System	Closeness of pairs on Banks & Gregg (1965) polity types (polarchic, centrist, personalist, elitist, traditional) computed as follows: $$\sum_{i=1}^{5} (x_i - y_i)^2$$ where x, y refer to nations and i=1, . . . 5, for five polity types.
System maintenance activities	Trade between pairs in a dyad	$\dfrac{\text{Total Trade}_{a-b}}{\text{Total Trade}_{a+b}}$
System maintenance activities	Trade between pairs in a dyad as percentage of sum of pair's GNP	$\dfrac{\text{Total Trade}_{a-b}}{GNP_a + GNP_b}$
System maintenance activities	Shared international organizations	Number of international organizations (universal & regional) to which both pairs in a dyad belong
Similarity of economic capability	The difference between pairs in a dyad in energy consumption	$\mid \text{Log ec/cap}_a - \text{Log ec/cap}_b \mid$
Conflict between dyadic pairs	Rummel FCB data (official acts only for 1953-55)	$(FCB_{A \rightarrow B}) + (FCB_{B \rightarrow A})$ for 1953-55
Past success	Separate shared conflict objects and total shared conflict objects 1953-55	Same as dependent variables
Proximity	Membership in same geographical region	Similar geographical regions as defined by Russett's (1967) analysis
Proximity	Distance between each pair of nations	Air miles between capital

they would encounter the same kinds of problems and threats. Whatever the explanation, it is hypothesized that nations which have agreed to form a formal military alliance will also tend to align themselves with respect to conflict objects.

Nations form a variety of relations in economic, political, technological, and social areas. Quite frequently, those relationships might be threatened by the actions of third parties in the international system. In an attempt to protect or maintain sub-system relationships, nations might find it necessary to align to ward off threats presented by such third parties. Put another way, it may be hypothesized that actions in one issue area, when threatened, may lead to a spill-over into another issue area.

In the literature on political integration, a controversy exists as to whether or not actions and agreements in one issue-area spill-over into another issue-area. [4] Proponents of the spill-over theory hold that cooperation in one issue area, such as trade, will facilitate, if not actually cause, cooperation in other areas such as military security. Russett and Lamb (1969), for example, found that nations that trade highly with each other also tend to exchange many diplomats. In regard to patterns of alignment, the question of spill-over is quite pertinent. Do nations with a variety of links, such as trade relations, membership in global international organizations, membership in regional, non-military organizations, tend also to share conflict and cooperation objects? [5]

The question of spill-over or system maintenance will be examined by considering two types of behavior or commitment. First, the tendency for nations which exchange relatively large amounts of trade also to share conflict objects will be explored. Second the impact of shared membership in regional or universal international organizations on informal alignments will be investigated. It is hypothesized that nations which exchange large amounts of trade will form alignments, in an attempt to insure that those existing relations will be maintained by warding off hostile third parties. Similarly, it is hypothesized that nations which share memberships in universal and regional international organizations may tend to share common conflict objects in an attempt to maintain the organizational aspect of their relationship against threats from other nations or other regions.

As indicated in Table 2, two measures of shared trade are employed in this study. The first determines the amount of trade exchanged between the members of a dyad relative to the total amount of trade each exchanged with other countries. Given that a nation is dependent to a certain extent on foreign trade for economic reasons relative to other nations, this measure indicates how much that nation is dependent on its dyadic partner for necessary trade. Russett

4. See Holsti and Sullivan (1969: 166) and the works of Deutsch and Haas cited therein.

5. Formal alliance commitments are a form of cooperation, and as such might be analyzed in terms of a spill-over theory. We have treated them separately because we hypothesize that they may be more directly related to alignments than spill-over.

has also proposed another measure which gets at a slightly different aspect of interdependence (1967a: 122-127). Stressing that trade should be considered an independent variable which can lead to political integration, he suggests that interdependence can best be measured by assessing the amount of trade between pairs of countries relative to the national income of each country. Thus, how much of a nation's total economy is dependent on the country's dyadic partner? Both measures provide different approaches to the problem of interdependence and sub-system maintenance. The other aspect of sub-system maintenance, shared international organizations, is measured by a count of the number of such organizations to which both parties in each dyad belong.

Many writers have stressed the importance of ideology and a sense of community on various aspects of alliances.[6] Russett (1968a) has summarized literature which considers bonds of community, such as ideology, similar institutions, similar language, and culture, are important in international politics. Gamson has utilized a concept of "non-utility preferences" by which players distinguish among coalition in the same pay-off class (Gamson, 1961; Russett, (1968a). Such preferences would include ideology as a factor. Dinerstein (1965) has placed heavy emphasis on the role of ideology as a factor in alliance formation and alliance transformation in the period since 1945. Elsewhere (Sullivan, 1969), by means of simple coding of ideological similarity, I found that this variable had very little impact on alliance maintenance in the period 1815 to 1939. This result may be, however, a function of the particular historical period.

Despite my negative findings for the pre-World War II period, there is strong support in the literature for the role of "bonds of community" or socio-political similarity in international politics. Russett and Lamb (1969), for instance, found a relationship, albeit rather weak, between socio-cultural groupings and diplomatic exchange. Russett (1967a), on the other hand, found that the existence of such bonds alone did not make conflict between nations less likely, but did do so in the absence of proximity or economic interdependence. We hypothesize, then that the existence of such socio-political bonds may increase the likelihood that nations will align with each other. For the purpose of this study, *socio-political* similarity is measured by determining the closeness of each dyad on the five Banks and Gregg (1965) polity types. This measure is described in Table 2.

There are numerous attribute dimensions other than ideological similarity along which pairs of nations may be similarly located, and which might have an impact on the tendency for such nations to share conflict objects. One is similarity in economic capability. Some observers have viewed this attribute as an indicator of development and it may also be viewed in some respects as an indicator of power. In regard to cooperative behavior between nations, one

6. The role of ideology in alliances and coalitions is discussed by a number of writers. See, for instance, J. Sullivan (1970), Russett (1968a), Gamson (1961), and Leiserson (1966).

might expect that developed, economically capable nations might tend either to share the same kinds of perceptions of international problems or to have similar types of international problems with which to cope. The sharing of similar views or of similar problems might lead such nations to form alignments with each other more frequently than they would with nations not as economically powerful as they. It is hypothesized, then, that nations which are similar to each other will tend to share foreign conflict objects more frequently than will nations which are dissimilar to each other. The measure employed here is energy consumption per capita.

In considering the tendency for pairs of nations to align with respect to common conflict objects, it is important to take into account the manner in which each member of the dyad relates to the other. The concept of alignment employed in this study involves explicit or implicit coordination of behavior and suggests that the members of each dyad have a relatively harmonious relationship. If, in fact, the nations in each dyad exhibit considerable intra-dyadic conflict, it would seem senseless to say that they are aligned. In order to take into account this factor, the amount of intra-dyadic conflict for each dyad was introduced into the analysis.

The role of proximity and regional affiliation have long been considered important in the behavior of nation-states.[7] In regard to alignment, proximity of nations may be particularly important. Actors proximate to each other may tend to view the world in a similar manner because their proximity may have exposed them to similar regional "experiences" and hence provide similar historical backgrounds. In addition, because they belong to the same region, proximate nations may tend to share the same problems with which they must cope. Thus, we hypothesize that regional affiliation and proximity of relationship may be good predictors.

It should be pointed out, however, that this variable may be confounded by the fact that some international actors appear to be "un-regional" in their behavior. Put another way, some actors in the present international system are truly "international" actors in that their concerns and interests are global, that is they extend to every part of the world. It may be, however, that these actors (which at a guess, include the United States, France, Britain, W. Germany, and the USSR) constitute a class by themselves, a class, that is, whose "region" is the whole globe.[8]

The first measure of proximity employed in this study will be air distances between capitols of each nation in a dyad. Using such distances, Russett has also identified various regions in the international system. While these regions are a function of the air distances, they correspond closely to what one would intuitively identify as "regions." But nations proximate to each other may, in

7. On regions in general and proximity see Russett (1967a), Chs. 1, 10.

8. Some support is given this assertion by Russett and Lamb (1969: 42-44) and for members in international organizations, by Russett (1967a: 102-104 and Ch. 8).

fact, not be in the same region and this, as we have hypothesized, may have an impact beyond that of simple geographical distance. To assess the effects of these two factors, both distance and shared regional membership will be included in the analysis.

The final variable is the past alignment patterns of an aligning pair. Nations which have been successful in cooperating in the past may seek each other out as alignment partners as in the future they attempt to cope with issues and problems. This, of course, may be a function of membership in formal alliances, spillover, or bonds of community. It might be, on the other hand, more a function of previous success in dealing with their problems while aligned. Whatever the explanation, this variable was included in the analysis in order to determine if there is some effect of earlier patterns of alignment on later patterns.

It will be useful at this point to make a distinction between these concepts which are taken to explain alignments and the concept of alignment itself. As is clear from Table 2, many of these concepts refer to one form or another of cooperative behavior. Trading, maintaining organizational commitments, and past successes in achieving goals through cooperative efforts are all patterns of behavior which are positive and cooperative in nature. At the same time, these forms of cooperative behavior may have occurred in the absence of some formal commitment between the nations involved. Thus, it might be thought that these types of international interactions ought to be called "alignments" also. It is important to make a distinction between these relationships and the concept of alignment as employed in this study. These types of interaction may well be "informal" in the sense that they are not regulated in any manner by a formal agreement, but they must be kept distinct from alignments as conceptualized in this study, however, which refer to a specific type of action directed at a common object. The actions contained in the Dimensionality of Nations data bank are exclusively conflictual behaviors and can be considered as of a political nature designed to influence the behavior of third parties in the international system.[9]

THE RESEARCH DESIGN

The research reported here has gone through a number of phases. For the purpose of this paper, two research designs were employed. The first involved what will be called the analysis of "great power dyads." A sample of dyads was selected according to the following criteria: the three major actors in terms of amounts of Foreign Conflict Behavior—Communist China, the Soviet Union, and the United States—were selected. These were paired with all other nations that had engaged in an average of four Foreign Conflict Behaviors for the years which

9. The limitation of this study to conflictual alignments was discussed above, p. 120.

the Dimensionality of Nations data existed. Thus, the dyads studied in this phase of the research included nations which were relatively active in terms of foreign conflict behaviors. The most active nations are listed in the Appendix. The second design involved an analysis of "most-active-nation-dyads" in general.[10] Because the number of most-active-nation-dyads was quite large, a random sample of 150 dyads was selected.

Data for each of the most-active-nation-dyads and the great power dyads were collected according to the operational procedures presented in Tables 1 and 2 above. Then two sets of analyses were performed. First, those variables which exhibited the best relationship with the dependent variable were identified. Then a series of additional analyses were performed in which the significant variables were explored.

Two additional aspects of this design should be noted. First, the set of objects for generating the two alignment scores included all of the nations employed as targets in the Dimensionality of Nations data bank. A previous analysis had been conducted with a very limited number of DON targets as objects in the alignment score. The inclusion or exclusion of targets from the computation of the alignment scores raises theoretical questions which will be discussed below.

Second, the theoretical orientation which guides this work specifies that past levels of alignments should be related to current levels. In order to assess the impact of this factor on alignments, the Foreign Conflict Behavior data were divided into two time periods. The data employed in this study covered the period 1963-1967. The measure of past levels of foreign conflict was generated from the years 1963-1965. The measure for the dependent variables were generated from data from the period 1966-1967.

ANALYSIS: GREAT POWER DYADS

The aim of this research is the identification of the sources of informal alignments among two types of nations, great power dyads and nations which are relatively active in the international system, that is, most active nation dyads. We presented above a series of factors which were hypothesized to be related to informal alignments. In addition, we identified two types of alignment, the scope of alignment or the number of different conflict objects each pair shared and the intensity of alignment, or the number of actions directed at each shared object. In this section we will discuss the results of the analyses performed on these data. The next two parts will examine the sources of alignment for the great power and most active nation dyads in that order. The final two parts of this section will explore more complex models of behavioral alignments.

As discussed above, the set of great power dyads consists of alignments between the United States, the Soviet Union, and Communist China and the

---

10. This sample also included some great power dyads.

most active nations in the Dimensionality of Nations data bank. This set of dyads also includes those between each of the three great powers. The relationships discussed in the first section were explored with the appropriate data for both aspects of informal alignments, the scope of alignment and the intensity of alignment. As the results presented in Table 3 indicate, seven of the eleven measures employed in testing these hypotheses proved to be significant in a simple bivariate analysis for both the intensity of alignment and the scope of alignment, although not the same variables were significant in each case. We will consider each aspect of alignment in turn.

Of the seven variables significantly related to the intensity of alignment of the great power dyads, the past level of intensity of alignment is clearly the most powerful. By itself, this factor accounts for 39 percent of the variance in current levels of intensity of alignment. In addition, the sign of the coefficient is in the hypothesized direction indicating that as past levels of alignment are high, so will be the current levels. Only two of the remaining significant variables account for any appreciable amount of current levels of alignment intensity. Past scope of alignment accounts for 15 percent of the variance and intradyadic trade (as normed by the total amount of dyadic trade) accounts for 14 percent of the variance. Again, both coefficients are positive, indicating that high levels of intra-dyadic trade and past levels of scope of alignment will lead to high current levels of intensity of alignment.

None of the remaining four significant variables accounts for any more than 7 percent of the variance by itself. Thus, while socio-political similarity, similar economic capability, trade/GNP, regional similarity, and proximity are significantly related to intensity of alignment, no one of these by itself accounts for any appreciable amount of the variance in that variable. While these variables

Table 3. Sources of Great Power Alignments

Independent Variable	Scope of Alignment (TSCO)		Scope of Alignment (SSCO)	
	t ratio	r^2	t ratio	r^2
Socio-political similarity	−3.25	.07 [b]	−1.95 [a]	.02 [b]
Similar region	−1.92 [a]	.02 [b]	−1.62	.02 [b]
Proximity (air miles between capitols)	2.08 [a]	.03	1.60	.01
Similar economic capability	−2.14 [a]	.03 [b]	−1.31	.01 [b]
Intra-dyadic trade	4.33 [a]	.14	4.07 [a]	.12
Trade/GNP	2.39	.04	2.12 [a]	.03
Shares IO memberships	.07	.00	.30	.00
Shared alliance since 1945	2.59 [a]	.05	3.95 [a]	.10
Past intensity of alignment	9.18 [a]	.39	4.81 [a]	.15
Past scope of alignment	4.84 [a]	.15	5.13 [a]	.17

a. Significant at the 0.05 level.
b. Negative relationship.

are not very good in terms of the amount of variance they account for, the coefficients are not always in the hypothesized direction. Sociopolitical similarity, similar economic capability, and similar region all have negative coefficients, indicating that the great powers tend to align with dissimilar and distant partners contrary to the hypotheses presented above. As discussed earlier, this may be explained by the fact that these three actors, as well as some others, are "global" actors in that they have interests and goals in all part of the world and that they are not limited strictly to local problems. Hence, regional identification or ideological orientation of the partner may often be irrelevant for these three nations.

A slightly different pattern emerges with respect to the scope of alignment of the great power dyads. Again, past scope of alignment is the most powerful but it accounts for only 17 percent of the variance in the dependent variable. Similarly, past level of intensity of alignment is a significant variable, but it accounts for only 15 percent of the dependent variable. While the coefficients are in the expected direction, neither variable is very powerful. Only two other variables account for any appreciable amount of the dependent variable. As was true with the intensity of alignment, intra-dyadic trade is significant but it accounts for only 12 percent of the variance. In addition, shared alliance membership, which was not related to intensity of alignment, is related to scope but it accounts for only 10 percent of the variance in that variable.

None of the other significant variables accounts for any more than 3 percent of the variance in scope of alignment by themselves. Two that are significant, however, again have coefficients that are opposite in sign from that predicted. Socio-political similarity is negative in sign, indicating that the great powers do not necessarily seek partners of similar orientations for informal alignments. In addition, the sign of intra-dyadic conflict is positive, contrary to what was expected. That may be due to a measurement problem in the data as presently coded. The DON data contain only conflictual actions between pairs of nations. Rather than a simple sum of intra-dyadic conflictual interactions, it might be better to normalize that sum to the total amount of interactions between each pair. At the present time it is not possible to develop this measure. In the conlusion of the paper we will discuss one alternative which may provide a better measure of the impact of intra-dyadic conflict on behavioral alignments.

For the scope and intensity of great power alignments, the following picture emerges. Past alignments are most powerfully related to current alignments. Bonds of trade are also positively related to intensity, and alliance bonds are related to scope of alignments. Other variables were significantly related to both dependent variables but the amount of variance accounted for was extremely small and hence the degree of fit, in such a bivariate analysis, is very poor. Thus, past experience and sub-system bonds were most important factors in Great Power dyads.

MOST ACTIVE
NATION DYADS

A second group of dyads was formed from the nations in this study. As discussed above, the yearly total of DON conflict acts for each nation was determined and the average per nation computed. The results suggested that nations with an average of four or more conflict acts per year should be considered the most active nations. Since the total number of possible dyads that could be formed from this group was in excess of 900, a random sample of 150 dyads was selected. Analyses similar to that done for the Great Power dyads was performed and the results are presented in Table 4.

Table 4. Sources of Most-Active Nation Alignments

| | DEPENDENT VARIABLE | | | |
| | Intensity of Alignment (TSCO) | | Scope of Alignment (SSCO) | |
Independent Variable	t ratio	r^2	t ratio	r^2
Socio-political similarity	.30	.00	.41	.00
Similar region	1.73[a]	.02	2.79[a]	.05
Proximity (air miles between capitols)	1.09	.00	2.91[a]	.05
Similar economic capability	1.61	.01	1.55	.01
Intra-dyadic trade	−.28	.00	.16	.00
Trade/GNP	−1.60	.02	−.54	.00
Shared IO membership	−.83	.00	−.09	.00
Shared alliance since 1945	1.83[a]	.02	1.62	.01
Past intensity of alignment	6.05[a]	.19	2.76[a]	.04
Past scope of alignment	3.83[a]	.09	2.44[a]	.03
Intra-dyadic conflict	1.50	.01	1.65[a]	.01

a. Significant at the 0.05 level.

At the outset, an examination of this table indicates that no one of the variables accounts for very much of the variance in either dependent variable. Nonetheless, patterns somewhat similar to the great power dyads do emerge. To begin with intensity of alignment, past intensity of alignment is significantly related to this variable and accounts for most of the variance, 19 percent. The next most powerful variable is past scope of alignment, which accounts for only 9 percent of the variance in intensity of alignment. The other two significant variables, similar region and shared alliance membership, each account for only 2 percent of the variance. Thus, while significant at the level chosen, the degree of fit is extremely poor—as was the case for the great power dyads.

Turning to the scope of alignment for the most active nations, the results are even less significant. Again past scope and intensity are significantly related to scope of alignment, but they account for only 3 percent and 4 percent of the variance respectively. The only other variable near this level is similarity of region which accounts for 5 percent of the variance. Again the degree of fit between the variables for the most active nation dyads is extremely poor. Note, however, that sub-system bonds of trade did not emerge as significant, while similar region did. This suggests that the distinction between the great power as global actors and other nations as having a more focused, regional perspective may be valid. While it is a very weak variable, similar regions emerged as significant for both dependent variables indicating that these nations seek as alignment partners those nations in their own region. This will be discussed more in the conclusion.

GREAT POWER DYADS:
COMPLEX MODELS OF ALIGNMENT

In this and the next section we will pose and analyze somewhat more complicated models based on the previous analysis. We will select those variables which appeared to be most strongly related to alignments and examine their combined impact.[11]

In the discussion of the intensity of alignment of the great power dyads, we noted that past levels of intensity, socio-political similarity, shared alliance, and intra-dyadic trade all showed some degree of relationship with that dependent variable. In order to explore this further, these variables were combined in a number of ways and the results are presented in Table 5. Each row is for a separate equation; a blank indicates that a variable was omitted from the particular equation. To begin, it is quite clear that the combination of both past experience and the three types of bonds adds little to the impact of past experience alone. For great power alignment intensity, past experience alone accounted for 30 percent of the variance. The addition of political and economic factors raises this by only 3 percentage points to 42 percent. Thus, the combined

11. The statistical procedure employed was a standard multiple regression model. Thus it was assumed that the independent variables had a linear, additive effect on the dependent variables. This statistical model permits an evaluation of the theoretical model underlying this research and allows one to identify those variables which are best predictors of the dependent variables. With a single exception noted below, multicollinearity among the independent variables is not a problem.

impact of these four factors accounts for hardly any more of the variation in great power alignment intensity than does past experience alone.

Table 5. Great Power Dyads-Intensity of Alignment (TSCO)

	Independent Variables[a]				
TSCO 63-65 [a]	Socio-political Similarity	Shared Alliance	Trade	R^2	F
b = .60 t = 7.33	[c]	b = − .04 t = − .94	b = .40 t = 3.15 [b]	.42	26.82 [b]
b = .63 t = 8.07 [b]	b = −.03 t = −.63			.39	40.61 [b]
b = .64 t = 8.57 [b]		b = .02 t = .57		.40	42.04 [b]
b = .60 t = 7.46 [b]			b = .17 t = 2.08 [b]	.42	41.73 [b]
	b = −.10 t = −1.54	b = −.04 t = −.73	b = .40 t = 3.30 [b]	.16	6.85 [b]

a. b refers to the coefficient for each variable, t is the ratio of each coefficient to its standard error, F is the ratio of the mean squared deviation due to the regression over the mean squared deviations due to error and deviations. The smallest degree of freedom in this table is 110.
b. Significant at the 0.05 level.
c. This variable accounted for less than .01 percent of the remaining variance and was excluded from the equation.

Beyond this, note that two of the variables which were only marginally significant in the previous analysis, socio-political similarity and shared alliance bonds, cease to be so in the larger analysis. Controlling for the effects of past experience and for intra-dyadic trade removes the small effect due to these two variables. This is further supported by the next three equations in which past experience is combined separately with the other three variables. Socio-political similarity and shared alliance membership fail to be significant. Intra-dyadic trade, however, remains significant although the additional amount of variance it accounts for is quite small.

The final equation examines the combined impact of the political and economic bonds. Together, these three variables account for only 16 percent of the variance in intensity of alignment but again, ideology and shared alliance members are not significant. In general, then, it appears that both past experience and economic bonds play a role in determining the intensity of great power alignments. While both of these variables are significant and their coefficients in the expected direction, together they account for only 42 percent of the variance in intensity of alignment. The more powerful is past levels of alignment, which accounts for 39 percent of the variance.

A slightly different picture emerges when we consider the scope of great power alignments. As the data in Table 6 indicate, no particular formulation of the past experience-current bond model accounts for very much. The combined impact of past experience and political and economic bonds accounts for only 23 percent of the variation in scope of alignment. In addition, the effects of both socio-political similarity and shared alliance membership are again removed when they are combined with past experience and intra-dyadic·trade. As was true with intensity of alignment, it appears that past experience and economic bonds best account for the scope of great power alignments.

Table 6. Great Power Dyads-Scope of Alignment (SSCO)

SSCO 63-65[a]	Socio-political Similarity	Shared Alliance	Trade	R^2	F
b = .28 t = 3.78[b]	[c]	b = .01 t = .62	b = .11 t = 2.14[b]	.23	10.98[b]
b = .32 t = 4.88[b]	b = .02 t = 1.13			.18	14.11[b]
b = .29 t = 4.46		b = .06 t = 3.11[b]		.23	18.09[b]
b = .29 t = 3.90			b = .14 t = 3.43[b]	.23	16.91[b]
	b = .0007 t = .02	b = .03 t = 2.26[b]	b = .12 t = 2.26[b]	.13	5.47[b]

Note: for footnotes see Table 5.

An examination of the next four equations, however, raises questions about this conclusion. It is clear that the effects of socio-political similarity are removed when past levels are introduced as a control. However, both shared alliance and trade are significant when separately combined with past levels of scope of alignment. Both equations account for the same amount of the variation in scope of alignment. However, in the final equation, when the three types of bonds are combined, only trade remains significant and the amount of variance accounted for is roughly what trade by itself accounted for (12 percent). This may be due, in part, to the fact that both intra-dyadic trade and shared alliance are fairly highly related to each other (r^2 = .41). Given this relationship between these two variables, the impact of shared alliances may be masked when combined with intra-dyadic trade. The relationship is not so strong, however, that one would want to use intra-dyadic trade as a substitute for shared alliance membership. Put another way, the political bond and economic bond for which these two are taken to be measures are conceptually distinct, as discussed above, and this empirical relationship indicates that one cannot be collapsed into the other. It does suggest, however, that the combined effect of these two factors cannot be assessed with a simple linear model.

The sources of great power alignments are, for both intensity and scope, largely the past levels of alignments between each pair and the economic bonds between each pair. The general past experience-bond model explored in this section was not fully supported by the data. For the scope of alignment, however, shared military alliance was also a significant factor, but its effects seem to be masked by its relationship with intra-dyadic trade. This suggests that a more complex model ought to be developed with attempts to separate out the effects of these two variables.

MOST ACTIVE NATIONS: COMPLEX MODELS OF ALIGNMENT

As noted above, none of the factors hypothesized to affect alignments was particularly strongly related to the alignment patterns of the most active nations. Three factors—past experience, similar region, and shared alliance—did exhibit some relationship with alignment patterns, however. In this section, we explore the combined impact of these variables. The models here are slightly different from those discussed in the previous section. Here the concern will be with the impact of past experience, military bonds, and shared region. The combined impact of these factors on both the scope and intensity of most active nation alignments is presented in Table 7.

As the results indicate, the combined impact of past experience, alliance bonds, and geography does not add much more than past experience alone. With respect to the intensity of alignments, these three factors account for 22 percent of the variation in the dependent variable. However, both shared region and shared alliance membership are insignificant in the equation, suggesting that their effects are removed when combined with past experience. Thus, past experience is the most important variable for intensity of the most active nation alignments.

A slightly different result arises for the scope of most active nation alignments. In this case, both past experience and shared geographical region are significantly related to scope of alignment. It is obvious, however, that the degree of fit is extremely poor as both variables combined account for only 9 percent of the variation in scope of alignment. In general then, the combined impact of these variables on both the scope and intensity of most active nation alignments is not much greater than the impact of the most powerful variable in each case, past experience. As was the case with the great power dyads, the factor most highly related to patterns of alignment is past levels of alignment.

Table 7. Most Active Nation Dyads-Past Experience and Proximity as Sources of Behavioral Alignments

A. Intensity of alignment

| | Independent Variables | | | |
TSCO 63-67	Similar Region	Shared Alliance	R^2	F
b = .56	b = .04	b = .04	.22	11.96
t = 5.52 [b]	t = 1.26	t = .75		
b = .57	b = .05		.22	17.75
t = 5.63 [b]	t = 1.55			
b = .54		b = .07	.20	19.43
t = 5.90 [b]		t = 1.43		

B. Scope of Alignment

| | Independent Variables | | |
SSCO 63-67	Similar Region	R^2	F
b = .19	b = .07	.09	6.22
t = 2.11 [b]	t = 2.44 [b]		

Note: for footnotes see Table 5.

DISCUSSION AND CONCLUSION

This paper has presented some results of a project designed to investigate one form of cooperative behavior among nation-states: patterns of informal, behavioral alignments. The concept was explicated and measures of it proposed. It is important to stress that this is only one step in the clarification of international cooperative behavior. This behavioral measure is very different from commitments which nations make with each other. It is to be hoped that other forms of cooperative behavior will be analyzed and investigated quantitatively.[12]

The results of the analyses performed on the data were somewhat mixed. In the analyses performed on each type of dyad, great power dyads and most active

12. In my opinion the present state of conceptualization and theory construction on cooperative behavior is rather poor. Once one leaves the arena of the formal, military alliance, the concepts employed are rather vague and operational measures are infrequently developed. In collaboration with Professor Nazli Choucri Field, I am attempting to clarify a set of of concepts which cover the spectrum of nation-state behavior from formal cooperation to complete non-cooperation. This will be reported in a future paper. With respect to formal alliances, Russett (1971) has performed analyses designed to identify empirically a typology of formal alliances.

dyads, it was hypothesized that a set of eight independent variables was related both to scope of alignment and to intensity of alignment. The analyses indicated that very few of these variables were in fact significantly related to alignment. In the case of great power alignments, past levels of intensity and scope of alignment were significantly related to patterns of alignment and to the amount of intra-dyadic trade. In the most active nation dyad analysis, past levels of alignment and residing in the same geographical region were significantly related to alignment.

In both types of dyads, the independent variable which accounted for most of the variance in the two kinds of alignment was past levels of alignment. This finding suggests that nations which have cooperated in the past are likely to do so in the future. From the present data, it is not possible to determine whether previous attempts at cooperation were in any way successful and thereby become the basis for future cooperation, or whether the aligning nations shared similar problems and cooperated regardless of past success. Factors hypothesized to be related to alignment—such as ideological similarity, similar economic power, and shared membership in international organizations—had little or no relationship with patterns of alignment. This, and the low relationship between alignment and trade and geographical region, indicate that these types of national attribute play a very small role in alignments, at least as that concept is measured in this research.

In the future this research will push in a number of directions. An early analysis of the data used in this paper, employing only 90 of the target nations in the DON data, produced for the great power dyads, results similar to those reported above with one exception (J. Sullivan, 1970). When total foreign conflict action was the dependent variable, similar economic capability proved to be significantly related to it. This was due in part to the nature of that sample, but it also suggests the possibility that alignments may be a function of the type of object involved as well as of the nature of the issue at stake. That is to say, in the preliminary analysis, only 90 target nations were employed and these tended to be nations active in the DON data bank. When the complete range of targets was employed the impact of economic similarity became relatively insignificant, suggesting that the addition of different types of targets made a difference. Put another way, alignment patterns may be a function of the characteristics of the target toward which the actions are directed as well as a function of the aligning nations. Thus, a typology of targets or objects should be developed and related to the other factors hypothesized to have an effect on alignments.

The design employed here also did not take into account, when the alignment scores were computed, the nature of the conflict act directed at each third party. All DON actions were included in the computations. The DON actions range from very conflictual actions to less conflictual words. One might reasonably expect that alignment patterns would vary in terms of the nature of the acts directed towards the object. This becomes increasingly important given the significance of past levels of alignment. By dividing the DON actions into groups, such as words and deeds, it would be possible to explore the effect of alignments characterized by much conflict and little conflict or alignments involving actions as opposed to words on future alignment patterns.

Finally, the problems associated with the measures of alignment employed in this study should be reiterated. The present measures suffer from drawbacks. It is not possible at the present time to determine if, when two nations share a conflict object, the same issue is involved in each pair of actions directed at a third party. Further development of this measure of alignment would necessitate developing some sort of issue scheme and including this information in the actions of each nation. Moreover, the present measures include only conflictual actions. A complete exploration of informal alignments would require that cooperative, as well as conflictual, actions should be included. Not only would this permit a more complete exploration of alignments, but it would also permit intra-dyadic conflict to be measured more accurately. [13]

Let us conclude this discussion with some thoughts on the policy relevance of this research. In the decision-making process, a decision-maker must define his problem and identify various alternative solutions to that problem. In addition, he must assess, in however imperfect a manner, what the likely consequences of each alternative will be and the costs or advantages to him of each alternative. To the extent that the student of quantitative international politics is able to establish, with some degree of reliability, relationships between sets of theoretically relevant factors, that information ought to enable the decision-maker to analyze his alternatives in a somewhat systematic manner. [14] From the perspective of the decision-maker, it would be most desirable that such relationships contain factors which he could manipulate and this effect the behavior and actions of others. Short of that, however, knowledge of systematic relationships among factors which he could not manipulate would be of importance to him as he considered various alternative allocations of future resources for foreign policy.

In this context, what might be said about the above research? To begin, it seems clear that the measures of alignment, in themselves, would be of interest to a decision-maker. As presently constituted, those measures indicate when two nations are sharing a smaller or larger number of conflict objects as targets of their actions. Put another way, they provide information as to tendencies for pairs of nations to escalate their conflictual words and deeds with respect to the same objects. Thus, a decision-maker might get important information relevant to his actions by monitoring these scores for pairs of nations whose actions and plans are relevant to his policies and future actions. [15] Knowing that pairs of

13. Although currently available, there are at present under way a number of data collections which will produce data which will not have these drawbacks and which will be compatible with the measures discussed above.

14. I have discussed this at greater length in J. Sullivan (1970).

15. While the present study has dealt with dyads, there is no reason why the measures could not be generalized to N nations thus permitting the decision-maker to examine the alignment patterns of some larger set of nations of interest to his nation's policy.

nations deemed relevant or crucial to his nation's policy are "pairing-up," so to speak, may permit him to eliminate certain courses of action unlikely to achieve his goals and force him to consider other alternatives, one of which might be the development of "counter" alignments.

The substantive findings themselves also have some policy relevance. They indicate that a kind of stability seems to exist with respect to the alignment patterns of pairs of nations. That is to say, if nations have aligned in the past, these findings suggest that they can be expected to align in the future. Other factors, even though significant, are so weakly related to patterns of alignment that they would be relatively useless in a decision setting.[16]

It is possible to identify the consequences of these findings for a decision-maker. First, it is quite clear that there is very little here that he can manipulate and which will have a wide-ranging effect on the behavior of other actors. He can, in an early time period, carefully assess potential alignment partners in terms of their desirability or usefulness in the future and use that assessment to determine his current alignment partners. The present findings suggest that he will probably align with present partners in the future and that he thus ought to pick current partners with that consideration in mind. Such analyses will, however, have an impact on only a small number of actors and will play a role primarily in their sharing of conflict objects with the decision-maker in question. The effects of current action will, furthermore, be realized primarily in the long run and uncertainty as to future problems and issues must be taken into account. There is little to be manipulated by the decision-maker that will have an immediate impact on his alignment patterns or on the alignment patterns of others.

From another perspective, however, the results of this research are of interest to a decison-maker. One aspect of the formulation of foreign policy is the identification of future possible antagonists among the members of the international system. Beyond that, any decision-maker will also be interested in potential "consortia" of antagonists likely to come into either verbal or physical conflict with him. To the extent that he is able to identify separate potential antagonists, this study of behavioral alignments permits him to assess the likelihood that those potential antagonists will link with each other to direct conflict at his nation or his allies or that they will seek as alignment partners nations currently friendly with his nation. Put another way, the decision-maker would be able to identify configurations of behavioral alignments of interest to him in one period and assess the likelihood that those patterns would persist into future time periods. Thus, knowledge of alignment patterns should help in a decision-maker's long-range planning and in his tentative decisions about the allocation of resources and appropriate defensive postures over long run. Monitoring alignment patterns of both friends and foes might permit him to play a role in conflict management and conflict resolution.

16. It is important to stress that these findings are derived from data limited to a short time frame. As soon as appropriate data over longer spans of time are available, these hypothesized relationships need to be re-examined to check their validity.

APPENDIX

DON Most Active Nations 1963-1967 (Average of 4.0 Actions or More Per Year)

I.D.	Country	Average Actions Per Year (1963-1967)	I.D.	Country	Average Actions Per Year (1963-1967)
2	Albania	7.4	65	Saudia Arabia	5.0
4	Australia	4.0	69	Syria	31.0
6	Belgium	4.4	70	Thailand	6.8
11	Cambodia	27.0	71	Turkey	19.8
15	China (PR)	136.0	72	Union of	
16	China (Taiwan)	4.2		South Africa	5.0
19	Cuba	27.0	73	USSR	109.4
20	Czechosolovakia	4.6	74	U.K.	36.4
24	Egypt	48.2	75	U.S.	113.0
26	Ethiopia	5.6	78	Yemen	5.4
28	France	19.6	80	Laos	4.4
29	E. Germany	11.8	81	N. Vietnam	43.4
30	W. Germany	7.2	82	S. Vietnam	14.2
31	Greece	8.2	86	Congoleo	12.4
36	India	37.4	90	Ghana	6.8
37	Indonesia	26.0	94	Malaysia	15.0
39	Iraq	8.0	97	Morocco	5.4
41	Israel	30.4	101	Somalia	4.0
44	Jordan	17.4	104	Tunisia	5.4
45	N. Korea	16.2	106	Alger	15.2
46	S. Korea	6.0	107	Cyprus	6.4
57	Pakistan	31.8	108	Zambia	6.0
62	Poland	7.8	117	Kenya	10.0
63	Portugal	6.6			

JEFFREY S. MILSTEIN

5. American and Soviet Influence, Balance of Power, and Arab-Israeli Violence

ABSTRACT

This research seeks to determine what the pattern of Arab-Israeli violence has been since 1948 and the extent to which that violence has been systematically influenced by economic aid, military aid, and trade from the United States and the Soviet Union, and by the balance of military power between Arabs and Israelis. Accordingly, the systematic effects of these large-scale American and Soviet actions and of the balance of military capabilities on five types of violence initiated by seven countries in the Middle East are separately measured and evaluated using quantitative data and statistical methods.

The years analyzed span three Arab-Israeli wars from 1948-1967. The violent actions initiated by Israel, Egypt (U.A.R.), Jordan, Iraq, Saudi Arabia, Syria, and Lebanon which are analyzed include: (1) encounters between government forces; (2) encounters between guerrillas and government forces; (3) attacks on civilians; (4) attacks on bases and strategic installations; and (5) mobilizations and alerts. Theoretical explanations of Arab-Israeli violence are also proposed and tested, including theories of hostile actions and reactions, balance, and learning.

Arab and Israeli violence is found to be primarily dependent upon the violence of the opposite side in a hostile action-reaction pattern resembling "an eye for an eye, a tooth for a tooth." The initiation of violence by Arabs and

Author's Note: This work has been supported by the World Data Analysis Program of Yale University under Grant 2635 from the National Science Foundation and Contract N-0014-67-A-0097-0007 from the Advanced Research Projects Agency, Behavioral Sciences, monitored by the Office of Naval Research. I wish to express my appreciation to Barbara Alexander, John Bolton, Lloyd Etheredge, Betty Hanson, Mary Huang, John Kirkwood, Robert Luft, Donna Lustgarten, Ann Morris, Robin Nadel, Michelle Press, Janet Seymour, and Thomas Sloan for the great assistance they gave me in the process of doing this research and preparing this manuscript. I am also indebted to Paul Berman and Joseph B. Kadane for their statistical advice. The responsibility for the work is, of course, my own.

Israelis is found *not* to be dependent on differences in military capabilities. United States and Soviet influences on Arab and Israeli violence, when controlling for other variables, are found to be very limited. Soviet and American leaders should realize how limited this influence is, or they risk an involvement in the conflict much graver than they would have intended.   ■

THE SUPER-POWERS
AND THE MIDDLE EAST

In a quick series of diplomatic actions, the United States and Soviet Union were able to induce Israel, Egypt, and Jordan to agree to a cease fire on August 7, 1970 after more than three years of violence. This successful effort raises the question of how consistant and extensive United States and Soviet influence has been on Arab-Israeli violence over the years. As a demonstration of the ability of the superpowers to control violence in the Middle East, is the 1970-72 cease fire a fortuitous event that one could not expect to be repeated, or is it an example of consistent influence the superpowers have over actions of Arabs and Israelis?

Both the United States and Soviet Union have an interest in controlling the violence between Arabs and Israelis. Of paramount concern to the superpowers is that they themselves not be drawn into armed conflict against each other as an outgrowth of the violent conflict between their clients. Both also have policy objectives in the Middle East which are affected by Arab-Israeli violence.

The United States Government has sought to keep Israel viable as a progressive democracy to satisfy an active Jewish constituency in the United States; to protect American economic investments, particularly in oil; and to retain a strategic presence for the United States and the NATO countries in the Middle East. Both the United States and the Soviets wish to have influence in the Middle East that would enable them to project their military forces into the region and to use bases there to send those forces into other geographical areas (Southern Europe for the Soviets, for example). Both have been greatly interested in building and maintaing naval strength in the Mediterranean Sea and in having access through the Suez Canal to project this naval strength to the Persian Gulf, East Africa, and Asia. In addition, both countries have sought to control the flow of oil to Western Europe and Japan. American corporations have more than three billion dollars invested in Middle Eastern oil and profit from that investment. The American Government seeks to protect that investment and to secure the needed oil supplies for its vital NATO and Japanese alliance partners. The Soviets have been interested in controlling this flow of oil as a basis for influencing NATO countries and Japan.

Both the United States and Soviet Union have sought to achieve their policy objectives by, aside from diplomatic means, supplying arms, other military assistance and economic aid, and by engaging in trade with the Middle Eastern countries. Economic and military aid has been used as both a carrot and a stick by the superpowers. Withholding aid—once a Middle Eastern country had become dependent upon it—could be used to influence that country's violent behavior. Both superpowers have sought to make the recipients of their military aid dependent upon them for necessary follow-up training in the use of the weapons they supply and for spare parts. Even the type of training received tends to tie the recipient country to the donor because military officers prefer to continue with the procedures that they have learned rather than change to new weapons systems provided by another country. A general hypothesis in this research is that any unique political influence demonstrated by the United States or the Soviet Union—the 1970-1972 cease fire, for example—is based upon long-standing commitments and support, such as those represented by long-term aid and trade.

The continuation of violence in the Middle East has been of some advantage to the Russians, for the radical Arab countries have become dependent upon them for military assistance to carry on the conflict with Israel, and have thus given the Russians an unprecedented strategic position in the Middle East. The United States has also benefited from the Arab-Israeli conflict, for the Israelis represent an anti-Soviet bulwark in the Middle East. The ability of the Israelis to reduce the military and political influence of the Russians by destroying Soviet-supplied arms to Arab countries and, since 1967, by preventing the passage of Soviet ships through the Suez Canal could be viewed as advantageous to the United States. Thus, Russians and Americans have had conflicting interests in escalating and de-escalating the Arab-Israeli conflict at various times over the years. It is assumed in this research, however, that the superpowers have used aid and trade to try to control Arab-Israeli violence as well as to achieve their other policy objectives.

The two superpowers have a vital interest in knowing to what extent they can systematically control the Middle Eastern conflict, for there is a great danger that the Arab-Israeli struggle could draw the United States and the Soviet Union into a confrontation with each other. The superpowers could be manipulated by the Middle Eastern countries so that the tail would be wagging the proverbial dog.

The deeply rooted conflict in the Middle East stems from such unresolved issues as the existence of the sovereign Jewish State of Israel and the counter claim of the Palestinian Arabs to all of Palestine as their own, as well as a host of disputed corollary issues: the territorial boundaries of the State of Israel; the official state of belligerency between Israel and the Arab countries; the right of Israel to navigate the Suez Canal and the Straits of Tiran; the independence, repatriation, resettlement, and compensation of the Palestinian refugees; and finally, the control of Jerusalem.

The Middle East raises some important theoretical questions: how autonomous is a pattern of interaction among a regional set of nations (a subsystem of the international system)? How much is the regional subsystem affected by interaction with superpower actors, whose actions in the regional subsystem are a part of the larger Cold War system? Put in another way, what is the effect on one subsystem of interaction when penetrated by a larger system of interaction? The general interactions considered in these questions and in this study are diagrammed in Figure 1.

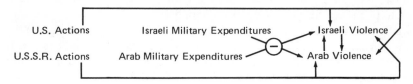

Figure 1. Systems of Interaction

Do the superpowers really have any control over the violent actions that stem from the conflicts noted above? Is all of the aid and trade between the superpowers and Middle Eastern countries of no effect on the violence between Arabs and Israelis? Do the United States and Soviet inputs of aid and trade encourage, by directly or indirectly escalating, Arab-Israeli violence?

DATA

Two types of data are used in this study. The first is a set of variables which already exist in quantitative form: miltiary expenditures, American economic aid, American military aid, Public Law 480 aid, Soviet loans, and special imports from the United States and the Soviet Union by each of the Middle Eastern countries. ("Special imports" are the same as general imports, except that they include imports for domestic consumption from free-trade zones or bonded warehouses.) The sources of these data are given in the Appendix.

The second type of data, that for Arab and Israeli violent actions, had to be coded to yield a quantitative measure. First, two coders established five classes of violent actions for each of seven Middle Eastern Countries (Israel, Egypt, Jordan, Iran, Saudi Arabia, Syria, and Lebanon). These five categories are:

1. Encounters Between Government Forces (GF). This category encompasses skirmishes between government troops, shelling of enemy positions and return of fire, aerial "dogfights", and any events at sea which involved official navies rather than civilian ships.

2. Encounters Between Guerrillas and Government Forces (GUER). This includes only skirmishes between Arab guerrillas and Israeli soldiers. Israeli commandos were classed as official soldiers rather than as guerrillas. Israeli police, except for "border police" (who are really soldiers), were classed as civilians; Arab "police," being paramilitary in organization, were classed as government soldiers. Occasionally, Israeli patrols kill a "suspicious" Arab who later proves to have been unarmed; this event was coded as an attack on civilians.

3. Attacks on Civilians (AC). This category includes any attack by regular soldiers or guerrillas on towns, kibbutzim, unarmed individuals, trains, etc. Also included are attacks on planes or trucks carrying supplies to United Nations

Emergency Force troops. A guerrilla raid on a town was coded under this category, rather than under category 2. The explosion of mines was generally placed here, although it might have gone under category 2 if soldiers were injured or under category 4 if the mine were set in a government installation. Generally no initiating country can be identified in mine cases.

4. Attacks on Installations (AI). Pipelines, electrical installations, water pumping stations, and railways are the principal targets here. Government buildings were included if it seemed clear that the attack was intended to destroy the building rather than to injure civilians. An attack on an army base would be both a category 1 and a category 4, assuming the attacked soldiers fought back. However, an event such as the Israeli raid on Beirut airport, while of military significance, was classified under category 4 only.

5. Mobilizations, Troop Movements, Declarations of Emergency, Alerts (M&A). This category included governmental actions which, while non-violent themselves, appeared to be asking for conflict. Verbal actions, such as threats, were not included.

Using two sources, the *Middle East Journal Chronology* and *The New York Times Index,* the coders recorded whether, within a given week, a country had initiated one or more acts of violence in each of the categories. Thus, the measure is not the number of violent acts engaged in, but the number of weeks each year during which a country engaged in each type of violent action.

Data from the two sources were merged so that an event reported in either, or both, would be recorded as one ("present") for that week. If an event was not reported by either source, a zero ("absent") was recorded. The number of weeks in which each country engaged in each type of violence was then totalled for every year from 1948 through 1969 (although the analysis reported here will cover only 1948 through 1967—the period during which three Arab-Israeli general wars were fought—because the most recent aid and trade data were unavailable.)

Coding the number of weeks per year that a country engages in a particular type of violence alleviates some of the more severe problems of coding events. The amount of time that a country engages in violence each year is used as a general indicator of the amount of violence that the country engaged in, making these data less dependent upon idiosyncracies of reporting. The measure—the number of weeks per year—is an integral number ranging from 0 to 52.

The methods used in this study include bivariate product moment correlation and bivariate and multiple regression analysis. The emphasis is on single equation regressions. Correlations among dependent variables (each country's violence) are not a serious problem, since independent variables exogenous to the Middle East are included. Future work might develop simultaneous equation models and use methods of simultaneous estimation of the parameters. In this study a particular Israeli action is explained in terms of a particular Arab action (plus some other factor, such as United States or Soviet aid), and that same Arab action by the Israeli one (plus other factors).

THEORY

One can assume that Middle Eastern leaders wish to minimize external attacks against their own people, if for no other reason than to protect their own popular support, the basis of their political power. Once their people are attacked, there are several theoretical explanations and predictions as to why and how national leaders will respond. The purpose of the following empirical analysis is not only to describe what the patterns of violent interaction between Israelis and Arabs have been, but also to use these patterns as evidence to support or deny certain general theoretical explanations and predictions of this kind of conflictual violent behavior. Briefly, these general theories are as follows.

The first is "hostile reaction theory" which states that people behave in direct response to impinging hostile stimuli without reference to any inner state, such as tension or pleasure. It is a mechanistic theory, positing hostile human behavior in terms of actions and reactions. It has, however, been hypothesized to be appropriate to such phenomena as fights, when the hostile action of one party stimulates the hostile response of the other in an upward spiral of hostile actions (Rapoport, 1960).

The second general theory, "balance theory," maintains that people seek to reduce stresses that result when outside events or conditions change the equilibrium, or balance, of the actor, and that the behavior exhibited is a function of such stresses. Actors are variously conceptualized as individuals, organizations, or nations. Various theories lie within this framework. "Cybernetic theories" conceptualize actors as servomechanisms who have set goals and who act purposely to reduce discrepancies between the current state of affairs and the desired state (Wiener, 1948). "TOTE (test-operated-text-exit) theory" is one such theory (Miller, Galanter, Pribram, 1960). Psychological theories of "cognitive balance, consistency, or dissonance" are also within this balance paradigm (Festinger, 1957; 1964). "Stress theory" (Howard and Scott, 1965) and "frustration-aggression" also lie within this framework. Frustration is conceptualized as a tension due to blocked impulses (Dollard, et. al., 1939).

The third general theory is "learning theory." It states that people adapt their behavior on the basis of past experience so as to achieve rewards and avoid punishments. People are conditioned to perform certain behaviors and avoid others on the basis of reinforcement, i.e., the rewards or punishments they have experienced in conjunction with, or as a consequence of, their behavior (Hull, 1943; Homans, 1961).

These three general theoretical paradigms are complementary. Balance and learning theories build on hostile reaction theory by providing intervening mechanisms by which stimuli produce responses. Balance theory and learning theory are further complementary in that reducing tension and achieving goals are themselves rewarding. Thus, balance theory stipulates a mechanism that initiates behavior, which is then conditioned.

One way in which national leaders think they can reduce attacks against their own people is to counterattack or preemptively attack the enemy. If the Middle Eastern leaders acted as theorized by hostile action theory, a "fight" involving an escalating number of attacks and counterattacks would occur in which Arabs and Israelis returned "an eye for an eye and a tooth for a tooth," or even "an eye for a tooth," i.e., more harmful attacks, such as those against civilians, for less harmful ones, such as those against military units. Positive statistical relationships between violent actions of Arabs and Israelis would provide empirical support for this theory.

According to balance theory, people act in response to increased tension. Assuming that attacks against their people increase the tension of national leaders and that counterattacks are a possible response, then one would hypothesize that the more they were attacked, the more leaders would respond with counterattacks. Thus, positive statistical relationships also support balance theory. Moreover, balance theory provides an explanation for an observed pattern of hostile interaction-tension. Israeli Foreign Minister Abba Eban is quoted as stating that the Soviet Union was interested in maintaining "controlled tension" in the Middle East (New York Times, March 31, 1970: 3).

According to learning theory, national leaders might respond to attacks on their people and country in two different ways. First, if counterattacks were successful in reducing the number of attacks on their own country, they would be repeated and possibly increased, since they were found to be rewarding. On the other hand, if counterattacks led only to an increase in the number of enemy attacks, the counterattacks would be reduced, since punished behavior tends to be extinguished. Thus negative statistical relationships would support this version of learning theory.

Secondly, if counterattacks were not successful, but were punished by an increase in the number of the enemy's attacks, the behavior involving a small number of counterattacks might be extinguished in favor of a larger number of such attacks, leading to an escalating spiral of violence. Positive statistical relationships would support this version of learning theory. It complements the explanation of violent behavior offered by balance theory: tensions are punishments which people seek to avoid by extinguishing behavior associated with them.

In the following statistical analyses, the reader should keep in mind the implications of positive or negative statistical relationships for the theoretical interpretation of the empirical patterns of violent interaction between Arabs and Israelis. These theoretical implications will be summarized at the end of each section.

ACTION AND
REACTION PATTERNS

Tables 1, 2, and 3 show the bivariate product moment correlations between Arab and Israeli violence over 87 quarters from 1948 through 1969 for like violent actions within the same quarter, as well as for actions in one quarter compared within similar enemy actions in the preceding and following quarters. Almost all the relationships are positive, especially the strong relationships with correlations greater than 0.50.

A comparison of Tables 1 and 4 shows that some Israeli violent actions correspond to different, rather then similar, types of Arab violence. The variables listed in Table 4 were selected because they are all highly

Table 1. Quarterly 1948-1969 Correlations Between Violent Actions of Israel and Arab Countries [a]

| | (Same Quarter) | | | | |
	GF	GUER	AC	AI	M&A
Egypt	0.75	0.47	0.43	0.67	0.46
Jordan	0.79	0.80	0.65	0.47	0.29
Iraq	0.26	0.01	0.29	0.25	0.29
Saudi Arabia	0.16	—	−0.02	−0.35	—
Syria	0.40	0.51	0.05	0.16	0.45
Lebanon	0.36	0.41	0.40	0.19	0.27

a. The following abbreviations are used throughout these tables: GF = encounters between government forces; GUER = encounters between guerrillas and government forces; AC = attacks on civilians; AI = attacks on installations; M&A = mobilizations, troop movements, declarations of emergency, and alerts.

Table 2. Quarterly 1948-1969 Correlations Between Violent Actions of Israel and Arab Countries

| | (Arabs Lagged) | | | |
	GF	GUER	AC	AI
Egypt	0.64	0.40	0.38	0.65
Jordan	0.63	0.67	0.55	0.27
Iraq	0.18	0.09	0.36	0.05
Saudi Arabia	−0.09	—	0.12	0.18
Syria	0.13	0.40	−0.02	0.18
Lebanon	0.25	0.44	0.31	0.30

Table 3. Quarterly 1948-1969 Correlations Between Violent Actions of Israel and Arab Countries

| | (Israel Lagged) | | | |
	GF	GUER	AC	AI
Egypt	0.56	0.35	0.34	0.50
Jordan	0.61	0.69	0.55	0.23
Iraq	0.19	−0.11	0.25	−0.05
Saudi Arabia	0.14	—	0.10	0.00
Syria	0.31	0.34	0.14	0.02
Lebanon	0.31	0.23	0.24	−0.07

Table 4. 1948-1969 Quarterly Correlations Among Violent Actions

	Isr GF	Egy GF	Jor GF	Isr GUER	Egy GUER	Jor GUER	Leb GUER	Isr AC	Jor AC	Leb AC	Isr AI	Egy AI
Isr GF	1.00											
Egy GF	0.75	1.00										
Jor GF	0.79	0.53	1.00									
Isr GUER	0.67	0.55	0.74	1.00								
Egy GUER	0.60	0.72	0.52	0.48	1.00							
Jor GUER	0.60	0.49	0.73	0.80	0.43	1.00						
Leb GUER	0.34	0.34	0.22	0.41	0.32	0.32	1.00					
Isr AC	0.68	0.55	0.63	0.65	0.46	0.51	0.32	1.00				
Jor AC	0.58	0.46	0.71	0.60	0.41	0.62	0.30	0.65	1.00			
Leb AC	0.47	0.50	0.36	0.51	0.53	0.34	0.48	0.40	0.51	1.00		
Isr AI	0.65	0.76	0.46	0.68	0.67	0.53	0.46	0.53	0.47	0.65	1.00	
Egy AI	0.53	0.63	0.38	0.46	0.62	0.38	0.44	0.45	0.53	0.61	0.67	1.00

intercorrelated. Table 4 shows also that the four types of Israeli violence listed correlate highly with each other. One finds too that most types of violence initiated by Israel, Egypt, and Jordan are highly correlated. Excluding mobilizations and alerts, which tend to be independent of the other four types of violent actions, these three countries have engaged in the four remaining types of violence during the same quarterly time period.

Table 5 gives correlations between Israeli and Arab violent action during each

Table 5. Yearly 1948-1967 Correlations Between Violent Actions of Israel and Arab Countries

	(Simultaneous)				
	GF	GUER	AC	AI	M&A
Egypt	0.82	0.18	0.64	0.74	0.51
Jordan	0.77	0.59	0.64	0.35	0.20
Iraq	0.19	0.23	0.56	0.45	0.31
Saudi Arabia	0.45	—	0.21	0.76	0.49
Syria	0.49	0.21	0.28	−0.02	0.63
Lebanon	0.16	0.03	0.37	0.32	0.47

year from 1948 to 1967, in contrast to the quarterly breakdown in the preceding tables. Not all of the Arab countries have had the same pattern of violent interaction with Israel. For example, encounters between government forces occur primarily between Israel and Egypt and Israel and Jordan. Only Israel and Jordan, however, have highly correlated encounters between guerrilla and government forces. These patterns of interaction will be more fully analyzed using regression analysis on the yearly data.

Table 6. Association Between Israeli and Egyptian Violent Actions[a]

		GF	GUER	AC	AI	M&A
Israeli	R	0.82	0.66	0.84		0.63
	a	−7.50	−1.96	−3.84		−0.24
GF	b	0.84	0.37	0.43		0.11
	SE	0.14	0.10	0.07		0.03
Israeli	R	0.49		0.58		
	a	1.89		0.59		
GUER	b	1.22		0.72		
	SE	0.51		0.24		
Israeli	R			0.64		
	a			−0.41		
AC	b			0.39		
	SE			0.11		
Israeli	R			0.87	0.74	
	a			1.01	0.11	
AI	b			0.95	0.38	
	SE			0.13	0.08	
Israeli	R	0.53				
	a	−0.29				
M&A	b	2.14				
	SE	0.81				

a. The following abbreviations are used throughout the remaining tables: R = multiple correlation coefficient; a = intercept; b = regression coefficient; SE = standard error of regression coefficient.

Tables 6-9 give the bivariate regression equations of each Arab country's violent actions on each of Israel's violent actions, and show which Israeli actions are associated with Arab actions. The multiple correlation coefficient R can be used to determine how good the linear fit is in the prediction of the dependent variables.[1] The regression coefficient b indicates the change in the dependent variable for each unit change in the independent variable; for

1. It should be noted that in the regression tables, the multiple correlation coefficient R appears without a sign. The direction of the bivariate relationship is indicated in every case by the sign of the regression coefficient b.

Table 7. Association Between Israeli and Jordanian Violent Actions

		GF	GUER	AC		M&A
Israeli	R	0.77	0.52	0.71		
	a	0.80	0.36	−0.90		
GF	b	0.44	0.22	0.43		
	SE	0.90	0.08	0.10		
Israeli	R	0.48	0.59			
	a	5.58	1.53			
GUER	b	0.68	0.59			
	SE	0.29	0.19			
Israeli	R	0.64	0.48	0.64		
	a	3.90	1.66	1.77		
AC	b	0.43	0.23	0.45		
	SE	0.12	0.10	0.13		
Israeli	R					0.71
	a					0.60
AI	b					0.25
	SE					0.06
Israeli	R	0.50				
	a	4.58				
M&A	b	1.13				
	SE	0.46				

Table 8. Associations Between Israeli and Syrian Violent Actions

		GE	GUER	AC	AI	M&A
Israeli	R	0.49				0.54
	a	2.90				−0.34
GF	b	0.29				0.10
	SE	0.12				0.03
Israeli						
GUER			No "significant" relationships			
Israeli						
AC			No "significant" relationships			
Israeli						
AI			No "significant" relationships			
Israeli	R		0.47			0.63
	a		−0.22			−0.04
M&A	b		0.68			0.44
	SE		0.30			0.13

Table 9. Association Between Israeli and Lebanese Violent Actions

		GF	GUER	AC	AI	M&A
Israeli	R			0.74	0.54	
	a			−0.71	−0.25	
GF	b			0.09	0.03	
	SE			0.02	0.01	
Israeli						
GUER		No "significant" relationships				
Israeli						
AC		No "significant" relationships				
Israeli						
AI		No "significant" relationships				
Israeli	R	0.65				
	a	−0.80				
M&A	b	0.49				
	SE	0.14				

example, per million dollars of U.S. economic aid. The size of the regression coefficients can be used to compare the effects of different independent variables on the same dependent variable when the units of the independent variables are the same, e.g. weeks of violence or dollars.

The a coefficients, the intercepts, in these regression equations may be interpreted as follows: negative values indicate that only above the threshold of a/b in the independent variable is there a response in the dependent variable. Positive values indicate that the violent action represented by the dependent variable was ongoing for a weeks even when the value of the independent variable was zero, and thus that however closely related to the independent variable, the dependent variable is dependent upon some other variable(s) as well. For example, one may interpret a positive a coefficient as indicating that Israel engaged in a certain number of encounters with Arab government forces while Egypt engaged in no similar encounters. On the other hand, a negative a coefficient indicates that Egypt initiated a certain number of guerrilla attacks (a) against Israeli government forces even when Israel initiated no similar guerrilla attacks against Arab government forces.

The "standard error of the regression coefficient (SE)" is given in the table so that comparison can be made with the regression coefficients, facilitating evaluation of the explanatory power of each independent variable. The t-ratios of the value of a regression coefficient to its standard error are not given because coefficients were not derived from a random sample and because the main determinant of a statistical significance level is the sample size. Calculating a precise probability, if the true t ratio were zero, of observing a sample t ratio at least as high as that observed is not informative, since we know that the probability is close to zero. What we have done, however, is to eliminate from the tables, as of little interest, all relationships where the t ratio is not at least 2.1. This ratio would be equivalent to statistical significance at the .05 level if the sample were random.[2]

A non-statistical measure of the importance of the regression coefficient of an independent variable is the "dollar cost/effectiveness" of various United States and Soviet actions. For example, where regression coefficients have relatively small standard errors, one can compare the cost of trying to affect Arab or Israeli violence using two different means.

Each type of Israeli violent action is highly associated with one or more Egyptian acts of violence. The relationship is particularly strong in cases of encounters between government forces and attacks on civilians and on strategic installations. In all these cases the b coefficients are positive, indicating an action-reaction type of relationship.

Israeli actions have a significant effect on each type of Jordanian action, with the exception of attacks on installations. In particular, Israeli-initiated encounters between government forces trigger similar Jordanian actions, and Israeli attacks on installations greatly affect Jordanian mobilizations and alerts. Israeli attacks on civilians cause a similar Jordanian reaction, as well as provoking guerrilla encounters.

Israeli actions seem generally to be independent of Iraqi or Saudi Arabian violence, so no tables are given.

Most Syrian violence appears to be independent of Israeli actions. However, attacks by Syria's government forces are in response to similar Israeli attacks, and Syrian guerrilla attacks appear to be affected by Israeli mobilizations and alerts. Syrian mobilizations and alerts appear to respond to Israeli mobilizations and alerts and encounters between government forces.

Lebanese-initiated violence also appears to be independent of Israeli actions. Exceptions inlcude Lebanese-initiated encounters between guerrillas and government forces, which are affected by Israeli mobilizations and alerts; and Lebanese attacks on civilians and installations are affected by Israeli-initiated encounters between government forces.

Ideally one would like to determine which particular Israeli action was most significant in provoking each type of Arab violent response. However, the high degree of intercorrelation among all types of Israeli actions precludes the use of

2. As an additional check on how good the bivariate relationships are, each relationship that had a t ratio greater than 2.1 in the bivariate regression analysis was cross-plotted and check visually to insure that a good general relationship existed, and was not due to outliers or clusters of observations. Only those relationships that passed this "eyeball" test appear in the regression tables and are discussed as significant in the text.

a multiple regression equation to determine the separate effect of each one upon Arab violence. The different violent actions of the Arab countries are similarly intercorrelated and thus subject to the same limitations. (The degree of correlation varies with the country. For example, Egyptian violent actions are more highly intercorrelated than are those of Syria.) Ignoring the individual regression coefficients in a multiple regression equation, one can still use the multiple correlation coefficients as an indicator of the extent to which each Israeli violent action is determined or predicted by the whole set of Arab violent actions operating together.

Table 10 shows the multiple correlation coefficients measuring the degree to which each Arab country's combined violent actions determine or predict each Israeli violent action. (Saudi Arabia has been omitted because it did not engage in all five types of violence.) The conventional warfare initiated by Israel—encounters between government forces and attacks on installations—is best predicted by Egyptian violent actions. Whereas less conventional maneuvers—encounters between guerrillas and government forces and attacks on civilians—are best predicted by Jordanian actions. These findings have significance for the cease fire begun on August 7, 1970. Israel, Egypt, and Jordan all agreed to the cease fire; Syria and Iraq did not. However, because Israel's violent actions seem to be in response mainly to Egyptian and Jordanian violence, and vice versa, the fact that these three nations agreed to the cease fire improved its chances of success.

Table 10. Multiple Correlations with Israeli Violent Actions

	GF	GUER	AC	AI	M&A
Egypt	0.86	0.81	0.83	0.93	0.60
Jordan	0.79	0.96	0.88	0.75	0.55
Iraq	0.66	0.84	0.70	0.80	0.41
Syria	0.70	0.69	0.72	0.45	0.73
Lebanon	0.80	0.68	0.72	0.74	0.71

The overall pattern of violent interaction between Israel and the Arab countries is clear: where there is interdependence, the statistical relationships are all positive. Violence begets more violence. "An eye for an eye; a tooth for a tooth," is and has been the dominant pattern of interaction between Arabs and Israelis.

Theoretically, these findings give support to and may be interpreted by hostile reaction theory, balance theory, and part of learning theory. According to "hostile reaction" theory, the parties to the Arab-Israeli conflict are responding to the violent actions of their enemies automatically, without thinking of the consequences of future escalated violent responses by the enemy. According to "balance" theory, violent attacks that are perceived to threaten the security, well-being, and survival of a country and its people increase the stress and tension felt by the national leaders and lead them to try to *force* the enemy to reduce violent attacks (and, consequently, the stress and tension) by means of violent attacks of their own. The stress and tension itself may be the cause of the automatic, unthinking, uncalculating, and irrational behavior theorized in hostile reaction theory. Under high stress national leaders are less likely to make rational calculations than they are under conditions of less stress.

Finally, according to "learning" theory, these patterns of violent interaction can be interpreted to support the proposition that national leaders, when punished for their own violent behavior by the violent behavior of their enemies, will actually *increase* their violent behavior. In an escalating conflict, parties remember past punishment for having engaged in less violent behavior. The only option is more violence, because that is the only untried alternative that has not already been punished. Thus, punishment from the more distant past, as well as from the recent past, affects the choice of alternative behavior. Such punishment, according to learning theory, could be the violent attacks themselves and/or the tension and stress induced by those attacks.

SOVIET AND AMERICAN EFFECTS ON ARAB-ISRAELI VIOLENCE

The dramatic cease fire engineered by the United States and Soviet Union during the summer of 1970 is a clear manifestation of American and Soviet political influence on Arab and Israeli violence. This cease fire represents such a departure from the previous 20 years of protracted Arab-Israeli violence that it may give rise to the assumption that until then the superpowers exercised no systematic influence on this conflict. We shall now test this assumption. In any case, we assume that the superpowers could have acquired and maintained long-term influence over Arab-Israeli violence only through sustained, large-scale interactions with the belligerents—economic aid, military assistance and training, and trade. We shall examine the effect of specific types of superpower input.

Some comment is required on the variables used to measure the large-scale Soviet and American inputs into the Middle East. The amount of military or economic assistance or trade in each year will be correlated with the number of weeks during which each Middle Eastern country initiated each of the five types of violent actions. It is assumed that the value of the aid or trade in a specific year is what affects the amount of violence initiated. It can be argued that because aid and trade agreements are made sporadically, influence over the Middle Eastern countries is also sporadic and occurs not at the time of the agreement but when the decision to extend such aid is made. (This argument would best apply to economic and military aid and trade by the "state" traders, such as the Soviet Union and most of the Middle Eastern countries.) The capability to engage in violent action, however, depends upon economic and military resources, and it is hypothesized here that the resources received from aid and trade could be used for violent actions. Whether they actually are or not is an open question, since the donor could use the threat of discontinuing the aid to influence the recipient to reduce his violence.

Only publicly available data have been used. Data for American military aid comes from "Overseas Loans and Grants" of the United States House of Representatives Appropriations Committee. Of course direct loans and grants do not represent the entire amount of American military assistance to the Middle East, but the figures for many types of military assistance, such as those for direct sales of ammunition and spare parts or direct sales facilitated by United States economic assistance, are classified by the American government. "Third nation" military assistance to Israel was at times stimulated, and frequently compensated for, by the United States; West Germany was allegedly reimbursed through the release of "surplus" United States/NATO stocks for its substantial assistance to Israel from 1958 to 1963. Similarly, in considering economic aid, one might wish to add to the official data on direct American assistance such indirect aid as encouragement and compensation to third countries for their assistance to Israel, for example, the large German reparation payments to Israel in the 1950's, and private donations to Israel.

Much of the data on Soviet aid, both economic and military, are not available. Thus, the figures for the United States and the Soviet Union that are public knowledge are like the tip of an iceberg, representing only a fraction of the whole which is submerged beneath the surface and invisible to the observer. We shall assume, however, that the visible portion is a constant proportion of the total cumulative amount. In making this assumption, we must still remain cautious about the kinds of inferences we draw using these quantitative indicators. Regarding the potential influence of trade, it is more directly apparent how the offering of trade deals could influence the behavior of those governments that are "state traders." For the non-state traders we must assume that trade influences the behavior of governments through their desire for markets, preferential tariffs, and credit terms.

Table 11 shows the effect on Israeli violence of the following independent variables: American economic aid in the current and past year, military aid, Public Law 480 aid, and special imports from the United States as well as the Soviet Union in the current and past year. If we assume that the correlations in some sense indicate influence, American economic aid within the same year consistently reduced the number of weeks in which Israel initiated encounters between government forces. When there was no American economic aid, Israel initiated encounters between government forces on an average of 32 weeks each year; for each $10 million in economic aid, such violence was reduced two weeks each year. One might infer that the United States has had a condition for giving such aid: that the Israelis decrease violence initiated against the Arabs. This reduction of violence would be in the interest of the United States, which wishes to maintain some influence in the Arab world and could ill afford Arab accusations of giving the Israelis economic aid when the Israelis subsequently engaged in more violence against the Arabs.

Table 11. Superpower Inputs and Israeli Violent Actions

		GF	GUER	AC	AI	M&A
U.S.	R	0.57				
Economic Aid	a	32.01				
(same year)	b	−0.23				
	SE	−0.01				
Imports from	R					0.61
Soviet Union	a					1.90
(same year)	b					4.22
	SE					1.39

No significant relations were found for any of these independent variables: U.S. economic aid (previous year), U.S. military aid (same or previous year), U.S. Public Law 480 aid (same or previous year), imports from the United States (same or previous year), and imports from the Soviet Union (previous year).

Israeli violent actions appear unaffected by U.S. military aid to Israel, either in the same or previous year. This might be the result of incomplete data, but is more likely attributable to the greater significance of other factors in determining Israeli violence—Arab violence, for example.

Imports appear to be generally unrelated to Israeli violent actions. However, Israeli mobilizations and alerts may be increased by special imports from the Soviet Union during the same year. There is no clear reason why this should be the case, and it may be a spurious relationship in which intervening factors cause the imports and mobilizations and alerts to increase simultaneously.

Table 12 gives the same information for the Arab states. Egyptian violent actions generally seem to be independent of most United States inputs. This is true of American economic aid both in the same and previous year and of Public Law 480 aid the same year. Imports from the United States, however, do seem to have a dampening effect on Egyptian-initiated encounters between government forces and attacks on civilians in the same year. Imports from the Soviet Union tend to decrease attacks on civilians in the same year. It may be that both the Soviets and Americans urged Egypt to decrease attacks in order to receive imports.

Soviet loans and military aid, in the current or previous year, seem to be unrelated to Egyptian violence. Thus, remembering the limits of quantitative data used here, it appears that contrary to what one might expect, the Egyptians have engaged in violent actions whether Soviet military or economic aid was increased or decreased. The finding might be explained by considering the type of violence and the weapons used. Soviet assistance may merely increase the sophistication of the weapons Egypt can use against Israel, but not necessarily the frequency or the length of the attacks.

Imports from the United States in the previous year tend to increase Jordanian attacks on installations. One might infer that Jordan obtained goods in this trade that allowed it to increase attacks. However, United States economic aid reduced Jordanian initiated encounters between government forces, and Public Law 480 aid reduced attacks on civilians. Iraqi violence appears essentially unaffected by any American or Soviet economic imputs. Saudi Arabian violent actions for which data exist seem largely unaffected by imports from the United States or the Soviet Union.

Syria's violent actions appear to be independent of American Public Law 480 aid or imports from United States. Imports from the Soviet Union in the same year, however, are associated with increased attacks on installations, and those

Table 12. Superpower Inputs and Arab Violent Actions

		EGYPT				
		GF	GUER	AC	AI	M&A
Imports from	R	0.48		0.51		
United States	a	12.76		6.77		
(same year)	b	−0.14		0.07		
	SE	0.06		0.03		
Imports from	R			0.49		
Soviet Union	a			7.02		
(same year)	b			−0.20		
	SE			0.09		

No significant relationships were found for any of these independent variables: imports from the Soviet Union (previous year), U.S. economic aid (same or previous year), U.S. Public Law 480 aid (same or previous year), imports from the United States (previous year), Soviet Union loans (same or previous year), and Soviet Union military aid (same or previous year).

		JORDAN				
		GF	GUER	AC	AI	M&A
U.S.	R	0.60				
Economic Aid	a	14.54				
(previous year)	b	−0.16				
	SE	0.06				
U.S.	R			0.56		
Public Law 480	a			10.33		
Aid (same year)	b			−0.55		
	SE			0.21		
Imports from	R				0.48	
United States	a				0.15	
(previous year)	b				0.42	
	SE				0.19	

No significant relationships were found for any of these independent variables: U.S. economic aid (same year), U.S. military aid (same or previous year), U.S. Public Law 480 aid (previous year), and Imports from the United States (same year).

		GF	GUER	AC	AI	M&A
SYRIA						
Imports from	R				0.73	
Soviet Union	a				−0.11	
(same year)	b				0.05	
	SE				0.01	
Imports from	R	0.57				
Soviet Union	a	6.46				
(previous year)	b	0.16				
	SE	0.06				

No significant relationships were found for these independent variables: Public Law 480 aid (same or previous year), and Imports from United States (same or previous year).

from the previous year with increased encounters between government forces. One might infer that Syria imported material which allowed it to initiate more of these encounters (see Table 13).

Lebanese violence is quite independent of imports from either the United States or the Soviet Union, and American economic aid.

While there are some large-scale Soviet and American actions that have influenced Arab and Israeli violence, that influence has been limited both in terms of the countries and the types of violence affected. Moreover, the effects are not always in one direction, that is, either intensifying or decreasing the violence. This might reflect super power ambiguity about the value of maintaining some Arab-Israeli conflict. The Arab-Israeli conflict thus appears to have a great deal of autonomy, which was also demonstrated by the action and reaction patterns described previously. Whether or not they were supplied by the superpowers with military assistance or even economic assistance and trade, the Arabs and Israelis probably would have engaged in violence with whatever means were available, including assistance from countries other than the superpowers. However, the effects that have been noted should not be overlooked, especially by policy-makers who might be in a position to use economic or military aid in addition to diplomatic pressure and persuasion to mitigate at least some aspects of this very dangerous conflict.

THE BALANCE OF MILITARY POWER

If the superpowers have any influence over Arab and Israeli violence (and we have seen that in some limited respects they do), that influence might be exerted on the military balance in the Middle East. Thus, we now turn our attention to the ways in which differences in military capability might affect Arab and Israeli violence.

Many people, including those involved in the Arab-Israeli conflict and President Nixon, have stated that an important determinant of the violent actions of Israel and the Arab countries is the balance of power—that is, the difference in military capabilities between Israel and the Arab states. Each side attempts to achieve superior military power in order to deter external attacks, to increase the prospects for survival in the face of military threat, to gain prestige, and to aid in achieving other objectives, including defensive and offensive military operations. A nation's security is potentially threatened by the military power of its enemy. In the Middle East we would expect a gap in military capabilities to put stress on the leaders to decrease the gap or, in more traditional terms, to return the balance of power. Traditional "balance of power" theory hypothesizes that if one side or the other tries to change the status quo, that is, the current balance of power, this attempt will set off a series of reactions in which each nation tries to re-establish the status quo. This behavior can be described theoretically by balance theory.

Violent actions themselves are a way for a country to decrease the difference in military capabilities between itself and its enemy. An attack on the enemy's strategic installations or bases will in fact decrease the enemy's capabilities and thereby increase its own relative position. There is, of course, an alternative way of trying to close the gap: obtaining military capabilities from external sources.

As an abstract concept "balance of power" can refer to a whole range of factors that deal with strategic and military considerations, all of which point to the relative potential for victory if an all-out war occurs, or to the potential for achieving objectives. Many of the things that might be included in the balance of power are intangible: quality of leadership, morale of fighting men, motivation of leaders. A statistical analysis using the balance of power must use some readily available quantitative indicators to express the difference in military capabilities.

In this study the military balance of power will be measured by the difference in military expenditures between Israel and each of the Arab countries, or Israel and all the Arab countries. These expenditures are measured in constant 1960 dollars and corrected for exchange rates; where applicable, the amount of military aid received is included. Thus, a country's military capability is indicated by that country's own military expenditures plus military assistance received during a given year.

The military capabilities of a country are actually a function of past, as well as current, expenditures. Weapons bought one or two years before remain usable. Thus, it is possible to measure the military balance as the difference in the expenditures and aid of the past two years in addition to the current year. This indicator will be tested to see if it yields results different from those in which expenditures and aid received during the current year only are considered.

The relationship between a country's military expenditures and its violent acts could be considered on the basis of the following simple hypothesis: the greater the proportion of total governmental expenditures for military expenses, the greater the amount of violence it will initiate and engage in. This simple hypothesis is not supported by the data, except in just one instance: the greater the proportion of total governmental expenditures that Egypt spends on military capabilities, the greater the number of attacks on installations that it initiates (R = 0.48, a = −1.38, b = 15.74, SE = 6.77). One might explain this relationship by maintaining that the greater proportion of military expenditures allowed Egypt to buy the military equipment necessary to initiate these attacks. However, the overwhelming evidence is against this hypothesis, for there seems to be no systematic relationship between military expenditures as a proportion of total governmental expenditures and the violent actions of any of the other countries, or even of the other violent actions of Egypt.

Since the proportion of total governmental expenditures for military spending does not determine the kinds of violent actions that the Middle Eastern countries engage in, one might hypothesize that the leaders of these countries are primarily concerned with the *difference* in military capabilities between themselves and their enemy. Differences in military capabilities can be measured as differences in military expenditures alone, or differences in expenditure plus aid. It is unlikely that Israeli or Arab leaders know the actual amount of military spending or aid of a country other than their own during the same year. However, expenditures and aid do pay for troops, training, and weapons. We would expect military intelligence to be able to supply information about the enemy's troops and weapons in any given year. The cost of obtaining and maintaining a given number of troops or a given weapons sytem can be determined; thus, a country's weapons and troops are indirectly indicated by that country's military expenditures and aid. Military capabilities will here be indicated (1) by expenditures plus aid for the current year, and (2) for a three-year period (the current and two past years). We will compare the difference in those relationships.

Since no data on Saudi Arabia's military expenditures were available, its violent actions will not be analyzed in this section. Some countries received military aid and some did not; the test of the balance of military capabilities model will be made only when relevant data are available for a pair of countries.

Egyptian violent actions are unrelated to the difference between Israeli and Egyptian military expenditures plus military aid received during one year (Table 13). But the greater Egyptian military superiority in expenditures and aid, the more encounters between government forces Israel initiated.

When Israeli and Egyptian military capabilities are measured for a three year period, one finds that the greater Egypt's superiority, the more Israel initiated encounters between government forces mobilizations and alerts. A comparison of the strength of the relationships using figures for a single year and for a three year period reveals that a single year's data give essentially the same results. Since the best measure of a concept is the simplest one that gives adequate results, these findings argue for measuring the difference in capability for one year's expenditures and aid. Hence we do not print the three-year results.

Considering the difference in just military expenditures within the same year, one finds that the greater Israel's superiority, the more Syria initiates encounters between government forces. No relationship emerges, however, for Israeli acts. Differences in military capability seem to have no systematic effect on violent actions between Israel and Jordan, Iraq, or Lebanon, so none of these results are recorded in Table 13.

Table 13. Military Balance: Differences in Military Expenditures and Aid Received

		GF	GUER	AC	AI	M&A
EGYPTIAN ACTS						
Egyptian military expenditures + military aid — Israeli military expenditures + military aid (one year)		No "significant" relationships				
ISRAELI ACTS						
Egyptian military expenditures + military aid — Israeli military expenditures + military aid (one year)	R	0.64				
	a	−7.98				
	b	0.06				
	SE	0.02				
DIFFERENCES IN MILITARY EXPENDITURES						
SYRIAN ACTS						
Syrian military expenditures — Israeli military expenditures (one year)	R	0.66				
	a	−4.52				
	b	−0.04				
	SE	0.01				

The difference in the level of military expenditures, or expenditures and aid, seems to determine some of the violent actions of Israel and Syria, but not of Egypt, Lebanon, Jordan, or Iraq. Because of the limited predictive and explanatory power of this model, we shall examine other balance of power models.

ANTICIPATED MILITARY BALANCE MODELS

An alternative to the above model is one that assumes that Middle Eastern leaders will act violently in response not only to differences in levels, but also to the rates at which these levels of military expenditures and aid are being used. One way leaders might estimate the future balance is to add to current military expenditures, or military expenditures and aid, the most recent annual increments to that level. Thus, a country superior in military capabilities might be more concerned about how rapidly the level of its enemy was approaching its own than about what those levels were. Moreover, the country inferior in military capability might determine its violent actions by the rate at which it was catching up with its enemy.

Table 14. Anticipated Military Balance and Violent Acts

		GF	GUER	AC	AI	M&A
		EGYPTIAN ACTS				
Egyptian military	R					0.54
expenditures and aid	a					−0.58
levels and increments	b					0.006
— Israeli military	SE					0.002
expenditures and aid						
levels and increments						
		SYRIAN ACTS				
Israeli military	R	0.67				
expenditure levels	a	4.69				
and increments —	b	0.03				
Syrian military	SE	0.007				
expenditure levels						
and increments						

Of all the possible relationships between Egypt and Israel only one seemed significant: measuring by levels plus yearly increments in both expenditures and aid, the more superior Egypt is, the more mobilizations and alerts in which it engages. The more superior Israel is in military expenditures plus change in expenditures, the more encounters between government forces Syria initiates. Israeli violence seems to be independent of this anticipated military superiority.

There appears to be no systematic relationship between differences in the anticipated military capabilities of Israel and Jordan, Iraq, or Lebanon. Because of the limited predictive and explanatory power of this model, still other models will be proposed.

Another model proposes that not the sum of military levels plus changes in levels, but the differences in the rates of change determine violent behavior. Here, the assumption is that leaders would react to sudden increases in enemy capabilities relative to the rate of increase of their own countries, not to the difference in the actual level. The difference between Israel and Egypt in the rates of military expenditures and military aid received does not affect encounters between government forces. But the difference in rates of increase in military expenditures between Israel and Syria has an effect on Syrian though not on Israeli violent actions. The more superior Israel is the more encounters between government forces Syria initiates (R = 0.46; a = 15.88; b = 0.06; SE = 0.03). The difference in rates of growth appears to have no systematic effect on violence between Israel and Jordan, Iraq, or Lebanon.

Of the many possibilities only a very few strong statistical relationships are apparent between military capabilities and the balance of military capabilities (as measured in several different ways) and Arab and Israeli violence. The strong associations include the proportion of total governmental expenditures Egypt spends for military purposes and Egyptian attacks on Israeli installations; anticipated Egyptian superiority and increased Egyptian mobilizations and alerts; Israeli superiority in terms of levels and rates of military expenditures and increased Syrian-initiated encounters between its governmental forces and Israel. Egyptian superiority increases Israeli-initiated encounters between government forces. No other strong associations are found between balance of military capabilities and other acts of violence initiated by Egypt or Syria. All the violence initiated by Jordan and Iraq seems independent of the balance of military capabilities. Thus, in general, the balance of military power does not in any systematic way affect the initiation of violence between Arabs and Israelis.

GETTING IT
ALL TOGETHER

Previous sections have demonstrated the separate effects of three factors determining Arab and Israeli violence: (1) the violent actions of the antagonistic parties, (2) Soviet and American aid and trade, and (3) the military balance of power. While bivariate regression analysis has indicated which of these variables are important factors determining Arab and Israeli violence, it makes the assumption that the independent variable in a bivariate regression equation is the only factor determining a particular violent action. We know, however, that all these factors are operating at the same time. Therefore, it is important to try to discern which of the separate factors remain significant when we consider all the important factors together and control for the effect of each. Multiple regression analysis is a method that can be used for this. In this section, where two or more independent variables were found significant in the bivariate regressions, they will be included in a multiple regression to determine which remain significant while controlling for the effect of the others. Where two or more independent variables are highly intercorrelated, the variable least plausible from a theoretical and substantive standpoint will be excluded so that the multiple regression results will not be confused by multicollinearity. The results are given in Table 15.[3]

The bivariate regression analyses have shown that independent variables affecting Israeli-initiated encounters between government forces include: (1)

3. In the following discussion the multiple regression results are shown in Table 15 only when two or more independent variables remained significant (t ratio ≥ 2.1) in the multiple regression. Standard errors are given in parentheses beneath the b coefficients. The relevant bivariate regression equations that are significant can be seen in the earlier part of the text.

Table 15. Multiple Regression Models of Israeli and Arab Violence

Israeli M&A = 1.5 + 1.0 [a] Imports from Soviet Union + 0.9 [a] Egyptian M&A
                        (0.4)   (0.3)
        R = 0.67

Egyptian A.I. = −1.6 + 0.35 [a] Israeli A.I. + 10.9 [a] Egyptian $\dfrac{\text{Military Exp.}}{\text{Total Exp.}}$
                           (0.08)   (4.8)
        R = 0.81

a. t-ratio $>$ 2.1.

Egyptian-initiated encounters between government forces, (2) Jordanian-initiated encounters between government forces, (3) U.S. economic aid to Israel, (4) and the difference in military expenditures and aid between Egypt and Israel.

In the multiple regression equation including U.S. economic aid to Israel and Egyptian-initiated encounters between government forces, the multiple correlation coefficient is 0.82. But the only significant variable is Egyptian-initiated encounters between government forces. Thus, the action-reaction cycle of hostility emerges as the most plausible explanation of this type of violent action of Israel.

Exports to Israel from the Soviet Union and Egyptian mobilizations and alerts were found in the bivariate analyses to influence Israeli mobilizations and alerts. The multiple regression analysis also shows both these factors to be significant (Table 15). The previous bivariate analysis showed that Israeli attacks on Egyptian installations, Israeli encounters with Jordanian guerrillas, and Israeli attacks on Jordanian civilians were affected only by similar Egyptian or Jordanian actions respectively. Thus in every instance the hostility cycle of action and reaction appears to offer the best explanation of Israeli-violence.

With one exception, the independent variables found to affect Egyptian encounters between government forces are intercorrelated. However, Israeli-initiated encounters between government forces still appear to be the most important factor determining the same type of Egyptian action, especially when one compares the regression coefficients of the independent variables.

Israeli-initiated encounters between government forces was the only significant factor increasing Egyptian encounters between guerrillas and government forces.

When controlling for the variables previously found to affect Egyptian attacks on civilians, Israeli attacks on installations appear to be the most important factor increasing these Egyptian attacks. Israeli-initiated encounters between government forces, Israeli attacks on civilians, and the amount of special imports by the Egyptians from the Soviet Union do not remain significant determinants. The hostility pattern between Israel and Egypt is in this case not an eye-for-an-eye, but rather an eye-for-a-tooth.

Both similar Israeli attacks and the proportion of total government expenditures which Egypt spends for military purposes remain significant factors in increasing Egyptian attacks on installations. Egypt apparently engages in this type of strategic attack more frequently when it is spending relatively more for military purposes, perhaps during periods when it feels more threatened by its enemy and is preparing for all-out war (see Table 15).

Israeli-initiated encounters between government forces and Israeli mobilizations and alerts were the two variables found to be important in determining Egyptian mobilizations and alerts. Neither factor appears significant when controlling for the other. Since the multiple correlation coefficient is only moderately high (r^2 = .29), other, unspecified factors are apparently also contributing to Egyptian mobilizations and alerts. One such variable, previously found significant in a bivariate regression, is the military balance between Israel and Egypt including levels and changes in levels of military expenditures and aid. This variable is highly intercorrelated with the other two independent variables reported here; even when added to a multiple regression, the squared multiple correlation coefficient is increased only very slightly, to .30. Again it is the hostility cycle of actions and reactions that seems best to explain Egyptian violence.

In the bivariate relationships, Israeli-initiated encounters between government forces, attacks on civilians, and mobilizations and alerts were strongly related to encounters with Jordanian government forces. Israeli mobilizations and alerts and attacks on civilians are correlated with the other independent variables; and because these variables are less closely related to Jordanian government encounters, and because they are less plausible causes of Jordanian-initiated encounters, they have been eliminated from the multiple regression. This elimination caused no decrease in the multiple correlation coefficient. Israeli-initiated encounters between government forces are the most important cause of similar Jordanian attacks.

In the bivariate examination, Israeli encounters between guerrillas and government forces were found to be the most important factor determining the same type of Jordanian action. In the bivariate relations, Israeli attacks on civilians were found to be the best predictor of Jordanian attacks on civilians. The "eye-for-an-eye" hostility cycle seems also to be the dominant pattern of violence between Jordan and Israel.

There were no multiple significant determinants of Iraqi, Lebanese, or Saudi Arabian violence to test.

In the bivariate relationships, Syrian-initiated encounters between government forces were strongly affected by: (1) Israeli-initiated encounters between government forces; (2) special imports from the Soviet Union in the previous year; and (3) the balance of military power as measured by the difference in the levels and rates of military expenditures. When these independent variables were entered into a multiple regression, the multiple correlation coefficient was .73. When controlling for all independent variables, no single variable remained a significant factor, however.

Syrian-initiated encounters between guerrillas and government forces were found to be affected only by Israeli mobilizations and alerts. Only imports from the Soviet Union were related to Syrian attacks on installations. Israeli mobilizations and alerts remain a significant factor affecting Syrian mobilizations and alerts. Imports from the Soviet Union do not.

SUMMARY AND CONCLUSIONS

The effects of three different types of variables on Arab and Israeli violence have been analyzed; (1) the violent actions of the enemy; (2) Soviet and American military and economic aid and trade; and (3) the military balance between Israel and each Arab country. Three general conclusions can be made.

First, "The violent actions of Israel and each Arab country can best be explained by the violent actions of that country's enemy." The violent behavior of the enemy appears to be significant far more often than is either the military balance or Soviet and American inputs. Thus, a major inference from the empirical findings is that Arab-Israeli violence stems primarily from the unresolved conflict issues: the existence of the state of Israel and the fate of the Palestinian Arabs. This inference is supported by the finding of a large number of action and reaction patterns of violence between Israel and all the Arab countries, but particularly between Israel and Egypt, and Israel and Jordan.

A second major conclusion is that "Arab and Israeli violence is generally independent of the weapons balance between Israelis and Arabs."[4] Thus, the leaders of the Middle East countries may be chasing a phantom in their attempts to achieve security from external violence by trying to acquire superior military power. Military superiority is as likely to provoke the enemy to attack as to deter that country from attacking. Nor does being militarily inferior mean that one will engage in less rather than more violence. These findings have important implications for the Middle East countries, as well as for the superpowers who supply them with arms. Maintaining a military balance of power does not necessarily decrease violence in the Middle East.

A third conclusion is that "the United States and the Soviet Union have had but limited influence on the "normal" Arab-Israeli violence that has characterized most of the past 23 years." Multiple regression analyses have shown only a few American and Soviet actions to have any strong relationship to Arab and Israeli violence; and the significant relationships that do occur are as likely to be due to the effects of third factors as to direct influence. For example, Egyptian-initiated encounters between its government forces and those of Israel have tended to increase as American exports to Egypt have decreased. This finding is possible evidence that the United States had a constraining influence

4. Note the mixed and sometimes conflicting results also in the Singer and Rummel chapters in this volume.

on Egypt when its trade contacts with Egypt were stronger and Egypt was more dependent upon American exports, such as wheat. Another example is Syrian attacks on installations, which have increased as Soviet exports to Syria have increased. With closer ties to and support from the Soviets, the Syrians have become more belligerent. However, it is possible that the Soviets could use their ties to constrain Syrian violence, as they reportedly did in influencing the Syrians to withdraw their tanks from Jordan during the 1970 clashes between Jordanians and Palestinians.

The superpowers may—by their military and economic assistance as well as their diplomatic effects—affect the degree of military preparedness of the parties to the Middle Eastern conflict and the types of weapons used by them. In this most basic sense they can make violence possible. From time to time they may even exercise a restraining influence upon the level of violence, perhaps especially in periods of crisis. However, this deeply rooted, emotionally based conflict, with its cycle of violent actions and reactions, is generated and maintained by conditions and antagonisms now largely beyond the control of the superpowers. If American and Soviet leaders are unaware of the actual scope and limitations of their influence, they face the danger of being drawn unwittingly into confrontation with each other in support of their clients.

APPENDIX:
DATA SOURCES

Military Expenditures: Stockholm International Peace Research Institute, *SIPRI Yearbook of World Armaments and Disarmament, 1968/69* (New York: Humanities Press, 1970). Expenditures expressed in millions of American dollars at 1960 prices and 1960 exchange-rates.

U.S. Economic Aid: U.S. House of Representatives Foreign Affairs Committee, U.S. Overseas Loans and Grants, 1966. U.S. House of Representatives Appropriations Committee, 1964-1968.

U.S. Military Aid: U.S. House of Representatives Appropriations Committee, Overseas Loans and Grants, 1964. Approximate value of equipment and training provided.

U.S. Public Law 480 Aid: U. S. House of Representatives Appropriations Committee, U.S. Overseas Loans and Grants, 1964.

Soviet Economic Loans to Egypt (UAR): U.S. Congress Joint Economic Hearings. Muller, Jurt, *The Foreign Aid Programs of the Soviet Bloc and Communist China.* (New York: Walker, 1967)

Special Imports from the United States: Department of Economic and Social Affairs, Statistical Office of the United Nations, *Yearbook of International Trade Statistics* (New York: United Nations). "Special imports" are the combined total of imports directly for domestic consumption (including transformation and repair) and withdrawals from bonded warehouses or free zones for domestic consumption.

Special Imports from the USSR: Department of Economic and Social Affairs, Statistical Office of the United Nations, *Yearbook of International Trade Statistics* (New York: United Nations).

STEVEN ROSEN

6. War Power and the Willingness to Suffer

ABSTRACT

Two types of theories of war power are identified, one emphasizing the importance of strength in producing victory, the other emphasizing the willingness to suffer. Reliance on force of arms is characteristic of conventional forces, such as those of the United States, while reliance on superior cost-tolerance is typical of guerrilla forces such as the Viet Cong. This paper tests the relative potency of strength and cost-tolerance as predictors of victory in a body of 40 historical international wars. It is found that cost-tolerance can be traded off against strength, but that wealth and the strength it produces resulted in victory in 80 percent of the cases. Superior cost-tolerance is no more a guarantee of victory than is strength, and probably less so. ∎

DAMAGE AND COST-TOLERANCE

The United States entered the war in Indochina with what now seem very optimistic assumptions about its ability to defeat the Communists quickly and at a low cost to itself. The United States, the conventional reasoning went, is after all the most powerful nation in the history of mankind, and a decisive application of its might against a fifth-rate power like North Vietnam should quickly convince them of the futility of struggle. Even with Russian and Chinese aid they could not hope to match American forces.

The North Vietnamese and the Viet Cong perhaps entered the American phase of the struggle equally confident. They did not doubt the manifest physical superiority of the United States, but rather took it for granted. The very essence of the doctrine of guerrilla struggle is that it is a form of struggle

Author's Note: I wish to thank the following people for comments on parts of this work: Michael O'Leary, Julian Friedman, Robert Gregg, and William Coplin of Syracuse University; Steven Brams, NYU; and Richard Cottam, John Tyler, Robert S. Walters, Douglas White, Ray Owen, Robert Donaldson, and Michael Margolis of the University of Pittsburgh.

167

designed to combat a materially stronger opponent; the basic idea is that the regime has the guns, but the guerrillas have the hearts of the people. The guerrilla's superiority is not in his ability to harm, but in his greater willingness to be harmed Ho Chi Minh formulated this in a classic way with his familar prediction that "In the end, the Americans will have killed ten of us for every American soldier who died, but it is they who will tire first " This was the model of Algeria, where the vastly superior French were eventually exhausted by the cost-tolerance of the Algerians. The Algerians suffered in a ratio of perhaps 10 to 1, but valued their goal much more deeply than the French did theirs. In a sense, the Communist victory at Dienbienphu was also of this type. It did not really destroy the French forces as much as it demonstrated to France that victory could not be obtained at a price commensurate with the value of Indochina to France.

So while the strategic theory of the United States was derived from a model of war power based on the ability to harm, the strategic theory of the guerrilla is based on the willingness to suffer. Arab guerrillas recognize the critical place of cost-tolerance in war power by calling themselves "fedayeen"—the sacrificers. An Irish revolutionist said, "It is a question which can last longer, the whip or the back." Castro's victory in Cuba, the Communist victory in China, and perhaps even the revolutionists' victory in the American colonies were won by sheer persistence in the face of overwhelming odds. In each case, a highly committed party exhausted a materially stronger opponent by making the costs of victory exceed the privileged party's willingness to suffer.

So while the United States expected victory on the model of the World Wars or Greece or Malaya, where superior force prevailed, the Communists expected victory on the model of Algeria or Dienbienphu, where the willingness to suffer gave an edge to the weaker party. It appears at the time of this writing that the confident expectations of victory by both sides were wrong. The Communists have demonstrated an unexpected and incredible willingness to suffer, but the United States has arrayed against them destructive power beyond anything previously imagined in so small a country.

The history of the War from 1965 thorugh 1971 may be summarized as the progressive disappointment of each side in the hope that its original model would prevail, but the defeat of neither side. The two have gained respect for each other, the Communists for the awesome wealth and technology of the American war machine, the Americans for the tenaciousness of the Communists' struggle. In a sense, the war power model of each side is being modified to give some effect to the theory of the other. In a very gross way, we can represent the synthesis of their theories as follows: [1]

1. This unusual double ratio is used rather than the identity:

$$\frac{\text{(Cost-tolerance of A)}}{\text{(Cost-tolerance of B)}} \qquad \frac{\text{(Strength of A)}}{\text{(Strength of B)}}$$

because the strength of A and the cost-tolerance of B are both measured in units of harm to

$$\text{Power ratio} = \frac{\text{Party A}}{\text{Party B}} = \frac{\text{Cost-tolerance of A/Strength of B}}{\text{Cost-tolerance of B/Strength of A}}$$

The ratio of power between A and B consists of A's ability to tolerate the costs that B imposes, against B's ability to tolerate the costs that A imposes. There is a trade-off: one may compensate for an opponent's strength, his ability to harm, by a greater willingness to be harmed. The formal expression above highlights the fact that greater cost-tolerance is no more a guarantee of victory than is greater strength. The question might be, does my willingness to suffer exceed his by more than my ability to harm is exceeded by his?

Is this a general theory of war power? Is every war a test of each side's ability to hurt against the other side's willingness to be hurt, to establish a ratio of power in proportion to which the contested values (e.g., land, degrees of control of the state) may be allocated? Is the subjective factor in war power usually as crucial as the simple theory suggests?

Testing the validity of this theory ideally would involve assembling aggregate data about a large number of wars, and testing the potency of "strength," the ability to harm, against "cost-tolerance," the willingness to be harmed, as predictors of victory and defeat. This is not fully possible for a number of reasons. Strength is itself an aggregate of many dimly understood factors. Those listed by Morgenthau (1967: 106-44) include geography, natural resources, industrial capacity, military preparedness, population, and others. Morgenthau gives none of these in terms of a single quantitative index, partly because each is again composed of a multitude of factors. Also, there is no simple formula by which we can assign an appropriate weight to each factor to develop an overall index of strength.

Cost-tolerance is even more difficult to measure as it is wholly subjective and sometimes not even an explicit or conscious property of the thinking of relevant individuals. Up to what cost in American lives should we have fought to prevent a Nazi conquest of Europe? One's cost-tolerance does have a limit, but most of the time it is not defined, and even when it is, without the opportunity to conduct interviews the researcher may not be able to discover it. I have nevertheless tried to find some available means of measuring strength and cost-tolerance to test their relative potency. Most of the rest of this paper will describe these operations and the reasoning behind them.

B (e.g., B lives lost) while the strength of B and cost-tolerance of A are measured in units of harm to A (e.g., A lives taken or lost). Consequently, the double ratio compares meaningful magnitudes while the simpler identity does not.

STRENGTH

I have chosen as an available measure of strength the wealth available to the government of a nation at war. This decision is based partly on the intuitive belief that national wealth can be shown to be the strongest correlate of a nation's destructive potential, and partly on the availability of wealth data. The subject of war power has received relatively little attention from scientific students of war behavior. Most research has been devoted to the study of the etiology of war, the search for factors associated with its outbreak. The subject of war power has been mainly the realm of the strategic studies research tradition, which has a strong "how-to" bias. There are, however, a few aggregate/empirical studies of war power, and these point to wealth as the single best gauge of strength.

One example is A.F.K. Organski's (1968: 189-220) development of an "index of national power." Organski first identifies the following as elements of national power on a deductive or inferential basis: size of territory, geographical location, natural resources, population size, age structure and growth rate, industrial development, urbanization, education, geographic and social mobility, family structure, innovation attitudes, religious beliefs, political development, diplomatic and propaganda skill, military strength, military and civilian morale, and political ideology. These are compressed through a process of intuitive factor reduction to the "three most important determinants of national power": population size, political development, and economic development. Political development is then excluded for lack of an adequate quantitative measure. Economic development is indexed by per capita Gross National Product (GNP). Multiplying this by population yields the GNP itself. Hence, Organski's initially quite elaborate scheme boils down to sorry old GNP. Organski then uses GNP as his sole index of national power.[2]

Another more elaborate study is that of F. Clifford German (1960), who develops measures of more than 20 factors (chosen on the basis of plausibility and what data is available), intuitively gives these factors mathematical weights, and thus develops an overall index as a "tentative evaluation of world power." For example, "working population" is corrected for "technical efficiency" by multiplying the working population "by 1 if the national consumption of energy is less than 0.5 ton of coal equivalent per head per year; by 2 if between 0.5 and 1.5 tons," etc. "Morale" is measured by inflating the working population of selected nations (e.g., Japan and Germany) by an increase of 1/3 to 1/2, again on an intuitive basis. For possession of nuclear weapons the entire index is doubled. The ranking of 19 countries in the late 1950's that results from use of this index is fairly plausible, but the index may have been manipulated exactly to achieve this result.

Since Organski's "index of national power" ranks the power of countries by GNP, and German ranks his "tentative evaluation of world power" by using a

2. See also Hitch and McKean (1960, ch. 1) and Russett (1965: 2-3).

much more complex list of economic factors, a rank-order correlation between the two may indicate whether it is necessary to use something more refined than crude wealth to measure the economic power of a state. The German and Organski indices result in power rankings that correlate with each other strongly (Spearman's rho = .89), though it should be emphasized that German ranked only the wealthiest and probably most powerful states, and that Organski considers his list more reliable at this end of the scale. Thus German's index tapped the same factors that are summarized by the GNP measure, or are highly correlated with it. This same result has occurred in a number of studies which have factor analyzed data on GNP along with many other size and capability indices (Rummel, 1969c; Russett, 1967a: 17-21, 41-46). The complexities of German's index do not seem. to yield results substantially different from GNP alone, and it would be preferrable not to introduce controversial assumptions of the type he suggests if nothing is gained thereby.

Recently Alcock and Newcomb (1970) have shown that GNP rankings are a good predictor of what lay subjects believe to be the relative power of states. Thirty eight Canadian subjects were asked to indicate what they believed to be the relative power rankings of groups of nations. The researchers compared these perceptions with GNP and found a .85 rank-order correlation. Also, GNP alone explained power perceptions as well as did an index based on GNP combined with national area and population measures. A measure of military expenditures had a slightly higher correlation with power perceptions than did GNP (.92). This might suggest the desirability of using military expenditures for the present study. However, we will be studying historical wars. for which such data are generally not available. Also, Newcombe and Alcock show a correlation of .89 between military expenditures and GNP, so wealth is strongly associated with the allocation of resources to war preparations. The few quantitative studies of war power, then, as well as the best non-quantitative studies (Knorr, 1970) point to GNP as the most useful simple measure of physical strength in war, though none of them has validated the GNP measure of war power by showing that it correlates with the winning of wars.

Despite the strong case to be made for GNP, we will in fact not be able to use it. The body of wars in this study begins in 1928. GNP data is a Keynesian phenomenon and is not available for most states before 1930 or later. The closest and most interesting gross economic measure is the revenue of the central government, which has been recorded by the *Statesman's Yearbook* since 1864. This is the portion of wealth that is available to the warring government itself for all purposes, including the conduct of war, so one may expect that it is both highly correlated with GNP and, perhaps, even more sensitive than GNP as a gauge of the influence of wealth on war power. For this study of 40 wars, interval comparisons were possible for the antagonists on 22 wars, ordinal comparisons ("more/less") were estimated with a high expectation of reliability for 17 others, and one case (the Russo-Turkish War of 1828) was excluded for lack of a reliable basis for estimation.

The potency of material capability in war power will hence be tested by finding the frequency with which the state with more government revenue won the war. But in doing so we must remain aware of the imperfections of this measure, not least of which are the complex ways in which the conduct of military operations far away from the center of a nation's power may diminish its capabilities (Boulding, 1962; Wohlstetter, 1968a).

COST-TOLERANCE

The second component of war power in our theory is cost-tolerance. Very little is known about the actual setting of cost-limits for goals by actors, despite the central nature of this question to utility theory. Much more research has been devoted to the identification of goals than to the question, "Up to what cost do you favor this goal?" Even for contemporary problems, there are few opinion surveys from which one might derive cost-tolerance estimates; for historical cases, the problem is much worse. An alternative might be to make inferences from existing records of opinion and values, i.e., content analysis. But content analysis in this field is extremely hazardous in that cost-limits asserted by parties engaged in struggle may be deliberately inflated as a bargaining tactic or to bolster one's own moral. It is easy and useful to assert that one will fight to the last breath, but parties seldom fulfill such promises.

Also, as noted earlier, actors may be only dimly aware of their own limits. In a recent study reported elsewhere (Rosen, 1971) I administered a survey instrument seeking cost-tolerance statements from 600 student subjects who were asked to express cost-limits in human lives for a number of foreign policy goals. One finding was a great resistance to setting life-prices; 1 in 6 of my respondents appended an unsolicited comment objecting to the idea of cost-limits in human lives. As Warner Schilling (1965: 389) suggested, "The objects for which statesmen contend are not easily weighed in human lives." Alden Voth (1967: 438) also found this resistance in a study of Vietnam opinion. In my study the cost-tolerance limits that were given were very much lower than those professed by American policy-makers. In a scenario featuring a Communist attempt to seize West Berlin, for example, the average maximum number of American lives that the respondents would give to stop the Soviets was under 5000. Contrast this with Herman Kahn's (1960: 29-30) estimate that Americans would give 1/3 of their population—70 million—or with contemporary American strategic assumptions that deterrence of the Soviet Union requires an "assured destruction capability" of 1/5 to 1/4 of the Soviet population and 1/2 to 2/3 of Soviet industry (Stillman, 1970). One discovers when he constructs a survey instrument of this type how complex questions become when even the simplest cost considerations are introduced. In any event, my study did not result in plausible expressions of the actual willingness to suffer. My subjects had fairly clear priorities in their foreign policy goals, but rather unclear cost-tolerance limits for these goals.

We do not, then, have a good way of gauging the cost-tolerance attitudes of parties in wars of the past. We do, however, know the cost that they actually did suffer, at least in terms of human lives. We may test our hypothesis about the importance of cost-tolerance by comparing the losses of the winner and the loser. If there is a very strong correlation between losing fewer lives and winning, then we may infer that cost-tolerance is not a major factor since the party that inflicted greater harm usually won. If on the other hand there is not a strong tendency for the party losing fewer lives to win, then the hypothesis is at least not disconfirmed. We cannot infer that it is confirmed because we are not really measuring cost-tolerance directly. One problem is that the war may have ended at the point where it is clear to the loser that he will suffer greatly in the future, his defenses having been penetrated, but he has not suffered greatly yet. If the amount of suffering that actually occurred determined the outcome, then the willingness to suffer could not have been very important. On the other hand, if the amount of suffering did not predict the outcome very well, the reason may be the endurance factor, but it may also be expectations about future suffering or another unmeasured factor.

Another problem is our measure of suffering. Life costs are not the only cost in war. There are also financial costs, the loss of common interests with the opponent, the diversion of resources from other goals to war, alliance costs, sometimes social dissolution at home (e.g., Vietnam), etc. In Algeria the main cost to France was probably political disintegration rather than the loss of life; in Angola, Mozambique, and Portuguese Guinea, the main costs to Portugal are probably inflation and economic retardation; in Vietnam some have argued that the main costs to the United States are the continued decay of American cities and the disillusionment of young people. Again, a strong correlation between loss of life and losing the war will disconfirm the hypothesis about the importance of cost-tolerance, but a lack of relation between the two may be due to the exogenous factor of other cost items rather than the cost-tolerance factor.

It might also be argued that absolute losses of life are less important than losses relative to population size. The significance of a cost relates partly to the size of the pool of resources from which it is drawn; this is the theory behind the graduated income tax. The argument on the other side is also compelling. Human lives are valued absolutely for many purposes. Even while tolerating the loss of huge numbers of lives in highway slaughter and cigarette-induced cancer, wide attention may focus on the fate of a single individual trapped in a mine. Systems which encourage thinking in terms of "tolerable" losses of life are despised by the layman, though in an unconscious way all social systems do exactly this. This factor of the absolute value of life makes it plausible that a nation of 200 million may experience the loss of 500 men quite as painfully as would a mini-state with a population in the tens of thousands.

We will try both measures of life loss, absolute and relative to population. But with all the caveats listed above, the sole aspect of cost-tolerance in this study will be lives actually lost in war. The data used include only battle deaths of military personnel; knowledge of civilian deaths would be important but the data are unreliable.

THE
WARS

The principle of cost-tolerance, as formulated in other language by guerrilla theorists, was intended originally as a theory of "internal" war (including colonial independence struggles). Here the control of populations is a central factor, so a willingness to suffer in resistance is an obvious asset. We are attempting to generalize the theory of cost-tolerance to all wars, civil and international, including those where population control is not a central factor. I have chosen to test the theory in a body of "international" wars, partly because these are the ones where its applicability is intuitively less clear, and partly because data are more readily obtainable for discrete national units than for struggles in which one party is not a state but a movement.

The body of cases is drawn fron Singer and Small's (1972) standard list of all international wars from 1815 to 1945, which is a total of 41 wars according to their definitions of "international" and "war." (One of these, the War of Spanish Succession, is excluded from the present study for lack of data, so we will have a total of 40.) For each of the 40 wars it was necessary to identify a "winner" and a "loser." Obviously these designations are crude. What is winning? If winning consists of accomplishing the general political objectives of the party, then Japan may be said to have won World War II in that many of her "Co-Prosperity Sphere" goals in that war have been realized since 1945. For present purposes, however, we are interested in the realization of goals directly through the application of war power. In other words, which of the parties at the time of the termination of the war came closer to accomplishing its goals in the war (i.e., achieving the distribution of the contested values that it sought)?

Another methodological problem is how to count coalitions. Who are the warring parties? For present purposes coalitions are limited to partners actively participating in the dispute by the direct application of military power. What if one member of the coalition is defeated while the other members fight on to a successful conclusion? For example, France was defeated in World War II, but her allies fought on to win. Nonetheless, we will adopt the convention of ascribing the gross coalition outcome to each of its members—French population, wealth, etc. will be taken as part of the winning Allied coalition. This assignment does not materially affect the statistical results to be reported, as the latter are exclusively concerned with ordinal, more/less comparisons between winning and losing coalitions, and in every controversial case herein the magnitude of the differentials between winners and losers is such that even wholesale reassignment of dubious cases to the opposite column would not change the ordinal comparison.

THE
FINDINGS

First, was there a very strong tendency for the party that suffered least in absolute terms to win the war? The answer is somewhat surprising: in only slightly more than half the cases (55 percent; 22 of 40) was the winner the party that suffered less in absolute life loss. In almost half the cases (45 percent; 18 of 40) the winner lost more lives in battle than the loser! (See Figure 1 and Table 1.) It definitely is not the case that the winner is usually the party who kills more of the enemy. Perhaps this finding would be even stronger if we looked at internal wars where the cost-tolerance factor is clearer.

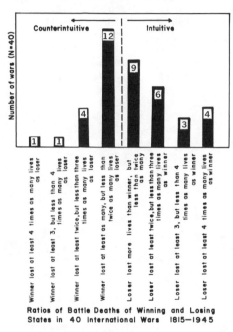

Ratios of Battle Deaths of Winning and Losing States in 40 International Wars 1815–1945

Figure 1.

We will turn to losses relative to population in a moment, but first it might be argued that while absolute losses are not a good predictor of victory in all wars, they are crucial in very large wars in which total societies are pitted against each other. I have tested this by correlating the size of wars against a ranking based on the winners losses as a percentage of the loser's losses (see Table 1, columns 2 and 3). The rank-order correlation is only .02. In other words, it definitely is not the case that absolute loss levels are more important in large wars than in small ones. The lack of relation between battle loss magnitudes and winning and losing is true throughout the size range of the sample.

Turning to battle losses relative to population, we see in Table 1 that there is a stronger relationship between relative suffering and victory and defeat. 30 of

Table 1. Does the Party Which Suffers Least Win the War?

War and date begun	Size of War (Total Battle Deaths 000)	Who lost more lives in Battle? (Winner/ Loser)	Who had more population? (Winner/ Loser)	Who lost more % of population in Battle? (Winner/ Loser)	Who had more Revenue?
(1)	(2)	(3)	(4)	(5)	(6)
World War II, 1939	15443.6	210.8%	470.1%	44.8%	Winner
World War I, 1914	8557.8	156.2	352.9	44.2	Winner
Sino-Japan, 1937	1000.0	33.3	15.1	220.2	Winner
Russo-Turk, 1877	285.0	72.7	304.2	23.9	Winner
Crimean, 1853	264.2	164.2	166.4	98.2	Winner
Franco-Prus, 1870	187.5	33.9	85.2	39.7	Loser
Russo-Japan, 1904	130.0	188.9	36.2	532.3	Loser
Chaco, 1928	130.0	62.5	39.5	157.8	Loser
Russo-Turk, 1828	130.0	62.5	182.9	34.0	—
Russo-Finn, 1939	90.0	125.0	4662.6	2.6	Winner
First Balkan, 1912	82.0	173.3	39.7	439.2	Loser
Second Balkan, 1913	60.5	236.1	832.2	28.2	Winner
Sino-Japan, 1931	60.0	20.0	14.6	136.3	Winner
Greco-Turk, 1919	50.0	66.7	441.2	15.1	Winner
Austro-Prus, 1866	36.1	63.3	148.0	41.7	Winner
Italian, 1859	22.5	80.0	167.4	45.7	Winner
Mexican, 1862 (Fr.)	20.0	150.0	21.5	714.2	Loser
Italo-Turk, 1911	20.0	42.9	145.5	29.3	Winner
Italo-Ethiop, 1935	20.0	25.0	413.9	5.6	Winner
Mexican, 1846 (USA)	17.0	183.3	261.0	70.1	Winner
Sino-Japanese, 1894	15.0	50.0	10.4	600.0	Winner
Pacific, 1879	14.0	27.3	46.2	58.6	Loser
Moroccan, 1859	10.0	66.7	577.3	11.4	Winner
Spanish Amer, 1898	10.0	100.0	398.1	22.2	Winner
Moroccan, 1909	10.0	25.0	394.2	6.2	Winner
Austro-Sardin, 1848	9.0	164.7	786.7	20.5	Winner
Danish, 1848	6.0	71.4	710.0	9.7	Winner
Schleswig-Holst, 1864	4.5	50.0	2102.4	1.7	Winner
Roman, 1849	2.2	2100.0	3198.4	50.0	Winner
Persian, 1856	2.0	33.3	427.2	5.8	Winner
Greco-Turkish, 1897	2.0	233.3	1504.4	12.5	Winner
Boxer Uprising, 1900	2.0	300.0	108.7	300.0	Winner
La Plata, 1851	1.3	160.0	16.0	1100.0	Winner
Roman, 1860	1.0	42.9	700.6	4.5	Winner
Sicilian, 1860	1.0	150.0	951.1	11.7	Winner
Colombian, 1863	1.0	42.9	228.0	18.8	Winner
Spanish, 1865	1.0	233.3	30.3	1400.0	Loser
Central Amer, 1885	1.0	25.0	45.9	55.1	Loser
Central Amer, 1906	1.0	66.7	115.7	56.7	Winner
Central Amer, 1907	1.0	150.0	269.3	56.0	Winner

Columns (2) and (3), Spearman's rho = .018.
Sources: Battle death data from Singer and Small (1972). Government revenue sources available on request from the author.

the 40 wars (75 percent) were won by the party which lost a smaller percentage of its population. Whereas absolute losses of life compared to those of the opponent was a poor predictor of success, percentage population loss is a fairly strong correlate of winning.

However, an analysis of these 30 cases shows that most of the effect indicated was not produced by the loss rate, but rather by mere population size; Table 2 breaks down the 30 cases of parties who won by losing a smaller percentage of their populations. This breakdown shows that population size explained 90

Table 2.

| | | LOST MORE LIVES | |
		Winner	Loser
Had More Population	Winner	12	15
	Loser	0	3

percent (27 of 30) of the cases in which the victor was the party with a smaller population loss rate. The relative magnitude of losses explained only 60 percent (18 of 30) of the cases. Putting it another way, if a victorious party lost a smaller percentage of its population than did the loser, chances were very good that it had a larger population, but only a little better than even that it lost fewer men. Overall, 70 percent (28 of 40) of the wars were won by the party with a larger population. This also shows the greater potency of population size compared to the loss rate.

To summarize, it is not the case that the winner is the party who suffers less. Often the winner suffers more than the loser in terms of battle deaths. It is possible that this paradox is explained by the cost-tolerance factor.

What about our measure of wealth as an index of strength, the ability to harm? How great was the tendency for the wealthier or stronger party to win? If strength explains most of the variation in winning and losing, then the factor of cost-tolerance cannot be very important.

Our principal finding is that 70 percent (31 of 39) of the wars were won by the wealthier party. There is an impressively strong relationship between wealth and victory. Only about 1 war in 5 was won by the party with less wealth. And Table 3 shows that there was a small tendency for wealth to be more important in large wars than small ones.

If strength predicts the outcome of 4/5 of all international wars, and is more important in large, costly wars than in small ones, then there is only a small range within which cost-tolerance factors could influence victory and defeat. On the other hand, the theory we suggested at the outset is consistent with this data. If we assume that the stronger party is as likely to have more cost-tolerance as he is to have less cost-tolerance, then the party with more strength should win 3 of 4 wars. (In half the cases he has more strength and more cost-tolerance; he

Table 3. Is Wealth More Important in Large Wars?

War and Date Begun	Size of War (Total Battle Deaths, 000)	Who had more Government Revenue (Winner/Loser) in Percentages
World War II, 1919	15443.6	124
World War I, 1914	8557.8	355
Sino-Japanese, 1937	1000.0	2197
Russo-Turkish, 1877	285.0	4021
Franco-Prussian, 1870	187.5	46
Russo-Japanese, 1904	130.0	55
Chaco, 1928	130.0	26
Russo-Finnish, 1939	90.0	2702
First Balkan, 1912	82.0	96
Second Balkan, 1913	60.5	1005
Sino-Japanese, 1931	60.0	1097
Greco-Turkish, 1919	50.0	120
Austro-Prussian, 1866	36.1	115
Sino-Japanese, 1894	15.0	978
Pacific, 1879	14.0	37
Spanish-American, 1898	10.0	248
Greco-Turkish, 1897	2.0	513
Boxer Rebellion, 1900	2.0	671
Spanish, 1865	1.0	16
Central American, 1885	1.0	75
Central American, 1906	1.0	343
Central American, 1907	1.0	2645

Spearman's rho = +.308.
Sources: Battle death data from Singer and Small (1972). Government revenue sources available on request from the author.

is the obvious victor in these cases. In the other half, he has more strength but the opponent has more cost-tolerance; ideally, he wins half of these.) If the cost-tolerance factor indeed accounts for the unexplained 20 percent of international wars, and a somewhat higher percentage of internal wars, the findings about strength are consistent with the theory.

We can submit the theory to one further simple test. Some researchers have asked whether there is a fixed level of population loss at which point warring states concede the issue. Such a "fixed" level of cost-tolerance would be a partial disconfirmation of our theory. The present theory argues that the willingness to suffer, like the ability to impose suffering, is highly variable, and that in fact differences between two states' willingness to suffer for their goals sometimes explain why one wins a war and the other loses.

Population losses were of particular interest to two previous researchers: Lewis Richardson and Frank Klingberg. Klingberg (1966: 147-148) concluded from a detailed study of a few cases that

"When population losses approach three or four percent, a critical period may have been reached in the nation's morale. . . . [Other factors must be considered, but] if one assumes that the given nation is losing productive power by steady attrition . . . and has lost hope of aid from other nations, then there may be a critical figure in population loss beyond which the nation will not go without surrendering."

Richardson (1960a: 299) searched for such a "critical" level of population loss. He found that "Defeat would usually occur when the less populous side had lost in dead some number between 0.05 percent and 5.0 percent of its population."

To analyze the relationship between population loss and defeat, Richardson's test was replicated for the present study, enlarging his sample of 21 defeated parties greatly to 77. Richardson's upper limit is indeed confirmed: in only 2 of the 77 cases did states suffer more than 5 percent population loss in battle before yielding (see Figure 2). On the other hand, his lower limit is definitely disconfirmed: in 23 of 77 cases the defeated party lost less than 0.05 per cent of its population in battle deaths. (An interesting implication of these figures is that war has not really functioned as a Malthusian population-limiting device in the past.)

Cost-tolerance levels do indeed seem to have had a fairly limited range of variance. But within this range there are great differences between individual cases. For example, the median of the highest decile of cases is 1000 times the median of the lowest decile (4.1 percent vs. .004 percent). (In Vietnam, we may crudely estimate that the North Vietnamese and Viet Cong have lost 800,000 men against a population base of over 20 million—about 4 percent. The U.S. has lost under 50,000 against a population of over 200 million—less than 1/4 of 1/000 of one percent. Their losses are 16,000 times ours in terms of population, but they are not more weary than we are.) Cost-tolerance does indeed vary greatly as measured by actual war losses.

This variation actually is not surprising, on careful theoretical consideration. There are a number of important elaborations of this simple theory that I have discussed elsewhere (Rosen, 1970). Both strength and cost-tolerance, particularly the latter, are subject to large changes over time, both before a war and within the span of a single war. Also, the two factors are inter-related. Strength, the ability to impose harm, is partly a function of the willingness to commit resources, which is itself a function of cost-tolerance. A sophisticated analysis thus might look at changes in government revenues as war progresses, to tap the ability of a government to persuade its people they should tighten their belts to achieve their war aims. Indeed, any full theory must recognize that cost-tolerance is a variable for different groups within a nation as well as varying over time and between nations. In large part it will depend on the alternatives to war that are available to a government and a people; rats in corners fight especially hard (Russett, 1963b, 1967b). The whole question addressed in this paper also gives rise to questions concerning counter-force vs. counter-value targeting. Even for deterrent purposes, is it likely to be more useful to direct one's strength

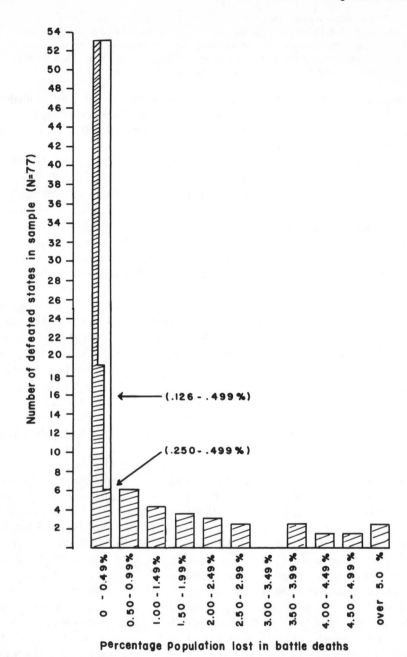

Figure 2.

against the strength of the opponent, or to impose costs against his cost-tolerance for civilian lives?

COMBINATIONS
OF FACTORS

It is obvious that war power is composed of many factors. Ideally some operational measure could be found for each factor and multivariate techniques of analysis be used to determine the weight of each and the degree to which factors covary. In this way factors might be combined to produce a war power index explaining a very large portion of the variance in winning and losing. This small study is concerned with only a few of the relevant variables, and the number of cases is much too small to employ high-powered multivariate techniques. It is possible, however, to examine a few combinations of factors using common-sense techniques (see Table 4).

Table 4. Summary of Data on Correlates of War Performance

In . . . wars	One of the parties had . . .	It won in . . .	Probability
39	more government revenue	31	.79
40	more population	28	.70
40	fewer battle deaths	22	.55
40	lower population loss rate	30	.75
31	both *more* revenue *and* *lower* population loss rate	26	.84
8	more revenue *but* a *higher* population loss rate	5	.63
35	more revenue *and* more population	27	.73
4	more revenue *but less* population	4	1.00
22	more revenue and fewer deaths	18	.82
17	more revenue but *more* deaths	13	.76
36	more population and a lower population loss rate	27	.75
4	*less* population but a lower population loss rate	3	.75
20	more population *and* fewer deaths	15	.75
20	more population *but more* deaths	13	.65
24	fewer deaths *and* lower population loss rate	18	.75
16	*more* deaths *but* lower population loss rate	12	.75
31	more revenue, more population *and* lower population loss rate	26	.84
19	more revenue, more population, fewer battle deaths and a lower population loss rate	15	.79

The strongest factors of the 4 we have examined are wealth (.79 probability of victory) and lower population loss rate (.75 probability). One way to test the combined predictive power of these 2 measures is to take all the cases in which one party had both more government revenue and a lower loss of life rate. There were 31 such cases, of which 26 were won by the party favored in both respects.

What if the party has more revenue but lost a larger percentage of population? There were only 8 such cases, of which 5 resulted in victory and 3 in defeat. There were 35 cases in which the party that had more revenue also had more population. It won 77 percent of these (27). There were 4 other cases in which the party with more revenue had less population. It won all 4 anyway. In this sample population is not important as a factor separate from revenue. Revenue predicts all the cases that population predicts plus some that it does not.

Revenue also predicts as well alone as it does in combination with absolute life losses. In the 22 cases in which one party had both advantages (more wealth and lower losses), it won 72 percent of the time (18 cases). The other 17 parties with more revenue but also higher losses won 76 percent of the time (13 cases). Adding the battle death factor to the revenue factor does not increase explanatory power, and of course revenue has the useful predictive quality of being knowable in advance of the war with some reliability.

The same lack of increase in explanatory power results from adding battle deaths to the rate of population loss (which is somewhat redundant anyway), and from adding population size to the population loss rate.

Given revenue data, the only other factor that seems to have a significant degree of statistical independence and to be important in predicting to victory or defeat is the population loss rate. To summarize: a party with either more revenue or a lower population loss rate is favored to win by about 3 or 4 to 1. A party favored in both respects gets odds of almost 5 to 1.

CONCLUSIONS

We have outlined a theory of war power in which the power of party A is a function both of A's ability to harm B and A's willingness to be harmed by B.[3] To validate the theory a number of attempts were made to disconfirm the importance of cost-tolerance in war power. The findings lend some credence to the theory, though they fall short of full validation: It is not the case that winners of wars were usually the parties who suffered less (in 18 of 40 international wars, the winner lost more lives than the loser). Strength alone, as measured by wealth, explained 80 percent of the victories, which is close to the theory's prediction that, assuming that each of the two parties is equally likely to have greater cost-tolerance, the stronger party should win in 75 percent of wars. Finally, there has been great variation in the level of population loss at which point defeated states conceded—cost-tolerance indeed varies greatly.

3. This theory is elaborated in Rosen (1970).

Pieces of these data reflect importantly on the strategic theories of both of United States and the Vietnamese Communists. The early confidence of the United States that it would prevail because of its vastly superior means might have been shaken by our finding that 1 of 5 international wars (and perhaps a higher percentage of internal wars) has been won by the weaker party. Also, it is significant that almost half of our international wars (18 of 40) were won by the party losing more lives in battle.

On the other side, the data shows that while superior cost-tolerance may occasionally give the advantage to the weaker party, having less strength but more cost-tolerance more often results in defeat. Our crude data suggest that the party superior in strength but inferior in cost-tolerance (e.g., the United States in Vietnam) is favored, at least by the odds (60/40) to win anyway. Cost-tolerance as a single factor is no more a guarantee of victory than strength, probably less.

Research on war power may aid forms of social engineering and political policy that will reduce the need for political violence. Given a political dispute over competing claims to an important value, the actual occurrence of a war often can be attributed to erroneous judgement by at least one of the parties concerning its military power. This proposition is based on the following reasoning: if two parties are in a dispute, but they both know in advance who would win should a war occur, they could settle the dispute without violence simply by simulating the decision that both know will result from war. Most wars occur because the two parties have very different expectations of the likely outcome. "The most effective prerequisite for preventing struggle, the exact knowledge of comparative strength of the two parties, is very often obtainable only by the actual fighting out of the conflict" (Simmel, 1904). Much fighting might be prevented if social scientists could devise a "yardstick of war power, some kind of measuring device that would enable parties to come to a common picture of the power situation in lieu of actual conduct of violent struggle" (Coser, 1961). A useful metaphor is the picture of men fighting in a darkened room. If the lights were turned on, and some of the combatants had a clearer picture of the hopelessly superior size of their opponents, much of the fighting would end. Some would continue to fight because there was still some prospect of victory, and others would defy from desperation at the alternatives or confident hopes of a miracle, but in at least some cases a quixotic struggle would be abandoned. Research on war power just might be as useful in reducing violence as research on war causation.

MICHAEL P. SULLIVAN with the assistance of William Thomas

7. Symbolic Involvement as a Correlate of Escalation: The Vietnam Case

ABSTRACT

Nations commit themselves to issues, to other countries, and to conflicts, and their foreign behavior will be to some degree dependent on their type of commitment. One way of differentiating types of commitment is along a symbolic-nonsymbolic continuum, and the following general hypothesis is investigated: international conflicts in which decision-makers are "symbolically involved" are especially likely to be escalatory.

The Vietnam War was chosen to test this general hypothesis. Data on escalation consisted of United States troops and casualties in Vietnam. Data on symbolic involvement were derived from a content analysis of President Johnson's speeches on Vietnam from 1964 to 1968. The entire list of symbolic tip-off words was broken down into "positive" or highly-valued symbols (such as "democracy," "freedom," "liberty," and "justice"), and "negative" symbols (such as "terror," "anarchy," "violence," and "aggression"). Finally, more specific hypotheses from the conflict literature suggested that sub-samples of the "positive" group of symbols might be related to escalation: two of these were "commitment" symbols (such as "determination" and "commitment"), and "status" symbols (such as "honor," "will," and "status").

Analysis of the entire five-year period showed a negative relationship: as escalation increased, President Johnson's use of symbols declined. However, when the five years were broken down into two different phases, 1964-1966 and 1967-1968 some very strong positive relationships were apparent. It was found that "positive" and "commitment" symbols were positively related to escalation

Authors' Note: we would like to thank Connie Wilde for assistance in the original formulation of the coding sheet for data collection. John Schwarz provided immeasurable assistance on early drafts. Gail Bernstein, Robert Lawrence, Edward J. Williams, and J. Richard Wagner also read and commented on earlier drafts. Barbara Harrison prepared the figures. Data generation was supported (in part) by the Voluntary International Coordination Project, the University of Michigan. Research time was provided by a grant from the Institute of Government Research, Department of Government, University of Arizona. Generous computer time was provided by the University of Arizona Computer Center.

185

during the first phase, while negative symbols were not. In addition, correlations were strengthened by lagging escalation. During the entire second phase there were no consistent relationships, but isolating the last eighteen months the second phase, and lagging escalation, showed strong positive relationships between the "commitment" and "status" symbols and escalation.   ∎

INTRODUCTION

One of the most intriguing questions in contemporary international politics concerns the escalation of international conflicts. Some crises, confrontations, disagreements, and conflicts erupt into serious violence, involve large numbers of fighting men, and are long in duration. Others, however, flare up briefly and then subside, never to be heard of again. Are there any systematic patterns in the escalation of international conflicts, and if so, what are the correlates of these escalatory patterns?

Escalation to high levels of violence can be a result either of large systemic forces which over a period of time exert certain pressures on conflict systems, driving them toward higher levels of violence; or it can be a result of interaction processes set up within a conflict itself and which may be unrelated to these systemic forces (M. Sullivan, 1969). This paper will concentrate on one aspect of these behavioral processes that occur during a conflict.

We will focus on the escalation of the Vietnam conflict from 1964 through 1968, and will investigate three questions. First, was there a change in the perceived U.S. involvement toward the conflict along a "symbolic" dimension? Second, if such a change did occur, was it related in any way to the escalatory process in the conflict? And finally, is there any evidence that would indicate which occurred first, the escalation or the symbolic involvement?

A country's perception of its involvement or "commitment"—either to an issue, to another country, or to a conflict—may change, and such changes may be related to its behavior. American decision-makers, for instance, have argued that this nation's involvement or commitment in the Vietnam conflict has remained the same throughout the course of the conflict, and that its actions have resulted from this consistent involvement.

Chester, Hodgson, and Page argue, however, that a "posterior rationalization" occurred in the escalation of the Vietnam conflict: "One of the most important political points about America's war in Vietnam was that, to an unusual degree, involvement preceded rationale: the war was well advanced before there was any structured national debate about its purpose (1969: 22, 28)." On a more general level, Werner Levi has argued that "objectives and actions are chosen and values then called upon to justify them . . . this belated reference to ideology often appears as an afterthought, . . . when the need arises to enlist public opinion in support of policy . . . (1970: 8)." Has the United States' commitment or involvement in Vietnam changed, and if so, has this change occurred along a symbolic dimension?

The answer to these questions can be of great policy importance. If states' perceptions of their commitments are strongly related to their behavior, then knowledge of such changing commitments may serve as indicators or cues to their foreign policy behavior. States continually interact with threats, denials, requests, attacks, rewards, and many other types of behavior. One type of interaction is the transmission to another state of one's perception of or commitment to an issue. Thus, use of differential commitments or types of involvement transmits different information. As Yakobson and Lasswell remark, "A detailed analysis of the changing trends in slogans could occasionally even facilitate the making of political weather forecasts (1949: 204)." Thus, if there are relationships between a state's behavior and what Yakobson and Lasswell call slogans, and what we label different commitments, then a careful reading of such changing commitments may give clues to present and future state behavior.

COMMITMENT

States become committed to issues, to other countries, and to conflicts. The traditional manner of noting a nation's depth of commitment is through the concept of "national interest." States see their national interest either as involved or not; if the former is the case, then action is called for, while if the latter is the case, then no necessary action is called for. In spite of the serious operational problems encountered by the researcher in working with this vague notion, it has been popular with statesmen and has been used in much of the traditional international relations literature and even some contemporary research.

Quincy Wright, for instance, utilized this notion in attempting to assess the probabilities of escalation of a large number of conflicts. He argued that once a country decided to take action in a conflict, it would develop forces "at a rate . . . in proportion to the intensity of its national interest in the issue . . . (1965a: 435-436)." Wright's definition of national interest was broad:

> "States seem to regard the spread of their ideologies, the observance of their commitments; the realization of their policies; the preservation of the national character; the gaining of prestige; the satisfaction of pride; the augmentation of power; the security of independence, territorial integrity, and continued existence as interests which usually increase in importance in somewhat this order" (1965a: 445).

In addition to this, Wright notes that other subjective interests, such as respect, pride, reputation, and prestige might come into play as part of the national interest.

National interest is, in a broad sense, an issue. Relatively simple issues in a conflict may "become encrusted with ideological verbiage" and become "harder to resolve through compromise because government officials and public alike tend to regard any withdrawal as a sacrifice of some great principle (Holsti, 1966: 277)." As issues change in this way, the "national interest" changes, and the perceived scope of a conflict becomes broadened (Coleman, 1957; M. Deutsch, 1965). Broad "status" issues become less amenable to compromise than more specific, tangible issues (Rosenau, 1966).

Just as national interests and issues may change, so also are there different types of commitments. Daniel Katz proposes three types of commitment that individuals may have to a political system. The first is a low-level, functional commitment, in which the commitment is made "because its demands are instrumental to an individual's needs." A normative commitment, on the other hand, is the "acceptance of specific legitimate requirements of the system necessary for system leadership." Finally, a symbolic commitment is one in which the symbolic values are "absolute values which have a life of their own (1967: 17-18)."[1] Comparing the three types of commitment in terms of nation-state action, Katz notes that:

> "With greater normative and functional involvement, there is more freedom of action than with symbolic commitment. Functional and normative nationalism can lead to other than military paths to objectives. It can lead to international negotiation and cooperation in situations in which symbolic patriotism would demand war" (1967: 18).

Mitchell and Mitchell also refer to the power of symbolic issues:

> "When the resolution of differences is defined in terms of quantitative benefits or costs, it is possible to compromise by either redistributing existing supplies or creating more for all.... The extraordinary power of ... symbolic issues is thus demonstrated by the greater incidence of violence in their resolution than is the case with purely material distributive problems" (1969: 147).

Just as Mitchell and Mitchell suggest that symbolic issues are more likely to bring about incidents of violence in their resolution than are purely distributive issues, so Katz suggests that states which are "symbolically" committed are more likely to resort to war than to negotiation and compromise.

Thus states act owing to "perceived issues," "national interests" or "commitments." These are not static variables, however. They change, and the changes either in the issues, the type of "national interest" involved, or in the type of "commitment" will affect states' behavior.

1. Weinstein makes a similar distinction between situational and non-situational commitments. A situational commitment is one which is "inherent in the situation" and its fulfillment depends on whether it "serves national interests in the situation" (1969: 40). Contrasted to this is a "nonsituational" commitment, which derives from the notion that a government must fulfill its "commitments" even though, if it could reverse the clock, it would not commit itself in the same fashion again. A nonsituational commitment, like Katz' symbolic commitment, "tends to acquire a life of its own, taking on significance as a symbolic demonstration of a country's dedication to principles, security interests, or other considerations removed from the situation with which the commitment is concerned" (1969: 41).

Unfortunately, all of these concepts are usually treated as static variables. National interest is usually conceived as present or absent. States are seen as committed or not committed. Wright assessed the "national interest" of a country along a 100-point scale at one point in time. Weinstein, applying his situational-non-situational dichotomy to France and the United States, argues that the United States has a nonsituational commitment to Vietnam, whereas France, in her general foreign policy orientation, usually becomes involved only in situational commitments. Although he argues that "A government's pronouncements with respect to various commitments . . . will often reveal a clear predisposition toward one of the two concepts (1969: 48)," he leaves out an entire range of possible explanations for state action deriving from changing interests or changing commitments.

A second and related problem is that no attempt has been made to put empirical reality into these conceptions, with the exception of Wright's attempt to operationalize "national interest." Weinstein categorized both the United States and France into either situational or nonsituational commitment categories, and thus implicitly suggests that other countries can likewise be categorized, but it is unclear exactly how this is to be done. In short, states do have commitments, but these are changing, dynamic entities, and it is these changes which may be crucial in explaining state action.

The above notions suggest propositions which relate different types of commitment or involvement to state action. They hypothesize a linkage between tangible issues and the ability to arrive at cooperative bargaining, on the one hand, and intangible issues leading to uncompromising political behavior, on the other (Rosenau, 1966). "Ideological verbiage," it is said, permits action that would not be permissible were this language and commitment not in force (Holsti, 1966), and this "verbiage" often comes to represent the "national interest." The nature of the issue in a conflict is important in determining a competitive or cooperative solution: "The greater the size and rigidity, the more difficult it will be to resolve [a conflict] cooperatively (Deutsch, 1965: 30)." Violence is more likely to occur where symbolic issues are at stake (Mitchell & Mitchell, 1969); escalation is more likely to occur where a country's "national interest" is involved (Wright, 1965a); war is more likely to follow from a symbolic commitment than from a functional or normative one (Katz, 1967); a nonsituational commitment poses certain risks for the international system: "If powerful nations regard their commitments as unalterable and interdependent, small wars are likely to become big ones (Weinstein, 1969: 55)."

Thus the more closely a state's commitment to an issue, to another country, or to a conflict becomes symbolic, the less likely is it to compromise, and the more likely to partake in violent as opposed to non-violent action. A state is thus more likely to escalate a conflict during periods of symbolic involvement and commitment, and to take de-escalatory action during periods of low or lessening symbolic involvement.

HYPOTHESES

A series of exploratory hypotheses are suggested by the notions just outlined. Issues are conceived to run on a spectrum from narrow, specific ones to broad, general ones. A very common way to broaden an issue is to treat it symbolically. One general hypothesis relates the use of symbols to behavior in a conflict: decision-makers become differentially committed or involved in conflicts, and as the level of escalation rises, their perception of commitment to the conflict will become more "symbolic."

Decision-makers may use different types of symbols at different times. On the one hand, it can be argued that politicians in western, democratic countries may use certain "democratic" symbols all the time; their resort to such terms as democracy, liberty, justice, freedom, may just be part of their working vocabulary, and external events will not affect their use of such symbols. On the other hand, if, as Snyder suggests, decision-makers communicate their perceptions of values to other decision-makers (Snyder, 1961), we could argue that we would find these highly-valued symbols occurring more often during escalatory periods of an on-going conflict. At these junctures, decision-makers would be attempting to communicate the seriousness of their commitment, and would do so by referring to highly-valued symbols. Thus we shall investigate whether these positive or highly-valued symbols, such as democracy, freedom, liberty, justice, are related to escalation.

Ted Gurr (1970: 225) suggests that an additional important element in the occurrence of violence, at least on the domestic level, is the communication of aggressive symbols, defined as "verbal or graphic representations of violence against political targets, including descriptions of actual violence, past or present . . ." The communication of aggressive symbols through the media, Gurr argues, can facilitate specific outbreaks of violence. By extension, we argue that a nation may use a greater proportion of "aggressive" symbols when it is partaking in violence, i.e., escalation of a conflict. Thus aggressive or negative symbols, such as aggression, enemies, anarchy, threat, oppression, and so forth, are hypothesized to be related to escalation.

Decision-makers may manifest different types of commitments or involvement in two other ways. First, they may simply announce that they are committed to an issue, a country, or a conflict. Second, they may commit their country's status or honor. By using such symbols as challenge, commitment, determination, and struggle at specific points in a conflict, the decision-makers' "commitment" has indeed changed, and we would hypothesize these changes to occur during periods of heightened escalation. Furthermore, symbols which denote the broad notion of "status," Rosenau suggests, are more likely to bring about non-compromising behavior than compromising behavior, and therefore we hypothesize that symbols of status—such as confidence, determination, national honor, image, or will—are more likely to occur during escalatory periods in an international conflict than during normal or de-escalatory periods.

A correlate of the escalatory process in international conflicts is the broadening of the perceived scope of the conflict, and one of the most basic ways in which this occurs is through the greater use of symbols. Thus the general hypothesis investigated is that symbols will rise during periods of escalation and decline during periods of de-escalation or negotiations.

DATA

Data to answer the questions outlined in the previous section must (1) be able to delineate different types of "involvement" or "commitment" parties may have in a conflict, and (2) be at least a potential communication from one party to another. This rules out diaries or memoirs which may provide information about an individual's feelings or psychological state but are not used to influence an adversary.

The content analysis is suggested by the literature presented earlier. Recall that Katz posited three types of "commitments" that individuals may have toward a political system: functional, normative, and symbolic. The same terminology can be applied to a state's commitment or involvement in a conflict. (From this point on, we will substitute the word "involvement" for Katz' "commitment" in order to lessen confusion later in analyzing the specific "commitment" symbols.)

Here we have concentrated on only one of Katz' three types of "involvement," the symbolic. It would be profitable to have a functional-to-symbolic or a less-to-more symbolic continuum, but previous research indicates that in doing this, the definition of, and differences between, the three types of involvement become somewhat blurred (see M. Sullivan, 1970). An alternative is to view the presence or absence of "symbols" in decision-makers' statements as indicative of their type of involvement. The more a decision-maker relies on symbols in his references to an issue or a country—or, in our case, a conflict—the more symbolically involved" he is, and the broader the scope of the conflict. The less symbolically an issue or a conflict is defined, the narrower the scope.

Although there is much discussion about what symbols are in a very general sense (Lasswell, et al., 1949; Lasswell, 1954; Edelman, 1964), there has been little or no attempt at an operational definition of a symbol. This is unfortunate because as Lasswell says, "It is apparent that changes in the spread and frequency of exposure to key signs is an exceedingly significant indicator of important social processes" (Lasswell, 1954: 201). Edelman has made the useful distinction between referential symbols and condensation symbols. "Referential symbols are economical ways of referring to the objective elements in objects or situations," he suggests, while condensation symbols "evoke the emotions associated with the situation. They condense into one symbolic event, sign, or act patriotic pride, anxieties, remembrances of past glories or humiliations, promises of future greatness: some one of these or all of them (Edelman, 1964: 6)." This paper focuses on the spread and frequency of such condensation symbols in President Johnson's documents on Vietnam from 1964 through 1968.

In an attempt to develop some idea of which condensation symbols might be involved in perceptions of a conflict, three investigators coded ten randomly selected statements by President Johnson in the 1964-1968 period. Each coder extracted from the documents words or phrases that he would classify as a condensation symbol. Those symbols on which all three coders agreed were included as valid; those extracted by only one or two were discussed and some retained, some discarded. There was no dispute about such symbols as honor, pledge, commitment, national interest, liberty. justice, peace, freedom, and so forth. The first tip-off word list, which comprised approximately 41 symbolic "tip-off" words, was then used in a pre-coding of another set of 10 randomly selected Presidential statements. The inter-coder reliability averaged approximately .80. After this second coding and discussions about problems in using the original list, a final list of 51 symbolic tip-off words was used to code 650 documents by President Johnson which had some reference to Vietnam.[2] In the final analysis, a total of 367 documents were coded. Speeches or remarks devoted to another subject but in which minor reference was made to Vietnam were not coded; only documents which were actually Vietnam documents or texts of which a substantial portion was devoted to Vietnam were coded. After completing approximately one-half of these documents, a revision was once again made in the codesheet in order to include items which had originally been excluded. All items coded prior to this revision were then re-coded. In the end, the inter-coder reliability averaged .85.[3] The final codesheet of symbolic tip-off words is presented in Appendix A, and they have been there broken down into the different types of symbols to be analyzed. Simple frequency counts were made of all these symbols occurring in all the documents coded, and the length of the document was recorded as a control.

The above content analysis data represents a preliminary attempt to measure the independent variable of a decision-maker's level of symbolic commitment to a conflict. This will be related to the dependent variable of escalation. Data on escalation are derived primarily from official Defense Department statistics (supplemented in some instances by New York Times reports) on the following indicators: number of United States troops in Vietnam (1964-1968), and United States deaths from hostile action (1964-1968).[4]

2. The source for the documents was Presidential Papers (1964-1968). All documents which were indexed under either Vietnam, North Vietnam, Asia, Southeast Asia, and any other relevant heading in the index was included. This insured a coding of all documents in which any reference whatsoever was made to any of these items. We are satisfied that we have tapped almost all openly released Presidential statements on Vietnam for the years mentioned, and we are convinced that we have the universe of his important statements.

3. This refers to within-document reliability; that is, coders were picking up the same symbols, and with almost the same frequency. An additional check was made on two coders for inter-document reliability, and the correlation on a small number of documents was .95.

4. An earlier paper (Sullivan, 1970) used two types of data to get at differing types of commitments: First, a content analysis of decision-makers' documents using Katz' functional-normative-symbolic trichotomy, and second, an analysis of the basic "issues" in a

ANALYSIS: CHANGES IN
SYMBOLIC COMMITMENT

We have posed three questions in this study. First, has there been a change in United States involvement along a symbolic dimension during the Vietnam conflict? Second, if such a change has occurred, has it been related to the escalation of the conflict? Third, which occurred first, the commitment or the escalation? In order to answer these questions, we have used seven-month moving averages to smooth out the rather large month-to-month fluctuations in the use of symbols. The same technique has been applied to the escalation data, and thus the analysis in this paper is confined to the trends both in symbolic commitment and escalation, and the relationship between these trends.[5]

Figure 1 shows all the symbols combined for the 54 time periods under study, and the moving average data for total troop commitment and monthly deaths. Figures 1a-1d in Appendix B present the four sub-types of symbols. Figure 1 indicates quite clear changes through the 54 time periods in the use of symbols by President Johnson. Recall that each data point represents an average for a seven-month period. There is first a fluctuating period from 1964 through early 1965. Beginning with the seven month data of February-August, 1965, the number of symbols changes from the up and down movement established to that point, and rises to a peak in the August, 1965-February, 1966 period. Use of symbols then drops off and halts near the peaks of the 1964 period. Through the latter part of 1966 symbolic usage rises again. Then, from May-November, 1966 to February-August, 1967 symbolic usage declines sharply. At that point it increases again until near the Tet Offensive and Johnson's withdrawal speech, and then declines with fluctuations near the end of 1968.

Figure 1 thus indicates three peaks in symbolic involvement: late 1965 through early 1966; the latter part of 1966; and finally, late 1967 through early 1968. With the exception of 1964, then, the data on symbolic involvement show definite trends and very little random fluctuation. It is only the first eight periods that could truly be described as "random"; the remaining 46 periods—although exhibiting fluctuations—are far from random. In fact, the smoothness of the trends after 1964 may be evidence that Johnson paid more

---

conflict as perceived by the decision-makers. This proved partially satisfactory; it indicated trends, for instance, in the Vietnam conflict showing a change from a functional commitment to a symbolic one during the 1961-1966 period. The theme content analysis utilized, and the small number of documents analyzed, however, could give little more than a general trend. In addition, no direct measure was made of escalation; it was simply assumed—an accurate assumption—that throughout the 1961-1966 period escalation did occur in Vietnam.

5. Moving averages is a simple technique whereby the data for the first seven months is averaged, and this average is used to represent this seven month period. Then, the data for the eighth month is added to the seven month total, and the first month is subtracted. A new average is computed, and this represents the second through the eighth month. This is done for the entire 60-month period, resulting in an "n" of 54, and provides a trend for the entire period.

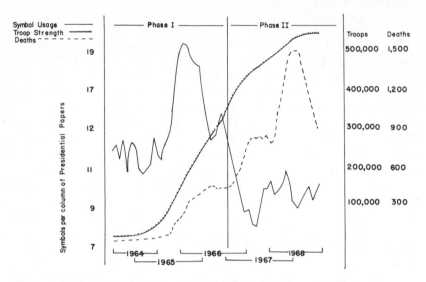

Figure 1. Changes in Symbolic Usage, 1964-1968. Data are 7-month Moving Average Trend Lines

consistent attention, and more careful attention, to Vietnam during the later years than earlier.

Thus, there is no doubt that President Johnson changed the extent to which he used verbal symbols over this five year period. It is far from a continual increase, and therefore does not parallel, for instance, troop strength, but the changes in symbols in Figure 1 appear to occur at points when escalation is also undergoing changes.

Figures 1a-1d in Appendix B show the trend in symbolic usage of the different types of symbols suggested earlier, and it is clear that there are slightly different trends for the differing symbols. "Positive" symbols comes closest to following the trend of all symbols combined. But negative symbols, contrary to what had been expected, declined throughout the five years of this analysis. There is some increased use in 1965-1966, but this hardly goes above the mid-1964 level. Also, contrary to positive symbols, which rise again in the latter periods of 1968, negative symbols decline during the last four time periods. Overall, negative symbols decline in a much clearer fashion throughout the five year period than any of the other types.

Commitment symbols fluctuate through the first 15 time periods, rise when most other symbols rise through the next seven periods, and then parallel, to a much less marked degree, all symbols for the remaining periods. Because of the smaller number of commitment symbols compared to all the other symbols, the changes in Figure 1c appear much smaller. The same applies to the status symbols. These, however, more than any other type separated here for analysis, appear to be relatively random.

In terms of percentage change of the different types of symbols, positive symbols rise over 70 percent from their low in 1964 to the peak shown in Figure 1a. Commitment symbols change 51 percent and the negative ones only 45 percent. All categories of symbols change, but positive symbols make the most dramatic change. It should be noted—and will be considered more extensively in the concluding section—that this change in positive symbols may be due partially to the "peace offensive" that the Johnson administration launched in late 1965. Since "peace" is considered a symbol, it was included in the symbolic word list. This raises the problem of whether the use of "peace" in such a context should be considered as symbolic involvement. We will treat this problem extensively below.

The first question, then, has been answered: if the frequency of use of the symbols presented in Appendix A accurately reflects differential involvement along a symbolic dimension, then there was a definite change in President Johnson's involvement toward Vietnam—along this symbolic dimension—during the 1964-1968 period.

SYMBOLIC COMMITMENT AND ESCALATION: FIVE-YEAR PERIOD

When we turn to the second question and analyze the relationship between symbols and escalation in Vietnam, Figure 1 suggests that overall correlations should be negative between symbols and escalation for the five year period. Table 1 indicates that this is the case, although to varying degrees depending on the type of symbol considered.[6] All symbols combined are correlated relatively highly with both troop strength and deaths (−.36 and −.40, both significant at the .01 level.) Breaking these down into types of symbols, however, shows that this high negative relation is apparently caused by declining negative symbols. Whereas the latter correlate at −.67 and −.70 with escalation (significant at .001 level), positive symbols drop to −.19 and −.23 (both insignificant). The overall tendency for symbols throughout the five year period of analysis, then, is to decline relative to the rising escalation, but this negative relationship is accounted for to a considerable extent by the negative symbols.

High and significant correlations are also found between "commitment" symbols and escalation. On the other hand, status symbols reflect the trend found in positive symbols: they are negatively related to escalation, but to a lesser degree.

6. The data from which these correlations were computed do not satisfy all the requirements for the use of correlations. All of the independent variable data have been normalized. The indicators of escalation, however, only approximate normality and in most cases deviate from such a distribution. Although numerous transformations were attempted on the data, none would produce normal distributions in the dependent variables. The significance levels noted in the text and in the tables should therefore be interpreted with caution.

Table 1. Correlations Between Symbolic Usage and Escalation, 1964-1968[a]

	ESCALATION			
	United States Troop Strength		United States Monthly Deaths	
All Symbols	−.36[b]		−.40[b]	
	−.33	−.38[b]	−.38[b]	−.42[b]
	−.31	−.40[b]	−.35[b]	−.44[c]
	−.28	−.44[b]	−.33	−.47[c]
	−.26	−.47[c]	−.30	−.49[c]
Positive Symbols	−.19		−.23	
	−.18	−.22	−.22	−.26
	−.16	−.24	−.20	−.28
	−.13	−.29	−.17	−.32
	−.12	−.32	−.16	−.35
Negative Symbols	−.67[c]		−.70[c]	
	−.65[c]	−.67[c]	−.68[c]	−.70[c]
	−.63[c]	−.68[c]	−.66[c]	−.71[c]
	−.61[c]	−.69[c]	−.65[c]	−.71[c]
	−.60[c]	−.69[c]	−.63[c]	−.71[c]
Commitment Symbols	−.53[c]		−.58[c]	
	−.51[c]	−.56[c]	−.56[c]	−.61[c]
	−.47[c]	−.59[c]	−.53[c]	−.63[c]
	−.44[b]	−.63[c]	−.51[c]	−.66[c]
	−.42[b]	−.65[c]	−.48[c]	−.67[c]
Status Symbols	−.35[b]		−.34	
	−.41[b]	−.33	−.38[b]	−.33
	−.41[b]	−.30	−.38[b]	−.31
	−.41[b]	−.31	−.38[b]	−.31
	−.42[b]	−.30	−.39[b]	−.30

a. N = 54. For each lag, n drops by 1.
b. Significant at .01 level.
c. Significant at .001 level (see Note 6).

The lagged relationships in Table 1 are very consistent. The lagged correlations are below the main ones: those to the right are correlations with symbols lagged behind escalation, while those to the left are those with escalation lagged behind symbols. In almost every category, as well as with all symbols combined, lagging of symbols raises the negative correlations, whereas lagging the escalation indicator drops the correlations. The sole exception is the group of "status" symbols. Thus, the consistent negative relationship between the President's use of symbols and escalation in the 54 periods of this analysis is made even stronger when symbols are lagged behind escalation.

It is clear from Figure 1, however, that although the overall relation is negative because of the declining trend in symbols, within this overall declining pattern there are nonetheless changes in symbolic usage which are related to changes in escalation. In order to discover the significance of these underlying relationships, we broke the 54 periods into two shorter periods, called Phase I and Phase II, and analyzed these separately. Tables 2 and 3 do this. Table 2 shows the period from 1964 through the point at which symbolic commitment receded to approximately its 1964 level, and Table 3 shows in general the 1967-1968 period.[7]

SYMBOLIC COMMITMENT AND ESCALATION: PHASE I (1964-1966)

Table 2 confirms the intuitive contention suggested by Figure 1: during the first 30 time periods almost all types of symbols are positively related to both escalation indicators, and, except for negative and status symbols, these relations are all significant. The symbols most closely related to escalation are "positive" and "commitment" symbols. The hypothesis suggested earlier concerning the relationship between negative symbols and escalation is not upheld in the 1964-1966 period. Whereas we had suggested that negative symbols would be manipulated and be responsive to aggression or violence in the international system, exactly the opposite occurs during this period.

The very significant relationship between escalation and positive symbols refutes the hypothesis that decision-makers in western, democratic countries would use such positive or "democratic" symbols consistently, regardless of events in the international system. At least in this case, the contrary hypothesis is confirmed: decision-makers will communicate their highly-valued symbols more frequently during times of escalation and crisis than during more normal periods. One conclusion from these data would be that positive and commitment symbols are likely to correspond to escalation during initial and dramatic changes in escalation; decision-makers thereby make their "commitment" more outstanding and clearer, and they indicate that highly-valued symbols are at stake. At the same time, status and negative symbols appear to play no role.

The lagged correlations in Table 2 show that the relationship between troop strength and symbols drops from .66 to .55 when lagging symbols, and the relation between casualties and symbols drops from .68 to .47. On the other

7. Recall that the data in Figure 1 and which were used to compute the correlations in the tables are all moving average data. Therefore each data point represents the average of seven months. For instance. the breaking point made between 1966 and 1967 in Figure 1 is really made between the seven month average of June-December, 1966 and July, 1966-January, 1967. Therefore this breaking point roughly approximates the latter part of 1966. In the text, therefore, when references are made to "December, 1966", for instance, this really refers to the average data for June-December, 1966. Wherever possible, references to such specific months have not been made, and rather attempts have been made to describe the seven month period that the data describes.

Table 2. Correlations Between Symbolic Usage and Escalation, 1964-1966[a]

	ESCALATION			
	United States Troop Strength		United States Monthly Deaths	
All Symbols	.66[c]		.68[c]	
	.68[c]	.65[c]	.71[c]	.64[c]
	.67[c]	.63[c]	.73[c]	.60[c]
	.68[c]	.59[c]	.73[c]	.53[b]
	.69[c]	.55[b]	.74[c]	.47
Positive Symbols	.69[c]		.72[c]	
	.71[c]	.68[c]	.75[c]	.68[c]
	.71[c]	.67[c]	.76[c]	.64[c]
	.71[c]	.63[c]	.76[c]	.57[b]
	.71[c]	.59[c]	.76[c]	.51[b]
Negative Symbols	.02		.02	
	.06	.08	.07	.04
	.05	.11	.07	.06
	.06	.11	.11	.06
	.11	.17	.18	.09
Commitment Symbols	.74[c]		.76[c]	
	.74[c]	.72[c]	.77[c]	.72[c]
	.74[c]	.70[c]	.78[c]	.68[c]
	.75[c]	.66[c]	.77[c]	.62[c]
	.76[c]	.62[c]	.78[c]	.56[b]
Status Symbols	−.06		.01	
	−.11	−.02	−.03	.02
	−.13	.04	−.06	.04
	−.13	.04	−.05	.00
	−.11	.05	−.06	−.01

a. N = 30. For each lag, n drops by 1.
b. Significant at .01 level.
c. Significant at .001 level (see note 6).

hand, lagging escalation behind symbolic involvement uniformly raises the correlations (.66 to .69 for troop strength, and .68 to .74 for casualties). Thus an increase in troop commitment and monthly deaths during this period was more highly correlated to a prior change in symbols than the reverse. These changes are far from drastic when lags are introduced, but their consistency leads us to conclude that the increase in symbolic commitment tended to precede greater troop involvement and deaths rather than the other way around. (An objection to this would be that such increases in symbolic involvement accompanied the actual decisions to commit troops or to raise the stakes in the war, and that our measures of escalation are naturally lagged behind these decisions. Unfortunately, we do not have data at this time to test this possibility. Nonetheless, even if that were shown to be the case, then the change in symbols would most likely accompany very closely the actual decisions to escalate the war. Such a finding would in no way lessen the significance of the results presented here.)

The same pattern in the lagged correlations occurs with the sub-group of positive symbols and commitment symbols. On the other·hand, the negative or aggressive symbols increase with each lag regardless of whether symbols or escalation is lagged, but none of these are significant. Status symbols remain insignificant when lags are introduced. The general conclusion is that not only do the positive and commitment symbols appear related to escalation during this period, but this relationship is heightened when escalation is lagged and diminishes when symbols are lagged.

In summary, the analysis of this period of time, contrary to what was found during the entire five year period, shows very strong relationships between escalation and some types of symbolic involvement. Positive symbols are very strongly related to escalation, as are commitment symbols. Of perhaps more interest, however, is the finding that, contrary to what Gurr suggests, negative symbols or symbols of aggression or violence are not related to escalation during this period.

SYMBOLIC COMMITMENT AND ESCALATION:
PHASE II (1967-1968)

When we turn our attention to the 1967-1968 period (Tables 3 and 4), we find that what appear at first to be generally negative relationships turn positive when part of this period is eliminated from the analysis. The most strikingly consistent pattern in Table 3—which presents correlations on data from very late 1966 to 1968—is that almost all correlations are negative; contrary to what occurred during the first period, there is a negative relationship between symbolic involvement and escalation during these 24 periods. The most strongly negative relationships during this period occur between the commitment symbols and troop strength and deaths, as well as between negative symbols and troop commitment.

The general findings here—in conjunction with the results presented in Table 2—lend support to the notion that decision-makers' symbolic involvement in a conflict changes most dramatically during initial periods of escalation but that at some point symbolic involvement drops off. Whether this decline in symbols derives from inability to sustain a high emotive output through the use of such symbols, or from a feeling that public support has already been garnered, is unclear. Note that the changes in symbolic usage in Figure 1 accompanying later escalatory action never quite reach the peaks attained during the original escalatory periods.

A more complex picture begins to emerge in the lagged correlations in Table

Table 3. Correlations Between Symbolic Usage and Escalation, 1967-1968[a]

	ESCALATION			
	United States Troop Strength		United States Monthly Deaths	
All Symbols	−.25		−.31	
	−.28	−.01	−.27	−.10
	−.25	.23	−.15	.08
	−.20	.45	−.02	.31
	−.19	.53	.18	.44
Positive Symbols	−.10		−.25	
	−.19	.15	−.23	.00
	−.19	.37	−.12	.19
	−.15	.53	.01	.39
	−.15	.59 [b]	.23	.53
Negative Symbols	−.38		−.22	
	−.29	−.22	−.18	−.13
	−.20	−.06	−.07	−.06
	−.12	.12	.03	.04
	−.12	.23	.17	.11
Commitment Symbols	−.60 [b]		−.49	
	−.58	−.47	−.40	−.42
	−.53	−.30	−.30	−.33
	−.47	−.04	−.23	−.13
	−.45	.20	−.14	.08
Status Symbols	.13		−.02	
	.01	.26	.10	.12
	.05	.34	.20	.18
	.08	.40	.29	.28
	.07	.54	.43	.49

a. n = 24.
b. Significant at .01 level.

3. All of the negative correlations between all types of symbols and both escalation indicators become positive when symbols are lagged. The few positive relations between symbols and escalation during this period become more significantly positive. The changes are dramatic. For instance, the relation of troop strength changes from −.25 to .53 after four lags and the relationship to monthly deaths changes from −.31 to .44. On the other hand, when lagging escalation, the negative correlations decline although none of these changes is as dramatic or as consistent as the changes when symbols are lagged. The least dramatic change occurs in the relation of negative symbols to both troop strength and monthly deaths. The only case that changes from negative to a

significantly positive relationship, regardless of what variable is lagged, is that between status symbols and deaths.

With the exception of the one case just mentioned, a fully consistent pattern in the lagged correlations of Table 3 leads very strongly to the conclusion that during this phase changes in escalation occurred prior to changes in symbols. Although there is only one statistically significant correlation in this table—the relationship of troop strength to positive symbols—the general conclusion just noted still describes the table. We have used a rather high cut-off level for significance, but other relationships in the table—such as positive symbols to casualties and status symbols to both troop strength and casualties—are fully consistent with this conclusion. It is abundantly clear from Figure 1 why these lagged correlations take on the pattern they do, for the escalation indicators change during this period and these changes are followed in a strikingly similar fashion by changes in symbols.

As described above, the relationship between symbolic commitment and the escalation of the Vietnam conflict during this two year period seems to be fairly simple. However, this analysis rests on the justification of breaking the Vietnam war into the two periods that we have where we have. To this point, all the data seem to show a clear relationship between symbolic commitment in Vietnam and escalation of the conflict: a significant positive relationship for three years, and then a basically negative—but not particularly significant—one for the two remaining years. This negative relationship, however, becomes positive in most cases when symbols are lagged. Table 4 and Figure 1 show why this is the case. Table 4 presents correlations between the same variables during the last 18 periods of the analysis, roughly from just before mid-1967 to late 1968. These correlations are in striking contrast to those in Table 3.

First, almost all relations in Table 4 are positive and for the most part high. This is not surprising when reference is made again to Figure 1. Table 4 eliminates the late 1966-early 1967 period, which was one of declining symbols. Thus the assertion of negative relationships during the last two years of the analysis depends on where we cut into it. By looking only at the last 18 periods, we find positive and strong relationships between symbolic usage and escalation. Furthermore, whereas Table 3 showed strong relations when symbols were lagged, Table 4 shows strong positive relationships when escalation is lagged. This suggests a leapfrog effect. Declining symbols and rising escalation in late 1966-early 1967 help to produce the negative correlations found in Table 3. However, this rising escalation is soon followed by rising symbols, which in turn are followed by higher movements in escalation.

The above description applies to almost all types of symbols in Table 4. Of specific note is the role of negative and status symbols. Recall that both of these were unrelated to escalation in the 1964-1966 period. In the last 18 periods of Phase II, however, both of these are highly related to escalation. Thus both Gurr's hypothesis concerning the effect of the communication of violent symbols on conflict, and the hypothesis linking status symbols to escalation

Table 4. Correlations Between Symbolic Usage and Escalation, July, 1967-1968 [a]

ESCALATION

	United States Troop Strength		United States Monthly Deaths	
All Symbols	.34		.07	
	.31	.18	.19	−.07
	.35	−.12	.36	−.42
	.42	−.33	.50	−.49
	.45	−.31	.73[b]	−.28
Positive Symbols	.43		−.07	
	.34	.32	.14	−.05
	.34	.12	.33	−.26
	.40	−.01	.46	−.22
	.41	.06	.73[b]	.05
Negative Symbols	.04		.29	
	.23	−.10	.37	.02
	.41	−.33	.49	−.30
	.54	−.51	.56	−.50
	.56	−.63	.68[b]	−.58
Commitment Symbols	.45		.45	
	.46	.25	.63	.21
	.58	−.04	.72[b]	−.21
	.70[b]	−.22	.74[b]	−.47
	.75[b]	−.26	.81[c]	−.47
Status Symbols	.60[b]		.18	
	.56	.54	.52	.18
	.61	.43	.61	.06
	.66[b]	.31	.69[b]	.01
	.69[b]	.31	.87[c]	.19

a. N = 18.
b. Significant at .01 level.
c. Significant at .001 level (see note 6).

seem to be validated in later periods of escalation in this on-going conflict, but not in original escalatory movements. A tentative implication would be that decision-makers—either in attempting to justify their own actions or in attempting to communicate with opponents—are more likely to use symbols of violence and to involve a country's status in later periods of a conflict than in earlier periods.

In summary, the entire 24 periods in Phase II exhibit a very interesting interrelationship between symbolic involvement and escalation. It is impossible in such situations—where we have cut into time series data—definitely to assert which variable was the original one causing this movement, but there is little doubt in Figure 1 and Tables 3 and 4 that there is a very close relationship between the two variables.

CONCLUSIONS

We have addressed ourselves to three questions. First, have there been changes in the United States' involvement in Vietnam (as expressed by its chief decision-maker) along a symbolic dimension? Second, if there has been such a change, is this related to the escalation of the Vietnam conflict in the 1964-1968 period? And finally, can any conclusions be drawn about whether this symbolic commitment occurred before or after the escalation?

There have indeed been changes in the "symbolic involvement" in Vietnam as expressed by President Johnson in his public speeches. Figure 1 showed clear changes through the 54 time periods for all symbols combined and for most of the different types of symbols that were isolated. The moving average data showed fluctuations through mid-1965, then a swift rise and peak sometime in early 1966, with a relatively rapid decline again, and then a small rise near the end of 1966. Once again there was a decline and a second peak near Tet of 1968. The different types of symbols isolated for analysis in this paper showed relatively similar patterns to all symbols combined. The only significant deviant case was the negative symbols, which decline throughout.

Thus, there is no doubt that President Johnson changed the extent to which he used verbal symbols during these five years. It is certainly not a continual increase and therefore does not parallel troop strength, for instance, but the changes in symbolic usage in Figure 1 appear to occur at points where escalation rises. Two questions, however, lend doubt to the validity of the general hypothesis investigated in this paper. First, if use of verbal symbols is related to increasing escalation and violence, why does the former variable decline sharply in the late-1966 to mid-1967 period while both indicators of escalation continue to rise? Second, if the peak around the Tet offensive is in fact related to the escalation at that point, why does it rise proportionately less than the earlier dramatic peak in 1965-1966?

We can, of course, offer only possible answers to these questions. First, the two peaks in symbolic involvement in late 1965 and late 1966 may have resulted from Johnson's need to garner public support for the escalation, which can be done by speaking of the conflict in "symbolic" terms. It may be impossible, however, to maintain symbolic rhetoric at a high level for prolonged periods, and after troop strength had reached over 250,000 in mid-1966 and casualties had leveled off during the mid-1966 period (Figure 1), there was a natural tendency to reduce symbolic rhetoric. Another factor is Johnson's popularity on Vietnam, as measured in periodic American Institute of Public Opinion surveys. This had fallen from 72 percent favoring his handling of the war in October, 1965 to just above 50 percent in August, 1966. This may help to explain the resurgence in late 1966 of symbols—the precipitous drop in popularity required further symbolic justification for the war. During the last six months of 1966 his popularity remained the same—just above 50 percent favoring his handling of Vietnam. Perhaps he felt a slim majority had been safely formed, and the declining popularity had been stemmed. It would be natural, then, to reduce symbolic usage, which explains the sudden drop through the next seven to eight periods while escalation was still occurring.

The second question concerned why symbolic usage around the Tet offensive did not rise to the earlier peaks of 1965-1966. First, it is clear that this change from mid-1966 through early 1968 parallels very closely the rise in casualties; deaths from hostile action had begun to rise dramatically four to five months earlier. In addition, however, Johnson's popularity on the war had continued to decline, until, by September, 1967, it was at an all-time low of 33 percent. Both of these variables help to explain Johnson's increased symbolic usage and also give some hints as to why the rise was limited. One possibility is that by this time Johnson himself was exhausted with the war and the criticisms of it. After carrying on a debate in favor of the war for more than three years, and encountering only more harsh and insistent attacks on his policy and a continually declining popularity, he simply was not capable of trying to do what he had done in 1965-1966. In this light, note that after his announcement of peace talks and of his withdrawal from the Presidential race in March 1968, symbols began to recede again. Thus the diminished rise in symbolic usage during this period may have resulted from Johnson's being caught in the middle. His declining popularity and the ever-rising death rates demanded that he do something to justify continuing the conflict, but at the same time both of these elements precluded his making an all-out attempt to vindicate an increasingly unpopular and devastating war.

Hence, it is clear that the changes in symbolic usage often parallel the changes in escalation but not always. Nonetheless, the deviations from this relationship are understandable, especially if we bring in other variables such as public opinion.

The second question under consideration was also answered in the affirmative; that is, there is a close correlation between symbolic usage and escalation, but the specific relationships depend on the type of symbol and the time period considered. It was clear from Figure 1 that the over-all negative relationships shown in Table 1 were not really descriptive of the interrelationships between the two variables, and it became necessary to split the entire five years of trend data into different periods in order to uncover the underlying relationships.

Some over-all impressions can be drawn. First, positive and commitment symbols seemed to play a very strong role in Phase I—the period of initial dramatic escalation. During Phase II positive symbols were related to escalation when lagged behind escalation, but this was not the case with commitment symbols. However, in the last 18 periods of Phase II, the commitment symbols once again play a strong role when escalation is lagged. The positive symbols are only moderately related to escalation. Thus on the whole, the commitment symbols seemed to come into play more often during the entire analysis than did any other type of symbol, being strongly related both during Phase I and during the last 18 periods of Phase II.

On the other hand, there was no relationship during Phase I and only a very moderate one during Phase II between escalation and such negative symbols as aggression, terror, and anarchy. Once again, we find that during the last 18 periods of Phase II negative symbols were very strongly related to escalation when the latter variable was lagged behind symbols. A very similar pattern occurs with status symbols. An overall negative relationship between status symbols and escalation for the entire five year period breaks down to no relation in Phase I, a moderate relation when lagged behind escalation in Phase II, and a very strong relation in the last 18 periods of Phase II when escalation is lagged. As noted earlier, perceptions of violence or aggression and perceptions of status correlated with escalatory actions in later periods of this conflict, but played no role in the initial escalation. In sum, the involvement of the chief United States decision-maker in the Vietnam conflict did change in his symbolic usage through the course of the conflict, and these changes were related to the escalation of the conflict. However, the relationships were different for different types of symbols and for different time periods. Whereas the positive symbols and the sub-set of these designated commitment symbols were related more strongly and more often to escalation, the negative and status symbols came into play more clearly in the later periods of the conflict.

The third question asked which came first, the symbolic commitment or the escalation. It makes very little sense to analyze the lagged correlations for the entire 54 time periods since these do not adequately describe the relationships between the variables. There is a consistent relationship in Phase I (1964-1966) where correlations become higher when escalation is lagged, and lower when symbols are lagged. One conclusion, then, is that initially there is a change in use of symbols, followed by a change in escalation. As noted earlier, however, this finding need not be interpreted as meaning that changes in the use of symbols somehow force decision-makers to escalate a conflict, since decisions to escalate may be made anywhere from one to six months before the actual escalation takes place (actual troop commitment or more active troop operations, for instance). Nonetheless, there would still be a clear relationship between the use of symbols and escalation. Symbolic usage would be related either to the escalation indicators used here or to the actual decisions which brought about the escalation.

Phase II (approximately 1967-1968) exhibits a consistent pattern in the lagged relationships (Tables 3 and 4). Lagging symbols during the entire Phase II period (Table 3) produces greater positive relationships, but if we eliminate the first six periods of this Phase (Table 4), we find higher correlations when lagging escalation. This is the pattern mentioned already where escalation seems to rise first, followed by a rise in symbols, which in turn is followed by higher levels of escalation. It is a leap-frog or feedback process, and although it is difficult to say conclusively which variable comes first, there is little doubt that the two are closely related.

There is very little evidence, then, in considering these lagged correlations, to support Levi's argument that there is a process whereby "objectives and actions are chosen and values then called upon to justify them (1970: 8)." The evidence from Phase I certainly does not support this argument, since the data for that period show that changes in symbols (Levi's "values" and "ideologies") were followed by changes in escalation (Levi's "actions"). However, there is some support for this argument later in the analysis—during Phase II—when the rise in escalation which began sometime in early 1967 was followed by the turnaround in symbolic usage.

IMPLICATIONS AND
ALTERNATIVE CONSIDERATIONS

We will focus on three questions in this section. How might we explain the patterns and relationships uncovered here? Are there any possible alternative explanations for these patterns? And finally, what are the implications of this study? The most obvious explanation for the two main upward thrusts in symbolic involvement is that they are related, as hypothesized, to escalation. The initial escalation of the Vietnam war occurred as President Johnson was becoming more symbolic in his pronouncements about the war. The second large change upward in use of symbols occurred approximately four to six months after the trend data on casualties begins to rise in early 1967. In addition, this turnaround in the use of symbols precedes an even greater increase in escalation in late 1967-early 1968.

Although the rather consistently downward movement of symbols through parts of 1966 and 1967 contradicts the hypothesized relationship between symbolic involvement and escalation, we have already suggested plausible reasons for this. First, it may not be possible for decision-makers who are involved in complex negotiations and activities every day to maintain for a long period of time a high level of symbolic output. Observers have noted that during this period Johnson was extremely concerned with the day-to-day activities of the war, even down to the choice of specific bombing targets (Kraslow and Loory, 1968: 43-54). It is difficult to imagine any President carrying on his regular duties, along with the concern about the specific activities of the war, and beyond all of this continuing a high level of symbolic justification for the war. Second, Johnson may have felt that he had garnered enough public support for his escalatory moves; if symbolic involvement is viewed at least partially as a patriotic rallying cry, then this was no longer needed if the public basically supported his moves.

Generally, we are more likely to find escalatory behavior when decision-makers are more symbolically involved.[8] Consideration should be given,

8. As someone once said, nobody believes the theory but the theorist, while everyone believes the experiment but the experimenter. Thus despite what we feel are fairly clear

however, to possible alternative explanations of changes in symbolic usage.[9] For instance, a most serious contender which might account for the initial rise in "symbolic involvement" is the fact that during the latter part of 1965 a "peace offensive" was launched by the Johnson administration. In fact, the monthly data on symbolic usage (not presented here) show that the two highest months of the entire 60 months are November and December, 1965. The problem, then, is whether this first large rise in symbolic usage is due to Johnson becoming symbolically involved or due to this "peace offensive." Since "peace" is one of the symbols included in the symbolic tip-off word list, might it not simply be more frequent reference to this symbol which causes changes in symbolic involvement? To investigate this, a sub-analysis of all "positive" symbols excluding the one symbol of "peace" was carried out. The change made little difference; the correlations between the positive symbols and positive symbols without "peace" was over .95. This initial rise in symbols, then, is not due solely to the use of "peace" as a symbol.

While this does not answer the question of whether it is simply this peace offensive which we are really correlating with escalation, it certainly lessens that possibility. In addition, however, we could argue that such "peace offensives" might themselves be used as types of symbolic involvement. By calling for peace and implying that one is looking for peace—and receiving no response from the other side—a decision-maker may feel further justified in escalating a conflict. As Tom Wicker noted concerning the bombing policy, "It became an article of faith in the Johnson administration that except for brief and fruitless propaganda 'pauses,' there could be no letup in the bombing, no matter how useless or unpopular, unless Hanoi would reciprocate in some unspecified way (Wicker, 1968: 270)." If bombing pauses were seen for their propaganda purposes, then "peace offensives"—which often coincided with these—might be viewed in the same way.

Other alternative explanations for the change in symbolic usage might be the domestic political situation either in the United States or in South Vietnam. In terms of the latter, it has been suggested that concern over "democracy" and

---

conclusions, the usual methodological caveats should be kept in mind. First, by dealing with trends we have left the large month-to-month fluctuations in symbolic usage unexplained. Future analyses will investigate whether these are simply random movements around the trends presented here, or whether they are related to other variables, such as diplomatic behavior. Second, we have been asserting a linear relationship between symbolic commitment and escalation, and in some cases there may rather be high and low periods of symbolic commitment. This is especially true for all symbols combined and for the "positive" group of symbols. Preliminary regression analyses have shown, for instance, that attempts to predict troop strength from the independent variables of positive or commitment symbols were sometimes quite far off the mark. Finally, any analysis limited to one decision-maker and one conflict is of course subject to the argument of "uniqueness." This objection can be countered only by extensive analysis of other conflicts and decision-makers.

9. We are indebted to James Stegenga and Timothy Luke for suggesting some of these possible alternative explanations.

democratic processes in Vietnam might evoke from United States leaders more references to symbols such as democracy, freedom, and liberty, which would effect changes in symbolic usage but would not necessarily be related to symbolic involvement in the conflict. This appears to be the case with the South Vietnamese assembly elections of September, 1966, which in Figure 1 roughly corresponds to the mid-1966 area, a point where symbols rise again after their precipitous decline. However, the monthly data (not presented here) show that although September, 1966 is slightly higher than July, August, October, and November, that month alone does not account for the rise in mid-1966. There is even less likelihood that the South Vietnamese presidential elections in September, 1967 are the prime cause of changes in symbolic usage in 1967, for that month is somewhat lower than numerous months surrounding it. Furthermore, it would be perfectly in line with the hypothesis investigated here to assert that Johnson's symbolic involvement was manifested in his concern over "democratic" and "just" processes in South Vietnam, and that the United States was involved in Vietnam in order to maintain such "justice" and "liberty" for its allies. Regardless of the specific empirical referent, it could still be construed as symbolic involvement.

Are there other alternative variables which might explain changes in Presidential use of symbols on Vietnam? Domestic public opinion has been mentioned as a plausible explanation both for the decline in symbolic usage over a year's period during which escalation was continuing, and for the small upturn in symbolic usage in mid-to-late-1966 and the more dramatic upturn in mid-1967. In the first instance, if public opinion supports a war the President can turn away from attempting to build support to more specific concern with the war. Both the latter instances—those of upward changes in symbolic usage—correspond to periods when support for the war had dropped off. Thus we find a pattern in which drastic dips in public opinion on the war seemed to correspond relatively closely with parallel or subsequent rises in symbolic usage. Is this, however, really an alternative variable which explains changes in symbolic usage, or it it rather simply a slightly different way of stating the same general hypothesis that we have been investigating? If symbolic involvement is used to justify escalatory actions, then it is still related to that escalatory behavior, and we would still conclude that to carry out escalation—and garner public support for such behavior—a decision-maker will become symbolically involved.

A final alternative explanation concerns two coincident events in the international system, neither of which was directly related to Vietnam: the June War of 1967 in the Middle East, and the Glasboro Conference. Perhaps as the Middle East situation exploded in early summer, 1967, Johnson turned attention away from Vietnam and towards the Middle East, and thus a decline in symbolic usage would be understandable at this point. Second, the occurrence of the "summit" meeting in Glasboro, also in June, 1967, might have necessitated a decline in the use of symbols. But the Middle East war was a sudden spurt of activity which for the most part was unpredictable and gave little advanced warning. Figure 1 shows, however that the decline in symbols began with the July, 1966—January, 1967 data, more than six months prior to the outbreaks of the war.

The same reasoning also applies to the Glasboro Conference, although to a lesser degree, but here a second point must be made. It would be perfectly consistent with the hypothesis investigated in this paper to argue that the Glasboro Conference necessitated a decline in the use of symbols. If decision-makers are interested in coming to agreements, if they want to discuss resolvable issues, then, we have argued, they will move away from symbolic issues. If Johnson's planning for the Glasboro Conference was concerned with attempting to arrive at some detente with the Soviets, then this would demand a lowering of general or symbolic concern with international issues, one of which was Vietnam. Thus the notion that international events unrelated to Vietnam caused the changes in symbolic involvement is in one case not a realistic alternative explanation, and in the second case actually supports the general hypothesis we have been investigating here.

In sum, these "alternative explanations" by no means invalidate the conclusions outlined in the last section. Instead, they add a great plausibility to the one change in symbolic involvement which goes against the hypothesis, for they make sense out of changes that—if the initially hypothesized simple relation were to be true in all instances—would not have occurred. Thus the great decline in symbolic usage while escalation was occurring does not make sense unless we take into account the fact that in some instances domestic public opinion may also affect symbolic usage. These alternative explanations—especially the role of perceptions of "freedom" and "democracy" in South Vietnam, and the possible role of the Glasboro Conference in reducing symbolic usage—actually enrich a very complex conflict process.

We have drawn no implications to this point concerning the motivation, if any, behind a decision-maker's use of symbols in his perception of and pronouncements about a conflict. Were the changes in symbolic commitment that we have noted here a result of conscious deliberation on the part of President Johnson and his advisors? Or were they, on the other hand, simply the result of an individual who found himself in what has often been called the conflict spiral? Furthermore, what implications do these findings hold for policy-makers and for policy analysts?

Unfortunately the data cannot provide any implications concerning the President's motivation. To answer this would require either in-depth interviews, or interviews with administration aides, and even if such interviews were granted, it is unlikely that the needed information could be obtained. But if our finding of a relationship between symbolic involvement and escalation were to be borne out in future studies of other decision-makers and other conflicts, certain generalizations might be drawn which would be more valid than this one-case study. If decision-makers are truly concerned that their actions might serve to escalate an on-going conflict or bring about an incipient conflict, they should be extremely cautious about the way they view a crisis or conflict. Although no conclusions about Johnson's internal mental processes were evinced from the data presented here, it is reasonable to assume that individuals can undergo a very subtle process whereby they become symbolically comitted to a conflict, in which their egoes may become involved even though they do not set out to do this. As was noted in a report on earlier research (M. Sullivan, 1970), President Kennedy during the Cuban Missile Crisis was very concerned that the issue in that confrontation not be generalized to anything more than the missiles in Cuba.

Knowledge about other decision-makers' perceptions of and commitment toward an on-going conflict might be of assistance in interacting with other countries. A change in commitments is a process which is internal to conflicts, and may be viewed as the "weather forecasts" that Lasswell referred to earlier. Just as escalation may be more likely when symbolic involvement is increasing, so de-escalation and moves toward negotiation may be more likely to succeed when symbolic involvement is decreasing. We noted the possibility that the decrease in symbolic commitment in 1967 might have partially resulted from the Glasboro Conference in June, 1967. If this relationship between commitment and these other processes were to be found in other conflicts—as well as in instances such as treaty negotiations—this might be one additional indicator which policy-makers could use to "read" the international system, both during periods of crisis and conflict as well as during periods when international negotiations are under way.

APPENDIX A

The following are the symbolic tip-off words used to analyze President Lyndon Johnson's speeches from 1964 through 1968. They have been grouped below into the categories which have been analyzed in the text.

Positive Symbols

allies	independence	religious
challenge	justice	responsibility
commitments	cause	rights
confidence	loyalty	rule of law
constitution	principles	sacrifice
cooperation	courage	security
democracy	humanity	self-determination
determination	equality	stability
dignity	liberty	support
fighting men	national interest	unity
flag	peace	way of life
free men	presidency	welfare
freedom	progress	will
honor	pride	"America"
image	reason	victory

Commitment Symbols	Status Symbols	Negative Symbols
burden	confidence	aggression
challenge	determination	anarchy
commitments	honor	communists
determination	image	conquest
responsibility	national interest	enemies
struggle	pride	force
cause	will	oppression
		revolution
		threat
		tyranny
		conquest

APPENDIX B

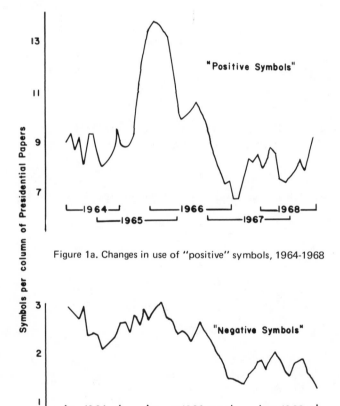

Figure 1a. Changes in use of "positive" symbols, 1964-1968

Figure 1b. Changes in use of "negative" symbols, 1964-1968

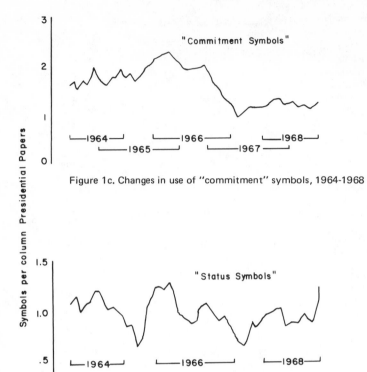

Figure 1c. Changes in use of "commitment" symbols, 1964-1968

Figure 1d. Changes in use of "status" symbols, 1964-1968

P. TERRENCE HOPMANN

8. Internal and External Influences on Bargaining in Arms Control Negotiations: The Partial Test Ban

[handwritten annotation: Short on the logic of the interactions]

ABSTRACT

Three questions relevant to bargaining in arms control negotiations were addressed. First, to what extent is behavior within negotiations affected by exogenous variables, especially by conflict in the relations among the participants outside the negotiating arena, as compared with endogenous variables, that is, the patterns of bargaining within negotiations? Second, what is the nature and direction of the impact, if present, of external conflict on the bargaining process? Third, what is the role of symmetry and reciprocity on the part of negotiators in their actions within arms control negotiations? These three questions were analyzed with data on the negotiations among the United States, the Soviet Union, and the United Kingdom in the Eighteen Nation Disarmament Conference in 1962-63, leading to the agreement on a Partial Nuclear Test Ban Treaty. Two primary methods were employed. The external factors, the degree of conflict and cooperation, were scaled using "events interaction analysis." Also, actions of these three actors within the negotiations were coded using a categorical content analysis of the verbatim texts of all Test Ban negotiations within the ENDC from March 1962 through July, 1963.

(1) Arms control negotiations were found to be affected both by the international environment within which negotiations took place and by the internal actions of participants in the negotiations. Endogenous factors accounted for the largest portion of the variance.

(2) Insofar as negotiations were affected by external actions, the degree of conflict or cooperation in the external interactions among negotiating opponents was related positively to their behavior within the negotiations. In general, more cooperative external behavior was followed by increased agreement on major

Author's Note: I am grateful to Barry B. Hughes, Charles Walcott, and Olin Bray for assistance in many aspects of this research, to the Graduate School and Office of International Programs at the University of Minnesota for financial assistance, and to the Data Analysis Center at the University of Minnesota for grants of computer time on the CDC/6600 for data analysis.

213

issues and by an increase in new proposals and concessions. Conversely, increased exogenous conflict between opponents was followed by increasing disagreement within the Test Ban negotiations, and by fewer new proposals and concessions and even some retractions from past positions.

(3) Actions of the negotiating parties were characterized by substantial symmetry and reciprocity. The internal actions of all actors tended to be strongly interrelated, so that mutual responsiveness was generally high.

(4) There were substantial differences in the patterns by which the three different countries responded to both internal and external factors in the negotiations. Specifically, the United Kingdom was most constrained by both internal and external factors, the United States was least constrained by either set, and the Soviet Union was relatively more affected by internal than external factors.

Several tentative implications were drawn: First, the actors' reciprocity appeared conducive to agreement; whether this is generally true can be determined only by comparing this case with other less successful arms control negotiations. Second, these data tended to question the general validity of the common assumption that a "hard line" foreign policy may provide an opponent with an "incentive" for agreement in negotiations. On the contrary, conciliatory gestures and improved Soviet-American relations outside the negotiations were related to greater agreement among parties within the Test Ban negotiations. ∎

INTRODUCTION

The arms race looms as one of the greatest threats to the stability and security of the world. While theorists of international relations have often disagreed as to whether the arms race is a cause or consequence of international tensions, few have denied its importance in leading to open conflict between nations. Not only are armaments a necessary condition for all armed conflicts, but they may be a sufficient condition under some circumstances. In particular the arms race itself may generate international tensions and feelings of mutual insecurity which become causes of war (Richardson, 1960b; Boulding, 1959).

This is a particularly serious problem in the current international system. Over the past 25 years the "peace" and "stability" of the international system have come to depend largely on the two great powers' threat to destroy one another totally. Yet a paradoxical system of "peace" based on the "balance of terror" between nuclear powers capable of destroying the world many times over is probably not stable over the long run (Russett, 1970: 229). For one thing, the arms race itself generates such tension, suspicion, and fear that conflict could conceivably occur as a result of decision-makers' panic or misperceptions in times of crisis. In addition, the constant fear of an arms breakthrough by one side or the other is a destabilizing influence and forces both sides to compete in an ever-spiralling race to build newer and more destructive armaments.

In the past decade, however, the two nuclear powers appear to have become more aware of the great dangers of the arms race. Perhaps more than any other single factor, the crisis in Cuba in October 1962 made it clear to both great powers that war in the nuclear age was possible, and this possibility seemed to have a sobering effect on their beliefs about the desirability of the arms race. One consequence of this has been the commencement of some serious arms control negotiations between the United States and the Soviet Union, resulting in a series of limited, but nonetheless significant, arms control agreements. The first major agreement of this type was the Partial Nuclear Test Ban Treaty signed in Moscow in July 1963. The purpose of this paper is to examine the process of negotiation leading to the conclusion of that treaty within the context of events occurring simultaneously in the international system. The nature of the influences, from both the international environment and from the behavior of other actors within the negotiations needs to be examined more fully. This may enable us to determine both the relative impact and the direction of influence which either set of variables may exert on negotiations leading to successful arms control agreements.

The specific substantive subject of this study is the negotiation process in the Eighteen Nation Disarmament Conference (ENDC) in Geneva in 1962 and 1963, leading up to the agreement between the United States, the United Kingdom, and the Soviet Union on a "Treaty Banning Nuclear Weapons Tests in the Atmosphere, in Outer Space, and Under Water." During 1962 most of these negotiations took place among the three nuclear powers in a Subcommittee on the Discontinuance of Nuclear Weapons Tests, and in 1963 they returned to the plenary sessions of the Eighteen Nation Disarmament Conference. Although the final agreement was produced at a secret conference in Moscow in July 1963, the substantive negotiations leading up to the agreement took place in the ENDC and in a few public communications between President Kennedy and Premier Khrushchev, which are the primary subject of analysis here. In addition, we have examined the direct international interactions among the three major participants during the period from January 1962 through August 1963 in order to determine the relationships between these systemic interactions and the actual processes of negotiation.

A THEORETICAL MODEL OF THE INTERACTION BETWEEN INTERNATIONAL EVENTS AND INTERNAL BEHAVIORS IN ARMS CONTROL NEGOTIATIONS

Iklé (1964: 3-4) has defined negotiation as "a process in which explicit proposals are put forward ostensibly for the purpose of reaching agreement on an exchange or on the realization of a common interest when conflicting interests are present." This definition implies several basic assumptions. For one, negotiations are possible only when two or more nation-states are interacting under conditions which combine elements of both conflict and cooperation. If the situation were purely cooperative, there would be no need for negotiation and all nations' behaviors would naturally intersect in a compatible manner. On the other hand, if the situation were purely conflictual, then there would be no basis for cooperation through agreement, as in almost all situations no agreement would be preferred to any agreement. Furthermore, this definition assumes that some degree of communication is possible between the nations in order for there to be an exchange or common realization of interests between them. Thus, the nature of the exchange between nations engaging in negotiations is the act of communication, either in a verbal or non-verbal form.

In general then, the negotiation process may be conceived as one in which two or more nations conduct communications about some objectives which combine conflicting and cooperative goals. As Iklé has suggested, at any stage in the negotiation process an actor has available to him three alternative strategies among which he must choose, according to the extent to which they enable him to maximize his goals. First, he may accept the available terms set forth in the present status of the bargaining process and settle at that point. Second, he may choose no agreement and bring the negotiations to a conclusion; this could presumably occur if he could achieve no settlement within some range which he defined as acceptable to himself. Or third, he may engage in further bargaining to try to achieve an acceptable final solution (Iklé, 1964: 60-61). But clearly at every point he must weigh the utility of the present alternative available to him against the utility of no agreement. Thus the purpose of negotiations is to attempt to find the range of common interests between two or more actors, where their common interests outweigh the alternative advantages of not agreeing.

This balance between common interests in an agreement versus the advantages or disadvantages of not agreeing may be directly affected by several different kinds of factors. For the present we shall consider two major factors, namely the events occurring outside of negotiations and the degree of symmetry in the negotiating behaviors of all participants within negotiations. In considering the relative impact of these two sets of factors, the major question involves the extent to which negotiations are autonomous from their external environment.

One general model of the bargaining process might emphasize a rather wide range of effects which the international environment has on negotiations. Clearly events outside negotiations may serve as intentional threats or warnings which are designed by one or more actors to have some impact on the negotiating behavior of other actors. These threats may be designed to emphasize the costs of no agreement to the actors or to encourage them to accept terms favorable to the threatening nation. Similarly, one nation may, through its actions, indicate a desire to reduce tensions as a reward for reaching agreement. Both threats and promises are designed to increase the relative value of agreement over nonagreement to the participants in negotiations.

Therefore, general actions outside of negotiations may affect the perceptions held by participants of the relative costs and gains which can be derived from agreement. However there is some disagreement about the direction of the effects which the external environment may have on negotiating behaviors.

One general orientation suggests that relatively conflictual behavior may actually be conducive to agreement because it provides an incentive for an agreement. In effect, a relatively "hard line" foreign policy may be perceived as serving the function of a tacit warning or threat. It implies that a general improvement in relations is contingent upon successful negotiation of an agreement, and the threat of continued hostility or the warning of a continued arms race is implied if the other party fails to reach agreement.

A contrary hypothesis would predict that conflictual international behavior may actually detract from the ability of the negotiating parties to reach an agreement. Negotiations depend essentially for success upon the communication of a common interest between the parties which overrides whatever conflicting interests they may have on the issues under negotiation. Conflictual behavior may retard this process in several ways. It may accentuate the conflicting interests in the attention of the negotiators, thereby overriding the common interests. Furthermore, it may impede the communications which are essential to negotiations. Since external behaviors themselves become a form of nonverbal communications, they may contradict the verbal communications presented in the negotiating session, especially if the former is characterized by conflict while the latter is characterized by professions of belief in peace and reduced conflict. This often leads to the breakdown of trust so that negotiating parties see the words of the other party as being contradicted by their deeds. In such a case, threatening and conflictual interactions outside the negotiations may reduce the likelihood of agreement within the bargaining process.

In order to examine the degree and nature of external influences we have developed a simple model diagrammed in Figure 1 which consists of two major sets of variables presumed to affect the negotiating process. The first stage, including the exogenous variables, refers to the direct relations outside negotiations among the parties to the negotiations. This may be conceptualized as falling along a dimension from conflict to cooperation. The second stage, including the endogenous factors, refers to the process of negotiation itself. For the purposes of this paper we have considered three components at this stage: (a) the attitudes of each party towards the position of the other, defined operationally as the extent to which they agree or disagree on substantive issues under negotiation; (b) the actual behaviors of the parties in the negotiations, that is, their propensity to make new proposals and concessions versus retractions of former concessions and proposals; (c) the responses of negotiators at any point in time, defined here as the extent to which the parties reciprocally acknowledge the contributions of the other side to agreement or accuse one another of being responsible for no agreement.

This simple model of the negotiating process also has a dynamic element, and these various stages and components of the model are assumed to be linked sequentially. Thus each stage is assumed to affect some change in the next,

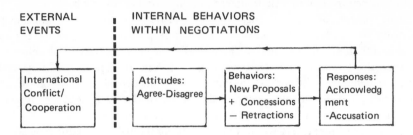

Figure 1. A Simple Hypothesized Model of the Effects of International Events on a Nation's Activities Within Negotiations

probably after some time lag, and the third component of stage two is hypothesized to feed back and to affect reciprocally the first stage. This produces a hypothetical model of the impact of exogenous variables upon the negotiating actions of each country treated individually. The relationships among these various components within each country may then be summarized by the following hypotheses:

Hypothesis 1.1: The degree of conflict in a nation's relations with its opponent outside the negotiations is related to its attitudes towards that nation within the negotiations: specifically, the greater the international conflict between a country and its opponent outside the negotiations, the greater the disagreement expressed by that country towards its opponent on substantive issues within the negotiations; conversely, the greater the international cooperation, the greater the agreement in negotiations.

Hypothesis 1.2: A nation's attitudes towards an opponent within the negotiations are related to its behaviors within the negotiations; that is, the greater the agreement by a country with its opponent on substantive issues of negotiations, the greater the new proposals and concessions and the fewer the retractions in its negotiating behavior; conversely, the more the disagreement, the more frequent are retractions, and new proposals and concessions are made less frequently.

Hypothesis 1.3: A nation's behaviors within negotiations are related to its responses to its opponent's behaviors: in other words, the more a country makes new proposals and concessions and the less it makes retractions in its negotiating position, the more it acknowledges the contributions of its opponent to agreement and the fewer the accusations of responsibility for no agreement; conversely the fewer the new proposals and concessions and the more the retractions, then the more frequent are accusations of responsibility for lack of agreement.

Hypothesis 1.4: A nation's responses within negotiations to its opponent's behaviors are related reciprocally to its degree of external conflict with that opponent: specifically, the more a country acknowledges the contributions of its opponent to agreement and the less it accuses its opponent of responsibility for lack of agreement, the more its international behavior will be characterized by cooperation with its opponent; conversely, the more a country accuses its opponent of responsibility for no agreement, the more its behaviors outside negotiations will be characterized by conflict.

These hypotheses assume that a nation's negotiating behavior will involve a consistent set of behaviors originally affected by the external relationships between itself and other parties to the negotiations with these effects being felt sequentially throughout the negotiating process itself. The endogenous aspects of the model may also be affected by the attitudes, behaviors, and responses of other actors within the bargaining process. We shall also examine the extent to which negotiations are an autonomous set of interactions, influenced primarily by the actions of all parties within the negotiations. Here again, several possible interpretations may be derived concerning the effects of these behaviors. One approach emphasizes the asymmetrical and discontinuous aspect of internal negotiating behavior. In such a model negotiations tend to remain stalemated until one actor makes a major new proposal which is either accepted by the other participants or perhaps forced upon them through some form of coercion. The stalemate may take the form of either inaction in negotiations or of a kind of approach-avoidance conflict in which actors step back from agreement whenever their positions become too similar. Such an interpretation of the Test Ban negotiations has been given by Jensen (1968).

The opposite approach emphasizes the symmetrical nature of successful negotiations. In this approach, successful outcomes in negotiations are made possible by the responsive behavior of all parties to the negotiations so that changes in the attitudes, behaviors, and responses of one actor are responded to by similar changes on the part of the other actors. This mutual responsiveness on the part of all actors is thus assumed to facilitate agreement. Taking this approach, we may suggest the following hypotheses about the effects of internal factors on the bargaining process:

Hypothesis 2.0: Negotiations between parties culminating in successful agreements will tend to be characterized by symmetry or reciprocity in attitudes, behaviors, and responses. In other words, positive attitudes, behaviors, and responses by one party are assumed to be related to positive attitudes, behaviors, and responses of the other party; conversely, negative actions by one will tend to be related symmetrically to negative actions of the others.

Hypothesis 2.1: In negotiations, relations between traditional allies will tend to be characterized by greater symmetry than relations between traditional enemies.

Hypothesis 2.2: Minor powers will tend to respond more to the endogenous factors, i.e., to the negotiating behaviors of the other actors in the negotiations, whereas major powers will be more directly affected by exogenous factors, i.e., by the international environment.

The model of negotiations developed in this project treats the negotiating behavior of a nation as a function both of its relations in the external international system with the other actors and as a function of the behavior of other actors within the negotiations themselves. For the purposes of these hypotheses, both types of relationships are assumed to be consistent, in the sense that positive and negative external relations, attitudes, behaviors, and responses are assumed to be interrelated directly both within each nation's negotiating system and in the relations among nations participating in negotiations. As treated in this idealized model, the set of variables represents a closed system, and the relationships have a deterministic bias. Clearly, however, the real world does not behave in all relevant respects exactly as predicted by this model. For example, the sequential processes suggested both in the within-nation model and the between-nation model tend to produce irreversible trends in one direction or the other, that is towards or away from agreement. Most negotiations do not proceed in such a one-directional manner, as many involve frequent fluctuation between agreement and disagreement.

Therefore, no relationship between the variables is meant to be completely deterministic; no one-to-one correspondence could be anticipated to link any pair of variables. The predicted relationships should be looked on as probabilistic rather than deterministic; furthermore, innovation should be able to enter the system at some points, since this is not in fact a closed system. But because present theories of bargaining provide little to suggest where such change and innovation is likely to enter the system, for purposes of setting up the basic relationships to be investigated we have treated the system as if it were closed. When testing it, however, we hope to be able to determine where important sources of change do enter the system and where other features of the highly simplified model are violated by the empirical data.

THE RESEARCH DESIGN

In order to test the hypotheses suggested above, it is necessary to collect data for two sets of variables included in the theoretical model: the degree of cooperation and conflict in the relations among participants outside negotiations and the behaviors of the parties in the actual negotiation process. The first set of variables was measured through the use of "events interaction data," designed to scale interactions between the participants along dimensions of conflict and cooperation. This procedure treats all major interactions between the actors as discrete events and attempts to place these events along scales to measure the content of these interactions.

The data were derived from chronologies reporting actions of the three major negotiating nations, the United States, the Soviet Union, and the United Kingdom towards each other for an 18-month period from January 1, 1962, through August 31, 1963. Each event was reduced to a series of separate simple dyadic interactions, namely an action connecting a single actor with a single target. Sources for these data included *The New York Times Index, Facts on*

File, and *Keesing's Contemporary Archives* for this period. The data were limited by the selective process employed by these sources, although the rather wide variation in events reported across these three sources may have contributed to the comprehensiveness of the data. All actions in these three sources listed under the headings of the three principal actors involving actions towards each other and their allies were extracted. These actions were then converted into simple dyadic interactions with the agents and targets masked. The only information provided, other than the action itself, was whether the target was an ally of the agent, a traditional enemy, or neither. Hence cards read like the following: "A holds maneuvers near the frontier of B" when B was an ally, "A holds maneuvers near the frontiers of X" if X was a traditional enemy, or "A holds maneuvers near frontiers of N" when the target was neutral.

A major limitation of this procedure was that this was all the contextual information which could normally be supplied easily without giving away the actual events being scaled. There is at least some reason to believe that bias may have resulted if the judges could identify the actors involved. But different discrete events may mean different things depending on the context, especially the chronological development of events, from which they were drawn. So the cost for preventing bias was the loss of such contextual information, requiring the scalers to treat events as discrete units.

All interactions reported in the above sources were recorded on 3x5 in. cards by date. Then another deck of cards was drawn up in which card order was randomized, the date removed, and the actors masked. These cards were then presented to four judges who were asked to scale them on scales developed by Corson (1970), two separate ratio scales for measuring the intensity of conflict and cooperation. The composite inter-judge reliability coefficient reached .88.

The original system was developed by Corson, who first had judges rank-order types of actions by intensity on both the cooperation and conflict dimension. Then other judges were presented with these rank-ordered scales and asked to assign the number one to the lowest intensity item; then all remaining actions were assigned numbers proportional to the increase in intensity over the previous. The final ratio scale was constructed through taking the geometric mean of the number assigned to each action by the respondents. Thus two scales resulted, ranging on the conflict dimension from 1 to 514, and on the cooperation dimension from 1 to 580.

This scale has several characteristics which differentiate it from other events interaction scales commonly used to measure conflict and cooperation in international relations (North et al., 1963; Moses et al., 1967). As a ratio rather than an ordinal or interval scale it is amenable to statistical manipulations not applicable to other techniques. It also may have reflected reality somewhat better than other scales because all events were not treated as if they were of equal intensity, but were rather weighted in a proportional manner. One limitation results from the fact that the rather wide range of intensities may have caused many small events to be washed out in the aggregate analysis by one or two high intensity events. It was virtually impossible to tell for sure to what extent this weighting distorted reality or actually reflected it more accurately.

The data, when scaled on these dimensions, were averaged across the four judges, and the numerical results were then reassociated with the original interaction card on which date, actor, and target could be identified. These data were aggregated on a monthly basis for each of the three dyads. A composite score for cooperation and conflict was then computed for each dyad, and a combined score consisting of the percentage of the interaction characterized by cooperation in each of three dyads connecting the United States, the Soviet Union, and the United Kingdom for each month from January 1962, through August 1963, served as the indicator for the interaction among parties to the Test Ban negotiations outside the negotiations.

The second set of variables, involving the bargaining processes within the formal negotiations, was measured through a thematic or categorical content analysis of the complete texts of all Test Ban negotiations in the Eighteen Nation Disarmament Conference from March 14, 1962, through July 30, 1963. These include the complete verbatim texts of the Subcommittee on the Cessation of Nuclear Weapons Tests which held 50 sessions on the Test Ban Treaty in 1962 and the plenary meetings of the ENDC in 1963, of which 28 sessions were at least partially devoted to discussion of the Test Ban Treaty.

For each session the various types of action included in our hypotheses were recorded whenever they occurred in the speech of a delegate. These procedures were similar to those employed by Jensen (1968) in his study of the Test Ban negotiations, except that some additional coding categories were employed and no attempt was made at this stage to weight different behaviors. For each session a record was kept for each of the three major actors, including each of the following types of statements or actions: (1) expression of agreement or disagreement on substantive issues of negotiation; (2) negotiating behaviors, including new proposals, concessions, and retractions as well as the use of threats or promises to support any of these actions; and (3) acknowledgment of the contributions of the other side to an agreement, and accusations of the responsibility of the other side for lack of agreement.

In addition, the number of pages of text covered in each session by each negotiator was recorded as a control for length. These data thus permitted us to measure the second set of variables found in the simple model. They too were aggregated on a monthly basis for every month except for January, 1963, when the ENDC was in recess. Thus, for each month we could determine for each country the average number of times per page of verbatim text that any negotiator engaged in any of the relevant behaviors or expressed any of the relevant attitudes. These data could then be related on a monthly basis over time with those obtained from the "events interaction analysis" to determine the relaionships between events outside negotiations and the bargaining processes within the negotiations.

For purposes of analyzing the data statistically, several alternative models were employed. In general, since our hypotheses implied that variables would be related sequentially, it seemed appropriate to analyze data in terms of several time lag models. Several models were tried, including no lag, a one month lag between all variables, and a decaying memory lag. The latter model was found to provide the best fit, and most results reported in this paper are based upon that analysis. This model assumes that each actor behaves in part on the basis of past information, although his memory of past events decays rapidly with time. Therefore, dependent variables are related to a composite independent variable, weighted to include present behavior as well as behavior during the two preceding months according to the following formula where Y represents the dependent variable, X represents the independent variable, and t represents one month time intervals:

$$.50X_t + .35X_{t-1} + .15X_{t-2} \rightarrow Y_t$$

In this model every variable may be related to every other variable in two directions, so that effects may be indicated with one variable acting on another, and, where actions proceed in both directions, the effects may be assumed to be reciprocal.

RESULTS: INTERNAL AND EXTERNAL FACTORS IN THE BARGAINING PROCESSES

Hypothesis 1, including its subparts, predicted that each individual nation's negotiating behavior would be directly related to the dyadic conflict between that nation and its opponent outside of the negotiations. Furthermore, it suggested that the effects of the external conflict behavior would be felt in a sequential pattern like that diagrammed in Figure 1. In examining the data for the three principal countries involved in the Test Ban negotiations we found that the external conflict did have a significant effect in all cases, but that the pattern of those effects was somewhat different for all three countries. The results for each of the three countries are diagrammed in Figure 2, parts a, b, and c, where the empirically derived within-country models are found. In these diagrams the lines represent relationships significant at the .10 level or better, and the arrows represent the direction of sequential ordering based on the decaying lag model. Values within each box below the title represent the extent to which each variable was related to itself in the lagged term. The value indicated by the symbol T = .xx is the correlation of the variable with time; if it has an asterisk, it means that the variable was significantly correlated with time at the value represented by .xx. The relationships between two serial values may be auto-correlated due to the common effects of time on both.

The empirical model for the United States found in Figure 2a indicates that conflict between the United States and the Soviet Union did not have a significant impact on any of the three components in their negotiating behavior

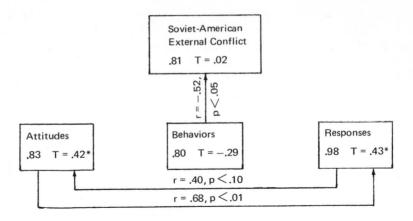

Figure 2a. Effects of conflict between the United States and the Soviet Union on bargaining actions of the United States in Test Ban negotiations, 1962-1963[a]

a. Data are analyzed using a decaying time-lagged model, with the direction of temporal sequence indicated by arrows.

at Geneva, using the decaying lag model. The primary reason for this seems to be that simultaneous correlations were very low or negative (.05 between conflict and attitudes, −.16 between conflict and behavior, and −.24 between conflict and responses). These results offset much higher lag correlations in the decaying memory model. In examining one and two month lags, somewhat stronger findings appear. Soviet-American conflict outside of negotiations appears to exert a significant relationship on American attitudes within negotiations after a one-month lag ($r = .36$, $p < .10$), and attitudes are weakly though insignificantly related to behaviors after an additional month ($r = .25$). The strongest relationship, however, was found between Soviet-American conflict and United States behavior in negotiations, with the latter value lagged a full two months behind the former ($r = .59$, $p < .01$). In many ways this aspect of the empirical model reflects the theoretical model fairly closely, inasmuch as effects of external variables seem to impinge on the attitudes of American negotiators in the first month, which in turn affect behaviors in the second month. One exception to the hypothesized model was that responses did not seem to follow after behaviors. Indeed, responses were related reciprocally to American attitudes, and the decaying lag correlations reached were significant in both direction ($r = .68$ and .40). Finally, there was no feedback in the American model from responses in the international environment. Rather what feedback did exist emanated from the behavior variable, although it was negatively related to Soviet-American conflict. Therefore, events outside of the negotiations tended to respond in the opposite direction from the behavior of the United States within the negotiations. The feedback loop thus did not tend to reinforce the previous patterns of behavior, enabling changes in behavior to enter the system. One reason for this is that many major American proposals and concessions were made early in the period under analysis in this study, especially in the summer of 1962. These new proposals were followed by the events of greatest conflict, particularly by the Cuban missile crisis, which perhaps accounts for the negative relationship in this case.

In general, however, the American model gave qualified support to hypothesis 1.1. Although the effects of Soviet-American conflict on American negotiating actions were often weak and delayed, the effects that did exist were in the predicted direction. As Soviet-American conflict decreased the United States tended, after some time lag, to agree more with them on specific issues, and, after an additional time lag, to make more frequent new proposals and concessions and fewer retractions. Thus, for the United States, a reduction in inter-system conflict appears to have increased somewhat the propensity towards agreement within negotiations after a time lag of several months.

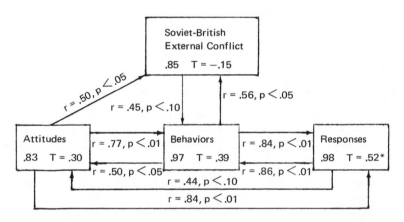

Figure 2b. Effects of conflict between the United Kingdom and the Soviet Union on bargaining actions of the United Kingdom in the Test Ban negotiations, 1962-1963[a]

a. Data are analyzed using a decaying time-lagged model, with the direction of temporal sequence indicated by arrows.

The empirical model for the United Kingdom, depicted in Figure 2b, is somewhat different from that for the United States and conforms more closely to the theoretical model. British conflict with the Soviet Union was a significant factor affecting British negotiating behaviors (r = .45). Thus at least some portion of the variance in British behaviors was accounted for by their relations with the Soviet Union outside negotiations, so that improved relations led to increased British initiatives in the form of new proposals and concessions combined with fewer retractions. The other components of the British model were highly interrelated. The three internal components were all related to one another strongly and reciprocally, with all six possible interrelations being statistically significant. Therefore, the internal aspects of British actions remain remarkably consistent and interdependent. Reciprocal effects were also exerted by several aspects of British actions back on the international environment. These reciprocal effects did not originate from the responses, as predicted by the theoretical model. Rather both the attitude and the behavior component had significant and positive effects on the international environment. Thus, although most correlations were well below 1.00, the pattern of interrelationships was very tight-knit, as predicted in the theoretical model, and all aspects of British behavior tended to be related to all others. The British system appeared to be far more closed to extraneous influences than was the American system.

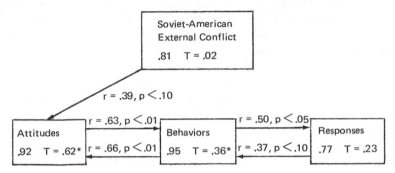

Figure 2c. Effects of conflict between the United States and the Soviet Union on bargaining actions of the Soviet Union in the Test Ban negotiations, 1962-1963[a]

   a. Data are analyzed using a decaying time-lagged model, with the direction of temporal sequence indicated by arrows

The empirical model for the Soviet Union, depicted in Figure 2c, also corresponds rather closely to the predictions of the theoretical model. The first relationship predicted in hypothesis 1.1 between Soviet-American external conflict and Soviet agreement with the United States on substantive issues of negotiations was confirmed ($r = .39$, $p < .10$). Here improved external relations between the super powers were reflected, after the decaying lag, in increased Soviet agreement (or reduced disagreement) with the United States on the issues under discussion in the Test Ban negotiations. The second sub-hypothesis, 1.2, predicted a positive relationship between attitudes towards the opponent in the negotiations and the behavior of the Soviet Union within the negotiations. This hypothesis too was confirmed reciprocally, with changes in attitudes related to later changes in behavior ($r = .63$, $p < .01$) and changes in behavior also affecting later changes in attitudes ($r = .66$, $p < .01$). Increased Soviet agreement on the issues with the West was related to an increased propensity to make new proposals and concessions combined with fewer retractions. The third hypothesis, 1.3, predicted a positive relationship between new behavioral initiatives taken by the Soviet Union in negotiations and increased recognition by them of the contributions by the West toward agreement and fewer accusations of Western obstinacy and obstruction of negotiations. This hypothesis too was confirmed in both directions, going from behavior to responses ($r = .50$, $p < .05$) and from responses reciprocally back to behaviors ($r = .37$, $p < .10$). Hypothesis 1.4, predicting a feedback relationship from these responses to events in the international system, was not confirmed. The unique aspect of the Soviet model was the total absence of any feedback relationships from their actions within negotiations to their relationships with the United States outside negotiations. Thus, in the Soviet case, negotiating behaviors were affected by external actions, but the internal actions of the Soviet Union exerted no reciprocal effects back onto the international environment.

Several conclusions may be drawn. First, in all cases the degree of external conflict and cooperation among participants was positively related to at least some aspects of the negotiating activities of all three nations, with different lag correlations applying in each case. Second, the pattern of interactions among the various components of the negotiating process differed somewhat for all three actors; therefore, the form through which external relationships affected the negotiations varied from country to country, even though the effects were present and were all in the same direction in every case. Third, in no case did the response, that is, the degree of acknowledgment of contributions by the other party versus accusations of responsibility for no agreement, mediate between attitudes and behaviors during negotiations and future external relationships. Rather, in all three cases it was related positively and reciprocally to attitudes (United States) or behaviors (Soviet Union) or both (United Kingdom). Therefore, the response seems to be related only to the internal dynamics of the negotiating process. Feedback to external relations which was found to be positive only in the British case, proceeded from both attitudes and behaviors, and in the American case proceeded negatively from internal behaviors.

The second set of hypotheses concerned the interrelationships endogenous to the negotiations, namely the relations among the three aspects of the negotiating acuvities of each state across all three dyads. The basic question to be examined thus involved the extent to which an actor's negotiating behavior was determined by the behaviors within the negotiations of the other actors rather than by the interrelationships among those actors outside negotiations. Therefore, hypothesis 2.0 suggested that the interrelationships among the negotiating actions of all three parties would tend to be characterized by reciprocity across all three components of the negotiating process, namely attitudes, behaviors, and responses. Thus, for every dyad there were nine possible two-way interrelationships (or 18 uni-directional relationships) among the three components. Furthermore, each component was treated in terms of basically positive or negative dimensions. That is, positive actions included agreement on substantive issues, more new proposals and concessions and/or fewer retractions, and more frequent acknowledgment of contributions to agreement or fewer accusations of responsibility for no agreement. Conversely, negative actions included disagreement on substantive issues, fewer new proposals and concessions and/or more retractions, and more accusations of responsibility for intransigence and/or fewer acknowledgments of contributions of the other side to agreement. Therefore, the hypothesis which predicted symmetry across the nine possible relations in each dyad suggested that positive-negative actions of each type (attitudes, behaviors, and responses) by each actor should have been positively related to positive-negative actions of each type by the other actor. The data to test this hypothesis were analyzed for each of the three dyads separately.

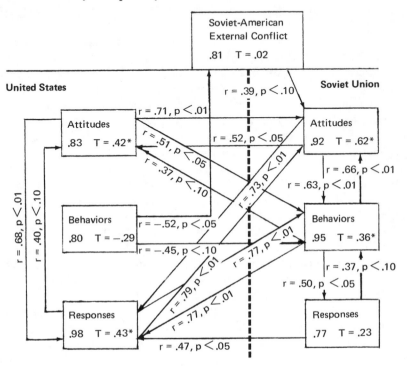

Figure 3a. Negotiating actions in the Soviet-American dyad during the Test Ban negotiations, using a decaying time-lagged model

The statistically significant relationships in the Soviet-American dyad are diagrammed in Figure 3a. Using a .10 level of significance one would expect about 2 relationships to be "significant" on the basis of chance. However, in this case 11 of 18 one-way relationships proved to be significant with 9 of those being in the positive direction. This gives strong support to hypothesis 2.0 in the case of the Soviet-American dyad. Two of these relationships could be partially accounted for by auto-correlation between two variables (U.S. responses and Soviet attitudes) which are both serially correlated. The coefficients of their relationship, however, are stronger than the serial correlation for either variable, so not all of the relationship could have been accounted for simply by time.

The only significant exception to the predictions of hypothesis 2.0 involves

all 6 relationships entailing American behavior. Four of these 6 were not significant, and the 2 which did reach high statistical levels were negative. This may be
accounted for largely by the fact that American behaviors were most positive
very near the beginning of the negotiations when the United States delegation
put forward numerous new proposals. These were responded to negatively by
the Soviet Union in the early phases of negotiation. Later, however, the United
States offered fewer new proposals when the Soviet Union began to make more
concessions and to respond more favorably to earlier proposals. This probably
largely accounts for the negative effects of American behavior on Soviet
behavior and responses. Other than this one case, and except for a negative
reaction to American behaviors within the negotiations, almost all other
interrelationships within the data were statistically significant, indicating
substantial reciprocity in Soviet-American actions. In particular, American
responses appeared to be strongly related to all aspects of Soviet action within
the negotiations as opposed to Soviet actions outside the negotiations to which
they were unrelated. Soviet responses, on the other hand, seemed to be less
responsive to American actions within the negotiations; indeed, they were
inversely related to American behavior. This may have contributed to stalemate
in the early stages of negotiations, although in the later stages it may have
contributed to a reversal in direction when American behaviors were characterized by few new initiatives.

Turning next to the data on the two allies in the negotiations, the United
States and the United Kingdom, one can see in Figure 3b that even greater
reciprocity existed in actions within the negotiations. In this case 12 of 18
relationships were statistically significant, with 11 being positive and only 1
being negative. All components of both nations' systems were interrelated with
one exception, namely American behavior. In this case only 1 of 6 possible
relationships involving U.S. behavior was significant, and that one was negative;
British attitudes responded inversely to American behavior within the negotiations. With the exception of this one case, 11 of the remaining 12 possible
relationships were significant and positive, demonstrating the high degree of
symmetry between British and American actions within negotiations. But here
again the lack of consistency in American behavior disrupted what is otherwise a
highly constrained system of negotiations between the two allies. The entire
British model is one of considerable constraint, as British behaviors are both
highly related to what their allies do as well as being highly consistent internally
and significantly related to their relations with the Soviet Union outside of
negotiations. Therefore, on the whole the British-American dyad is consistent
with the predictions in hypothesis 2.0.

The data for the third dyad, which relates the Soviet Union and the United
Kingdom, are found in Table 3c. Here hypothesis 2.0 is confirmed even more
strongly than in the two previous cases. Significant relationships among the
various internal components in the two nations' models are 14 out of 18
possible, and all are positive. Indeed, the only pair of variables which are not

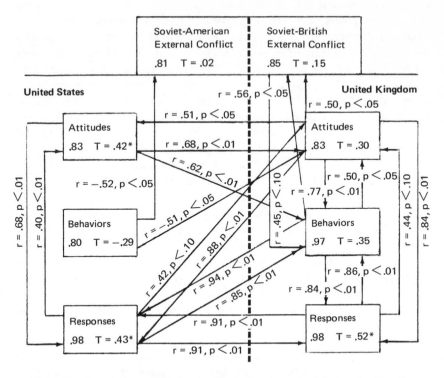

Figure 3b. Negotiating actions in the Anglo-American dyad during the Test Ban negotiations, using a decaying time-lagged model

significantly related by at least a one-way relationship is that involving Soviet responses and British behaviors. With this exception, the British and Soviet dyad approximates almost the closed system assumed by the hypothetical model. Not only are most of the correlations connecting these variables significant, but in many cases they are extremely high. British and Soviet actions within the Test Ban negotiations were very closely interrelated and symmetrical.

These results may be summarized in terms of hypothesis 2 and its subparts. Hypothesis 2.0 predicted symmetry among all three components of the activities within negotiations by all three actors across all three dyads. Thus, changes in a positive direction in a single component were predicted to be directly related to positive changes in all components of the negotiating actions of the other two actors. Of 54 possible relationships of this type (18 for each of three dyads), 34 were statistically significant in the predicted direction, and 3 were significant in the inverse direction, with 17 remaining insignificant. The number of significant positive relationships was far greater than would be predicted on the basis of chance, thereby giving substantial support to this hypothesis. In all three dyads actions tended to be highly symmetrical and interrelated, and our theory would tend to suggest that this reciprocity probably

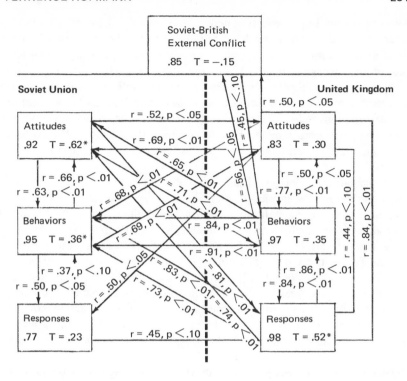

Figure 3c. Negotiating actions in the Anglo-Soviet dyad during the Test Ban negotiations, using a decaying time lagged model

contributed to the attainment of a successful agreement in the Test Ban negotiations.

Hypothesis 2.1 suggested that traditional allies would tend to demonstrate greater symmetry in their negotiating activities than would traditional enemies. The results on this hypothesis differed between the United States and the United Kingdom. In neither case were the differences great, although for the American case the results were slightly consistent with this hypothesis. There were 11 positive relationships between the United States and its ally, Great Britain, in contrast with 9 such relationships with the enemy, the Soviet Union. In the British case, however, there were even more positive relationships between its own activities and those of its enemy, the Soviet Union, totalling 14 in contrast to 11 with the United States. These weak and mixed differences cast considerable doubt on the validity of this hypothesis as applied to the Test Ban negotiations.

Hypothesis 2.2 predicted that relatively minor powers, in this case Great Britain, would respond more to the negotiating actions of other actors within the negotiations rather than to external events, whereas the great powers would be affected more by their external relations with one another. These data did not confirm the hypothesis as stated although they did suggest an interesting modification of it. The general results indicated that the minor power, namely Great Britain, was far more responsive to or constrained by both external actions and internal behaviors than either of the other two actors. Therefore, British behaviors were generally more determined by both internal and external variables, whereas other factors outside of these models seemed to account more for the variations in Soviet and American behaviors. The setting and interactions within negotiations are more likely to constrain the behavior of minor actors, while the great powers have more freedom for maneuver and initiative in their actions.

At the outset we suggested that one major objective of our research was to determine the relative impact of internal and external factors in the negotiating behaviors of nation-states in arms control negotiations. To aid in this task we have done some multiple regression analysis to attempt to determine the percentage of variance in the behaviors of the three actors which could be determined by three sets of factors: (1) the external conflict between each country and its opponent; (2) the within-nation model for each country, including both external conflict and the two other components of internal action, namely attitudes and responses; and (3) the between-nation model, that is, the behaviors of other actors in the negotiations. Results for this analysis are contained in Table 1. Since the three sets of independent variables are somewhat

Table 1. Multiple regression analysis of the effect of combined independent variables upon the behavior component of each nation's actions within negotiations, using a decaying time-lagged model [a]

	DEPENDENT VARIABLE: BEHAVIOR IN NEGOTIATIONS					
	United States		Soviet Union		United Kingdom	
Independent Variables	r	r^2	r	r^2	r	r^2
External Conflict	.05	.02	.34	.12	.45	.21
Own System (Conflict plus attitude and response)	.02	.004	.68	.47	.92	.85
(External Conflict)	.08		.25		.60	
(Attitude)	.15		.50		−.27	
(Response)	−.27		.26		.79	
Behaviors of Others	.29	.08	.88	.77	.91	.83
(Country 1)	−.27 (USSR)		−.46 (U.S.)		.09 (U.S.)	
(Country 2)	.21 (U.K.)		.85 (U.K.)		.90 (USSR)	

a. Multiple regression coefficients are given for the effect of each combined independent variable at the lagged time upon the behavior component as the dependent variable. Components of each combined independent variable are then broken out in parentheses, where partial correlation coefficients are presented.

correlated with one another, they represent overlapping, not entirely exclusive, explanations.

Nothing explains United States' behavior adequately. As we noted previously, although U.S. behavior is somewhat related to external conflict after a two-month lag, almost nothing else seems to account for it. The greatest variance in Soviet behavior could be accounted for by the behavior of the other actors in the negotiations. These variables alone accounted together for 77 percent of Soviet behavior; this variance is explained both by the positive relationship of Soviet behavior to British behavior and its negative relationship to American behavior. Alternatively, about 47 percent of Soviet behavior may be accounted for by its own internal actions combined with its external relations with the United States, and only 12 percent of its behavior is directly accountable for by relations with the United States outside negotiations. Therefore, while Soviet behavior is positively related to external variables, it is clearly more responsive to actions within the negotiations themselves.

In the British case, again, we find a similar conclusion. However, as noted previously, British behavior is far more constrained by both internal and external factors, in contrast to the other two nations. In comparing the effects of the within-nation model and the between-nation model, we find that each accounts for very high percentages of the variance in British behavior, namely 85 percent and 83 percent respectively. By contrast, the external conflict variable acting alone accounts for only 21 percent of British behavior, although the relationship is clearly in the predicted direction.

We conclude that the Test Ban negotiations were more affected by the behavior taking place within the negotiations than by events outside. However, they were not completely autonomous from external events, as all three countries were affected in some way by the degree of conflict/cooperation with their enemies, and the effects did proceed in the predicted direction. Insofar as external conflict did have an effect, the direction was one in which increased cooperation contributed to more positive internal interactions, whereas increased conflict led to more negative interactions, including disagreement.

Yet the general pattern which emerges is one of a set of negotiations proceeding in a generally upward progression toward more positive activities. Although few correlations with time were statistically significant, all internal variables except American behaviors had positive serial correlations. American behaviors, as we have already noted, started out with numerous proposals, and from that point on the United States undertook fewer initiatives. The serial correlation for American behaviors was $-.31$, which probably explains why it was negatively correlated with so many other variables. Except for this case, however, all variables showed some more positive actions over time, which were generally reinforced by the reciprocal responses of the other actors, thus leading to a general positive spiral towards agreement. Certainly there were setbacks along the way and periods when stalemate seemed to have taken hold; yet the positive outcomes were perhaps largely a consequence of this symmetrical behavior. One other factor may have been related to the attainment of a successful outcome. While external behaviors had been rather cooperative at the onset of negotiations in 1962, they deteriorated significantly midway through the negotiations in the period surrounding the Cuban missile crisis and extending even into early 1963. In March of 1963, U.S.-Soviet relations were characterized by only 16 percent cooperative interactions, and no cooperative interactions were recorded between the United Kingdom and the Soviet Union. But from that point on the deteriorating trend was reversed suddenly, and cooperation in the Soviet-American dyad increased to 62 percent in April, 93 percent in May, 91 percent in June, 85 percent in July, and 100 percent in August, after the Test Ban Treaty was signed. While the external system may not have been the most important factor explaining behavior throughout the entire negotiation process, it did appear to be an important contributing factor to breaking the stalemate and making agreement possible in the summer of 1963.

CONCLUSION

This research produced several major findings. First, arms control negotiations were found to be affected by both the international environment within which negotiations took place and by the internal actions of participants in the negotiations. While the endogenous factors seemed to account for the largest proportion of the variance in the behaviors of all three actors, all three countries were affected in some significant manner by the level of conflict/cooperation among negotiating nations outside of the negotiations.

Second, insofar as negotiations were affected by external actions, the relationship was a positive one between the degree of conflict or cooperation in the external behaviors of the opponents and their activities within the formal negotiations. In general, more cooperative external behaviors were followed by increased agreement among parties and by an increase in new proposals and concessions. Conversely, increased conflict between opponents was also followed by increased disagreement within the Test Ban negotiations and also by fewer new proposals and concessions and even some retractions.

Third, the endogenous actions of the negotiating parties were found to be characterized by substantial symmetry and reciprocity. The internal actions of all actors tended to be strongly interrelated, so that mutual responsiveness was generally high. The extent to which these factors actually contributed to an outcome of agreement can only be determined with confidence by comparing the results from the Partial Test Ban case to other cases of less successful arms control negotiations.

Fourth, this study also indicated that there were substantial differences in the patterns with which different countries responded to negotiations, and especially to the relative impact of endogenous and exogenous variables. In the case of the Test Ban negotiations the United States remained surprisingly independent in its actions from both internal and external influences; external conflict affected

American behavior only indirectly through its impact on attitudes and only after a two-month lag, while the United States was less responsive to internal actions of the other parties than either of the other two actors. The Soviet Union was more directly affected by both external actions and by the actions of other parties within the negotiations. Soviet attitudes and behaviors both tended to be highly responsive to the actions within negotiations of the other two parties. Finally, the actions of the United Kingdom tended to be the most directly affected by all of the variables analyzed in this study; they were most strongly affected by the external environment, by a consistent set of internal actions, and by the attitudes, behaviors, and responses of the other actors. Great Britain's behavior was more constrained overall by the variables included in this study than was the behavior of either superpower, since the latter undoubtedly had more flexibility and room for maneuver.

There are several limitations to this study which necessarily qualify the types of generalizations that can be derived from it. First, it suffers from all the limitations of any case study, and the relevance of its findings beyond the single case can be established only by further research. Nevertheless, the methods and hypotheses are in a sufficiently generalized form to permit comparative analysis. The need for further work is particularly severe in the light of attempts made herein to develop a dynamic model of the negotiating process, given the limitations of an eighteen month time span. I am presently extending the time range covered in this study throughout the entire 1960 period as well as developing experimental procedures to test many of these hypotheses in a controlled environment (Hopmann and Walcott, forthcoming). Second, the methods employed in this research are still in a relatively experimental stage of development, and further experience with these methods may be necessary before we have greater confidence in them. Nevertheless, they did prove to be useful in measuring relevant concepts and testing the major hypotheses examined in this study.

In spite of these rather serious limitations, we may attempt to speculate about a few implications of this research. First, the data uncovered tentatively suggest that negotiations are more likely to reach agreement if the negotiators maintain a high degree of responsiveness or reciprocity to changes in attitudes, behaviors, and responses of their negotiating partners. This type of reciprocity appears to be conducive to a convergence of negotiating positions. Second, these findings tended to indicate that any efforts to improve the general state of international relations between negotiating parties should be conducive to increased agreement within the negotiations. This would seem to cast doubt on the frequently held assumption that threats, warnings, and other belligerent behavior outside of negotiations actually contribute to agreement. In no case did our data support this assertion, as correlations between external actions and internal behavior were always positive, even though not always significant. In the Test Ban case increased levels of conflict were always related to decreased levels of agreement. Perhaps the most clearcut substantive illustration of this was the use by the United States of atmospheric testing as a threat applied in the negotiations.

When President John F. Kennedy announced that American nuclear tests were to resume in late April 1962 (in a speech on March 2, 1962), he made specific reference to the effect of this action on Soviet bargaining behavior in the ENDC:

> "As new disarmament talks approach, the basic lesson of some three years and 353 negotiating sessions at Geneva is this—that the Soviets will not agree to an effective ban on nuclear tests as long as a new series of offers and prolonged negotiations, or a new uninspected moratorium, or a new agreement without controls, would enable them once again to prevent the West from testing while they prepare in secret.
>
> "But inasmuch as this choice is no longer open to them let us hope that they will take a different attitude on banning nuclear tests—that they will prefer to see the nuclear arms race checked instead of intensified, with all the dangers that intensification is likely to bring: the spread of nuclear weapons to other nations; the constant increase in world tensions; the steady decrease in the security of us all." (ENDC/113: 8)

Kennedy concluded by informing the Soviets that they had two months, until the end of April, to accept the American draft treaty before testing would begin and its consequences unleashed. The Soviets refused to accept this proposal and the United States resumed its nuclear tests. In our data, the percentage of Soviet-American cooperation on the Corson scale fell progressively from a high of 100 percent in April 1962, to 6 percent in September 1962, before the Cuban missile crisis. This was accompanied by a reduction of agreement in negotiations which has already been indicated. The Soviets consistently denounced the resumption of American tests in the negotiating sessions and described them as a major obstacle to agreement.

Apparently Kennedy changed his view on this issue during the next year. In his speech at American University on June 10, 1963, he announced that high level discussions would begin shortly in Moscow to attempt to reach agreement on a Test Ban Treaty. He added:

> "To make clear our good faith and solemn conviction in this matter, I now declare that the United States does not propose to conduct nuclear tests in the atmosphere so long as other states do not do so. We will not be the first to resume. Such a declaration is no substitute for a formal binding treaty—but I hope it will help us to achieve one."(ENDC/95: 6)

According to our data, this speech was preceded by an improvement in Soviet-American relations, moving from a low of 16 percent cooperation in March 1963, to 91 percent by June, and, following the Test Ban agreement, it rose to 100 percent in August. While the issue of nuclear testing itself may not have made all the difference, and while the early threat may have dramatized the dangers of a Soviet-American competition in nuclear testing, the cessation of tests combined with more general changes over time in Soviet-American relations seems to have contributed to the actual outcome.

This case study suggests that greater belligerency in foreign policy, especially when tied by threats to the actual negotiations, seems to detract from agreement. This finding is contrary to the assumption upon which policy makers often seem to be operating, and may therefore challenge the generality of their assumption even if it is not completely generalized itself. For example, a recent report by the U.S. Senate Armed Services Committee argued that expansion of the American Safeguard Anti-Ballistic Missile system would contribute to agreement in the Strategic Arms Limitations Talks (SALT) between the United States and the Soviet Union:

> "As one of the central limitations to be negotiated in conjunction with limitations of offensive forces, Safeguard is essential to the American position. Without Safeguard the Soviets would have little incentive to agree to constrain increases to their offensive forces. The progress thus far in the SALT talks has served to confirm this view that Safeguard is essential to their successful conclusion." (Quoted in International Herald Tribune, July 17, 1970: 5.)

While the data obtained in our research may not completely disprove this assertion that threats of an expanded arms race may at times contribute to agreement, they at least throw into question its generality.

APPENDIX:
DATA SOURCES

Eighteen Nation Disarmament Conference, *Documents,* ENDC/1-95. Geneva: 1962-1963.

Eighteen Nation Disarmament Conference, *Verbatim Records,* ENDC/PVI-148. Geneva: 1962-1963.

Eighteen Nation Disarmament Conference, Subcommittee on the Cessation of Nuclear Weapons Tests, *Verbatim Records,* ENDC/SCI/PVI-50. Geneva: 1962.

NAZLI CHOUCRI with the collaboration of Robert C. North

9. In Search of Peace Systems: Scandinavia and the Netherlands; 1870-1970

ABSTRACT

This investigation draws upon conflict theory and analysis for insights concerning the development and maintenance of peace systems.

Peace systems are not devoid of conflict. Conflict emerges whenever individuals, groups, or nations come into contact. One distinguishing characteristic of a peace system is the institutionalization of non-violent modes of behavior and conflict resolution. Testing for the prevalence of peace systems is based on three distinct but related considerations: first, isolating the determinants of warfare; second, identifying those situations which do not conform to what are thought of as conflict and war-prone systems; and finally, examining the relationships among those variables that are crucial in conflict systems and noting the extent to which their behavior does not conform to a conflict model.

The investigation centers around three Scandinavian countries and the Netherlands. The former provide a marked contrast with major powers, and the latter serves as something of a contrast to the Scandinavians. The analyses combine an historical approach with more recent empirical methods of inquiry. Causal modelling procedures are employed to estimate the parameters of a conflict model (partially validated in earlier analyses) while employing data for these four countries. Our results indicated that most links in a war-prone conflict model do not hold for Sweden and Norway and few links are significant for Denmark and Holland. The variable effects of population dynamics and technological development become apparent as do alternative "paths" to military preparedness. ∎

Authors' Note: We would like to acknowledge the research assistance of Raisa Deber and Panayiotis Momferratos whose careful work and sense of precision were invaluable in the course of our investigations. We are also grateful to Hayward Alker and J. S. Nye for criticism of an earlier draft. Research support from the Center for International Studies at MIT facilitated the background investigations.

239

POPULATION, RESOURCES, TECHNOLOGY, AND INTERNATIONAL BEHAVIOR

This chapter represents a convergence of two intellectual traditions—conflict analysis and peace research. On the one hand we have an interest in identifying the origins, nature, and dynamics of conflict and warfare among nations; and on the other a deep concern for peace systems. Our purpose is to work toward an operational theory of international dynamics—one which will account for the peaceful resolution of conflict and the absence of war as well as for conflict and warfare. In any investigation of this kind the "causes" of war and the conditions for peace become highly interdependent, as they are in the "real" world.

We proceed from the assumption that the roots of conflict lie deep in the configuration of national attributes and, by extension, in the relative distributions of national capabilities within the international systems. These two sets of considerations define the parameters within which psychological, sociological, and political variables become important determinants of actions and reactions. Differences in national capabilities are therefore related and sometimes give rise to differences in behavior. Major Powers tend to have certain types of capabilities and they behave and are expected to behave in some ways and not in others. Historically, for example, Great Powers (as well as many Lesser and Small Powers) have tended to be war-prone. Thus, certain characteristic attitudes and behaviors on the part of the world's strongest Powers are likely to be markedly different from those exhibited by Lesser or Small Powers.[1] These attitudes and behaviors and also some of the influential attributes are also likely to be quite different from the attitudes, behaviors, and influential attributes of countries that are candidates for consideration as "peace system" nations.

We would expect a peace system to be characterized by the institutionalization of non-violent modes of international behavior and conflict resolution. For purposes of analysis, however, peace systems must be further identified in terms of particular kinds of (1) national attributes, (2) behavioral predispositions, and (3) patternings across national predispositions.[2]

The analysis that follows focuses on four Small Powers—Sweden, Norway, Denmark, and the Netherlands (at least three of which suggest rough approximations of peace systems nations) and searches for stable relationships among various indicators of national capability as well as changes over time and evidence for the existence of a national profile that is empirically distinguishable from those of the Major Powers. To the extent that the behavior of these states as Small Powers differs from the behavior of Major Powers, we would expect

1. The relationship between national capability and international behavior is a central theme in the International Relations literature (Aron, 1967, Organski, 1968; Renouvin and Duroselle, 1967; Rosecrance, 1963; Wright, 1965a). The essays in the volume, especially those by Wallace and by Rummel, bring the empirical perspective to bear most directly upon this issue.

2. There have not been any satisfactory definitions of peace systems, partly because of the nature of the phenomenon. (See Galtung, 1969, for a treatment of this problem.)

their attributes and characteristics also to differ; hence, uncovering the nature of these differences is an important, if only preliminary, step toward the identification of peace systems.

The development of conflict and war-prone systems is predicated, in large part, on the gradual convergence of determinant variables. Such systems crystallize to the extent that the "causes" of violence are neither weakened nor transformed into conditions for non-violent modes of behavior. In the same fashion, the development of peace systems is predicated on the absence of significant convergence or mutual reinforcement among various "causes" of violence and on the extent to which habitual modes of international behavior are non-violent in nature. Peace systems, however, are not devoid of conflict. Conflict emerges as soon as, and as long as, two or more individuals, groups, or nations come into contact.[3] But a unique characteristic of a peace system is the non-violent nature or mode of involvement in conflict.

Testing for the prevalence of peace systems is based on three distinct considerations: first, isolating determinants of warfare; second, identifying those situations which do not conform to what are thought of as violent conflict or war-prone systems; and, finally, examining the relationships among those variables that are crucial in a war-prone system and noting the extent to which the behavior of these variables in a peace system deviates from their behavior in a violence model. Thus, a model of peace systems will be one in which the greatest number of links in a war-prone conflict model appear to be non-significant or to provide negative effects on conflict-related variables.

The model used in our subsequent analysis is based on the proposition that the roots of international violence can be found in the distribution of attributes and capabilities of individual nations insofar as these continue to have an impact on, and even perhaps condition, their position relative to others in the international system. The crucial variables are population, resources, and technology, where technology refers to the general level and rate of development of human knowledge and skills in a society. A combination of growing population and developing technology imposes rapidly increasing demands upon resources. To meet these demands a society tends to develop specialized capabilities. The greater the unsatisfied demands and needs in a society and the greater the capabilities, the higher is the likelihood that national activities will be extended outside territorial boundaries.[4] Such efforts undertaken beyond the home territory may be expressed in any one or a combination of different modes—exploration, commerce, investment, extraction of minerals, warfare, and so forth. The mode (or combinations) of such external behavior will condition both eventual outcomes and the nature of relations among nations. Historically, many such expansions of effort beyond home territories have given rise to colonial-type wars against low-capability people and sometimes indirectly to wars with a rival Power.

3. See McNeil (1965) for different perspectives on conflict behavior.
4. See North in collaboration with Choucri (1971) for an extended discussion of the effects of population in the international system.

War-prone systems thus tend to develop when two or more countries with high capabilities and unsatisfied demands extend their interests and psycho-political borders outward and develop the feeling that such interests ought to be protected. There is then a strong probability that sooner or later the two spheres of interests will intersect. The more intense the intersections, the greater is the likelihood that competition will assume military dimensions. When this happens we may expect the competition to become transformed into conflict and perhaps an arms race or cold war. Thus, as we have argued elsewhere, major wars often emerge by way of a two-step process: in terms of internally generated pressures or external expansion of interests and activities and in terms of reciprocal comparisons, rivalry, and conflict between two (or more) Great Powers on a number of salient dimensions (Choucri and North, 1972),

Conflict relationships may be depicted, in a highly simplified way as follows in Figure 1.

Peace systems represent a variant of this basic model and are likely to develop when modes of international behavior generated by internal demands and pressures are such as to avoid giving rise to spheres of influence that need to be defended and thus to intersections among such spheres or to military competition. This does not mean that competition is avoided altogether, but rather that it is channelled through non-violent, low-threat modes of action. In

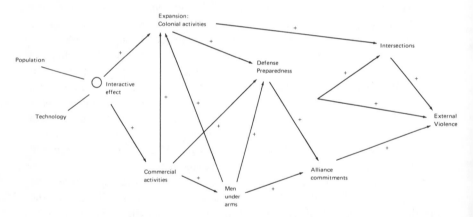

Figure 1. Linkages Between National Capabilities and External Behavior: A Conflict System Model [a]

a. This diagram is presented for illustrative purposes only. It is a simplified statement of the dynamics under consideration. For the sake of brevity further interactions, feedback effects and mutual dependencies are omitted although it should be recognized that they operate at every stage. It might also be noted that the expansion variables are bound by our empirical analysis of a specific conflict situation (Europe, 1870-1916) and that at different periods and with different nations other variables may be more appropriate. However, the general sequence of the dynamics pointed is independent of operational definitions. Finally, the diagram is meant to summarize the theoretical arguments in the text and not to provide an arrow diagram for direct translation to statistical equations.

the context of Figure 1, such relations are characterized not by positive feedback and explosive dynamics but by inverse effects and negative feedback loops at some critical junctures.

We suggest that the differences between war-prone and peace systems might be attributed to four considerations: the type and extent of demands that are generated internally; the general capability of the system to translate demands into actions; the nature and characteristics of the capabilities which the system has developed; and the modes within which international behavior is undertaken. Therefore, theoretically at least, the underlying structure of variables in a war-prone conflict system is similar to that of peace systems; the difference lies in initial values, coefficients, and levels and rates of change.

Our emphasis on internal capabilities should not be construed to imply a necessary one-to-one correspondence between population level, technological achievement, military capability, and so forth on the one hand and international behavior on the other. It may be obvious to assert, for example, that the behavior of a Major Power is determined in large part by those attributes that make it a Major Power (and similarly for smaller states). But changes in a nation's attributes may well be conducive to changes in behavior.

At the same time, however, we also recognize that the perceptions of a nation's capabilities held by its leaders (accurate or inaccurate as the case may be) are equally, or perhaps more, critical than "reality" (White, 1968; De Rivera, 1968). This latter consideration is likely to be especially important in the shaping of a policy, whereas outcomes are conditioned more by the "reality" of things and only secondarily by the perceptions of national leaders. The two tend to be highly interconnected. The nature of the dependency is, of course, an important question, but it far exceeds the limitations of the present study.

The following analysis is concerned primarily with the effects of population growth, resources, and technological development on (1) the consolidation of military capabilities (reflected in budgetary allocations to defense and in the size of the armed forces), (2) the pursuit of two different modes of external behavior (commercial activities versus colonial expansion), and (3) the relationships between these two factors.

INTERNATIONAL DYNAMICS: LINKAGES IN A CONFLICT SYSTEM

Our recent efforts to untangle initial dependencies among variables have centered around the Major European Powers during the forty years or so prior to the outbreak of World War I. These analyses have been tentative and have indicated that deeper and more complicated dynamics were involved than we had initially thought. We attempted to measure the properties of particular war-prone conflict systems in terms of the configuration of coefficient characteristics, but we have not as yet extended our analysis to other domains nor demonstrated empirically the differences, if any, between Major and non-Major Powers. Nonetheless, our investigations have yielded important methodological and substantive results.

We have examined mutual dependencies between internal and international variables by specifying key links in the chain of developments leading to international conflict and by constructing equations for domestic capabilities, extnesion of a nation's activities outside its own boundaries, the types of behavior that immediately precede violence, and then violence. We have also experimented extensively with alternative formulations of the basic theoretical framework and have submitted different models to the empirical test. The strength and direction of coefficients relating key variables yielded some indication of relative fits (Choucri and North, 1969). The most significant variables contributing to colonial expansion were population growth, technological development, and the interactive effect of population and technology. These linkages seem to hold for the six Major Powers and "explain" much of their expansionist thrusts at various periods from 1870 to 1914.[5]

At the same time it also became apparent that there were some significant links between technological growth and colonial expansion on the one hand and defense preparedness on the other. Of course mutual dependencies are not to be precluded, and evidences of simultaneous effects are pronounced. On balance, however, the most important "causes" of increasing defense allocations appeared to be both internal and external to the nation state. The internal variables are predominantly technological, in combination with the bureaucratic effects associated with defense preparedness (best represented by the constraints on this year's budget imposed by last year's allocations). The external factors appear to be twofold: first, the gap or difference between a nation's defense preparedness and that of its rivals, and second, the intensity of intersections among their respective spheres of influence.[6]

5. The results have been presented and discussed fully elsewhere (Choucri and North, 1971; North and Choucri, forthcoming.) The dependent variable employed in this analysis was colonial population (as an indicator of expansion) although colonial area is equally appropriate, and the independent variables are home population, home area, steel production, and interactive effect of population and production, imports and exports, and defense expenditures. We found strong evidence for the prevalence of break points (or shifts in the underlying dynamics) with the empirical data producing better "fits" at different sub-periods than for the forty-five years as a whole. For example, between 1870 and 1900 the colonial populations under British control more than double in size, and 75 percent of the variance in this expansion can be accounted for mainly by the differences between population growth in relation to home territory, by technological advancement, by the combined effect of population and technology, and by military preparedness. For France about 85 percent of the variance in colonial expansion from 1902 to 1914 can be accounted for mainly by technological advancement, by the interactive effect of population, and by military capability. Well over 60 percent of the variance in German expansion until 1892 can be accounted for by these variables. Similar patterns are evident for Russia, Italy, and, to a lesser extent, Austria-Hungary as well, although in the latter case expansion was severely constrained by geographical and political considerations.

6. The analysis of armament competition has been given considerable attention among more empirically oriented scholars (Alker, 1968; Caspary, forthcoming; Lagerstrom and

Not unrelated to the above are the considerable effects of defense preparedness and intersections among spheres of influence on the intensity of violent interactions among nations. One critical junction, therefore, seems to be the point at which nations extend their behavior outside territorial boundaries and the mode of behavior selected. Intersections thus follow directly from expansion; expansion is conditioned by internal demands for resources (and markets) and by defense preparedness; expansion of interests contributes to violence; and defense preparedness contributes, in turn, both to expansion and to external violence.[7]

The dependence of external behavior on internal attribute characteristics thus becomes a partially validated hypothesis. While we recognize that the 1870-1914 conflict situation cannot be generalized indiscriminately to all conflict systems, the implications of such empirical relations should not be minimized. How the nature of these relationships changes over time and across nations is still very much of an empirical question, but we expect the coefficient characteristics relating attribute variables for the smaller states to differ from those for Major Powers. Thus, as noted earlier, the types of linkages between domestic and external variables for nations in a peace system are likely to be different than those for nations in a conflict and war-prone system.

Peace system nations, such as the Scandinavian countries, deviate sharply from the Major Power pattern in that they have consciously endeavoured not to become involved in ongoing global conflicts nor to engage in international warfare. Thus, the possibility of finding alternative patterns of international relations which minimize the probabilities of violent eruptions is convincingly raised by these countries' behavior. For example, the reciprocal dependencies between expansion, military preparedness, and external violence evident between the Major Powers do not hold, if only because the Scandinavians have

North, 1969; Mitchell and Choucri, 1969; Moll, 1968). Our own analyses have concentrated on systematic comparisons of three different types of military competition equations, comprising the results and evaluating these accordingly. The first, a national dynamics equation, stipulates that military competition results primarily from dynamics internal to the nation-state; the second, an interaction equation, suggests that military competition results from comparisons of gaps or differences between a state's defense capabilities and those of its adversaries or rival; and the third, that competition and arms race dynamics result primarily from processes of an international nature. The results indicated that each set of dynamics (as represented by those equations) provided some explanatory power. Over 80 percent of the variance in the dependent variable is accounted for by this equation for each of the Major Powers. The incorporation of break points in the analysis by redefining the adversaries to reflect the changing political situation resulted in consistently good "fits" for the period as a whole.

7. These interdependencies were apparent in the results for the equations depicting expansion, intersections, military competition, and violence (North and Choucri, forthcoming). Furthermore, changes in the explanatory power for each equation supported the hypothesis that different dynamics operate at different stages in the development of a conflict system (see Choucri and North, 1972, for comparative R^2; North and Choucri, forthcoming, Part V, for coefficients and related statistical data and information).

not at any time in the past century initiated organized external violence or colonization ventures. Furthermore, their dominant modes of external behavior appear to be limited to commerce, shipping, involvement in international organizations, peacekeeping, and similar enterprises which minimize the probabilities of intersections with other powers and, by extension, the development of the causal sequence associated with the eruption of large scale violence and warfare. For our purposes the Scandinavian regional sub-system may best be considered as a partial, or imperfect yet prototypical, peace system, leaving the concept still not fully defined but nonetheless clearly enough distinguishable from the conflict and war-prone system characteristic of Major Power interactions between 1870 and 1914.

To the extent that these states reflect a distinct profile of national attributes, capabilities and purposive behavior, the investigations reported in this paper should shed light on some important issues relevant to conflict and cooperation, peace and war, theory and analysis. Our purpose is to move toward empirically-based assessments of some of the properties of a peace system without claiming as yet deep insight into the "causes" of the emergence or decline of such a system.[8]

The Netherlands present an additional perspective on the issue of war-prone and peace systems. On the one hand, Holland today shares Small Power status with the Scandinavian countries; on the other, it has, until very recently, shared with the Major Powers the status of Colonial Power. Two-way comparisons of this nature are likely to be extremely useful, a consideration which we return to in a subsequent section when explicit comparisons of the attributes, capabilities, and the behavior of the four countries in this study are undertaken.

THE SCANDINAVIAN COUNTRIES AND THE NETHERLANDS: HISTORICAL OUTLINE

Essentially, the Scandinavian countries "opted out" of ongoing conflict and war-prone systems long ago and as a result of internal and external transformations have substantially modified the patternings of their international relations. This process took place over a considerable span of time with several turning points at different historical periods, each of them resulting in a considerable reduction of external violence (Woods and Baltzly, 1915; Wright, 1965a). From the mid fifteenth century to the early 1700's, Sweden, Denmark and Holland were almost continuously involved in war—a pattern extending several centuries back.[9] Especially in the case of Sweden, this aggressiveness coincided with

8. For a discussion of the Scandinavian countries from the perspective of integration theory see Deutsch et al. (1957). Haas (1970) and Nye (1970) provide important theoretical insights.

9. Sweden was almost constantly in a state of war or turmoil (civil as well as external) from 800 to 1814. The Viking period (800-1060) best illustrates this above judgment: Scandinavia was relatively overpopulated; methods of agriculture and cattle breeding were

rapid population growth (with overpopulation relative to domestic resources available at the time), and in a search for external resources. At the turn of the eighteenth century, however, their war involvements diminished gradually, though consistently. For the Scandinavian countries, especially, the Napoleonic wars marked a turning point in terms of the direct participation in warfare and conquest (Wright, 1965a: 641-647). The change is not central to our discussion, but it does point to the adaptive capability of nations, a capability which may have important implications for the potential development of peace systems. Danish foreign policy in the mid-nineteenth century followed a sharp military defeat and a substantial loss of territory and resources.[10] Increasingly, the Scandinavian countries thus diverted their capabilities to predominantly non-violent patterns of international behavior (Wuorinen, 1965, Oakley, 1966).

By the outbreak of War in 1914 "the foreign policies and relations of the Scandinavian nations . . . had long been such as to place them outside the mainstream of Big-Power agreements or alliances; they were designed to maintain peace and neutrality and to avoid undertakings likely to create friction or endanger cordial relations with other states" (Wuorinen, 1965: 29). It appears, therefore, that the transition from war-prone to peace systems had been largely completed by that time.

When war broke out in 1914, Denmark, Norway, and Sweden declared a position of neutrality—a status that left them vulnerable to the point where their rights as neutrals were repeatedly violated by the belligerents. During the Second World War the Scandinavian countries were even less fortunate than in the first. Russian pressures culminated in the invasion of Finland, and Germany occupied Denmark and Norway. Only Sweden remained relatively uninvolved. But Swedish neutrality was predicated almost entirely on Russian and German benevolence, and the price of neutrality was high.

Differences in World War II experiences contributed—along with differences in attributes and in earlier experiences—to the adoption of different post-war international postures. In 1948, Sweden, Norway, and Denmark entered into discussions concerning the possibility of military cooperation and reciprocal alignment. Attempts to develop regional organizations were unsuccessful, however, and subsequently Denmark and Norway—the two Scandinavian countries overcome and occupied by Nazi forces—turned to NATO. The international cleavages penetrated deep into regional politics, and therefore they

---

impractical, and produce was insufficient on a per capita basis. For a general survey of Swedish and Scandinavian history and political development see Andersson (1956) Shirer (1955), Wuorinen (1965), Oakley (1966), and Scott (1950). Changes in Norway's international status over the past centuries do not allow ready comparison with Sweden and Denmark.

10. The war with Prussia in 1864 was the only large scale conflict following the 1814 watershed and resulted in a substantial loss of territory for Denmark—about one third of the pre-war area. Following this war Denmark undertook a concerted effort to modernize (Lauring, 1960).

perceived their own security in a cold war period as not guaranteed either by their own capabilities or by a regional alliance, particularly at a time when United States policy was to make military supplies available only to countries directly associated with its own military alliances. The decision to join NATO, to acknowledge formally the prevailing ongoing military defense system and to participate in it, marked a distinctive new trend for these two countries. In contrast, Sweden's neutrality had, by then, become a well-established policy and prevented the government from envisaging any alliance with the West. From the perspective of the present analysis, Sweden alone remained outside the ongoing Major Power conflict system—the cold war—and, in doing so, continued a pattern of international behavior that had been adopted well over a century earlier.

In 1914 Holland too adopted a neutral position which officially placed the country outside the parameters of the war-prone system. When war broke out again in 1939, Holland's position became untenable, and its neutrality shortlived. When NATO was formed at the end of the war, the Dutch, who had experienced Nazi occupation along with the Danes and the Norwegians, were one of the earliest signatories.

Despite differences in official posture—and to some extent in domestic attributes as well—Denmark, Sweden, Norway, and the Netherlands do not, at the present time, differ significantly in their respective budgetary allocations to defense. The reasons for this similarity might be the following: three of them are in NATO; in Holland's case the loss of colonies necessitated a change in its defense allocations; and Sweden's defense preparations are made in anticipation of NATO assistance in times of crisis. But these considerations do not detract significantly from the basic question of how or why the Scandinavian countries, at least, have worked so consistently to avoid war. Why did they "opt out" after the Napoleonic wars?

An obvious consideration might involve their position as Small Powers hemmed in by Major Powers such as Russia, Germany, Great Britain, and, to a lesser extent, France. But other countries perceiving themselves as "surrounded" have built up their military capabilities, sometimes at the expense of domestic benefactors, and have enhanced their positions further by allying themselves with Great Powers or with coalitions of Lesser Powers. The question remains whether domestic attributes peculiar to the Scandinavian countries have shaped their behavior, or whether the answer lies in some other characteristics of their history or culture or in an accumulation of military experience that persuaded them that warfare was not worth the cost of the effort, resources, and human lives. The following analysis seeks to provide some clues into the nature of peace system nations by identifying some of their distinctive attributes and capabilities.

THE SCANDINAVIAN COUNTRIES AND THE NETHERLANDS: NATIONAL ATTRIBUTES AND EXTERNAL BEHAVIOR; 1870-1970

A first step in the analysis is a comparison of the Scandinavian countries and the Netherlands with each other and with the Major Powers in terms of some critical internal and external variables. The domestic variables to be considered are population, density, national territory home area, and budgetary allocations to defense. External variables include expansion in terms of colonial area and control of colonial populations, and commercial activities in terms of imports and exports and the size of the merchant marine. Table 1 represents some basic data on the levels of some variables for the Scandinavian; Holland, and the Major Powers.

Perhaps the most important variable, and the one showing the greatest contrast between the Scandinavian countries and the Major Powers, lies in the area of numbers. The combined population of Norway, Sweden, Denmark and Finland amounted to no more than 21 million in 1960—approximately 10 million less than Great Britain's population one century earlier, and 17 million less than that of France one century earlier (Wuorinen, 1965: 10). Data on population and density for the 1870-1914 period further illustrate the magnitude of the difference. This is not to imply that the key to peace systems lies solely in small numbers. Neither population nor any other variable, taken by itself, is likely to explain much about the complexities of war, peace, or other aspects of international behavior. But in the long run, over years and decades, we expect outcomes to be partially determined and severely constrained by variable population dynamics (Ehrlich and Ehrlich, 1970).

In more specific terms, the effects of population levels, densities, and rates of growth are mediated by technology and resources, together with the specialized capabilities developed by the society, and these constitute important variables in the pressure calculus.[11] The means by which resources are acquired constitutes a key consideration. For over a century now the Scandinavian countries have channeled their energies toward such activities as commerce, shipping, and shipbuilding, and have placed heavy emphasis on these modes in their efforts to supplement their essentially agricultural economies. Sweden is one of the largest shipbuilding nations in the world, sharing in the equipment of the Norwegian fleet with Holland. At the same time, Norway, Denmark, and Sweden all rank among the ten largest trading nations in the world. Indeed, revenue from shipping has traditionally offset trade deficits. Thus, commerce

---

11. Although the Scandinavian countries do have something of an internal resource base it is limited and they have traditionally been dependent on external resources. Sweden and Norway are both rich in timber and in certain minerals. Both rely heavily on water power for energy and on dairy produce for food and exports. Denmark is more severely constrained in natural resources, and national production is weighted heavily on the agricultural side. The government publications of these countries provide detailed data and discussion of resources and the level of technological advancement. Additional historical material is provided in the *Statesman's Yearbook* and in Mulhall (1880).

Table 1. Levels of National Capabilities: Some Basic Comparisons, 1870-1914[a]

	Home Population	Density	Home Area	Colonies[b] Population	Colonies[b] Area	Merchant Marine	Defense as % of Budget Expenditure	Defense as % of National Production
Sweden	4.9	28.5	171.5	–	–	575.00	33.96	2.05
Norway	2.1	16.9	123.5	–	–	1,506.09	20.03	1.31
Denmark	2.2	156.1	14.5	.13	880.3	355.17	27.67	1.76
Netherlands	4.8	381.7	12.6	31.58	740.0	402.74	35.86	2.18
Britain	38.6	319.2	120.9	335.4	9,773.3	8,413.4	38.68	2.96
France	38.3	187.2	204.6	29.9	2,386.3	1,152.0	26.66	4.06
Germany	52.1	248.7	209.9	6.8	778.6	1,173.0	47.99	2.35
Russia	103.4	50.3	2,085.0	121.5	8,540.0	506.7	29.24	3.48
Austria-Hungary	42.6	177.2	240.6	–	–	320.2	86.67	–
Italy	30.7	275.1	111.9	1.4	284.9	973.5	18.67	2.95

a. These figures represent long term averages for the period as a whole.

b. Swedish colonies included St. Barthelemew, 35 square miles and a population of several thousand. Denmark's colonies include Greenland. In the case of Austria-Hungary one might consider Bosnia-Herzgovenia in the context of a colonial relationship, an area of about 22.3 thousand square miles and a population averaging 1.6 million for the period as a whole. Moravia, Croatia and other Balkan areas might also be viewed as colonies. Calculated from 1900-1914; reliable GNP data are unavailable for the earlier years.

Units: Population—in millions; Density—per square mile; Area—in thousand square miles; Colonial population—in millions; Colonial Area—in thousand square miles; Merchant Marine—in thousand metric tons; Defense Budget—as percentage of total budgetary expenditures; —as percentage of GDP for Scandinavian countries and Netherlands and as percentage of national income for major powers.

Sources: The Statesman's Yearbook (1870-1920); Annuaire Statistique de la France (Paris: Imprimerie Nationale, 1932, 1954, 1961); Data for European states reported from national government sources; Almanac de Gotha (1870-1920); and the national Yearbook for individual countries. See references for Scandinavian and Dutch sources and North and Choucri (forthcoming) for detailed discussion of major power sources and data bases.

and shipping provided the main vehicle for international behavior and the acquisition of resources, without the accompanying patterns of conquest, territorial expansion, and colonial domination characterizing Major Powers in the past, and seemingly also without some of the modified war-prone patterns characterizing Major Powers since World War II.[12]

The Dutch case presents a "mixed" profile partly illustrated in Table 3. Holland shares with the Scandinavians a long tradition of commerce and shipping, but it differs from them in terms of population levels, densities, and growth rates, in terms of the internal resources base, and in terms of the modes of external behavior adopted to meet internally-generated demands. With the Major Powers Holland shares a long history of colonization and expansion, but differs primarily in domestic size, level of technology, and industrialization.

The particular combination of Dutch national attributes, characteristics, and external behavior can again best be explained in terms of numbers. Holland is one of the most densely populated areas of the world, and limitations of the internal resource base result in demands and pressure far outstripping available resources. "The Dutch found their country had no stone, no iron, no coal, no timber, and therefore they began the world as fishermen" (Mulhall, 1880: 325). Although fishing has traditionally provided an important backbone for the Dutch economy, land-based produce has always been important. Efforts to increase the total land area by creating polders began as early as the seventeenth century. By the year 2000 approximately 1255 square miles will have been added from all reclaimed lands (Williams, 1963). But land area still remains the single most serious constraint, especially in an agricultural economy. In view of these considerations the Dutch government has traditionally encouraged diverse forms of lateral expansion, such as emigration, commerce, shipping, and colonization.

Dutch colonial expansion began as early as 1602 with the acquisition of the Dutch East Indies. In 1870 Holland controlled over 600,000 square miles of overseas territory, with a population of over 18 million. At the outbreak of World War II Holland controlled about 840,000 square miles and a population of well over 70 million. At its height the empire included Indonesia, Surinam, and the Netherlands Antilles. Although the Dutch Empire never approximated the British or French in size, its possessions were strategically located, densely populated, and a ready source of raw materials.[13]

12. The contrast in terms of territorial expansion is especially worthy of emphasis. Norway controls three uninhabited Antarctic islands and several similarly populated Arctic territories. Sweden has, in the past century, had no colonies aside from a brief control of St. Bartholomew—a total area of 35 square miles. Sweden's historic union with Norway, 1814 to 1905, might be mentioned, although Norway was not in this case a colony. Denmark controls Greenland (about 84,000 square miles) and the Faroe Islands (540 square miles). The Islands of St. Thomas, St. John, and St. Croix in the Virgin group (within an area of 100 square miles) constituted a Danish colony from 1754 until 1919, when they were bought by the United States. Denmark also controlled Iceland until 1944.

13. For data on the resource base of the Netherlands East Indies see Boeke (1946). It might also be noted that two Caribbean colonies, Curacao and Aruba, have a higher per

Table 2. Rates of Change: Some Basic Comparisons, 1870-1914[a]

	Home Population	Prod.[c]	Colonies Area[d]	Colonies Pop.[d]	Imp.[c]	Exp.[c]	M.M. ton	Army[c] Budget	Navy[c] Budget	Defense as % of Budget Expenditure	Defense as % of National Production
Sweden	.69	3.13	–	–	3.81	3.63	3.07	4.40	4.77	.22	1.27
Norway	.80	3.89	.00	.29	3.69	4.54	1.49	3.11	5.92	-1.29	.79
Denmark	1.09	4.15	–	–	3.70	4.05	2.71	.98	.28	-.19	-1.57
Netherlands	1.12	2.06	.44	2.10	2.14	2.25	3.49	2.20	1.09	-.05	-.25
Britain	.89	2.24	.71	3.30	2.26	4.41	1.80	4.41	22.30	.63	1.92
France	.13	3.04	6.08	5.57[b]	1.55	1.37	2.80	6.55	3.82	2.10	2.37
Germany	1.15	2.49	6.20	9.11	2.36	2.12	1.40	11.91	3.82	9.97	10.96
Russia	1.46	2.32	.08	1.79	3.15	2.15	2.90	6.45	6.38	2.60	5.26
Austria-Hungary	.80	–	–.43	–	3.59	3.35	1.50	6.89	6.39	5.55	–
Italy	.65	2.84	5.60	19.75[b]	3.96	3.95	.50	3.98	7.11	1.93	2.05

a. These figures represent the average percentage change over the 45 years. See Table 3 for additional comments.

b. For Germany the rate is calculated as of 1885, for Italy as of 1890.

c. Rates of change are based on value expressed in standardized 1906 values in U.S. dollars. Undeflated figures in native currencies show slight discrepancies for imports and exports, and army budget. Discrepancies in navy budget are most evident for Germany where the deflated figures standardized to comparable 1906 U.S. dollars are higher than the undeflated figures in German marks. The advantage of transforming all budgetary or monetary data to a common and standard currency lies in the resulting comparability thus allowing for common interpretation of statistical analysis. The trends for the deflated and undeflated values are identical. Wholesale price indices for 1901-1910 = 100 were used for deflation and then conversion to common currency was subsequently undertaken. This second step is not necessary when comparing rates for change, but only when comparing absolute levels in actual currency value (and not as a percentage of national GNP). For the four smaller countries production is indicated by GNP; for the six Major Powers the indicator is national income. National income statistics are not readily available for Austria-Hungary.

d. By 1877 Sweden no longer possessed colonies, so that presenting a rate of change might lead to misspecification.

Sources: Same as Table 1.

The loss of colonies after World War II necessitated a considerable readjustment on the part of the Dutch. This readjustment took primarily the form of further industrialization, industrial investments, technical developments in agriculture, greater reliance on the productivity of the national rather than the colonial population, and a shift of emphasis from the colonies to western Europe. Although the loss of colonies marked an important turning point in Holland's international orientation, the Dutch adjustment to this change demonstrates once more the adaptive capability of nations.

As might be expected, the levels for most variables are significantly higher for the Major Powers for Holland and the Scandinavian countries—except perhaps in the case of merchant marine tonnage. Surprising is the fact that, with all the other differences among Holland, the Scandinavian countries, and the Major Powers, their respective percentage budgetary allocations to the military during the 1870-1914 period do not differ greatly.

The key to this paradox might be that allocations to defense in peace system nations are characterized not so much by distinctive levels or percentage of total budget or of national product but by low rates of change. Although their percentage military allocations were not significantly different from those of the Major Powers for 1870-1914 period the rates of change for Holland and the Scandinavian countries were markedly lower. The periodic sharp increases characterizing Major Power budgets are not apparent for the other four states. In fact, Norway, Denmark, and Holland all exhibit negative rates of change (decreases in percentage allocations), and Sweden's increases are quite marginal. Thus, there is little evidence of the escalatory reaction processes of the pre-World War I Major Power conflict system.

Comparative rates of change in allocations to the military, rates of change in trade, in shipping, in population, and in expansion are presented in Table 2. For the Scandinavian countries the most rapid growth is to be found in imports, exports, and merchant marine tonnage; for Holland it is to be found in imports and exports, but also in colonial expansion. For the Major Powers, colonial expansion and the percentage of total budgetary allocations to defense underwent the most rapid growth. Despite the previously-noted vast discrepancies in population levels, the rates of change on that dimension are not significantly different.

During the 1950-1967 period Norway, Denmark, and the Netherlands contributed substantially lower proportions than did the Major Powers or most other NATO members.[14] Although the average levels of Defense/GNP were

---

capita income than Holland (*New York Times Almanac,* 1970: 922). See Vandenbosch (1955) for a survey of Dutch Foreign Policy over the past century.

14. For example, in 1955 the figures for Norway (4.4 percent), Denmark (3.6 percent), and the Netherlands (6.2 percent) contrasted sharply with the figures for the United States (11.1 percent), Great Britain (9.4 percent), or France (7.6 percent). These figures are quite representative of the differences in defense allocations during the post-war years (1950-1967).

markedly lower, the mean percentage rates of change were not. One obvious reason for this incongruity lies in the initial levels: with considerably lower levels and Defense/GNP ratios, any increases or decreases represented comparatively greater changes.[15] While these differences in levels can be explained largely in terms of size in conjunction with the rationale of alignment, they might also be attributed to the hypothesized structure of peace system nations. In this case, unfortunately, the imperatives and consequences of alliance policies become theoretically and empirically confounded with the expected attributes of peace system nations.

Viewed from a slightly different perspective—defense allocations as a percentage of total budgetary expenditures—this general pattern exhibited by Norway, Denmark, and the Netherlands is apparent as far back as 1870; with few exceptions, defense allocations over the past century have been relatively stable and even declining as domestic social-welfare programs have risen. For Sweden the pattern is slightly different—initial increases until mid 1920's and then sharp decreases thereafter, followed by a rise for World War II and a decline since 1950. (See Table 3 for comparative rates of change.) The percentage defense/total budgetary expenditures for the Scandinavian countries and Dutch are presented in Figure 2.[16]

THE SYSTEMATIC ANALYSIS OF INTERNATIONAL DYNAMICS

Our investigations of the 1870-1914 war-prone Great Power system yielded evidence of strong linkages among the determinant variables. We would therefore expect a peace system to be characterized by relatively weak linkages

15. These comments should not detract from our earlier discussion of the 1870-1914 period. The inferences drawn in the two contexts are not strictly comparable. In the pre-1914 case the long range levels of defense expenditures (as a percentage of total budgetary expenditures) were not dissimilar for the Major Powers and the peace system nations, but the rates of change were markedly and significantly lower for the Scandinavians and Holland. In the post World War II case the levels of defense expenditures (defense/GNP) are vastly different, but rates of change are not. Thus, while we have argued earlier that rates might provide some clues into the structure of peace system nations, tnese should properly be considered in the context of appropriate levels. (Statements concerning levels and rates are made from calculations of Defense/GNP data presented in Russett, 1970: 103-104.)

16. Percentages such as these are, at the very best, rough approximations. Differences in definitions, operational measures, budgetary categories, and organization account for a margin of error, the exact nature of which is difficult to determine. Differences in sources may account for an additional increment of error. For example, Norwegian government statistics calculate percentage allocations at an average of 5 to 8 percentage points lower than in Figure 2 (*Norway Historical Statistics,* 1968: 450-53). We have chosen the higher figure as a more stringent standard of comparison with other Powers. The same general observations hold for the Netherlands as well. The use of GNP as a common denominator alleviates this problem to some extent.

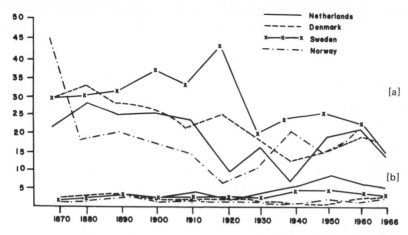

Figure 2. Military Expenditures as a Percentage of Total Budgetary Allocations[a] and as a Percentage of Gross Domestic Product [b]

Source: Same as Table 1.
a. Calculated on the bases of data for defense expenditures and for total budgetary expenditures.
b. Calculated on the basis of GDP and defense data.

throughout this whole process or by negative linkages (thus contributing a reversal, or diffusing the process before it becomes expressed in additional increments of allocations to defense needs). In short, where links are strong and significant, a war-prone conflict system is considered to prevail or, perhaps more accurately, a potentially war-prone system. Where links are weak, non-significant, or negative, the conflict system is called to question and a peace system is posited. Different national profiles and different patterns of international behavior may thus result from different combinations of attributes and capabilities.

The investigations reported in this chapter are restricted to one set of relationships depicted earlier in Figure 1. We shall be concerned primarily with the effects of population and technology on allocations to defense and on the pursuit of different modes of external behavior, and with the interrelationship among these variables. The final dependent variable in this analysis is the defense budget. At the theoretical level, however, we are interested in drawing inferences regarding the nature of peace systems and the underlying attributes and capabilities of peace system nations, and therefore the linkages between theoretical concerns and operational procedures are less direct than would be optimally desirable. Nonetheless, a first order approximation of the underlying theoretical dynamics may clarify some of the issues at hand.

Internal demands and pressures do not necessarily result directly, if at all, in territorial expansion, or in a growing military establishment, or in violence. However, expanding patterns of commercial, financial, diplomatic, and other

Table 3. Three Scandinavian Countries and the Netherlands: 1870-1970 Average
Annual Percentage Rates of Change for Different Time Periods[a]

	Sweden	Denmark	Norway	Netherlands
Population—Home				
1870-1966	.65	1.02	.80	1.23
1870-1914	.69	1.09	.80	1.12
1916-1938	.44	1.18	.73	1.35
1940-1966	.77	.78	v84	1.31
Area—Home				
1870-1966	.04	.15	.04	.04
1870-1914	.07	.05	.06	.02
1916-1948	.01	.48	.01	.04
1940-1966	.01	.01	.02	.07
Imports				
1870-1966	5.61	6.76[a]	6.25[a]	16.98[b]
1870-1914	3.79	3.70[a]	3.69[a]	2.16
1916-1938	8.19	7.34	4.18	19.53
1940-1966	6.23	8.68	10.03	22.21
Exports				
1870-1966	5.82	5.32[a]	5.35[a]	10.77[b]
1870-1914	3.62	4.05[a]	4.54[a]	2.26[b]
1916-1938	5.54	5.42	2.36	15.22
1940-1966	9.50	6.22	8.55	11.21
Merchant Marine (ton)				
1870-1966	3.22	3.34	3.40	4.00
1870-1914	3.07	2.71	1.49	3.49
1916-1938	2.72	3.60	5.08	7.12
1940-1966	3.87	4.12	4.97	2.14
GDP				
1870-1966	3.65	4.32[a]	3.73[a]	4.33[b]
1870-1914	3.12	4.15[a]	3.89[a]	2.08[b]
1916-1938	4.83	4.60	3.05	5.24
1940-1966	3.48	4.20	4.20	4.68
GDP per capita				
1870-1966	2.96	3.31[a]	2.86[a]	2.92[b]
1870-1914	2.40	2.93[a]	2.92[a]	.60[b]
1916-1938	4.34	3.55	2.30	3.85
1940-1966	2.66	3.39	3.29	3.28
Defense Budget % of total exp.				
1870-1966	1.08	2.38	.71	.08
1870-1966	.22	−.19	−1.29	−.05
1916-1938	2.90	6.03	−.56	1.01
1940-1966	.88	3.29	4.93	−.50

	Sweden	Denmark	Norway	Netherlands
Defense Budget				
% of GDP				
1870-1966	3.19	2.40	2.79	1.98[b]
1870-1914	1.27	−1.57	.79	−.25[b]
1916-1938	3.59	4.57	−1.38	2.06
1940-1966	5.86	6.79	9.51	3.04

a. Based on deflated values starting 1890 for Norway and Denmark and 1900 for the Netherlands. The unavailability of wholesale price index makes it difficult to push the deflated series back to 1870. Equivalent rates of change for undeflated prices are generally slightly lower except for the interway period when undeflated figures are consistently higher.

b. Monetary values are standardized to base year 1953 = 100 and the rules of change are computed on the basis of standardized native currencies. Slight discrepancies with rates in Table 2 are due to the conversion factor.

Sources: See Table 1 and Bibliography.

activities often create expanding areas of national interest, which may serve as substitutes for expansion of territory. It is quite possible that such activities may provide—as do all expansionist tendencies—claims for national defense and for a growing defense establishment. Still, some nations may select modes of behavior which do not require as great a dependence on defense preparedness, and it is precisely the weakness of links to defense that might yield useful insights into the structure of peace systems.

In the context of this study, war-prone dynamics can be evaluated in terms of the comparative effects of two alternative paths to defense: from population and technology through colonial expansion, or from population and technology through commerce and shipping—or variations thereof. These are, of course, not the only relevant paths, but they provide a useful point of departure. When translated in operational terms for empirical analysis these lines of inquiry give rise to the following system of equations: [17]

17. It is assumed, first, that the key relationships are additive both in coefficients and in co-terms (although interactive effects may be incorporated in an additive framework); that all relationships are linear; that the error or disturbance terms are uncorrelated with each other; and that the disturbance term is uncorrelated with the independent variables. Also assumed is the absence of collinearity among the independent variables, as well as the absence of severe autocorrelation within each time series.

Data for each observation are recorded at two year intervals, from 1870 to the present, yielding a total of 49 data points. We are not entirely satisfied with this bi-annual recording, nor are we satisfied with the specific choice of measures for some of the variables. For example, to maintain some consistency with earlier Major Power analysis we operationalized production (or technology) as the total output of iron and steel in metric ton, although we also employed GNP as a more direct measure of this variable (as noted below). Furthermore, in cases where colonial expansion is absent we have omitted both the variable and the corresponding equation. This decision is based on the consideration that serious problems arise with matrix inversion and with collinearity when a variable remains at a constant zero over time.

$$X_2 = P_{21}X + u$$
$$X_4 = P_{42}X_2 + u$$
$$X_5 = P_{52}X_2 + P_{53}X_3 + u$$
$$X_6 = P_{63}X_3 + P_{64}X_4 + P_{65}X_5 + u$$
$$X_7 = P_{75}X_5 + P_{76}X_6 + u$$
$$X_8 = P_{83}X_3 + P_{85}X_5 + P_{86}X_6 + u$$

where

X_1 = ΔPopulation

X_2 = ΔProduction (as an indicator of technology)

X_3 = ΔThe interactive effects of population and production

X_4 = ΔMerchant marine (tonnage)

X_5 = ΔExpansion (colonial population)

X_6 = ΔTrade (exports-imports)

X_7 = ΔMen under arms

X_8 = ΔDefense (percentage of budgetary allocations accorded to the military)

P = path coefficient or standardized beta weight.

While the "real" world is not easily decomposable as implied here, it is still possible to isolate, with a minimum of distorting effects, some empirical interrelationships and causal dependencies. One such perspective underlying causal modeling or econmietric analysis is that the "real" world is indeed decomposable and that unidirectional equations capture something of this reality. A second perspective views reality as more dynamic and less readily decomposable and thus stresses reciprocal effects.[18] In the first case, relationships are conceived as essentially hierarchical, and in the second as simultaneous or mutually dependent. While these two approaches are not mutually exclusive, as Franklin Fisher (1963) points out in this discussion of block recursive systems, and each has certain advantages and limitations, they do lead to different modelling procedures.[19] In the hierarchical case the appropriate statistical method for estimating the coefficients by regression analysis is ordinarily least squares. In the reciprocal case alternative procedures are adopted depending on the nature of the reciprocity and on the dynamic relationships modelled.

The model in Figure 3 approximates more closely the first perspective in that a series of sequences is posited and the flow of causal reasoning is depicted as unidirectional (frequently a necessary simplification at early stages of investigation.) At the same time, however, any causal interpretations of the model rest upon the a priori restrictions in each equation (in terms of zero coefficients and

18. This is a brief and highly simplified statement of these arguments. A more extensive treatment of these issues is discussed elsewhere (Choucri, 1970). The most authoritative sources are to be found in the econometric literature over the past two decades (see especially Ando, Fisher and Simon, 1963; Liu, 1955, Wold, 1953).

19. Franklin Fisher's resolution of this issue in terms of block recursive systems has important theoretical and empirical significance (Fisher, 1963; Blalock, 1969).

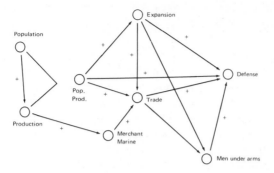

Figure 3. Linkages for Comparison with Peace System Nations: A Hypothesized Structure of International Dynamics[a]

a. In Figures 3-10 solid lines represent statistically significant paths and broken lines signify hypothesized but not empirically verified relationships. We have used t = 2.0 as a rough approximation of the critical region for significance rather than more rigid and formalized decision criteria. Solid lines with no coefficients indicate that there were very small (less than 0.001) though larger than the standard errors. Plus and minus signs indicate the direction of the effect. It might be recalled that for our purposes the absence of significant links is just as important, if not more so, than the presence of statistically significant paths.

relations among the variables) and upon the assumptions underlying the structure of each equation (in terms of linearity, additivity, and the nature of the disturbance or error.)[20] Although identifiability is generally thought of in the context of complex models, fulfilling the requirements for identifiability constitutes an important component of any model-building and estimation effort, as is the specification of reciprocal effects and mutual dependencies.[21] (These issues are discussed later.)

Our use of delta or change variables $(X_t - X_{t-1})$ is based on the consideration that changes tend to delineate international dynamics more precisely than do absolute levels. This is particularly important in view of our initial proposition—that differentials in rates of change are conducive to eventual outcomes, and that imbalances in rates of population growth and technological advances provide the initial impetus for the development of conflict systems.

In the effort to decompose our problem it has become necessary to experiment with lagged relationships and with systematic comparisons between rates of change and absolute levels. In each equation the independent variables were lagged by one time period (an admittedly simplified lag structure) for both

20. It might be noted that path analysis and econometrics both converge around the use of regression algorithms. The differences lie in the interpretation and assumptions, and not in the statistics themselves.

21. The problem of identifiability refers to the limits of inferential analysis: whether or not the parameter of a model or an equation can be estimated at all. A clear discussion of the necessary and sufficient conditions for identifiability is provided in Christ (1965), and a more technical presentation in Fisher (1966).

change (first difference) and absolute levels, although for theoretical reasons our preferences have been for the change expressed as $X_t - X_{t-1}$. We worked with standardized variables—zero mean and unit variance, a transformation which greatly facilitates both manipulation of variables and evaluation of coefficients with either path analysis or econometric interpretations, and compared the results with those yielded by non-standardized variables.[22]

In the following section we shall proceed by examining first one way effects and then, later on, mutual dependencies and reciprocal causation. In each case we shall focus primarily on change variables. This is important because one way dependencies allow us to examine relationships piece by piece on the basis of which it may then become possible to develop a viable overall model, individual components of which have been initially scrutinized. In many cases, however, one way effects tend to overshadow more intricate types of dependencies and it therefore becomes necessary to look for mutual causation or simultaneous effects. Although hierarchical models are not strictly causal, these can be interpreted as such only if the appropriate a priori restrictions and assumptions are made (Ando, Simon and Fisher, 1963).

Our thinking at this point is incomplete in at least one important respect: we have not taken into account external effects, such as rivals, alliances, and so forth, which may condition the development of war-prone or peace systems. This omission can be justified on the grounds that the Scandinavian situation throughout the past century does not provide a ready analogue to the World War I situation or to most war-prone systems, where alignment patterns are clearly delineated and, by extension, readily incorporated into any systematic analysis of international behavior (Singer and Small, 1968). In the case of the Scandinavian countries, the whole concept of institutionalized adversary is not entirely appropriate, nor have these nations been involved, until very recently, in any alliance—defensive or offensive. This is not to minimize the importance of Germany or Russia or other states in performing the role of an adversary at different historical periods. However, the problems involved in defining the adversary in the Scandinavian case are considerable and might only detract from the main objectives of this analysis.

Summary statistics presented in Tables 3 and 4 provide some insights into the nature of the variables on which the following analysis is predicated. The entries in Table 3 refer to the average annual percentage change throughout the century as a whole and during the 1870-1914, 1916-1938, and 1940-1968 periods. The values in Table 4 represent the correlation coefficients among the variables in

22. Regression coefficients yielded when utilizing standardized variables will be identical to those yielded by absolute levels only if the standard deviation for unstandardized variables were close to 1. The greater the departure from 1—in either direction—the greater will be the difference in the magnitude of coefficients yielded when utilizing absolute levels as opposed to standardized variables. What this means, essentially, is that the strength of estimated relationships may vary in accordance with the properties and structure of the data. Hayward Alker's clarification of this issue is gratefully acknowledged.

model (Figure 3). Table 3 summarizes the extent of variation among the four countries in terms of changes over time, and Table 4 summarizes the extent of interrelationships among key variables.

In Table 3 the least amount of variation over time is exhibited by the population and area variables. The growth in productivity and technology (expressed in terms of GNP and GNP per capita), in trade (imports and exports), and in the size of the merchant marine, though to a lesser degree, provide sharp contrasts to the population and area profiles. (Density rates can, of course, be inferred from these last variables.)

The most striking factors that emerge from Table 4 are, first, that the correlation coefficients drop substantially when computed on the basis of rates of change (perhaps not an entirely unexpected phenomenon); second, that interrelationships between the commerce and defense variables are generally negative and also fairly weak. Strong and positive relationships between trade and defense would have undoubtedly raised serious questions concerning the hypothesized relationship between trade and defense in the attribute profile of peace system nations.

A cautionary note on data and measurement might be advisable. The collection, processing, and analysis of longitudinal data is fraught with problems and with the possibilities of accumulated error. Discrepancies among sources and inconsistencies among data bases make such an undertaking difficult and sometimes hazardous. It is sometimes possible to develop alternative data series for each variable (drawn from different sources), to undertake parallel analyses, and to compare the results (as we have done to some extent with the Major Power data, 1870-1914). However this is often a difficult undertaking. Nonetheless, insufficient attention is generally accorded to measurement error, and to problems of theory and assumptions underlying data collection and processing. Although we are deeply concerned with this set of issues we have not as yet developed adequate estimates of measurement error nor explicit measures of the divergence among data sources. However, we have credited our sources with a certain degree of reliability and consistency, enough to allow us to proceed with some preliminary investigations and to draw some tentative conclusions.

FOUR NATIONAL PROFILES: SWEDEN, NORWAY, DENMARK AND THE NETHERLANDS

Because models specifying one way dependencies do not, by their very nature, take into account reciprocal influences and mutual causation, they represent less than a complete picture of the dynamics at hand. Nonetheless, one way dependency models (estimated through ordinary least squares) do provide some useful insights into the structure of the national systems in question. And in this respect, certain results deserve mention.[23]

23. Those comments are based on an analysis of rates of change. Level variables tend to obscure pertinent relationships, particularly in view of pronounced positive serial correla-

Table 4. Profile of Interrelationships: Correlation Coefficients for Levels and Annual Percentage Rates of Change[a]

	Population Home	Area Home	Production	Merchant Marine	Exports	Imports	Men Under Arms	Defense
				Sweden (1870-1966)				
Population—Home	1.00 (1.00)							
Area—Home	.80 (−.18)	1.00 (1.00)						
Production	.94 (.10)	.64 (.09)	1.00 (1.00)					
Merchant Marine	.90 (.11)	.60 (.31)	.97 (.17)	1.00 (1.00)				
Exports	.85 (.22)	.56 (−.06)	.95 (−.52)	.97 (−.04)	1.00 (1.00)			
Imports	.87 (.21)	.57 (−.06)	.96 (.65)	.98 (.12)	.99 (.75)	1.00 (1.00)		
Men Under Arms (1870-1914)	−.47 (−.09)	−.49 (−.32)	−.55 (−.35)	−.39 (−.09)	−.42 (.50)	−.49 (−.07)	1.00 (1.00)	
Defense	−.55 (−.03)	−.25 (.08)	−.59 (.19)	−.55 (−.05)	−.54 (−.11)	−.52 (.32)	−.54 (−.35)	1.00 (1.00)
				Denmark (1892-1966)				
Population—Home	1.00 (1.00)							
Area—Home	.87 (.44)	1.00 (1.00)						
Production	.86 (−.56)	.63 (−.19)	1.00 (1.00)					

	Population Home	Area Home	Production	Merchant Marine	Exports	Imports	Men Under Arms	Defense
Merchant Marine	.88 (−.18)	.63 (.27)	.97 (.12)	1.00 (1.00)				
Exports	.74 (.13)	.53 (.65)	.94 (.16)	.93 (.33)	1.00 (1.00)			
Imports	.73 (.06)	.51 (.64)	.94 (.05)	.93 (.25)	.99 (.76)	1.00 (1.00)		
Men Under Arms (1892-1914)	.27 (.10)	.12 (−.07)	.08 (−.57)	.23 (−.21)	.03 (−.69)	.05 (−.23)	1.00 (1.00)	
Defense	−.32 (−.05)	−.48 (−.26)	−.32 (−.20)	−.31 (−.12)	−.31 (−.38)	−.30 (−.22)	.11 (−.06)	1.00 (1.00)

Norway (1892-1966)

	Population Home	Area Home	Production	Merchant Marine	Exports	Imports	Men Under Arms	Defense
Population—Home	1.00 (1.00)							
Area	.73 (.49)	1.00 (1.00)						
Production	.93 (.04)	.72 (−.15)	1.00 (1.00)					
Merchant Marine	.87 (−.10)	.68 (−.10)	.98 (.18)	1.00 (1.00)				
Exports	.85 (.23)	.70 (−.16)	.97 (.35)	.95 (−.04)	1.00 (1.00)			
Imports	.86 (.26)	.72 (−.07)	.96 (.27)	.95 (−.14)	.99 (.90)	1.00 (1.00)		
Men Under Arms (1892-1908)	.007 (−.17)	−.18 (−.03)	−.28 (−.73)	.36 (.52)	.32 (.68)	−.06 (.20)	1.00 (1.00)	
Defense	−.06 (−.03)	.03 (.21)	.10 (.06)	.15 (−.03)	.22 (−.05)	.24 (−.12)	−.27 (−.55)	1.00 (1.00)

Netherlands (1900-1966)

	Population Home	Area Home	Production	Merchant Marine	Exports	Imports	Men Under Arms	Defense
Population—Home	1.00 (1.00)							
Area	.51 (−.25)	1.00 (1.00)						
Production	.87 (−.29)	.65 (.16)	1.00 (1.00)					
Merchant Marine	.98 (.22)	.54 (−.16)	.90 (.24)	1.00 (1.00)				
Exports	.50 (−.39)	.51 (−.07)	.77 (.67)	.55 (.11)	1.00 (1.00)			
Imports	.50 (−.41)	.52 (.17)	.78 (.18)	.54 (.02)	.99 (.64)	1.00 (1.00)		
Men Under Arms (1900-1914)	−.80 (−.14)	.50 (−.23)	−.80 (−.21)	−.80 (−.25)	−.63 (−.09)	−.55 (.09)	1.00 (1.00)	
Defense	−.52 (.08)	−.39 (−.25)	−.40 (.24)	−.49 (.01)	.06 (.11)	.06 (.36)	.82 (.35)	1.00 (1.00)
Population—Col.	−.50 (−.13)	−.14 (.52)	−.58 (−.03)	−.51 (.04)	−.80 (−.10)	−.79 (−.01)	−.81 (−.05)	−.15 (−.40)

a. The first coefficient is for absolute levels and the second, in parentheses, for rate of change. The actual data base for these computations is 1874-1964, since missing observations in some variables necessitated the loss of some data points and the reduction of the base. The production (technology) indicator is GNP standardized to the base year of 1953. Men under arms coefficients are calculated only for the pre-World War I period. Data for subsequent years are contradictory and incomplete. Defense variable is Defense/Total Expenditures. Colonial variables are omitted for the sake of consistency across countries.

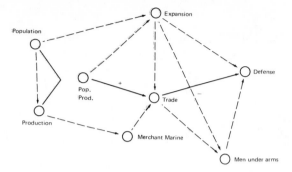

Rates of change and Lagged Independent Variables: the Netherlands

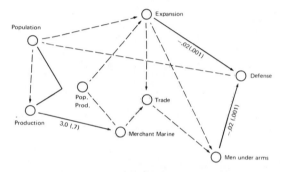

Rates of change and Lagged Independent Variables: Denmark

Figure 4. The Paths to Defense

First: few links in the basic war-prone conflict model appear to be at all significant for any of these countries. Strong effects are scarce, and for each state weak linkages seem to be the rule rather than the exception. This appears to be particularly true when the independent variables are lagged; whatever significant relationships exist tend to wash out by this process of adjustment. It is only when lagged dependencies are omitted—and unlagged independent variables are used—that some semblance of the war-prone conflict model is replicated by the data. Paths to defense are in evidence for the Netherlands and Denmark (Figure 4), but in the case of Norway and Sweden, the only salient paths are from production to trade via the merchant marine (Figure 5).

tion. Various dependencies have become clear when utilizing rates as opposed to levels. However, we have conducted parallel sets of analyses to verify our choice of delta values, a choice which we feel has been justified. There is no evidence of positive or negative serial correlation (as tested by the Durbin-Watson statistic) when utilizing first differences. The resulting coefficients are not distorted by the effects of serial correlation. The assumption underlying the d statistic is that rho, the autocorrelation parameter, is close to 1, an assumption which is often not valid. In such cases it is advisable to respecify the model so as to include variables "causing" serial correlation of the term, and/or to employ iterative algorithms for estimating rho and adjusting accordingly.

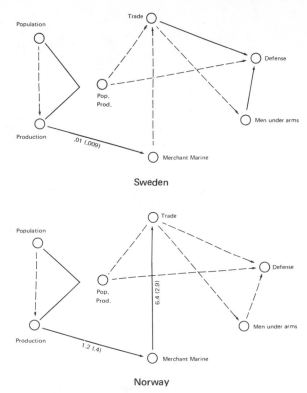

Sweden

Norway

Figure 5. Rates of Change and Lagged Independent Variables

Second: at the same time, however, relationships that are statistically significant are very small. With few exceptions coefficients generally range from .01 to .0001. Nonetheless such orders of magnitude can be important, especially when variables are defined as increments of change.

Third: general patterns that do emerge reflect two types of profiles—one characterized by Norway and Sweden, the other by Denmark and the Netherlands. More is involved here than simply a difference in colonial expansion. For the Norwegian and Swedish profiles there do not seem to be any significant linkages to defense regardless of whether lags are or are not utilized (Figure 6). In the case of Denmark and the Netherlands, linkages do appear, and frequently these are both strong and significant (Figure 7). For Holland, the paths to defense are from population to expansion and then to defense, from population expansion to men under arms and to defense, and from population and production to trade to defense. In each case the linkages are positive and significant, though not always large in magnitude. In the Danish case a similar pattern emerges, but the linkage from men under arms to defense is negative.[24]

24. The linkages to and from men under arms are restricted to the pre-World War I period. The discrepancy of estimates for subsequent periods dictated a more cautious

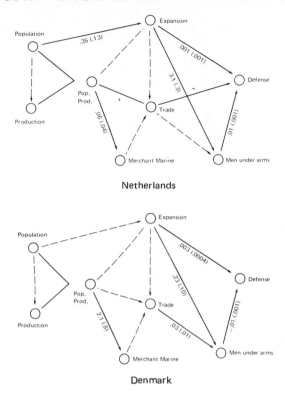

Netherlands

Denmark

Figure 6. Rates of Change

These findings suggest that Norway and Sweden do not, in fact, conform to the model of a war-prone conflict system whereas Denmark and Holland are somewhat closer. The absence of significant linkages among key variables thus underscores the inappropriateness of a war-prone conflict model for the analysis of the first two Scandinavian countries. To infer the structure of a peace system simply from the absence of linkages in a conflict model would be consistent with our initial theoretical specifications, but perhaps premature at this point. Yet the fact that linkages to defense are absent is encouraging—particularly in view of the contrast with the Netherlands. Why this difference arises is still an open question. Again comparative levels and rates of change might provide useful clues.

Identifying variables that can be manipulated for prescriptive purposes is not an easy matter, in part because of the nature of the model, in part because in the "real" world the variables of population and technology and so forth cannot be easily manipulated, and in part because in the case of Norway and Sweden most

approach. We therefore omitted both the variables and the equation for estimation of longer periods.

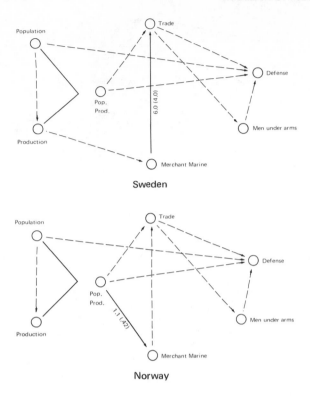

Figure 7. Rates of Change

empirical linkages (though statistically significant) are, at the same time, small in magnitude. This means that even if the first two issues were not problematic in their own right, weak linkages would further hinder our ability to manipulate key variables. But the fact that they are weak is important here. More basic is the consideration that these vairables provide the parameters within which day-to-day decisons are made, and within which a national leader has to formulate official policy. In this respect some variables today are relatively less amenable to manipulation than in earlier decades. National territory is one such example, since colonial expansion is no longer regarded as a viable means of national aggrandizement or modes of lateral pressure, whereas trade and overseas investments do provide more acceptable vehicles for the extension of national influence. That the path from trade to defense is weak is an encouraging finding in any speculations of this kind, thus making explicit the consideration that whereas defense preparedness may be an all too frequent consequence of commercial activities it is not a necessary one. Again, post World War II Dutch adjustment to the loss of colonies provides a useful example.

These observations are predicated on the initial effects of population growth and technological development. For this reason we proceeded to modify the basic model by reformulating the defense equation in a way as to include both

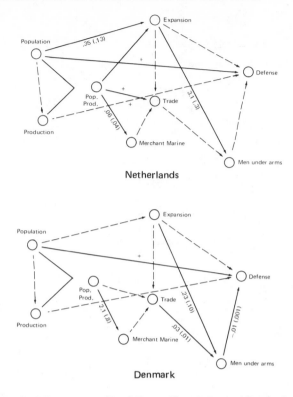

Netherlands

Denmark

Figure 8. Rates of Change, Including Effects of Population and Production (As Indicated by GNP)

population growth and GNP (as a more direct measure of technological achievement). When this is done two effects become apparent. First, in the case of Denmark and the Netherlands the inclusion of these paths does not change the initial profiles as specified by the basic model (Figure 8). On the other hand, the nature of the Swedish and Norwegian profiles seem to undergo a notable change (Figure 9). Now there does appear to be a direct and significant link from population to defense, but the effects, though positive, are very small in magnitude. Second, in both cases the link from technology (as indicated by national income) is significant—fairly strong, but negative in nature.

We shall discuss some of the further implications of these findings later on. The point to be emphasized here is that, unlike several cases among the Great Powers, overseas commercial activities of the Scandinavian countries have not contributed to the growth of military establishments or led to war.[25]

---

25. The theoretical linkages for the role of trade in integration and in conflict theories have not been adequately worked out as yet. There is considerable disagreement among scholars concerning the effect of trade on international behavior. (See Russett 1967a: chs. 8, 12.) Many theories of imperialism of course stress the role of trade-seeking in promoting war.

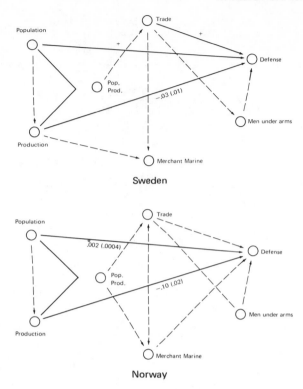

Figure 9. Rates of Change, Including Effects of Population and Production (As Indicated by GNP)

An examination of the residuals in each case yields some indication of the "best fitting" periods—although these are not documented in the above figures—and conversely of the extent to which the resulting diagrams depict generalized relationships. For each of the four states the figures represent dynamics that seem to have been operative from 1870 to about 1948.[26] The post-war period yields a wider scatter of residuals suggesting that inferences drawn for the earlier years need to be modified for the period after 1948.

A second method of inquiring into the validation issue is to estimate the parameters of the models for different periods and then compare the results. When this is done differences among the four countries do tend to disappear after World War II, as does the distinctiveness of the Dutch and Danish profiles. Generally, however, differences between the Scandinavian countries on the one hand and the Netherlands on the other are considerably more pronounced before the Second World War than after.

26. Exactly when the breakpoint occurred would be difficult to determine. Our guess is anywhere between 1940 and 1950.

In what ways are these findings modified when taking into account mutual dependencies and reciprocal relations?

We tried to determine whether the empirically delineated profiles depicted above persist when certain mutual dependencies are taken into account. Needless to say, it is possible to specify the structural relations of a model in very many different ways and with equally numerous assumptions and implications, the only requirements being those for identifiability. A model is identifiable if the number of variables is equal to or greater than the number of coefficients to be estimated. As a general rule, a model is over-identified if the number of regression coefficients exceeds the number of path coefficients, or, alternatively, if the number of predetermined variables exceeds the number of explanatory variables.[27] In such cases as these, more information is available than in cases of just-identifiable models where the number of variables is identical to the number of coefficients to be estimated. At this point, our problem was one of solving for an over-identified model, and one appropriate procedure is two stage least-squares.[28]

Briefly, this mode of parameter estimation involves the following:[29] (1) selecting one dependent variable; (2) computing the reduced form equation for the other jointly dependent variables in the equation using all predetermined variables in the model (this is the first of the two stages); (3) using the computed estimates in conjunction with the predetermined variables to calculate the least squares regression of the selected dependent variable (this is now the second step); and (4) the resulting coefficients are the two-stage least-squares estimates of the parameters in question. The nature—sign and magnitude—of these coefficients becomes the determining criteria for evaluating the results.

More specifically, we have reformulated the basic model as follows:

27. Endogenous variables are those which are explained in terms of other variables in the model; exogenous variables, on the other hand, are predetermined and therefore not defined in terms of any others. One necessary condition for identifiability is that the number of variables excluded from a particular equation be at least equal to the total number of equations less one. This is the order condition. The rank condition stipulates that at least one non-zero determinant of the order $(G-1)$, the number of structural equations less 1, out of the coefficients with which the variables excluded from a particular structural equation, appears in the $(G-1)$ other equations. Hence, in constructing equations for key relationships, it is empirically distinguishable from every other. Equations that are expressed in reduced form—whereby each of the dependent (endogenous) variables is explained in terms of exogenous or other endogenous variables—serve as an empirically based procedure of solving for multiple dependencies. That not all variables are exogenous or endogenous is a function of the particular problem at hand, but that a specific "mix" among these variables be specified is necessary for achieving identifiable parameters and thus isolating those relationships consistent with both model and structural equations, (see Ando, Fisher and Simon, 1960.)

28. Accordingly, ". . . when a relationship is one of several in a simultaneous system, classical least squares estimates of its coefficients will in general be inconsistent. The underlying reason is that some regressors are jointly determined with the regress and hence are dependent on contemporaneous disturbances" (Goldberger, 1964: 292).

29. This discussion is based on Christ (1965: 432-453).

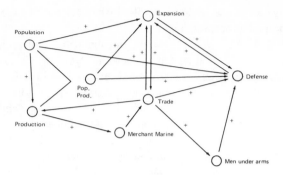

Figure 10. Some Reciprocal Effects and Mutual Dependencies

$$X_2 = P_{21}X_1 + P_{25}X_5 + u$$
$$X_4 = P_{42}X_2 + u$$
$$X_5 = P_{51}X_1 + P_{53}X_3 + P_{56}X_6 + P_{58}X_8 + u$$
$$X_6 = P_{63}X_3 + P_{64}X_4 + P_{65}X_5 + u$$
$$X_7 = P_{76}X_6 + u$$
$$X_8 = P_{81}X_1 + P_{83}X_3 + P_{85}X_6 + P_{87}X_7 + u$$

These relationships are depicted in Figure 10. When the colonial expansion variable is zero, the variable X_5 is omitted from the model as is the equation X_5.

Because Norway and Sweden seem to conform least to the model of conflict and war-prone systems—as depicted earlier in our analysis—we shall devote the remaining discussion to these two countries. What emerges from the resulting analysis appears to be consistent with the earlier discussion of one-way dependencies. Again, the paths to defense from population and from production are significant. Again, these are very small in magnitude. Again, the path from commerce to defense is neither significant nor strong, although the coefficient does approach significance in the case of Sweden. And, again, there does not seem to be evidence of a profile that is at all similar to that of Major Powers.

The implications for the development of peace systems are not entirely clear. in part because of the nature of the final dependent variable, defense, and its relationship to peace system dynamics.[30] Aside from the semi-obvious, namely that a minimal degree of imbalance in rates of change of national

30. Many of our theoretical difficulties in this chapter might be attributed to the discrepancy between the final dependent variable in our statistical analyses and the dependent variable at the theoretical and conceptual plane. At the empirical level we have employed defense budget as a first order approximation of military preparedness and, by extension, of conflict and war-prone processes. At the theoretical level, however, we are basically concerned wih the phenomenon of peace systems, where the dependent variable is actual behavior. Despite these difficulties, our lack of success in replicating the model of a conflict and war-prone system with data from the Scandinavian countries might have important theoretical implications pointing to the possibly fundamental differences between war-prone and peace systems which need further exploration.

attributes and capabilities seems to be a necessary condition, that favorable trade may serve to channel external behavior in non-violent directions and that increasing military preparedness does not come as a necessary correlate; what the sufficient conditions are is still unclear. Possibly the one immediately relevant insight emerging from this analysis is that of the various alternative network of relationships that have their origins in population dynamics, some do not result in increasing defense allocations. To suggest that greater emphasis should be placed on paths such as these may be trite, but at least it does assume that the conduct of purposive behavior may, at some point, be predicated on empirical realities.

THE SEARCH FOR PEACE SYSTEMS: SOME SUGGESTIONS AND TENTATIVE CONCLUSIONS

The above analysis does not diminish the probability that a combination of factors, such as their location relative to certain Major Powers and the lessons learned from attempts at conquest and territorial expansion during earlier centuries, strongly influenced the Scandinavian countries toward "opting out" of military alliance and other war-prone arrangements. But the pattern of strong and weak linkages—especially in the Swedish and Norwegian cases—does suggest some further possibilities with respect to the profiles of potential peace system nations. These are admittedly speculative, but they call attention to considerations that may be useful for further research, modeling, and simulation

In our investigations of the Major Powers we have found throughout the model strong linkages among key variables. In the cases of Norway and Sweden—our best rough approximations of peace system nations—linkages were far fewer, and those that emerged were comparatively weak. More specifically, the direct paths from population and technology to defense were weak for Norway and Sweden, but strong and significant for Germany and Great Britain (1870-1914). Thus on the one hand, these direct paths, however weak, tend to reinforce the basic proposition that population growth and technological advancement exert a strong influence in the direction of defense activities and war-prone arrangements. On the other hand, the fact that the linkages exist in the Swedish and Norwegian cases (together with other Swedish and Norwegian military phenomena) suggest that defense activities are not in themselves necessarily incompatible with rough first approximation peace systems.

As compared with Major Power patterns, a notable aspect of Scandinavian military expenditures has been their generally level or even downward trends—with increases in times of general war (and some aberrations for Norway and Denmark, the occupied countries, during and after World War II). These considerations suggest a Scandinavian disposition to adjust military expenditures in terms of fairly realistic appraisals of external threat. The tendency to bring military budgets down after the termination of war contrasts rather sharply with a frequent tendency, revealed by some of our ongoing research, for Major

Powers either to lower their post-war budgets only part way, thus establishing a new plateau well above pre-war levels, or to bring their budgets quite far down immediately after a war, but then to begin increasing them again after a year or two.

Among Major Powers prior to 1914 (and for some of them on up to World War II) there was a strong tendency to expand their national interests by territorial expansion or colonial domination and maintenance as well as through commerce and other forms of overseas activity and investment. In the case of pre-World War I Germany, the leadership decided also that a strong navy was necessary to protect an expanding commerce; in the British case, the Admiralty insisted that the commercial "lifeline" made continuing British naval supremacy mandatory. Since World War II the tendency for some of the Major Powers has been to press overseas trade, aid, and other investment, and also to establish overseas military bases and surveillance. Again, the Scandinavian pattern stands in sharp contrast: Norway, Sweden, and Denmark have developed and maintained vigorous world trade with a minimum of territorial expansion or colonial domination and with virtually no military or colonial domination and with virtually no military or naval protection or surveillance. Holland has been somewhat closer to the Major Power model.

In these terms it appears that during the nineteenth and early twentieth centuries the Scandinavian countries, with uneven success, found ways of satisfying with some degree of adequacy the demands for resources generated by their populations and by the requirements of their respective technologies without much reliance on territorial acquisition or military protection. Admittedly, a part of their success can be attributed to the forebearance (or the "peace-keeping" of other deterrent or equilibrium-maintenance activities) of some of the Major Powers. On the other hand (at least in some instances) their successes stemmed in large part from their determination and ingenuity.

With respect to Norway and Sweden, the combination of relatively low population levels with relatively high levels of technology (knowledge and skills) may have facilitated the task: by wise determination of technological emphasis and judicious use of domestic resources it was possible to supply the populace with basic goods and, especially in the Swedish case, to obtain gratifying returns on investment without the establishment of far-flung spheres of economic and political interest requiring surveillance and defense. Elsewhere, in reporting on the Major Powers prior to World War I, we have referred to the "satisfied" as those empires (like the British and French) that were able to expand their colonies and spheres of interest for decades at a time without serious constraint or other interference by a more powerful rival, and to the "dissatisfied" as those (such as Germany prior to both World Wars and Japan prior to Pearl Harbor) as those which, while expanding, nevertheless found their ambitions and activities blocked by real or perceived opponents. Here, in reporting on the Scandinavian states, we have evidence of countries having established and maintained quite distinguishable patterns of relative non-violent behavior—although not, in the Norwegian and Danish cases, without having paid considerable penalties.

JONATHAN WILKENFELD

10. Models for the Analysis of Foreign Conflict Behavior of States

ABSTRACT

This study investigates the extent to which a state's level of foreign conflict behavior is a function of prior or present levels of domestic conflict. The basic hypothesis is that a relationship between conflict behavior in the two spheres does exist, and that it takes various forms depending upon (1) the type of state under consideration, (2) the type of conflict behavior involved, and (3) the type of temporal relationship.

A series of Markov models are developed to cope with various types of lag situations. These models impose one and two year lags between the occurrence of prior and subsequent levels of foreign conflict behavior, as well as zero, one, and two year lags between levels of domestic and foreign conflict behavior. Six years of data for 74 states are arrayed in matrices, based on the probabilities associated with transitions from one level of foreign conflict in a given year to another level in the following year.

The findings indicate that among polyarchic states there is an overriding tendency to pursue a policy of foreign conflict behavior which matches their previous foreign conflict level. While a similar tendency is noted among the centrist states, they are to a certain extent better-equipped to change levels of foreign conflict behavior from year to year. The personalist states indicate only a few cases in which there is a tendency to perpetuate levels of foreign conflict from year to year.

For the polyarchic states, there are only rare instances in which the level of domestic conflict appears to play a significant role in the determination of a level of foreign conflict. The centrist states appear to be slightly more influenced by domestic conflict levels, particularly when a one-year lag is involved between domestic and subsequent foreign conflict. The personalist states indicate in a few instances a substantial impact of domestic conflict levels on subsequent levels of foreign conflict. ∎

Author's Note: I wish to express my appreciation to Dina A. Zinnes, Richard H. Van Atta, Nazli Choucri, Roy E. Licklider, and Frederic Pearson for their helpful comments on earlier drafts. I also wish to thank Virginia L. Lussier for her assistance in the computations.

TYPE OF STATE, TYPE OF CONFLICT,
AND TEMPORAL RELATIONSHIPS

Much recent research dealing with the determinants of national conflict behavior has focused upon the possibility of a relationship between the domestic and foreign conflict behavior of states. One commonly held notion is that the leadership of a state, under conditions of a deteriorating position at home, will seek to divert the attention of the population by engaging in some form of foreign violence. This is the idea of uniting a divided people behind the banner of a common cause (Farrell, 1966a; Wright, 1965a; Rosecrance, 1963; Denton, 1966; Haas and Whiting, 1956).

While the above notion has received a good deal of attention and support on a theoretical level, several recent data-based studies have reached somewhat different conclusions. Thus, R. J. Rummel found that "foreign conflict behavior is generally completely unrelated to domestic conflict behavior" (Rummel, 1963a: 24). Subsequent studies by Rummel (1963b, 1968), Raymond Tanter (1966), and Michael Haas (1965, 1968), all have substantially confirmed the original Rummel findings. A third set of studies (Wilkenfeld, 1968, 1969; Zinnes and Wilkenfeld, 1971) appear to occupy something of a middle ground between the two preceding groups. In these studies, the authors found that while there was no generalized relationship between the two types of conflict behavior, there were certain circumstances under which the two were related.

As in my earlier studies just cited, I will attempt here to assess the relevance of several intervening factors to the possible linkage between domestic and foreign conflict behavior. Thus, I contend that the relationship between domestic and foreign conflict behavior exists and that it takes on various forms, depending upon (1) the type of state under consideration, (2) the type of conflict behavior involved, and (3) the type of temporal relationship. Of these three factors, the first is perhaps the most crucial. The key supposition of this study is that taking into consideration type of state as measured by differences in governmental structures will enable us to isolate relationships between various types of conflict behavior. Furthermore, it is postulated that these relationships will be dependent upon specific time lags.

There is evidence in the literature that the governmental structure of a state is crucial to an understanding of both the process and the nature of domestic and foreign policy making. A state with a pattern of successful resistance to severe domestic conflict may be able to withstand large amounts of domestic disorder without resorting to attention-diverting devices such as foreign violence. The capacity to deal with domestic conflict may be related to the type of governmental structure.

In this regard, several recent studies have attempted to show that the supposed differences between democratic and totalitarian systems are not as great as would be imagined. Although decision makers in a totalitarian system are not motivated by the necessity of re-election to espouse foreign policy positions with an eye to the ballot box, they nevertheless do perceive international policy as one that can be manipulated to serve domestic intents (Farrell, 1966a). Milton J. Rosenberg (1967) contends that given the general anti-Communist trend of public opinion in the United States, conciliatory moves on the part of the government would be considered gross violations of the public trust. These dynamics are present in the Soviet Union as well. With its lack of institutions guaranteeing high office for fixed terms, the leadership must remain sensitive to public opinion among the subelite, the military, and provincial functionaries in the party system.

The more conventional view, that differences in states do influence the extent to which the domestic and foreign spheres are linked, is expressed by Joseph Frankel:

> "One of the most significant relationships within the environment is the interaction between domestic and foreign affairs. On the basis of relative security and isolation from foreign affairs, it has been customary for British and American thinkers and statesmen to believe that the two domains are separate and that domestic affairs prevail. Very different is the tradition of the continental countries where such separation has never taken place." (Frankel, 1964: 54)

It is in the area of conflict linkages that we find the greatest tendency among scholars to argue for the importance of differentiating among types of states. Farrell (1966a) declares that the use of international crises to divert attention away from internal problems is a device most commonly found in the totalitarian system. However, he warns against assuming that the democratic system is completely immune from this type of linkage. Differentiation of states according to level of economic development has also been cited in this connection. James Rosenau (1966) has observed that the literature on economic and political development often refers to the ways in which foreign policies of modernizing societies are shaped by their internal needs, such as the need of charismatic leaders to sustain their charisma, the need of elites for identity and prestige, and the need of in-groups to divert attention away from domestic problems and thereby to placate their opposition. Elsewhere, Rosenau has noted:

> "The leaders of underdeveloped countries ... often seem to be better able to overcome domestic strife and inertia by citing the hostility of the external environment than by stressing the need for hard work and patience at home. In effect, they attempt to solve domestic issues by redefining them as falling in the foreign policy area." (Rosenau, 1967: 25)

Finally, in this regard Pablo Gonzales Casanova (1966) speaks of the need for national unity within developing nations. He feels that the policy best suited for development is that provided by national unity and a "nationalist anti-imperialist front." This policy of nationalism is least understood in the developed world, and most directly binds the problems of internal and external politics.

A second major assumption of this study is that the relationship between domestic and foreign conflict behavior differs, depending upon the type of conflict behavior under consideration. It is the contention here that certain types of conflict occurring within a nation may provoke foreign conflict reactions, while the pressures of other types of conflict do not necessitate a foreign conflict response. It is also assumed that states differ in the extent to which certain types of conflict provoke conflict responses. Of course, our focus on the foreign conflict of a state as determined by its domestic conflict behavior means that we shall thereby be neglecting other very important determinants of conflict behavior. Positing linkages between conflict behavior in two spheres does not deny the possibility of conflict behavior in one sphere resulting from other conflict behavior in that same sphere.

The third element introduced into the present analysis is a temporal, or lagged, relationship. In this sense, we are introducing the notion of a directed relationship to what has heretofore been treated merely as an association. Thus, we can investigate the possibility that the occurrence of one type of conflict behavior systematically precedes the occurrence of the other. If in fact conflict in one sphere is viewed as a reaction to conflict in the other, then we can note and differentiate those types of conflict which engender immediate reaction from those which involve a time lag.

The present study has as its purpose to further explore relationships which were isolated earlier between certain aspects of domestic and foreign conflict behavior. In an earlier study (Zinnes and Wilkenfeld, 1971), the authors proposed a Markov model to account for the level of intensity of foreign conflict behavior engaged in by a state. The model attempted to predict the level of foreign conflict for any given year on the basis of the prior levels of both domestic and foreign conflict. In the present paper, several additional Markov models will be formulated and tested with the same data, in order to determine the best fit between model and data for various types of conflict situations.

THE
DATA

The models, to be described below, were tested using the combined Rummel and Tanter conflict behavior data for 1955-1960. These data consist of nine measures of domestic conflict behavior and thirteen measures of foreign conflict behavior for 74 states.[1] Adequate descriptions of the nature of these data have been provided elsewhere (Rummel, 1963a, Tanter, 1966).

1. For the period between 1955 and 1957, 77 states met Rummel's definition of a state. For the 1958-1960 period, 83 states met this definition. Of the original 77 states, three were excluded in the present study. Syria and Yemen were excluded, since Tanter included them together with Egypt in the U.A.R. and did not collect data on them individually. China (Formosa) was excluded since it had not been included in the study used below to classify states into groups.

The measures of domestic and foreign conflict behavior were separately factor analyzed, using a principal component solution and an orthogonal rotation, in order to determine the patterns of conflict for the six-year period (Wilkenfeld, 1969).[2] Tables 1 and 2 present the results of these factor analyses.[3] For domestic conflict behavior, two factors emerged from the analysis, using the eigenvalue-one criterion, with each accounting for about 50 percent of the common variance. The internal war factor appears to represent an organized, violent type of domestic conflict, grouping such variables as revolutions, guerrilla warfare, and purges. The turmoil factor represents a non-organized, spontaneous type of conflict, and includes such variables as demonstrations, riots, and strikes.

Three foreign conflict factors emerged from the analysis. The war factor, which accounts for 38.8 percent of the common variance, groups those variables which represent the most violent forms of foreign conflict behavior, such as wars, military actions, and mobilizations. The belligerency factor, accounting for 30.4 percent of the common variance, groups somewhat less violent manifestations of foreign violence. The diplomatic factor, accounting for 30.8 percent of the common variance, groups the least violent forms of foreign conflict, such as accusations, threats, and protests.

Table 1. Factor Analysis of Domestic Conflict Behavior Variables, 1955-1960, Orthogonal Rotation

Variables	Factor 1: Internal War	Factor 2: Turmoil	h^2
Assassinations	.30	.47	.31
Guerrilla Warfare	(.72) [a]	.09	.52
Government Crises	(.53)	.35	.40
Revolutions	(.80)	.12	.65
Strikes	.25	(.62)	.44
Purges	(.53)	.15	.30
Riots	.23	(.81)	.71
Demonstrations	.02	(.85)	.72
Domestic Killed	(.67)	.42	.63
Percent Common Variance	50.6	49.4	100.0
Percent Total Variance	26.3	25.7	52.0

a. Parenthesis indicates loading $\geqslant$.50.

2. The factor analyses performed in this study were done using the Biomedical Computer Program BMD03M. In order to maintain a parallel between this and the earlier Rummel and Tanter analyses, communalities of 1.00 were used for the diagonal elements in the correlation matrix.

3. The principal differences between this and earlier factor analyses performed on the same data are: (1) All 6 years of data were analyzed here, rather than only 3 years at a time. (2) Data were kept on a yearly basis, so that a lagged analysis could be performed. Thus, the present factor analysis is based on an N of 74 (nations) x 6 (years) = 444.

Table 2. Factor Analysis of Foreign Conflict Behavior Variables, 1955-1960, Orthogonal Rotation

Variables	Factor 1: War	Factor 2: Belligerency	Factor 3: Diplomatic	h^2
Severance of Diplomatic Relations	.14	(.64)	−.32	.54
Expulsions and Recalls— Ambassadors	.09	−.03	(.55)	.31
Military Actions	(.62) [a]	.17	.18	.45
Wars	(.80)	−.04	.16	.67
Troop Movements	.08	.09	(.62)	.40
Mobilizations	(.56)	.25	−.05	.38
Anti-Foreign Demonstrations	.21	(.56)	.13	.38
Negative Sanctions	.16	(.64)	.21	.48
Protests	.34	.26	(.66)	.62
Expulsions and Recalls— Lesser Officials	−.23	(.56)	.38	.51
Threats	.40	.48	(.51)	.66
Accusations	.47	.42	(.50)	.65
Foreign Killed	(.77)	.09	.21	.65
Percent Common Variance	38.8	30.4	30.8	100.0
Percent Total Variance	20.0	15.7	15.9	51.6

a. Parenthesis indicates loading ⩾.50.

The basic data for the present study were the factor scores which were computed for each state, for each of the six years, on each of the five conflict behavior factors. For purposes of testing the models, it was necessary to convert these factor scores into levels of intensity of conflict behavior. The D = 0 (domestic) and F = 0 (foreign) levels were those in which, for a given year, the factor scores indicated that there was either no domestic or no foreign conflict of the type grouped by the particular factor in question. It was less easy to define levels 1 and 2 of intensity. The factor scores were plotted for each factor, using the smallest reasonable interval. An inspection of these plots indicated an appropriate point at which the intensity of conflict became quite high, while at the same time the number of cases at this level dropped sharply. This point was chosen to differentiate between levels 1 and 2 for each particular factor. [4]

4. The following table indicates, for each of the five factors, the range of factor score values appropriate for each level of conflict.

Factor Score Ranges

	Level 0	Level 1	Level 2
Internal War	−1.697 to −0.444	−0.440 to 1.250	1.265+
Turmoil	−1.541 to −0.511	−0.474 to 0.750	0.765+
War	−1.726 to −0.291	−0.288 to 1.000	1.021+
Belligerency	−2.339 to −0.554	−0.547 to 1.250	1.304+
Diplomatic	−2.951 to −0.443	−0.440 to 1.250	1.263+

As indicated earlier, the intervening factor of nation type is included in the present analysis. The classification of states into types was accomplished using the factors extracted in the Banks and Gregg study (1965), in which a Q-factor analysis was performed on the political variables included in *A Cross-Polity Survey* (Banks and Textor, 1963). This technique of factor analysis results in the grouping of states according to similarities across the variables. Of the five groupings of states which emerged from that analysis, the three labelled personalist, centrist, and polyarchic were found to be useful in the present study. These groupings, together with their factor loadings, are presented in Table 3.[5]

As Table 3 indicates, the personalist group is composed of 15 states, and is by far the smallest of the three. Ten of the 15 personalist states are Latin American. An additional 3 states are Asian, and 2 are Middle Eastern. These states are personal dictatorships of one sort or another but are more "sporadically authoritarian" and less bureaucratized than the centrist states. The centrist group is composed of 26 states; 12 had Communist regimes during the period under consideration, and these states generally have the highest loadings on this factor. The rest are a mixed group of totalitarian, semi-totalitarian and authoritarian states; 4 are Middle Eastern. In general, these states exhibit dictatorial and highly centralized leadership patterns. Finally, we note the polyarchic group with 33 members. Virtually all the states correlating above .80 with this factor are economically developed, western nations. Furthermore, those states in the polyarchic group with lower loadings (below .80) usually exhibit at least one of these characteristics.

Note the rankings of these three groups of states on factors extracted by Russett (1967) from a different set of data. Table 4 indicates the mean of the factor scores for the personalist, centrist, and polyarchic states on three central factors extracted by Russett: economic development, communism, and size. There are rather sharp differences among the three types of states on these factors.

THE
MODELS

The models developed and examined in this study relate to the determination of the level of intensity of foreign conflict behavior engaged in by a state in a particular year. The assumption is that this level of foreign conflict is in part determined by some combination of prior and present levels of domestic conflict behavior being experienced by a state, as well as prior levels of foreign conflict

5. While I am acutely aware of the shortcomings of the Banks and Textor data, there was one important reason for using this scheme in the present study. Since it had already been used in the earlier study (Zinnes and Wilkenfeld, 1971), it was felt that if proper comparisons were to be made among the various models employed, the scheme adopted for the classification of states should remain constant.

Table 3. Groupings of Nations

Personalist	Loadings	Centrist (Cont.)	Loadings
Guatemala	.78	Iran	.48
El Salvador	.68	Pakistan	.48
Panama	.68´	Cambodia	.47
Peru	.68	Burma	.41
Honduras	.67		
Argentina	.66	*Polyarchic*	
Korea Rep.	.65		
Nicaragua	.64	Norway	−.92
Ecuador	.59	Ireland	−.92
Lebanon	.59	W. Germany	−.92
Paraguay	.58	Sweden	−.92
Iraq	.57	Australia	−.92
Haiti	.53	Netherlands	−.91
Thailand	.50	Denmark	−.91
Indonesia	.35	New Zealand	−.91
		Finland	−.90
Centrist		Switzerland	−.87
		Italy	−.86
Bulgaria	.90	U.K.	−.86
Albania	.89	U.S.	−.86
E. Germany	.88	Canada	−.85
Hungary	.86	Belgium	−.84
Mongolia	.86	Costa Rica	−.81
Czechoslovakia	.86	Uruguay	−.81
N. Korea	.85	Japan	−.79
USSR	.85	Greece	−.77
Rumania	.84	Israel	−.75
Poland	.83	France	−.75
Yugoslavia	.82	Chile	−.74
Spain	.80	Dom. Rep.	−.74
Portugal	.77	Philippines	−.73
China	.76	Turkey	−.72
Cuba	.69	Colombia	−.66
Afghanistan	.64	Mexico	−.65
Saudi Arabia	.63	Venezuela	−.63
U.A.R.	.62	India	−.62
Liberia	.58	Brazil	−.62
Jordan	.58	Bolivia	−.57
Nepal	.53	S. Africa	−.55
Ethiopia	.52	Ceylon	−.50

behavior for that state. The original model, tested by Zinnes and Wilkenfeld (1971), postulated the following relationship:

$$F_n, D_n \rightarrow F_{n+1}.$$ (1)

F_n is the level of intensity of foreign conflict in year n, and D_n is the level of

Table 4. Group Means of Factor Scores on Russett Factors

	Economic Development	Communism	Size
Personalist	−0.83	−0.39	−0.16
Centrist	−0.06	0.84	0.31
Polyarchic	0.52	−0.36	0.43

intensity of domestic conflict in year n. F_{n+1} refers to the level of foreign conflict in the subsequent (n+1th) year. The basic assumption of the model is that F_{n+1} is revised on the basis of F_n and D_n.

This model deals with a one-year lag situation between prior and subsequent levels of conflict behavior. There are, however, additional models that may be formulated to introduce different types and combinations of lags. First, we can alter the time sequence between domestic and foreign conflict. In the original model, the level of foreign conflict in year n+1 is in part a function of the level of domestic conflict in the prior year. A second formulation of the model can impose no time lag at all between the two variables. Thus,

$$F_n, D_{n+1} \rightarrow F_{n+1}. \tag{2}$$

indicates that the level of foreign conflict behavior in any given year is a function of the level of foreign conflict one year prior and the present level of domestic conflict being experienced by the state. In other words, there is no lag between domestic and foreign conflict behavior.

An additional model can be formulated to cope with another lag situation:

$$F_n, D_{n-1} \rightarrow F_{n+1}. \tag{3}$$

In this case, F_{n+1} is determined by the prior year's level of foreign conflict, and also by domestic conflict which occurred two years prior.

Furthermore, we can introduce a two-year lag between prior and subsequent levels of foreign conflict, and alter the models accordingly:

$$F_{n-1}, D_{n+1} \rightarrow F_{n+1}. \tag{4}$$

In this model, the assumption is that the level of foreign conflict behavior in a given year is a product of the levels of foreign conflict two years prior and the present level of domestic conflict. This model is then similar to model 2, in that there is no lag between domestic and foreign conflict.

$$F_{n-1}, D_n \rightarrow F_{n+1}. \tag{5}$$

Here, the level of foreign conflict is a function of the level of foreign conflict two years prior and the level of domestic conflict one year prior. In terms of the lag between domestic and foreign conflict behavior, this model is most similar to model 1.

$$F_{n-1}, D_{n-1} \rightarrow F_{n+1}. \tag{6}$$

In this final model, there is a two-year lag between the prior levels of domestic and foreign conflict behavior and the subsequent level of foreign conflict. It is similar to model 3.

The motivation behind the development of these additional models was the fact that the original model 1 did not seem to describe adequately the relationship under investigation. In particular, it was found that the crucial variable in determining the level of foreign conflict in a given year was the prior year's level of foreign conflict. In only a few cases was there found to be an apparent relationship between the prior level of domestic conflict and the subsequent level of foreign conflict. This finding appears to run counter to earlier results, based on correlations between domestic and foreign conflict factors (Wilkenfeld, 1968, 1969).

The second cause of dissatisfaction with the earlier model was that it did not seem to explain adequately the relationship between foreign and domestic conflict levels among the personalist states. While these states exhibited several interesting relationships when correlations were computed between factors representing the two types of conflict behavior, the Markov analysis did not show any such relationships. The possibility exists that a different model may be more appropriate for these nations.

THE TRANSITION MATRICES

In order to analyze each of the six models, the data were arranged in transition matrices. These matrices record the probabilities associated with various transitions in levels of foreign conflict behavior from one year to the next. Due to the rather large number of models being analyzed in the present study, the data as arranged in these transition matrices will not be reported, except where appropriate for explanatory purposes.

As an example, let us take the centrist group, for model 2, and examine the transition matrices for the situation in which the domestic conflict factor is internal war and the foreign conflict factor is war. Recall that model 2 postulates the following relationship:

$$F_n, D_{n+1} \rightarrow F_{n+1}.$$

In this case, this is equivalent to the statement:

$$War_n, Internal\ War_{n+1} \rightarrow War_{n+1}.$$

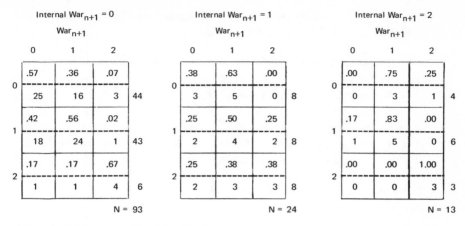

Figure 1. Trichotomous Transition Matrices

The transition matrices for the centrist group for the above model are presented in Figure 1.

The number in the upper left hand corner of a cell is the proportion of cases in that cell, summing to 1.0 across the rows. The number in the lower right hand corner of a cell is the actual frequency. The first matrix contains the transitions in the war type of foreign conflict from year n to year n+1, when the level of internal war in year n+1 is held constant at level zero. The second matrix again shows the transitions in war, when internal war in year n+1 is constant at level one. Finally, the last matrix holds internal war in year n+1 constant at level two.

Moving back to the first matrix, we can note that the proportion in a cell can be interpreted as the probability of a particular transition in foreign conflict from year n to year n+1. Thus, there is a probability of .57 that if the level of war was zero in year n, it will remain at level zero in year n+1, in those cases where internal war in year n+1 is also zero. There is a probability of .36 that the nation will move up to level one of war, and a probability of .07 that it will move up to level two.

Chi square tests are performed on these matrices in order to determine whether a relationship exists between prior and subsequent levels of foreign conflict behavior. That is, is there a significant difference in the configuration of cases in the three rows of the matrix? This series of tests is referred to as the order test, in which the null hypothesis is that when the level of domestic conflict is held constant, there is no relationship between the level of foreign conflict in year n and the level of foreign conflict in year n+1.

A second series of tests, referred to as the equality test, holds the level of prior foreign conflict constant, and attempts to determine whether the level of domestic conflict is related to the level of foreign conflict. In this situation, the null hypothesis is that when the level of prior foreign conflict is held constant, there is no relationship between domestic and foreign conflict behavior. Technically, this test involves pulling off the corresponding rows from each of the three original transition matrices and forming new 3 x 3 matrices, one for each set of $F_n = 0$, $F_n = 1$, and $F_n = 2$ rows.

The transition matrices are trichotomous, in that each defines three different levels of conflict behavior. In some cases, it was felt that additional information might be elicited if dichotomous transition matrices were also examined, similar to those analyzed in a recent study of the 1914 crisis (Zinnes, Zinnes, and McClure, 1972). In the dichotomous situation, level zero of conflict behavior remains the same, while the former levels one and two are combined. That is, we are here simply differentiating between the conflict/no conflict situations. Taking once again the example of the centrist states used earlier, the dichotomous transition matrices are presented in Figure 2. As was the case with the earlier 3 x 3 transition matrices, the 2 x 2 matrices were also subjected to the order and equality tests.

RESULTS: THE
ORDER TEST

Due to the large number of tests generated by the above analyses, only summary tables will be presented in the present paper.[6] Tables 5 and 7 summarize the findings for the trichotomous (3 x 3) case, while Tables 6 and 8 summarize the results for the personalist group for the dichotomous (2 x 2) case. Only those observed relationships which appear to be particularly important will be discussed in any detail.

It will be recalled that the order test holds the level of domestic conflict constant at levels 0, 1, and 2, and investigates the extent to which there is a relationship between prior and subsequent levels of foreign conflict behavior. Models 1 - 3 impose a one-year lag between levels of foreign conflict, and models 4 - 6 impose a two-year lag between levels of foreign conflict.[7]

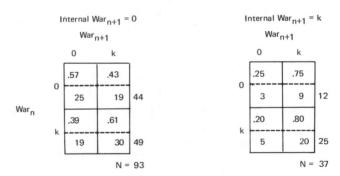

Figure 2. Dichotomous Transition Matrices

6. More detailed tables are available from the author upon request.

7. For those models in which there is a one-year lag between prior and subsequent foreign conflict levels, the total N for all three relevant transition matrices is: personalist = 75, centrist = 130, and polyarchic = 165. For the two-year lag case: personalist = 60, centrist = 104, and polyarchic = 132.

It becomes immediately obvious that the polyarchic group exhibits strong relationships for all six of the models. Thus it appears that the level of foreign conflict in year n has an effect on the level of foreign conflict in years n+1 and n+2. As we noted earlier in Table 4, the polyarchic states are predominantly large, economically developed, and for the most part open societies, and changes in the level of foreign conflict behavior from year to year do not appear to occur with a great deal of ease. Once a state of this type becomes committed to a certain level of conflict behavior, it tends to remain at that level in the following years.

This generalization, however, does not hold equally for all three levels at which domestic conflict is occurring. When the level of domestic conflict is held constant at level two, its highest level, there is an apparent lessening of the relationship between prior and subsequent levels of foreign conflict behavior. It would appear that when these states are experiencing a high level of domestic violence, the relationship between prior and subsequent levels of foreign conflict breaks down. With regard to this aspect there appears to be a difference between the two sets of models. In Models 4-6, in which there is a two-year lag between prior and subsequent foreign conflict, the breakdown of the relationship is more apparent than in Models 1-3. In certain cases, the occurrence of large scale domestic conflict does not immediately break the link between levels of foreign conflict, but this breaking does occur in the following year.

One such link which always appears for the polyarchic group is that involving the domestic conflict factor turmoil and the foreign conflict factor war. In this case, the relationship between prior and subsequent levels of war, with either a one or a two-year lag, is rarely altered as a result of the level of the turmoil type of domestic conflict. Even when turmoil is at its highest level, the link between prior and subsequent levels of war is retained, whether this be for a one or two-year lag. This finding should not be terribly startling. We have already noted a propensity among polyarchic states to become committed to a certain level of foreign conflict and to maintain that level unaltered over the years. Without attempting to evaluate the advantages and disadvantages for a state in operating in this manner, it does seem that this type of trend would be least likely to break down when the war type of foreign conflict is involved. The types of behavior exhibited by this factor, such as wars, military actions, and mobilizations, would likely be most resistant to domestic pressures. To some extent, a polyarchic state would have greater ease in manipulating the diplomatic and belligerency factors.

Turning now to the centrist group, we note that the order test does not produce as many significant relationships between prior and subsequent levels of foreign conflict as were apparent for the polyarchic group. Also note that we can begin to differentiate among the six models in terms of their relative goodness of fit to the data. Both Models 1 and 6 stand out as exhibiting fairly consistent relationships between prior and subsequent levels of foreign conflict. These models are, respectively:

Table 5. Order Properties of the 3x3 Transition Matrices

	Model 1			Model 2			Model 3			Model 4			Model 5			Model 6		
	D=0	D=1	D=2	D=0	D=1	D=2	D=0	D=1	D=2	D=0	D=1	D=2	D=0	D=1	D=2	D=0	D=1	D=2
Personalist																		
D = Internal War																		
War-War																		
Bel-Bel			‡			‡		‡	†					†	‡			
Dip-Dip																		
D= Turmoil																		
War-War								†	‡	‡		‡						
Bel-Bel					‡									‡				
Dip-Dip	‡		‡	‡									†					
Centrist																		
D = Internal War																		
War-War	†		‡	‡	‡		†			†			†		‡	†	‡	
Bel-Bel		‡		‡	‡		†	‡‡‡		†			‡	‡‡		‡	‡‡	
Dip-Dip		†		‡			†	‡‡‡		‡			‡	‡‡‡	‡	‡‡	‡‡‡	
D = Turmoil																		
War-War		‡	†	‡	‡		‡	‡	†	‡	‡	†	‡	†		†	†	
Bel-Bel		‡	‡	‡			†	‡	‡	†	‡	‡	†	†	‡	†	‡	†
Dip-Dip		‡		‡			†	‡‡‡		†	‡		†	†		†	†	
Polyarchic																		
D = Internal War																		
War-War	†		‡	‡	†		†	‡		†			†	†		†		‡
Bel-Bel		†		‡	†		†	‡‡‡		†	‡		‡	‡‡		‡	‡‡	
Dip-Dip		‡		‡			†	‡‡‡		‡			‡	†		†	‡‡‡	
D = Turmoil																		
War-War	†		‡	‡‡‡‡‡‡	†	†		†			†		‡	‡		‡	‡	‡
Bel-Bel	†		†	‡										†			†	
Dip-Dip	‡		‡	‡					‡‡					†			†	

Note: † = p ≤ .05; ‡ = p ≤ .10.

Table 6. Order Properties of the 2x2 Transition Matrices

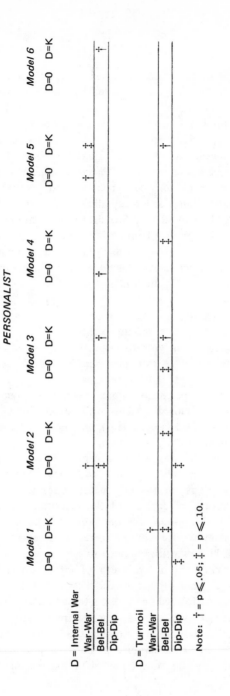

PERSONALIST

	Model 1		Model 2		Model 3		Model 4		Model 5		Model 6	
	D=0	D=K	D=0	D=K	D=0	D=K	D=0	D=K	D=0	D=K	D=0	D=K
D = Internal War												
War-War		†	†						†	‡		‡
Bel-Bel		‡	‡	‡		‡		‡				
Dip-Dip	‡		‡									
D = Turmoil												
War-War		†		‡		‡		‡		‡		
Bel-Bel		‡	‡		‡		‡					
Dip-Dip	‡											

Note: † = p ⩽ .05; ‡ = p ⩽ .10.

$$F_n, D_n \rightarrow F_{n+1}. \tag{1}$$

$$F_{n-1}, D_{n-1} \rightarrow F_{n+1}. \tag{6}$$

Examination of these two models reveals that in each case, prior domestic and foreign conflict behavior are measured for the same year. That is, these two models are equivalent, with the exception that Model 1 implies a one-year lag, and Model 6 implies a two-year lag in foreign conflict. The two models which appear least appropriate for the centrist nations are Models 4 and 5, both involving a two-year lag between prior and subsequent foreign conflict levels. In particular, the belligerency type of behavior appears never to be related to its subsequent level, no matter what type of domestic conflict is occurring.

The personalist states, as already alluded to in the earlier study (Zinnes and Wilkenfeld, 1971), exhibit very few significant relationships between prior and subsequent levels of foreign conflict behavior. In fact, these relationships are so few as to lead one to speculate that there is something in the makeup of the personalist states which allows them a relatively higher degree of freedom in the exercise of foreign policy than is apparent among the centrist and polyarchic states.

Perhaps the outstanding feature of this table is that it indicates in the polyarchic case, and to a certain extent in the centrist case, a tendency to perpetuate policies from year to year, at least in the area of foreign conflict behavior. Since we have examples here of both open and closed political systems, it would appear that in this area the two types of states are similar. On the other hand, the personalist states, being somewhere in between the ideal types of open and closed systems while at the same time smaller and less economically developed (see Table 4), tend not to be under as many constraints to perpetuate policy from year to year.

While it might be possible to accept the above argument as a plausible explanation for the phenomenon, additional investigation might uncover possible relationships for the personalist states which were obscured in the analysis. Therefore, an analysis of the dichotomous transition matrices was undertaken for this group, on the grounds that for this type of state, a dichotomous analysis differentiating merely between situations of conflict versus no conflict might be sensitive enough to isolate relationships. The thought here is that any change from level zero of either domestic or foreign conflict represents a significant occurrence for these states. Table 6 presents the results of the order test performed on the 2 x 2 transition matrices.

Table 6 does not reveal any startling new trends, but there are a few individual relationships worth noting. In the case of the turmoil-belligerency pair, there are, for 5 of the 6 models, relationships between prior and subsequent levels of foreign conflict. By the same token, 4 of the 6 models indicate relationships between prior and subsequent levels of belligerency when the domestic conflict factor held constant is internal war. It would appear then that the personalist states, while free to alter policy in the areas covered by the war and diplomatic factors, are operating under some constraints to perpetuate belligerency from year to year. The belligerency factor includes severance of diplomatic relations, negative sanctions, anti-foreign demonstrations, and expulsions and recalls of lesser officials. Anti-foreign demonstrations, the only variable reflecting public opinion and attitudes in the foreign conflict area, are included in this factor. It may be that while the personalist governments are free to change policy from year to year, unencumbered by prior levels, the public may not be able to shift gears as rapidly. Thus, if the public is aroused to a certain level of anti-foreign feeling, it may tend to remain at that level for some time, much longer, in fact, than its more flexible government might wish it to do.

Turning back to Table 5, there is one final aspect worth noting. For all three groups, the preponderance of relationships between prior and subsequent levels of foreign conflict occur when the domestic conflict factor involved is turmoil. As noted earlier, the turmoil factor loads the least violent of the domestic conflict variables, i.e., riots, strikes, and demonstrations. This is in contrast to internal war, which loads the more violent types of domestic conflict, such as revolutions, guerrilla warfare, and domestic killed. In general, no matter what type of state is under consideration, when it is experiencing the more violent forms of domestic violence, it is more likely to break with established patterns of foreign conflict behavior. Thus, it is perhaps more likely to divert attention and effort from the domestic to the foreign sphere.

EQUALITY
TEST

Thus far, we have been concerned only with the relationship between prior and subsequent levels of foreign conflict, while the level of domestic conflict has been held constant. In the equality test, we will be concerned with the possible relationships between levels of domestic and foreign conflict, when the level of prior foreign conflict is held constant. The summarized results of the chi square tests performed on the equality matrices are presented in Tables 7 and 8.

Looking first at the polyarchic group, in only a few cases is there a relationship between domestic and foreign conflict behavior. By far the strongest of these relationships occurs when the domestic conflict factor involved is turmoil and the foreign conflict factor is diplomatic. Thus, for the polyarchic group, the less violent of the two domestic conflict factors appears to produce some minimal effects upon the least violent type of foreign conflict engaged in by a state.

While the differences are not sharp, we can note that Models 1 and 5 produce relatively more significant relationships between domestic and foreign conflict than do any of the other four models. Both these models involve a one-year lag between the prior occurrence of domestic conflict and the subsequent

Table 7. Equality Properties of the 3x3 Transition Matrices

	Model 1			Model 2			Model 3			Model 4			Model 5			Model 6		
	F=0	F=1	F=2	F=0	F=1	F=2	F=0	F=1	F=2	F=0	F=1	F=2	F=0	F=1	F=2	F=0	F=1	F=2
Personalist																		
Int-War						‡							†	†				
Int-Bel																		
Int-Dip				‡									†					
Tur-War							‡			‡								
Tur-Bel					†		‡	†		‡						†		‡
Tur-Dip	‡					‡												
Centrist																		
Int-War	†				†		‡			‡			‡					
Int-Bel				‡			‡											
Int-Dip				‡		‡				‡								
Tur-War			‡	‡				‡	‡					‡				‡
Tur-Bel			‡	‡				‡						‡			‡	‡
Tur-Dip				‡		‡				‡								
Polyarchic																		
Int-War	‡																	
Int-Bel		†			†													
Int-Dip				†														
Tur-War	‡							‡					†				‡	
Tur-Bel		‡						‡				‡		†			†	
Tur-Dip		‡		†							†		†				†	

Note: † = p ≤ .05; ‡ = p ≤ .10.

Table 8. Equality Properties of the 2x2 Transition Matrices

PERSONALIST

	Model 1		Model 2		Model 3		Model 4		Model 5		Model 6	
	F=0	F=K	F=0	F=K	F=0	F=K	F=0	F=K	F=0	F=K	F=0	F=K
Int-War				‡					†			
Int-Bel			‡‡		†	†	‡‡					
Int-Dip												
Tur-War				†								
Tur-Bel					†	†			‡		‡	‡
Tur-Dip		†								†		†

Note: † = p ⩽ .05; ‡ = p ⩽ .10.

occurrence of foreign conflict. Polyarchic states apparently do not experience the effects of domestic conflict on the foreign sphere for more than one year.

Notwithstanding the few individual relationships of note, domestic conflict behavior has very little effect upon the present and subsequent levels of foreign conflict behavior for the polyarchic states. If we consider the combined results of the order and equality tests, the conclusion is inescapable that the dominating influence on the level of foreign conflict to be engaged in by a polyarchic state is its prior year's level of foreign conflict. In only a few instances is this pattern altered as a result of the level of domestic conflict behavior.

The centrist group exhibits only a slightly larger number of relationships between domestic and foreign conflict behavior than did the polyarchic group. These relationships are concentrated in Models 1 through 3, those involving a one-year lag in foreign conflict transitions. These three models are by no means equivalent in terms of the types of relationships they produce. For Model 2, when domestic and foreign conflict are measured for the same year, the strongest relationship occurs between internal war and diplomatic. When one and two-year lags are imposed between domestic and foreign conflict (Models 1 and 3), the strong relationships involve the turmoil factor only. While these results are not strong enough to indicate a substantial trend, it is interesting that for the centrist states, the most violent forms of domestic conflict are associated with the co-occurrence of foreign conflict, while the less violent forms of domestic conflict are associated with the occurrence of foreign conflict only after one or two years have elapsed.

In comparing the results for the polyarchic and centrist groups, note that the polyarchic states produced more relationships for the order test than did the centrist states. The results for the equality test indicate more significant relationships occurring for the centrist group than for the polyarchic. Overall, it must still be concluded that for both types of states, the crucial variable in determining the level of foreign conflict is in fact the prior level of foreign conflict. However, the centrist states do appear to indicate a greater ability to respond to changing levels of domestic conflict by altering the level of foreign conflict than was apparent for the polyarchic group.

We must deal finally with the personalist states. Once again, the dichotomous analysis was more appropriate in analyzing the foreign conflict transitions for this group. This analysis is presented in Table 8. While the results are again not particularly strong, the sharp decrease in the number of significant cases as we move from the order to the equality test, noted for the centrist and polyarchic states, does not occur for the personalist states. Thus, although the relationships are not strong, the personalist group more than either of the other two groups does exhibit the influence of domestic conflict levels on the level of foreign conflict. Unlike the other two groups, the crucial variable in determining the level of foreign conflict is not necessarily the prior level of foreign conflict.

The relationship between domestic and foreign conflict levels is particularly notable in those cases where the belligerency factor is at issue. In Models 3 and

6, which involve a two-year lag between the occurrence of domestic and foreign conflict, both types of domestic conflict behavior are strongly associated with the subsequent occurrence of belligerency. In the order test, we noted earlier a strong tendency among the personalist states for prior and subsequent levels of belligerency to be related. Recall that the belligerency factor produced no particularly strong relationships for either the centrist or the polyarchic groups.

One final point is in order. In the earlier paper (Zinnes and Wilkenfeld, 1971), only Model 1 was examined. There we concluded that the personalist states were indeed atypical, since only one possible relationship had emerged between the two types of conflict behavior. Examination of the five additional models investigated in the present study indicates that at least two of them are more appropriate for purposes of explaining the patterns of behavior of the personalist states.

Thus far, the six Markov models have been examined and evaluated using the chi square statistic and tests of significance. While this has provided us with a measure of the strength and significance of the observed relationships, it cannot provide information concerning the direction of these relationships. In order to get at this sort of information, we must examine the actual probabilities associated with various transitions in foreign conflict behavior from one year to the next.

The most efficient method for evaluating the directions of the transition probabilities is through the postulation of several sets of inequalities. Based on the theoretical implications of the model, it is possible to hypothesize which of the transitions, under particular circumstances, should be more probable than other transitions. These postulated inequalities are then compared with the data, in order to determine the direction of the observed relationships.

To evaluate these inequalities, some additional notation must be introduced. We will let $p(F_{ij}/D_k)$ indicate the probability of a nation moving from foreign conflict at level i in year n to foreign conflict at level j in year n+1 or n+2 (depending upon the model under consideration), when the level of domestic conflict in year n is k. For example, $p(F_{00}/D_0)$, for Model 1, indicates the probability of a transition from $F_n = 0$ to $F_{n+1} = 0$, when the domestic conflict level is zero (i.e., $D_n = 0$). In addition, a "correct" transition is one in which the level of foreign conflict in year n+1 matches the level of domestic conflict in year n. In the present context, the probability of a certain transition is given by the proportion of cases which fall in a particular cell of a transition matrix.

The first set of inequalities will be referred to as the "correct-versus-more-correct" analysis. Here we will be looking at sets of three equally correct transitions, in the sense that the level of foreign conflict matches the level of domestic conflict. These sets of transitions are as follows:

$$p(F_{00}/D_0) > p(F_{10}/D_0) \text{ and } p(F_{20}/D_0). \tag{1}$$
$$p(F_{11}/D_1) > p(F_{01}/D_1) \text{ and } p(F_{21}/D_1). \tag{2}$$
$$p(F_{22}/D_2) > p(F_{12}/D_2) \text{ and } p(F_{02}/D_2). \tag{3}$$

While all three transitions in each inequality are equally correct, they are not equally probable. In some cases, following the matching criterion, a correct transition involves maintaining the prior year's level of foreign conflict, while in other cases a change is required. It is postulated that the probability of repeating a "reinforced" response will be greater than the probability of correctly changing responses.[8]

With regard to the polyarchic group, examination of the transition matrices indicates that the data for the most part conform to the predictions in this first set of inequalities. That is, polyarchic states find it easier to maintain correctly the prior level of foreign conflict than to change levels correctly. For the centrist group, the data also conform to the predictions in the inequalities. For both groups, this finding is not as strong when conflict behavior is at level two.

In general, then, we have found that not only does earlier foreign conflict behavior affect subsequent foreign conflict behavior, but the effect follows a specific matching pattern. For example, if a state has experienced no previous domestic conflict, and did not engage in foreign conflict in the previous year, our best prediction is that it will remain at level zero of foreign conflict behavior in the subsequent year.

A second sort of matching phenomenon may also be present in the transition matrices. In the correct-versus-more-correct analysis, we were dealing with inequalities composed of three equally correct transitions in the level of foreign conflict. Here, in an analysis termed the "correct-versus-incorrect" case, we will examine situations in which the nation must choose between one correct and two incorrect alternatives. Once again, correct will be used in the sense that the level of subsequent foreign conflict matches the prior level of domestic conflict. The assumption is that correct transitions should be more probable than incorrect ones. Thus, the level of foreign conflict behavior should not increase or decrease in the absence of an increase or decrease in the level of domestic conflict. Also, changes in foreign conflict levels will in fact reflect changes in the level of domestic conflict.

From the above assumptions, the following predictions can be made:

$$p(F_{00}/D_0) > p(F_{01}/D_0) \text{ and } p(F_{02}/D_0). \tag{4}$$
$$p(F_{11}/D_1) > p(F_{10}/D_1) \text{ and } p(F_{12}/D_1). \tag{5}$$
$$p(F_{22}/D_2) > p(F_{21}/D_2) \text{ and } p(F_{20}/D_2). \tag{6}$$

For the polyarchic group, when domestic conflict is at level zero or one, all

8. Analysis of the inequalities will be limited to the polyarchic and centrist states, since the earlier chi square analysis indicated few significant relationships for the personalist group.

six models exhibit patterns matching those postulated. That is, a polyarchic state is more likely to remain at level zero or level one of foreign conflict, when these are in fact correct moves, than it is to move incorrectly to another level. Correct moves are more probable than incorrect moves. However, the data also indicate that when polyarchic states are experiencing very high levels of domestic and foreign conflict behavior, there is a tendency to decrease the level of foreign conflict involvement.

The centrist group performs differently for the two sets of models. Models 1-3, which impose a one-year lag between prior and subsequent levels of foreign conflict, indicate a tendency to perpetuate the prior year's level of foreign conflict. However, Models 4-6 do not indicate this sort of relationship. As was the case with the polyarchic group, inequality 6, which deals with level two of conflict behavior, indicates a tendency to move back to a lower level of conflict in the following year. That is, centrist states also find it difficult to maintain high levels of foreign conflict behavior in the face of high levels of domestic violence and unrest.

A final set of inequalities is based on the equality properties of the transition matrices. In the chi square tests we noted only a very few instances in which a significant relationship between prior domestic and subsequent foreign conflict occurred. Here we will attempt to see whether the data were at least in the predicted direction. The following inequalities are proposed:

$$p(F_{00}/D_0) > p(F_{00}/D_1) \text{ and } p(F_{00}/D_2). \qquad (7)$$
$$p(F_{11}/D_1) > p(F_{11}/D_0) \text{ and } p(F_{11}/D_2). \qquad (8)$$
$$p(F_{22}/D_2) > p(F_{22}/D_1) \text{ and } p(F_{22}/D_0). \qquad (9)$$

These inequalities postulate that the probability of remaining at the same level of foreign conflict behavior should be greatest when that level is reinforced by the same level of domestic conflict behavior.

For both the polyarchic and centrist groups, no clearcut pattern emerges in connection with this set of inequalities. Few cases conform to the predictions. One possible generalization from these results is that for the most part, regardless of the level of domestic conflict, states tend to perpetuate from year to year their level of foreign conflict behavior. This finding is in line with the earlier results based on the chi square tests.

CONCLUSION

Perhaps the most important finding in this study was the isolation of differences in the way different types of states behave in the sphere of foreign conflict behavior. While the results are far too diverse to be reviewed at this point, there is no doubt that each of the three groups of states reacts differently to various domestic and foreign inputs.

In particular, among the polyarchic states there is an overriding tendency to pursue a policy of foreign conflict behavior that matches the state's previous foreign conflict level, i.e., to perpetuate the existing level of foreign conflict. A similar tendency was noted among the centrist states, although these states were somewhat better equipped to change levels of foreign conflict from year to year.

On the other hand, among the personalist states, the crucial variable determining the level of foreign conflict was not necessarily the prior level of foreign conflict; these states were not under as many constraints regarding the perpetuation of policy from year to year except in the case of belligerency. Furthermore, the personalist group more than either of the other two groups does exhibit the influences of domestic conflict levels on the level of foreign conflict, particularly when the belligerency factor is involved.

These findings suggest that the structure of the personalist states gives their leaders a relatively higher degree of freedom in the exercise of foreign as well as domestic policy than is apparent among the centrist and polyarchic states. Thus for the personal ruler, relatively free to make foreign policy decisions and alter them, the prospect of diverting attention from his deteriorating domestic situation by engaging in a mild form of foreign conflict is a tempting policy alternative and one not difficult to pursue. However, the discovery of significant relationships between prior and subsequent levels of belligerency indicates that this particular course of action may be more difficult to terminate than to initiate. Having focused public attention upon a hostile opponent, the personal ruler may be constrained by the very public attitudes he had sought to generate. In any case, the tendency of states to use a foreign policy crisis to divert attention away from internal problems would appear from the results to be a more common attribute of personalist states than of the polyarchic or centrist types. This observation contrasts with the notion that this form of behavior is most commonly found among totalitarian (primarily centrist) states.

Except for this relationship between domestic conflict levels and belligerency among personalist states, domestic conflict in general appears to be only minimally related to foreign conflict behavior. The discovery of an overriding tendency among polyarchic states to perpetuate existing levels of foreign conflict lends credence to the notion that large, democratic, economically developed states find it exceedingly difficult to extricate themselves from wars; it should perhaps serve as a warning regarding future foreign conflict involvements. The extent of the difficulty may be indicated by the further observation that the link between prior and subsequent high levels of war and belligerency appears to break down only in circumstances of internal war or revolution, but remains unaffected by even a high level of turmoil type of domestic conflict. Thus the tendency is to remain committed to a high level of foreign conflict even in the face of widespread domestic pressures. However, the fact that centrist states also tend to perpetuate existing policy levels suggests that the flexibility of a state to alter its foreign policies—at least in the area of conflict—is more a function of the complexity and centralization of its political institutions than of their democratic character.

BRUCE M. RUSSETT

11. The Revolt of the Masses: Public Opinion on Military Expenditures

ABSTRACT

From the beginning of scientific opinion sampling until the 1960s, popular attitudes toward military spending in the United States were very permissive. Only a small minority ever favored reducing the armed forces. A somewhat larger minority rather consistently advocated expanding the military, but at most times a majority of the population either expressed satisfaction with the existing defense effort or was indifferent to the question. By the late 1960's, however, this situation had changed markedly. In recent soundings a near-majority of the entire populace has regularly advocated a reduction in military spending.

Several possible explanations for changing attitudes toward defense are considered. No relationship emerges between popular attitudes and actual levels of military spending. Long wars do seem to generate some opposition to defense spending, but that explanation is incomplete. Mass attitudes and those of the political elite (in this case Senators) rather closely coincide, but it is not obvious which is leading which. Insofar as the current high, and apparently fairly stable, level of mass opposition to the military is politically effective, there will be important pressures for reduction in arms levels and perhaps in the likelihood of war. ■

Author's Note: This article was written while I was Visiting Professor at the University of Brussels on Fulbright-Hays and Guggenheim awards, and the research was supported in part by Grant No. 2635 from the National Science Foundation. I am indebted to Philip K. Hastings of the Roper Public Opinion Research Center, Williams College, for providing me with most of the survey material cited here, and to Alfred O. Hero tor bringing some of it to my attention. Philip Converse made available material from an SRC survey under his direction. H. W. Moyer provided valuable assistance in a seminar paper at Yale. Moyer, Arnold Kanter, Michael Sullivan, and H. Bradford Westerfield offered useful comments. Of course no person or agency is responsible for anything I express here.

MYTHS ABOUT
POPULAR CONCERN

Many theories about the sources of national security and foreign policy stress the limiting, and occasionally the initiating, effect of public opinion. Certainly explanations solely in terms of external stimuli are inadequate, even for such phenomena as military expenditures and arms races.[1] A search for determinants within a nation's domestic political system may concentrate upon governmental or interest elites, as is done in the variants of theories about a "military-industrial complex," or it may probe deeper to include mass attitudes. Among analysts who have considered the question, there are a number of conflicting views. Some formerly well-regarded beliefs have been shown to belong largely in the category of mythology; others were probably correct in their time but need sharp revision under conditions of the new politics of the 1970s.

Political leaders have sometimes assumed that mass opinion constituted a major constraint on the choice of military policy, and have hesitated, for fear of popular reaction, to pursue policies they thought desirable. But in the past, public opposition to military spending really was not widespread. At the beginning of World War II President Roosevelt led very cautiously toward intervention because he thought the majority of the people were not initially ready to support a large defense program and aid to the Allies. Yet in fact a program of rearmament, at least, was very widely desired in the late 1930s. In other periods differing arms policies have been pursued within the context of fairly stable mass opinion. For example, during the entire cold war period from 1946 to 1960 repeated national surveys always found a substantial majority of the population in favor of a large army and navy. Despite this relative constancy of preference on the mass level, national policy varied from initial disarmament, through the beginnings of a cautious buildup, the exertions of the Korean War, and the cutbacks associated with the "new look" of the Eisenhower administration, to the makings of a new buildup at the beginning of the Kennedy years. The pattern of mass preference on military spending has changed drastically, however, very recently. For the first time in more than 30 years a majority of the population has come to advocate reduction in military expenditures, becoming, as never before, a serious potential constraint on national security policy. This article examines relevant data on several assertions concerning the state of public opinion toward defense spending over the last four decades.

The myth of public constraint was expressed clearly by Walter Lippmann (1955: 19-20):

> "At critical junctures, when the stakes are high, the prevailing mass opinion will impose what amounts to a veto upon changing the course on which a government is at the time proceeding. Prepare for war in time of peace? No. It is bad to raise taxes, to unbalance the budget, to take men away from their schools or their jobs, to provoke the enemy."

1. This argument is developed at much greater length in Russett (1970).

Two specific propositions are embedded here. First, government decisions, including military policy, are shaped and limited by public opinion. Second, at most times ("time of peace") public opinion serves to restrict and reduce the level of defense spending. The public is allegedly insensitive to the requirements of national security and requires that the defense budget be curtailed in favor of tax reductions or popular domestic programs.

Senator J. William Fulbright, on the other hand, more recently typified the view that mass opinion serves as a primary impetus to military spending and a barrier to its reduction. In 1964 he castigated

> "the readiness with which the American people have consented to defer programs for their welfare and happiness in favor of costly military and space programs. Indeed, if the Congress accurately reflects the temper of the country, then the American people are not only willing, they are eager to sacrifice education and urban renewal and public health programs—to say nothing of foreign aid—to the requirements of the armed forces and the space agency." (Quoted in Duscha, 1965: 18)

Although there is some ambiguity about whether popular opinion is correctly perceived ("if the Congress accurately reflects the temper of the country") this is nevertheless a fairly clear statement of a widely held view. Moreover, while the systematic literature on arms races considers various sorts of possible restraints on expenditures, mass attitudes are seldom among them.

EARLY PERMISSIVENESS
AND PRO-PREPAREDNESS

The first careful study of the survey data on this matter very firmly and convincingly rejected the proposition that public opinion restricts military spending. According to Samuel P. Huntington (1961: 235), Lippmann and others of like mind attributed to the mass public "a view which it did not possess and an attitude it did not hold." Huntington found in the surveys that on military programs and the defense budget the public tended to follow the lead of the Administration when the Administration took a definite position. In situations where the Administration did not take a strong stand public opinion was, at the least, passive and permissive and, at the most, very favorably disposed to stronger defense. A similar view, but stressing the general preference for a large defense establishment, emerged from a more recent review by Alfred O. Hero.[2]

The general public acquiescence in heavy defense spending up to the late 1960s, with occasional but not common very heavy pressures for increases, is documented clearly also below, in Figures 1 and 2 and Tables 1 and 2. Only the

---

2. In Robinson, Rusk, and Head (1968: 29-31). Caspary (1970a) shows evidence that a conviction that the United States has made "too many sacrifices for defense" was in the 1950s frequently associated with opposition to foreign military and economic assistance, and to international commitments more generally.

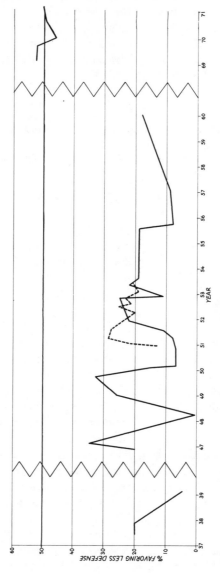

Figure 1. Percentage of Respondents Favoring Less Defense Spending

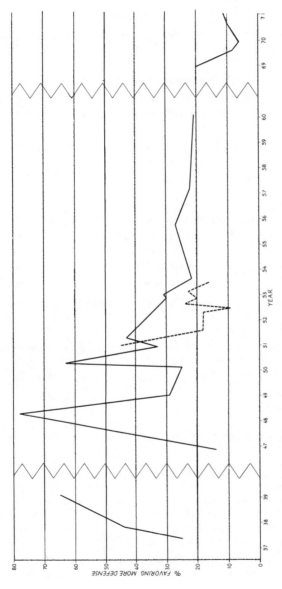

Figure 2. Percentage of Respondents Favoring More Defense Spending

Table 1. National Surveys on Defense Spending, 1937-1971

May 1937 (AIPO 82): "Do you think the amount of money we are now spending on the Army and Navy is too much, too little, or about right?"

Too much   20 percent

*October 1937 (AIPO 101): "Do you think government expenditures should be increased or decreased for the Army and Navy?" (Remain same not offered, but coded)

Decreased   20 percent

*January 1939 (AIPO 143): "Do you think government spending should be increased or decreased for national Defense?" (Remain same not offered, but coded)

Decreased   8 percent

January 1939 (AIPO 145): "Should government spending for national defense be increased, decreased, or remain about the same?"

Decreased   3 percent

. . .

*November 1946 (AIPO 385): "About half the cost of our government today goes to support the Army and Navy. Which of these do you think should be done—

"Reduce taxes by cutting down our Army and Navy/Keep our Army and Navy as they are for another 3 years?" (Increase not offered or coded)

Reduce taxes by cutting   20 percent

November 1946 (NORC 146): "This year the United States is spending about thirteen billion dollars on our armed forces. Which of these things do you think Congress should do next year—

"Reduce the size of our armed forces, in order to save money/Keep them at their present size, *or increase* the size of our armed forces, regardless of cost?"

Reduce   21 percent

**February 1947 (AIPO 391): "Have you followed the arguments in Congress for and against cutting down on the money for the Army and Navy?"
If yes: "Do you think Congress should reduce the amount of money which the Army and Navy have asked for?" (Increase not offered or coded)

Yes   35 percent

Note: This response is very unusual, because the respondents with college education are much more likely (by about 13 percent) to favor reduction than are those with only grammar school education. Ordinarily there is a slight *negative* relationship between education and favoring reductions. Since those with higher education are more likely to answer *yes* to the first part of the question, it is clear there is in this formulation a bias toward reduction.

March 1948 (Roper Fortune 64): "Do you think our military strength should be increased at the present time, left about the same as it is now, or do you think it should be cut down?"

Cut down   1 percent

January 1949 (NORC 163): "Last year the United States spent about thirteen billion dollars on our armed forces. During the coming year, do you think we should spend more than this amount, or less, on our armed forces?"

Less   26 percent

**September 1949 (AIPO 447): "Do you think it is a good idea or a poor idea to cut down on expenses in the U.S. military defense setup at this time?" (Increase not offered or coded)

Good   33 percent

February 1950 (AIPO 453): "Do you think the amount of money we are now spending on the Army, Navy, and Air Force is too much, too little, or about right?"

Too much   15 percent

March 1950 (AIPO 454): "Do you think U.S. Government spending should be increased, decreased, or remain about the same on the following:
  National Defense?"

Decreased   7 percent

*November 1950 (AIPO 467): "When the Korean war began, the United States had about one and a half million men in the armed forces. It has been decided to increase this number to three million men. Do you think this number is too high or too low?" (About right not offered, but coded)

Too high   7 percent

April 1951 (NORC 303): "During the coming year, do you think we should cut down the amount we are spending on our rearmament program, keep it about the same, or spend even more on our armed forces?"

Cut down   8 percent

*July 1951 (AIPO 447): "If the Korean war is brought to an end soon, do you think the United States should continue our defense program as planned, or do you think the defense program should be reduced?" (Increase not offered or coded)

Reduced   11 percent

*December 1951 (NORC 315): "Do you think our government should keep on building up our defenses and helping our allies, even if it means continued high taxes for you? ("Keep on building" is ambiguous.)

No   22 percent

*November 1952 (AIPO 508): "Do you think the government should spend more money or less money for defense purposes?" (Same not offered, but coded. Includes qualified less)

Less   25 percent

December 1952 (NORC 334): As in April 1951

Cut down   11 percent

*April 1953 (AIPO 514): "At present there are about 3½ million men in our Armed Forces, both in the United States and overseas. If a truce is reached in Korea, do you think we should cut down the size of our Armed Forces, or not?" (Increase not offered or coded. Includes qualified should)

Should   22 percent

*August 1953 (AIPO 519): "Do you think too much of the taxes you pay is being spent for defense, or is too little being spent for defense?" (About right not offered, but coded)

Too much   19 percent

*September 1955 (AIPO 553): "Do you think we should keep on spending as much as we do now for our defense program, or should we cut down on the amount we spend for defense?" (Increase not offered or coded)

Cut down   19 percent

October 1955 (NORC 378): "During the coming year, do you think we should cut down the amount we are spending on our arms program, keep it about the same, or spend even more on our armed forces?"

Cut down   8 percent

February 1957 (AIPO 579): "The biggest part of government spending goes for defense. Do you think this sum should be increased, decreased, or kept about the same as it was last year?"

Decreased   9 percent

February 1960 (AIPO 625): "There is much discussion as to the amount this country should spend for national defense. How do you feel about this—do you think we are spending too little, too much, or about the right amount?"

Too much   18 percent

*December 1968 (AIPO 773): "More than half of the money spent by the U.S. government goes for military defense. Looking ahead the next two or three years, would you like to see this amount increased or decreased?" (Same not offered, but coded)

Decreased   53 percent

July 1969 (AIPO 784): "There is much discussion as to the amount of money the government in Washington should spend for national defense and military purposes. How do you feel about this: do you think we are spending too little, too much, or about the right amount?"

Too much   53 percent

November 1969 (AIPO 793): As in July 1969

Too much   46 percent

September 1970 (AIPO): "Congress is currently debating how much money should be spent for military purposes. Would you like to have your congressman vote to keep spending for military purposes at the present level, increase the amount, or reduce the amount?"

Reduce   49 percent

March 1971 (AIPO): As in July 1969

Too much   50 percent

* or ** indicate bias in question wording.

Table 2. NORC Surveys on Defense Spending, 1950-1953

"Do you think the people in this country have been asked to make too many sacrifices to support the defense program, not enough sacrifices, or about the right amount?"

Too many		
	#295 December 1950	13 percent
	#298 January 1951	22 percent
	#300 March 1951	29 percent
	#312 August 1951	28 percent
	#323 April 1952	20 percent
	#327 June 1952	25 percent
	#329 August 1952	21 percent
	#333 November 1952	23 percent
	#337 February 1953	19 percent
	#341 June 1953	21 percent

percentages favoring a reduction in defense spending are given in the tables since that will be our primary interest, but those favoring an increase are shown graphically in Figure 2. The solid lines in both figures show responses over time to somewhat differing questions in a variety of AIPO, NORC, and Roper national surveys from Table 1; the dashed lines between December 1950 and June 1953 indicate, from Table 2, responses to an identical question asked in ten NORC surveys.

First and most obviously, except for the most recent years mass opinion certainly never really constituted a constraint on the level of military spending or the size of the armed forces. Save in the responses to a couple of questions seriously biased against military spending, in Figure 1 we see that those in favor of reducing the resources going to defense always numbered less than 30 percent of the population, with the remainder wishing an increase, expressing satisfaction with current levels, or indifferent and uninvolved (don't know). At times the percentage wanting less military spending fell very low indeed, below 10 percent—and this was usually precisely at times when the political leadership considered external threats to be especially serious and the need for a military buildup to be greatest; e.g. 1939, the beginning of the cold war in 1948, and the first year of the Korean War. (The 1939 case is perhaps especially poignant, given President Roosevelt's difficulties with Congress in pushing Selective Service and rearmament. Similarly, the lack of actual constraint in March 1950, before the Korean War, is noteworthy. That was about the time of NSC-68, the conviction of many in the government that American defense forces should be dramatically expanded, and a great fear that the populace would be unwilling to bear the burden. For many of these leaders the Korean War, despite its costs and dangers, at least had the virtue of providing an occasion for the buildup they wanted and hesitated—probably unnecessarily—to embark upon.)

Figure 2 shows the proportion of the population favoring an increase in the military establishment. This percentage was always, again except for the late

1960s, higher than the corresponding percentage who wished for a reduction, but still it too normally held at a level of well under half the population. The only exceptions to this last statement are clear external threats: 1939, March 1948 (immediately after the Communist coup in Czechoslovakia, and at the time of increasing threat to Berlin—but before the blockade); and, more surprisingly, March 1950 before the Korean War.[3]

This characterization is further supported by the only series we have of identical questions asked over a number of surveys to the same kind of sample: the NORC material from Table 2. Again the proportions favoring a change in the status quo, either for an increase or a decrease in defense spending, remain well under half—typically about 20 percent for each. The only serious exceptions are the number in the first two surveys (45 and 36 percent) who favored more defense in the first months of the Korean War. After 1951 the figures fluctuate within a very narrow range, and the differences from one survey to the next are usually not statistically significant.[4]

Thus, regardless of political leaders' perceptions, we have a picture of a public that was generally ready to rely on the judgment of the political leadership, to acquiesce in existing or planned levels of military strength. Only a minority of the populace favored change in either direction. This is true generally across the population by income and educational levels. On education, for example, between the college-educated and those with only grammar school education there was at most a difference of about 15 percent between the percentages who wished defense spending to be cut, virtually always with the better-educated more favorable toward the military.[5] (That is, 20 percent of the college-educated might favor a reduction where 35 percent of those with grade school education held that opinion.) To the degree popular dissatisfaction with arms levels existed, pressures for increase were more widespread than for decreases. *Hence when spending did go up there was greater resistance to cutting it back to its original level than there had been to the initial boost.*

Some other evidence supporting an image of public permissiveness is as follows:

3. Not all the data points represented in Figure 1 (favoring reductions) are found in Figure 2, since some questions did not offer an increase in spending as an option. Relevant questions were not asked during World War II nor, regrettably, between 1960 and the end of 1968.

4. For these sample sizes, the typical marginals we are dealing with, and the sampling methods used during most of the period, it seems appropriate to consider differences of less than 5 percent from one survey to another (that is, for example, 23 percent giving one answer in one survey and 19 percent giving the same answer in another) as not statistically significant at the .05 level, and hence perhaps due to sampling variation. Where the questions vary, as in Table 1, of course even 5 percent difference will not be significant. On these problems see the discussion in Glenn (1970).

5. This bias is not great enough to affect the trend analysis except perhaps to undervalue by no more than 1 percent the extent of anti-military feeling in the earlier surveys when better-educated people were oversampled (see Glenn, 1970).

1. When asked generally whether they were "satisfied with the way" America's military strength was being handled, the overwhelming majority usually expressed substantial contentment. For example, even in May 1966, during the Vietnam War, in an AIPO survey 88 percent declared themselves "extremely well," "considerably well," or "somewhat" satisfied.

2. The low salience of the defense spending issue is shown in the responses to open-ended questions asking whether, without suggesting items, there was any category of government spending that the respondent thought ought to be increased or decreased. Military expenditures were rarely mentioned. For instance, in AIPO surveys in January 1959, April 1963, and October 1963 neither the percentage for increase nor for decrease in defense ever reached as high as 7 percent. By contrast, typically one-third of the respondents volunteered foreign aid as a candidate for the axe, and in April 1963, 15 percent of the sample wanted public spending for education to be increased.

3. Over the years, congressmen have reported relatively little correspondence on the issue of military expenditures. (Huntington, 1961: 249).

4. There is substantial, if perhaps shallow, support for mutual disarmament. In response to repeated AIPO and NORC questions between 1946 and 1963 asking whether the United States should agree to reduce its armed forces if other countries (or specifically the Russians) cut down theirs, typically about half the sample, and almost always a majority of those with opinions, approved. The level was almost entirely independent of changes in opinion about the desirability of building or reducing the American armed forces taken alone, and was particularly strong even in 1951 and 1952 when our data in Figure 2 showed more than 30 percent of the respondents in favor of greater American military spending. This state of affairs gave political leaders a good deal of freedom to promote disarmament, perhaps even at the same time they advocated increased military expenditures.

POSSIBLE CAUSES
OF VARIATION

A second important element in these data concerns the wide swings in attitudes toward military spending in the early years, but then the way the fluctuations evened out and opinion became quite stable during the 1950s. For the entire 1947-1960 period both the highs and the deepest lows in both graphs come before 1951; after that the entire range of fluctuation is only about 20 percent, despite substantial variation in the form of the question. The only later fluctuations even that big involve the lows of December 1952 and October 1955, each of which has an unbiased question preceded and/or followed by biased ones. This is what we would expect with an issue that is at first new, or seen in a new context—the emerging cold war—but later becomes embedded in a structured set of attitudes toward the new situation. The early oscillations in attitude toward military spending perhaps reflect the great swings in mood and salience of foreign policy noted in Gabriel Almond's classic study (1960), which also seem largely to have settled down and to respond less to dramatic external events.[6]

Much of the variation that does exist must be due to substantial changes in the way the question about military spending or preparedness is phrased. I have noted with asterisks those questions in Table 1 which seem to me to be seriously biased—always, incidentally, against high levels of military spending. Types of biases at issue include:

1. In question wording, offering only increase or decrease, not retaining the current level. ("Remain the same" is always coded, even if not offered explicitly.) This tends to inflate answers in both the increase and decrease categories, perhaps by about 5 percent in each. Two AIPO surveys in January 1939 asked otherwise quite similar questions, except that one did not offer "remain the same" explicitly. The one offering only change produced percentages of 8 for decrease and 67 for increase; where the status quo was offered the percentages were 3 and 62 for change respectively.

2. Offering only decrease or status quo, not offering or coding increase. With "increase" not offered, "keep about the same" may lose some of the attractiveness it would have as a middle course, and some people may then choose "decrease" instead.

3. Explicit reference to the possibility of reducing taxes, or to the desirability of "cutting down on expenses," can be expected to prejudice many answers against high spending levels.

4. One survey, that by AIPO in February 1947, asked a two-part question in which the attitude portion was addressed only to those who acknowledged paying attention to the Congressional debate about defense spending. This survey, and another (AIPO in September 1949) which both failed to offer "increase" and asked simply whether the respondent thought it a good idea "to cut down on expenses in the U.S. defense setup," mark the pre-1968 highpoints of opposition to military spending. It is very possible that the bias there is so serious that the responses should be removed from the trend study, though I have left them in with cautions.

5. Explicit reference to the current or planned size of the armed forces or military spending might, at least relative to the stripped-down question, impress the respondent particularly with the burden at issue. Relevant phrasing includes references to "about half the cost of our government today," "thirteen billion dollars," "the biggest part of government spending," "and 3 1/2 million men." This seems, however, not to be a notable biasing factor if adjacent surveys November 1950-April 1951, October 1955-February 1957-February 1960, and December 1968-July 1969 are compared. Hence such phrasing alone does not suffice to award an asterisk.[7]

6. See also Deutsch and Merritt (1965). For some evidence that Almond exaggerated swings in mood, see Caspary (1970b).

7. This also suggests that merely "knowing the facts" does not itself produce any

Because of the relatively few data points available, and much more importantly because of the variation in question wording, it is impossible to apply a very sophisticated trend analysis.[8] Some hypotheses can nevertheless be suggested and some points made. Two hypotheses about the possible effects of war occur. One is that at the inception of war or severe external crisis, the popular response is one of patriotic rallying round the flag, with an immediate jump in opinion very favorable toward expanding the military to deal with the threat, and a drop in the number of people wishing to curtail defense spending. While we must be very careful about post hoc attribution of the label "severe crisis" to those events corresponding to increased public sentiment for military spending, some of this phenomenon seems to be present in 1939 and the time of the Czechoslovak coup in 1948.

The effect of the Korean War is harder to pin down. As manifested by both the February and March 1950 surveys in Figure 1, and the March survey in Figure 2, opposition to military spending had *already* dropped very sharply just before the onset of the war, perhaps in reaction to announcement of the first Russian atom bomb test in late 1949, and then remained low for more than a year thereafter. The war probably helped retain a climate of opinion very favorable toward greatly expanding the military, but preceding lows are more puzzling. Here, however, it is essential to pay close attention to the questions' wording. The February and March 1950 questions are essentially unbiased, and again are preceded and followed by surveys using queries which tend to exaggerate opposition to the military. The preceding survey (September 1949) is a particularly grave offender. Thus the immediate pre-Korean lows are probably deceptive, and it is likely that the war really did create a substantial change in opinion—that the November 1950 low, on a question that might be expected to inflate the proportion favoring a smaller army by perhaps 5 percent, is a true low in large part induced by earlier wartime conditions. This would be predicted by most of what we now know about popular response to international crises. A similar situation seems to have arisen in the enormous—and short-lived—upsurge in preparedness sentiment early in 1948.

A second war-related hypothesis, especially reflecting the apparent building of public distrust and hostility toward the military over the course of the long current conflict in Indochina, is that as any war (in this case the Korean conflict) drags on, public opposition to the military will mount. The evidence supporting this hypothesis is nevertheless extremely slim. Anti-military sentiments did seem to build up over the course of the latter half of 1951, but there is no apparent change thereafter. Even the rise in anti-military feeling in 1951 is dubious because much of the shift in the solid line in Figure 1 may be accounted for by

---

particular attitude for or against military spending. Note too, below, that while education is associated with approval of military spending in the early cold war years this relationship has reversed in the very different context of 1968-1971.

8. For an excellent example of what can be done with many data-points and fully comparable questions, see Mueller (1970).

the insertion of important bias in all but one of the questions from July 1951 through September 1955. The one unbiased question in this set appears in December 1952, and the percentage then expressing a desire for a smaller army is very markedly lower than before and after. About all that is clear is that in Figure 2, measuring the proportion who want a larger army, there is indeed a substantial and pretty steady drop that cannot be attributed to question bias.

Thus, the effect of the war was to produce a popular frame of mind that neither supported further expansion in the armed forces nor generated sentiments for reducing the army. And the latter cannot be simply attributed to war-time patriotism ("Don't cry out against the armed forces while a war is going on") either, since no new anti-military sentiments surfaced after the war despite the efforts of the Eisenhower administration to cut the military budget and reduce military manpower.

The failure of opposition to the military to emerge in mass opinion is especially striking since presidential popularity is generally considered to be a victim of extended wars. Harry Truman's popularity rating dropped from over 40 percent at the beginning of the Korean war to 23 percent in early 1952 (though it then rose again into the low 30's) and Lyndon Johnson's fell from about 70 percent just after his election to under 40 percent in 1968. This last should not be taken too seriously, however, because domestic events and a "normal" decline in a president's esteem greatly compound and confuse the effects of war. Our impressions that long wars severely damage leaders' popularity are actually very hard to document convincingly (Mueller, 1970).

Another plausible set of hypotheses concerns the relation of actual levels of military spending to the publicly-desired level. One might suppose (a) that there is a close positive association between actual and desired levels, probably because mass opinion perceives and responds to the same external events that cause political decision-makers to raise or lower the military budget, or (b) that actual and desired levels are negatively related, as mass opinion holds a fairly stable image of a desirable level of military spending and reacts against sharp changes in either direction. Further, the above hypotheses might apply to a more or less simultaneous association, or to a lagged one either way. Mass opinion might follow after the elite's changes in response to threat, or in a political system very sensitive to mass opinion it might first be necessary to have change in mass opinion before the political leadership would be willing to vary military spending importantly.

Figure 3 shows the level of military spending as a percentage of gross national product (GNP) over the period 1946-1970. Precise tests of the above hypotheses are impossible because of variation in the questions and the incomparability of data points for the two variables—survey responses perhaps two or three times a year, expenditure data on an annual basis. But even on inspection it is apparent that there is little support for any of the above hypotheses. A simple sign test for a concurrent relationship in the direction, up or down, of annual changes in each variable (correlation of the magnitudes of changes would be too powerful for

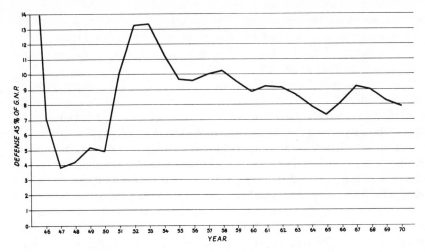

Figure 3. Defense as a Percentage of GNP, 1946-1970

Sources: 1946-1967, Russett (1970: 132); 1968-1970 from Survey of Current Business.

these data) also shows no relationship. For 11 years where one can match changes in the two variables, they are positively related in 5 and vary in opposite directions in the other 6. Introduction of a one-year lag either way does little better. Nor does it improve matters to use the total military budget, or the military proportion of government spending, instead of the military share of GNP. No simple explanation of public attitudes toward defense expenditures is adequate, and the puzzle becomes even more perplexing as we look at more recent events.

THE SLEEPER
AWAKES

The general image we have now built up—of a public usually rather indifferent to the size of the armed forces and the level of military spending, uninvolved and basically prepared to follow the political leadership, if anything more disposed toward building a larger army than toward reducing it—makes very strange reading in light of the data for mass opinion since 1968. Recent anti-military feeling is absolutely unprecedented from the beginning of scientific opinion-sampling. What had been a less than 20 percent minority who wanted to reduce the defense budget has become approximately half the populace; whereas two decades ago nearly a quarter of the population could always be counted on to support increased military spending, those ranks have shrunk to only one American in ten. The recent questions are essentially "perfectly straight" without any notable biases. Also remarkable is that this happened at a time when military expenditures were decreasing slightly and, though higher than they had been since the early 1960s, were far below the exertions characteristic of the Korean War and even lower than those of 1954-1959. (See Figure 3.) And opposition has remained at a stable high level for more than two years—a striking difference from earlier patterns.

Moreover, popular disenchantment with the military currently permeates all sections and levels. In the AIPO survey of July 1969, for instance, none of the standard major population categories—sex, race, education, occupation, age, religion, politics, region, income, or community size—shows fewer than 45 percent of its members responding that too much of government money goes to national defense, and none greater than 60 percent. This is a remarkably even distribution. The widest differential is for education, with 60 percent of the college-educated group declaring that too much money went to defense, as compared with only 46 percent of the population with only a grade school education holding that opinion. This spread increased in September 1970 to 60 percent among college-educated and 40 percent among those with only elementary schooling.

Such a clear association of education with opposition to defense spending is also new: it suggests that *anti-militarism is now strongest in the attentive public,* where it is likely to be politically effective, and that the salience of military spending as a political issue has become very high.[9] Supporting evidence can be found in a Survey Research Center study of October 1968. Respondents were asked to indicate their generalized sentiments toward "the military" on a 0 to 100 scale called a "feeling thermometer." Of those with only a grade school or high school education, 39 percent placed their sentiments in the "warmest" or most favorable decile of the scale, but only 18 percent of those with some college education did so. Similarly, favorable attitudes toward the military were negatively associated with information on the extent of military spending. Another question on the SRC survey asked respondents what proportion of the national government's budget they thought went to defense. The correct answer was just under 40 percent; the median answer was 50 percent. Of those who thought less than 20 percent of the budget was devoted to defense, a full 40 percent scored themselves in the warmest decile of the feeling scale toward the military. Even those who thought defense took between 80 and 99 percent of the budget tended to have favorable attitudes toward the military—37 percent of

9. This is much more typical of the situation in other countries. Huntington (1961: 243) reports that in a nation-wide survey asking Britishers; "If the government wants to cut down its spending, which of these would you put first?" the defense option was chosen by 32 percent. Similarly, in France, Norway, and Poland a proportion ranging from nearly half to over two-thirds of those with opinions preferred to cut defense spending rather than leave it at current levels or raise it (see Galtung, 1967: 173). Of course these countries can, if they choose, in large part rely on stronger allies for protection, as the United States cannot.

those put themselves into the top decile. But only 29 percent of respondents with an at least remotely accurate image of the military establishment's true size (placing it from 20 to 79 percent of the budget) were in the most approving decile.

It seems very unlikely that this astonishing shift, especially among the attentive public, can be attributed solely to the Indochina war. We have just seen how the Korean War, though it was also—in lesser degree—drawn-out and unpopular, failed to stimulate major opposition to military spending. Further-more, despite the regrettable absence of survey material for the early and middle 1960s there is some reason to suspect that anti-military sentiments have been building for a long time. In the last three surveys we have for the Eisenhower years, question bias is slight or non-existent. Yet a clear increase in preference for a smaller army is nonetheless apparent. The 18 percent figure for February 1960 marked an 11 year high for an unbiased question. President Eisenhower's farewell warning about the "military-industrial complex" came in the context of growing, if still modest, public concern. By the end of the 1950s and the 1960s the cold war had become less salient to many Americans; particularly after the Cuban missiles crisis of 1962 images of stability, parity, and low threat became generally accepted. The lower salience of the cold war may well have made possible a reexamination of its assumptions, providing the basis for very different opinions at the end of the 1960s when defense and foreign policy questions once more seemed pressing.

It might be hypothesized either that popular sentiment produces or that it follows high-level political anti-militarism. Figure 4 graphs the ups and downs of one measure of legislative opposition to defense spending over the period 1946-1970. It shows the highest percentage of the Senate recorded in favor of any reduction in military authorizations or appropriations below the level requested by the executive branch, as manifested in each session of Congress.[10]

As with the graph of actual military spending, there is no consistent relationship between year-to-year changes in congressional resistance to defense spending and such resistance in the mass public. An increase in Senate votes to cut the defense budget was about as likely to coincide with a decline in popular preference for such a move as with a similar increase. The search for a lagged relationship, however, turns up something a bit more promising. In six out of eight cases where one can match an increase or decrease in Senate anti-militarism

10. Thus votes merely in opposition to increases volunteered by congress are not shown. I use percentage of the Senate, rather than total votes, to allow for the expansion of the Senate with the admission of Alaska and Hawaii. Also, I use only the number of Senators so recorded on a roll-call vote, omitting pairs and later announcements of position, on the grounds that on those roll-calls that are deemed really important and politically salient (e.g. in 1969 and 1970) most Senators will appear. Inclusion of pairs and announcements would somewhat raise the more-than-zero levels of opposition that appear in most of the earlier years, but not greatly change the pattern.

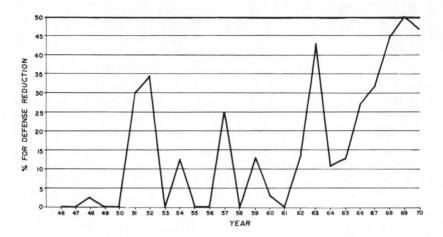

Figure 4. Highest Senate Votes for Cutting DOD Expenditures, 1946-1970

Items:

1946, 1947	No negative votes.
1948	Supplemental Defense appropriation; adopted 74-2.
1949, 1950	No negative votes.
1951	Flanders motion to recommit DOD appropriation with instructions to cut total to $55 billion; rejected 29-49.
1952	Morse amendment to reduce Air Force appropriation by $200 million; rejected 33-43.
1953	No negative votes.
1954	Long amendment to reduce by $45 million funds for barracks program; rejected 12-63.
1955, 1956	No negative votes.
1957	Dworshak amendment reducing DOD funds by $182 million; rejected 24-49.
1958	No negative votes.
1959	Young motion that Senate recede from its amendment to increase by $15 million House-approved funds for civil defense; rejected 12-72, Senate increase merely restored House cut, did not exceed original executive request [a].
1960	Appropriate $40 billion to DOD for fiscal 1961; adopted 83-3.
1961	No negative votes.
1962	Young amendment to delete $94 million appropriated for civil defense; rejected 14-68.
1963	Saltonstall amendment to cut DOD procurement appropriation by 1 percent; rejected 43-45 [b].
1964	Nelson amendment to reduce DOD appropriation by 2 percent; rejected 11-62.
1965	Young amendment to reduce civil defense funds by $35 million; rejected 13-72, p. 1058.
1966	Young amendment to reduce by $15 million appropriation for civil defense; rejected 27-59.

1967	Young amendment to reduce civil defense allotment by $20 million; rejected 32-55.
1968	Williams amendment to reduce defense authorization by $700 million; adopted 45-13.
1969	Smith amendment to delete funds for Safeguard ABM system while allowing development of other ABM systems; rejected 50-50.
1970	Hart-Cooper amendment deleting $322 million for deployment of Safeguard ABM system in Missouri and Wyoming; rejected 47-52.

a. 1959: I did not consider Thurmond's motion to reduce MATS funds by $20 million since his primary motivation was not a reduction in defense spending. Rather, Thurmond was against spending the money in the civilian sector, which he felt would impair the development of military air transport capabilities. See "Congressional Record" July 13, 1959, pp. 13202-13208 and July 14, 1959, pp. 13291-13316; particularly p. 13202 and p. 13315.

b. 1963: Another motion to show fairly strong anti-defense feelings was Young's motion to reduce civil defense funds by $47 million; rejected 28-48.

with subsequent popular changes, the two correspond. Nevertheless, the number of cases is too small to allow us to take the finding very seriously.

More impressive is the overall similarity in pattern between Figure 4 and the relevant portions of Figure 1. Both mass and political elite showed some opposition (stronger in the latter case) as the Korean War continued, and both reached their peak at the end of the 1960s as the Indochina War dragged on. Whereas in the initial post-World War II decade it was common practice for not a single Senator to be recorded in favor of reducing the defense budget, from 1966 onward more than a quarter of the legislators took such a position. Ignoring the wide fluctuations in mass opinion as registered in the polls of the 1940s (due in substantial measure to changes in question wording), the only important divergence between the elite and popular patterns probably occurred in 1963, when considerable sentiment emerged in Congress for reducing military spending. Even here we cannot be sure that such a divergence occurred because we lack proper measures of popular sentiment for that period. But the fact that Senate opposition quickly fell off again until several years later suggests that the legislative doves failed to strike an immediate chord of popular resistance.

Yet by the end of the 1960s opposition to defense expenditures had become widespread at all levels of the political system, and it is by no means obvious who was leading whom. It seems quite likely that in the recent phase Congressional anti-militarists were responding to public opinion as much as they were molding it. While the Senatorial doves doubtless made opposition to the military respectable in a number of less-exalted quarters, it is also true that many of those Solons either took up an already popular issue or used the new sentiment as an opportunity to express some latent feelings about defense spending that they previously feared to speak about. The precise mechanism triggered by this mass sentiment is unclear and doubtless varies for different politicians.

If the new attitude toward the military cannot be attributed solely to political leadership from the top nor to simple fatigue with war or opposition to extraordinarily high military budgets (compared with past budgets either as a share of total government spending or of GNP those of 1968-1970 are not extraordinary), where does it come from? Here one can only speculate. We should not, from mere temporal distance, forget that the Korean War was an unpopular conflict which produced a good deal of scepticism at home about American political and military leaders. But the Indochina war almost certainly reached much lower depths of public esteem. It dragged on twice as long, brought more casualties, and resulted in a much less favorable gain/loss balance for American foreign policy than did the Korean conflict. Despite some ambiguities and hopes for re-unifying Korea, the war of the 1950s did achieve the minimal goals of the government and of most Americans—the repulse of communist aggression. The same cannot be said for the 1960s war in Indochina; whatever the ultimate outcome the communists almost certainly will play a major role in the government or in much of the territory of each of the three Indochinese states, and the avowed aim of the American government—establishment of a democratic regime in South Vietnam—seems very distant. The Indochina War is the clearest failure of American foreign and military policy in 150 years. A special casualty perhaps has been popular respect and awe for the efficiency of the American professional military, and hence there is a new willingness to cut military funds. The McNamara years of new-style civilian analysis of military budget proposals may also have contributed somewhat to a general scepticism of military demands.

Furthermore, disillusionment with the military arises at a time of domestic crisis and new needs for government spending. The 1950s in large part constituted a period of reaction against big public expenditure programs, of fears of big civilian government. Thus, at least on the public expenditure level, there were few popular competitors to the defense budget. But with current requirements for better health, better cities, pollution control, and a fight against hunger, new demands, widely considered legitimate, are being made for public funds. Some programs initiated or expanded in the Eisenhower administration, for example, the great post-Sputnik inputs into education and research, contribute now to this climate.

Another probable contributing factor is the presence in the electorate of a whole generation with no adult memory of intervention in World War II or even of the beginnings of the cold war. This new cohort of voters is thus less ready to accept the standard arguments for an interventionist foreign policy or the need for large armed forces.[11] In the September 1970 survey 60 percent of voters under 30 wanted to reduce military spending, whereas only 46 percent of those 30 and over gave such an answer. And in an article published two decades ago Frank Klingberg (1952) presented some fascinating evidence for generation-long cycles of involvement-withdrawal in American foreign affairs—a cycle which he predicted to move into its withdrawal phase in the late 1960s.

11. A good systematic analysis of the effect of different life-experiences on opinion can be found in Bobrow and Cutler (1967).

In any case, what is clear is that the former popular permissiveness toward military spending is gone. Should the new climate of mass opinion be politically influential we will have to revise our conceptions about the determinants of military and foreign policy. Implications for the likelihood of violent international conflict are not hard to draw. Research is increasingly establishing a causal link from high arms levels to war.[12] If politically effective, mass resistance to military spending may therefore help avoid not just wasteful arms races, but war itself.

12. For example, see the contributions by Choucri, Milstein, and Wallace in this volume.

BIBLIOGRAPHY

Adams, J. S. (1965) "Inequity in Social Exchange." In Berkowitz (ed.), *Advances in Experimental Social Psychology.* Vol II. New York: Academic Press.

Alcock, N. and A. Newcombe (1970) "The Perception of National Power." Journal of Conflict Resolution 14, 3 (September): 335-343.

Alker, H. R., Jr. (1968) "The Structure of Social Action in an Arms Race." Prepared for delivery at the Sixth North American Peace Research Conference. Peace Research Society (International), Cambridge.

Alker, H. R., Jr. and B. Russett (1964) "On Measuring Inequality." Behavioral Science 9, 3 (July): 207-218.

Almond, G. A. (1960) *The American People and Foreign Policy.* New York: Frederick A. Praeger.

Andersson, I. (1956) *A History of Sweden.* London: Widenfeld and Nicholson.

Ando, A., F. Fisher, and H. A. Simon (1963) *Essays on the Structure of Social Sciences.* Cambridge: MIT Press.

Aron, R. (1967) *Peace and War.* New York: Frederick A. Praeger.

Banks, A. S., and P. M. Gregg (1965) "Grouping Political Systems: Q-Factor Analysis of *A Cross-Polity Survey."* American Behavioral Scientist 9 (November): 3-6.

Banks, A. S., and R. B. Textor (1963) *A Cross Polity Survey.* Cambridge: MIT Press.

Bentley, A. F. (1954) *Inquiry Into Inquiries: Essays in Social Theory.* S. Rutner (ed.). Boston: Beacon Press.

Berelson, B., and G. A. Steiner (1964) *Human Behavior: An Inventory of Scientific Findings.* New York: Harcourt, Brace and World.

Berkowitz, L. (1962) *Aggression: A Social Psychological Approach.* New York: McGraw-Hill.

Berry, B. J. L. (1966) *Essays on Commodity Flows and the Spatial Structure of the Indian Economy.* Chicago: University of Chicago Press.

Blalock, H. M. (1961) "Evaluating the Relative Importance of Variables," American Sociological Review 26, 1 (December) 866-874.

——(1965) "Theory Building and the Statistical Concept of Interaction." American Sociological Review 30, 3 (June): 374-380.

——(1966) "The Identification Problem and Theory-Building: The Case of Status Inconsistency." American Sociological Review 31 (February): 52-61.

——(1967) "Causal Inferences, Closed Populations, and Measures of Association." American Political Science Review 61, 1 (March): 130-136.

——(1969) *Theory Construction.* Englewood Cliffs, N.J.: Prentice-Hall.

Bleicher, S. (1971) "Intergovernmental Organization and the Preservation of Peace: A Comment on the Abuse of Methodology.' International Organization 25, 2 (Spring): 298-305.

Bobrow,˙D. and N. E. Cutler (1967) "Time-Oriented Explanations of National Security Beliefs: Cohort, Life Stage, and Situation." Peace Research Society (International) Papers 8: 31-57.

Boeke, J. H. (1946) "The Evolution of the Netherlands Indies Economy." New York: Netherlands and Netherlands Indies Council, Institute of Pacific Relations Research Series.

Bogardus, E. S. (1925) "Measuring Social Distance." Journal of Applied Sociology 9: 299-308.

——(1933) "A Social Distance Scale." Sociology and Social Research 17: 265-271.

Boudon, R. (1968) "A New Look at Correlation Analysis." In H. M. Blalock and A. B. Blalock *Methodology in Social Research.* New York: McGraw-Hill.

Boulding, K. E. (1959) "National Images and International Systems," Journal of Conflict Resolution 3, 2: 120-131.

——(1962) *Conflict and Defense.* New York: Harper and Row.

Brams, S. (1968) "Measuring the Concentration of Power in Political Systems." American Political Science Review 62, 2 (June): 461-475.

Bremer, S., J. D. Singer, and U. Luterbacher (1972) "Crowding and Combat in Animal and Human Societies: The European Nations, 1816-1965." In Albert Somit et al. (eds.) *Biology and Politics.* Chicago: Aldine.

Buchanan, W. and H. Cantril (1953) *How Nations See Each Other.* Urbana: University of Illinois Press.

Burton, J. W. (1962) *Peace Theory.* New York: Alfred A. Knopf.

Butterfield, H. (1959) *The Origins of Modern Science.* New York: Macmillan.

Campbell, D. T. (1958) "Common Fate, Similarity, and other Indices of the Status of Aggregates of Persons as Social Entities." Behavioral Science 3, 1 (January): 14-25.

Caspary, W. R. (1970a) "Dimensions of Attitudes on International Conflict, Internationalism and Military Offensive Action." Peace Research Society (International) Papers 13: 1-10.

——(1970b) "The 'Mood Theory': A Study of Public Opinion and Foreign Policy." American Political Science Review 64, 2 (June): 536-547.

—— (ed.) (forthcoming) *Reaction Process Models of International Conflict.* New York: Free Press.

Catton, W. R., Jr. (1965) "The Concept of 'Mass' in the Sociological Version of Gravitation." F. Massarik and P. Ratoosh (eds.) *Mathematical Explorations in Behavioral Science.* Homewood, Ill.: Richard Irwin.

Chester, L., G. Hodgson, and B. Page (1969) *An American Melodrama: The Presidential Campaign of 1968.* New York: Viking Press.

Choucri, N. (1970) "Applications of Experimental Econometrics to Forecasting in Political Analysis." Paper written for the Conference on Forecasting International Relations: California.

Choucri, N. and R. C. North (1969) "The Determinants of International Violence," Peace Research Society Papers 12: 33-63.

—— (1972) "Dynamics of International Conflict: Some Policy Implications of Population, Resources, and Technology." In World Politics, supplementary issue.

Christ, C. F. (1965) Econometric Models and Methods. New York: John Wiley.

Claude, I. L. Jr. (1962) *Power and International Relations.* New York: Random House.

Cofer, C. N., and M. H. Appley (1964) *Motivation: Theory and Research.* New York: John Wiley.

Coleman, J. (1957) *Community Conflict.* New York: Free Press.

Connery, D. S. (1966) *The Scandinavians.* New York: Simon and Schuster.

Corson, W. H. (1970) "Measuring Conflict and Cooperation Intensity in East-West Relations: A Manual and Codebook." Ann Arbor: Institute for Social Research, University of Michigan.

Coser, L. (1961) "The Termination of Social Conflict." Journal of Conflict Resolution 5, 4 (December): 347-353.

——(1963) "Peaceful Settlements and the Dysfunctions of Secrecy." Journal of Conflict Resolution 7, 3 (September): 246-253.

De Rivera, J. (1968) *The Psychological Dimensions of Foreign Policy.* Columbus, Ohio: Charles E. Merrill.

Denton, F. H. (1966) "Some Regularities in International Conflict, 1820-1949." Background (February): 283-296.

Deutsch, K. W. (1966) "Power and Communication in International Society." In A.V.S. de Reuck and J. Knight (ed.) *Conflict in Society.* Gloucester Place, London: J. and A. Churchill.

——(1957) *Political Community and the North Atlantic Area: International Organization in the Light of Historical Experience.* Princeton: Princeton University Press.

Deutsch, K. W., and R. L. Merritt (1965) "Effects of Events on National and International Images." In H. Kelman (ed.) *International Behavior: A Social-Psychological Analysis.* New York: Holt, Rinehart and Winston.

Deutsch, K. W., J. D. Singer, and K. Smith (1965) "The Organizing Efficiency of Theories: The N/V Ratio as a Crude Rank Order Measure." American Behavioral Scientist 9, 2 (October): 30-33.

Deutsch, M. (1965) "Conflict and Its Resolution." Paper presented to the Annual Meeting of the American Psychological Association. Chicago, Illinois (September).

Dinerstein, H. S. (1965) "The Transformation of Alliance Systems." American Political Science Review, 54, 3 (September): 589-601.

Dodd, S. C. (1947) *Dimensions of Society*. New York: Macmillan.

Dollard, J., et al. (1939) *Frustration and Aggression*. New Haven: Yale University Press.

Duscha, J. (1965) *Arms, Money, and Politics*. New York: Ives Washburn.

East, M. A. (1969) "Stratification and International Politics," Ph.D. dissertation. Princeton: Princeton University.

——(1971) "Stratification in the International system: An Empirical Analysis." In V. Davis et al., *The Analysis of International Politics*. New York: Free Press.

Easton, D. (1953) *The Political System: An Inquiry Into the State of Political Science*. New York: Alfred A. Knopf.

Edelman, M. (1964) *The Symbolic Uses of Politics*. Urbana: University of Illinois Press.

Ehrlich, P. R., and A. M. Erlich (1970) *Population, Resources, Environment*. San Francisco: W. H. Freeman.

Etzioni, A. (1965) *Political Unification: A Comparative Study of Leaders and Forces*. New York: Holt, Rinehart and Winston.

Ezekiel, M. and K. A. Fox (1959) *Methods of Correlation and Regression Analysis*. New York: John Wiley.

Falls, C. (1962) *A Hundred Years of War, 1850-1950*. New York: Collier Books.

Farrell, R. B. (1966a) "Foreign Politics of Open and Closed Political Societies " In Farrell (ed.) (1966b) *Approaches to Comparative and International Politics*. Evanston: Northwestern University Press.

——(1966b) (ed.) *Approaches to Comparative and International Politics*. Evanston: Northwestern University Press.

Festinger, L. (1957) *A Theory of Cognitive Dissonance*. Stanford: Stanford University Press.

——(1964) *Conflict, Decision, and Dissonance*. Stanford: Stanford University Press.

Fisher, F. M. (1963) "On the Cost of Approximate Specification in Simultaneous Equation Estimation." In A. Ando, F. M. Fisher, and H. A. Simon, *Essays on the Structure of Social Sciences*. Cambridge: MIT Press.

——(1966) *The Identification Problem in Econometrics*. New York: McGraw-Hill.

Fisher, R. (1969) *International Conflict for Beginners*. New York: Harper and Row.

Forbes, H. D. and E. R. Tufte (1968) "A Note of Caution in Causal Modeling." American Political Science Review 62, 4 (December): 1258-1264.

Fossum, E. (1967) "Factors Influencing the Occurrence of Military Coups d'Etat in Latin America." Journal of Peace Research 3: 225-251.

Frankel, J. (1964) *International Relations*. New York: Oxford University Press.

Friedheim, R. L., and J. B. Kadane (1970) "Quantitative Content Analysis of the United Nations Seabed Debates: Methodology in a Continental Shelf Case Study." International Organization.

Fucks, W. (1965) *Formeln zur Macht.* Stuttgart: Deutsch Verlagsanfalt.

Galtung, J. (1964a) "Summit Meetings and International Relations." Journal of Peace Research 1: 36-54.

——(1964b) "A Structural Theory of Aggression." Journal of Peace Research 2: 95-119.

——(1966) "Rank and Social Integration: A Multidimensional Approach." In J. Berger et al., *Sociological Theories in Progress* Vol. I. Boston: Houghton Mifflin.

——(1967) "Public Opinion on the Economic Effects of Disarmament." In E. Benoit (ed.) *Disarmament and World Economic Interdependence.* Oslo: Universitetsforlaget.

——(1969) "Violence, Peace and Peace Research." Journal of Peace Research 3: 167-191.

Galtung, J., M. Mora y Araujo, and S. Schwartzmann (1966) "The Latin-American System of Nations: A Structural Analysis." Journal of Social Research.

Gamson, W. A. (1961) "A Theory of Coalition Formation." American Sociological Review 26, 3 (June): 373-382.

German, F. C. (1960) "A Tentative Evaluation of World Power." Journal of Conflict Resolution 4, 1 (March): 138-144.

Glenn, N. (1970) "Problems of Comparability in Trend Studies with Opinion Poll Data." Public Opinion Quarterly 21, 1 (Spring): 82-91.

Gleditsch, N. P. (1969) "Rank and Interaction: A General Theory with Some Application to the International System." Paper presented at the Third Conference of the International Peace Research Association. Karlovy Vary, Czechoslovakia (September 21-23).

Gleditsch, N. P., and J. D. Singer (1972) "Spatial Predictors of National War-Proneness, 1816-1965." Oslo: Peace Research Institute.

Goldberger, A. S. (1964) *Economic Theory.* New York: John Wiley.

Gonzales Casanova, P. (1966b) "Internal and External Politics of Underdeveloped Countries." In Farrell (ed.) *Approaches to Comparative and International Politics.* Evanston: Northwestern University Press.

Gulick, E. V. (1955) *Europe's Classical Balance of Power.* New York: Norton.

Gurr, T. (1970) *Why Men Rebel.* Princeton: Princeton University Press.

Haar, J. E. (1969) *The Professional Diplomat.* Princeton: Princeton University Press.

——(1970) "The Issue of Competence in the Department of State." International Studies Quarterly 14 (March): 95-101.

Haas, E. B. (1953) "The Balance of Power: Prescription, Concept, or Propaganda." World Politics 5, 3 (April): 442-477.

——(1964) *Beyond the Nation-State.* Stanford: Stanford University Press.

——(1970) "The Study of Regional Integration: Reflections on the Joy and Anguish of Pretheorizing." International Organization 24, 4.

Haas, E. B. and A. S. Whiting (1956) *Dynamics of International Relations.* New York: McGraw-Hill.

Haas, M. (1965) "Societal Approaches to the Study of War." Journal of Peace Research 4: 307-323.

——(1968) "Social Change and National Aggressiveness, 1900-1960." In J. D. Singer (ed.) *Quantitative International Politics.* New York: Free Press.

Hall, E. T. (1959) *The Silent Language.* Garden City, N.Y.: Doubleday.

——(1969) *The Hidden Dimension.* Garden City, New York: Doubleday-Anchor.

Harris, C. (ed.) (1963) *Problems in Measuring Change.* Madison, Wisconsin: University of Wisconsin Press.

Heintz, P. (1969) *Ein Soziologisches Paradigma der Entwicklung mit Besonderer Berucksichtigung Lateinamerikas.* Stuttgart: Ferdinand Enke Verlag.

Hitch, C. J., and D. McKean (1960) *The Economics of Defense in the Nuclear Age.* Cambridge: Harvard University Press.

Holsti, K. J. (1966) "Resolving International Conflicts: A Taxonomy of Behavior and Some Figures on Procedures." Journal of Conflict Resolution 10, 3: 272-296.

Holsti, O. R., and J. D. Sullivan (1969) "National-International Linkages: France and China as Nonconforming Alliance Members." In J. N. Rosenau (ed.) *Linkage Politics.* New York: Free Press: 147-195.

Homans, G. C. (1961) *Social Behavior: Its Elementary Forms.* New York: Harcourt, Brace and World.

Hopmann, T. P., and C. E. Walcott (forthcoming) *Bargaining in International Arms Control Negotiations.*

Howard, A., and R. A. Scott (1965) "A Proposed Framework for the Analysis of Stress in the Human Organism." Behavioral Science 10, 2 (April): 141-160.

Huddleston, S. (1954) *Popular Diplomacy and War.* Rindge, N.H.: Richard R. Smith.

Hula, E. (1959) "Comment." Social Research 26 (Summer): 154-161.

Hull, C. L. (1943) *Principles of Behavior.* New York: Appleton-Century-Crofts.

Iklé, F. C. (1964) *How Nations Negotiate.* New York: Frederick A. Praeger.

Jacob, P. E., and H. Teune (1964) "The Integrative Process: Guidelines for Analysis of the Bases of Political Community." In P. E. Jacob and J. V. Toscano (ed.) *The Integration of Political Communities.* Philadelphia: Lippincott.

Jensen, L. (1968) "Approach-Avoidance Bargaining in the Test Ban Negotiations." International Studies Quarterly 12: 152-160.

Johansson, O. (1967) *The Gross Domestic Product of Sweden and its Composition 1861-1955.* Stockholm Economic Studies 18. Stockholm: Almquist and Wikfell.

Johnston, J. (1963) *Econometric Methods.* New York: McGraw-Hill.

Kahn, H. (1960) *On Thermonuclear War.* Princeton: Princeton University Press.

Kaplan, A. (1964) *The Conduct of Inquiry.* San Francisco: Chandler.

Katz, D. (1967) "Group Processes and Social Integration: A System Analysis of Two Movements of Social Protest." Journal of Social Issues 23: 3-22.

Kimberley, J. C. (1966) "A Theory of Status Equilibration." In Joseph Berger et al. *Sociological Theories in Progress.* Vol. I. Boston: Houghton Mifflin.

Kissinger, H. (1957) *A World Restored; Metternich, Castlereagh, and the Problems of Peace, 1812-22.* Boston: Houghton Mifflin.

Klingberg, F. L. (1952) "The Historical Alternation of Moods in American Foreign Policy." World Politics, 4, 2: 239-273.

——(1966) "Predicting the Termination of War" Journal of Conflict Resolution 10, 2 (June): 147-148.

Knorr, K. (1956) *The War Potential of Nations.* Princeton: Princeton University Press.

——(1970) *Military Power and Potential.* Lexington, Mass.: D. C. Heath.

Kraslow, D., and S. H. Loory (1968) *The Secret Search for Peace in Vietnam.* New York: Vintage Books.

Lagerstrom, R. P., and R. C. North (1969) "An Anticipated Gap, Mathematical Model of International Dynamics." Stanford: Stanford University.

Lagos, G. (1963) *International Stratification and Underdeveloped Countries.* Chapel Hill: University of North Carolina Press.

Landis, J. R., D. Datwyler, and D. S. Dorn (1966) "Race and Social Class as Determinants of Social Distance." Sociology and Social Research 51, 1: 78-86.

Langer, W. (1931) *European Alliances and Alignments, 1871-1890.* New York: Alfred A. Knopf.

Larsen, K. (1948) *History of Norway.* Princeton: Princeton University Press.

Lasswell, H. D. (1954) "Key Signs, Symbols, and Icons." In L. Bryson, et al. *Symbols and Values: An Initial Study.* New York: Harper.

Lasswell, H. D., and A. Kaplan (1950) *Power and Society: A Framework for Political Inquiry.* New Haven: Yale University Press.

Lasswell, H. D., N. Neites, and Associates (1949) *Language of Politics: Studies in Quantitative Semantics.* Cambridge: MIT Press.

Laumann, E. O. (1965) "Subjective Social Distance and Urban Occupational Stratification." The American Journal of Sociology 71 (July): 26-36.

Lauring, P. (1960) *A History of the Kingdom of Denmark.* Copenhagen: Host and Son.

Leiserson, M. (1966) "Coalitions in Politics: A Theoretical and Empirical Study." Ph.D. dissertation. New Haven: Yale University.

Leng, R., and J. D. Singer (1970) "Toward a Multi-Theoretical Typology of International Behavior." Ann Arbor: Mental Health Research Institute (April).

Lenski, G. (1966) *Power and Privilege: A Theory of Social Stratification.* New York: McGraw-Hill.

Lerche, C. O. (1956) *Principles of International Politics.* New York: Oxford University Press.

Levi, W. (1970) "Ideology, Interests, and Foreign Policy." International Studies Quarterly 14 (March): 1-31.

Lewin, K. (1964) *Field Theory in Social Science.* Dorwin Cartwright (ed.). New York: Harper Torchbooks.

Lippmann, W. (1955) *The Public Philosophy.* Boston: Little, Brown.

Liska, G. (1956) *International Equilibrium.* Cambridge: Harvard University Press.

——(1962) *Nations in Alliance.* Baltimore: Johns Hopkins Press.

Liu, T. C. (1955) "A Simple Forecasting Model for the U.S. Economy." In International Monetary Fund. Staff Papers: 434-466.

McNeil, E. B. [ed.] (1965) *The Nature of Human Conflict.* Englewood Cliffs, N.J.: Prentice-Hall.

Margenau, H. (1950) *The Nature of Physical Reality.* New York: McGraw-Hill.

Marsh, R. M. (1967) *Comparative Sociology.* New York: Harcourt, Brace and World.

Merton, R. K. (1957) *Social Theory and Social Structure.* New York: Free Press.

Midlarsky, M. (1969) "Status Inconsistency and the Onset of International Warfare." Ph.D. dissertation. Evanston: Northwestern University.

Miller, G. A., E. Galanter, and K. H. Pribram (1960) *Plans and the Structure of Behavior.* New York: Holt, Rinehart and Winston.

Mitchell, J. M., and W. C. Mitchell (1969) *Political Analysis and Public Policy: An Introduction to Political Science.* Chicago: Rand McNally.

Mitchell, R. (1964) "Methodological Notes on a Theory of Status Crystallization." Public Opinion Quarterly 28 (Summer): 315-325.

Mitchell, W. C. and Nazli Choucri (1969) "Armaments Behavior Among Competing Nations. Simulating the Naval Budgets of Major Powers: Europe 1870-1914." Center for Advanced Study in the Behavioral Sciences: International Systems Workshop.

Moll, K. (1968) The Influence of History on Seapower: 1865-1914. Stanford: Stanford Research Institute.

Morgenstern, O. (1963) *On the Accuracy of Economic Observations* (2nd edn.). Princeton: Princeton University Press.

Morgenthau, H. J. (1967) *Politics Among Nations* (4th edn.). New York: Alfred A. Knopf.

Morse, E. L. (1970) "The Transformation of Foreign Policies: Modernization, Interdependence, and Externalization." World Politics 22, 3 (April): 371-392.

Moses, L. E., R. A. Brody, O. R. Holsti, J. B. Kadane, and J. S. Milstein (1967) "Scaling Data on Inter-Nation Action." Science 156 (May 26): 1054-1059.

Mueller, J. (1970) "Presidential Popularity from Truman to Johnson." American Political Science Review 64, 1 (March): 18-34.

Mulhall, M. G. (1880) *The Progress of the World.* London: Edward Stanford.

North R. C. (1967) "Steps Toward Developing a Theory." Stanford: Studies in International Conflict and Integration.

North, R. C. (1971) In collaboration with Nazli Choucri. "Population and the Future International System." International Organization.

North, R. C. and N. Choucri (forthcoming) *Nations in Conflict: Prelude to World War I.*

North, R. C., O. R. Holsti, M. G. Zaninovich, and D. A. Zinnes (1963) *Content Analysis.* Evanston: Northwestern University Press.

Norway (1968) *Historical Statistics.* Oslo: Statistisk Sentralbyra.

Nye, J. S. (1970) "Comparing Common Markets: A Revised Neo-Functional Model." International Organization 24, 4: 796-835.

Oakley, S. (1966) *A Short History of Sweden.* New York: Frederick A. Praeger.

Ogburn, C. Jr, H. F. Haviland, Jr., and Associates (1960) *The Formulation and Administration of United States Foreign Policy.* Report for the Committee on Foreign Relations of the United States Senate: Brookings Institution.

Olsson, G. (1965) *Distance and Human Interaction: A Review and Bibliography.* Philadelphia: Regional Science Research Institute.

Organski, A.F.K. (1968) *World Politics* (2nd edn.) New York: Alfred A. Knopf.

Park, T. W. (1969) "Asian Conflict in Systemic Perspective: Application of Field Theory (1955 and 1963)." Ph.D. dissertation and Dimensionality of Nations Project Research Report No. 35. University of Hawaii.

Parkman, M. A. and J. Sawyer (1967) "Dimensions of Ethnic Intermarriage in Hawaii." American Sociological Review 32 (August) 592-607.

Patel, J. J. (1964) "The Economic Distance Between Nations: Its Origin, Measurement and Outlook." The Economic Journal 74 (March): 119-131.

Phillips, W. P. (1969) "Dynamic Patterns of International Conflict." Ph.D. dissertation and Dimensionality of Nations Project Research Report No. 33: University of Hawaii.

Platig, E. R. (1967) *International Relations Research.* Santa Barbara: Clio Press.

Poincaré, H. (1952) *Science and Hypothesis.* New York: Dover Publications.

Pool, I. de S. (1951) *Symbols of Internationalism.* Stanford: Stanford University Press.

Popper, K. R. (1961) *The Logic of Scientific Discovery.* New York: Science Editions.

Public Papers of the Presidents of the United States, containing the public messages, speeches, statements of the President: Lyndon B. Johnson (1964-1968). Washington: U.S.G.P.O.

Rapoport, A. (1960) *Fights, Games, and Debates.* Ann Arbor: University of Michigan Press.

——(1970) "Is Peace Research Applicable?" Journal of Conflict Resolution 14, 2 (June): 277-286.

Renouvin, P., and J. B. Duroselle (1967) *Introduction to the History of International Relations.* New York: Frederick A. Praeger.

Richardson, L. F. (1960a) *Statistics of Deadly Quarrels.* Pittsburgh and Chicago: Boxwood and Quadrangle Presses.

——(1960b) *Arms and Insecurity: A Mathematical Study of the Causes and Origins of War.* Pittsburgh and Chicago: Boxwood and Quadrangle Presses.

Robinson, J. P., J. Rusk, and K. Head (1968) *Measures of Political Attutides.* Ann Arbor: University of Michigan Institute of Social Research.

Rosecrance, R. N. (1963) *Action and Reaction in World Politics.* Boston: Little, Brown.

Rosen, S. (1970) "A Rational Actor Model of War and Alliance." In J. Friedman, C. Bladen, and S. Rosen (eds.) *Alliance in International Politics.* Boston: Allyn and Bacon.

——(1971) "Cost-Tolerance in Human Lives for Foreign Policy Goals." Peace Research Society (International) Papers 15.

Rosenau, J. (1966) "Pre-Theories and Theories of Foriegn Policy." In R. B. Farrell (ed.) *Approaches to Comparative and International Politics.* Evanston: Northwestern University Press.

——(1967a) "Foreign Policy as an Issue Area." In Rosenau *Domestic Sources of Foreign Policy.* New York: Free Press.

——(1967b) "Of Boundaries and Bridges: A Report on a Conference on the Interdependencies of National and International Political Systems." Center of International Studies Research Monograph No. 27. Princeton University.

Rosenau, J. (ed.) (1969) *Linkage Politics: Essays on the Convergence of National and International Systems.* New York: Free Press.

Rosenberg, M. J. (1967) "Attitude Change and Foreign Policy in the Cold War Era." In J. N. Rosenau (ed.) *Domestic Sources of Foreign Policy.* New York: Free Press.

Rummel, R. J. (1963a) "Dimensions of Conflict Behavior Within and Between Nations." General Systems Yearbook 8: 1-50.

——(1963b) "Testing Some Possible Predictors of Conflict Behavior Within and Between Nations." Peace Research Society Papers: 79-111.

——(1965) "A Field Theory of Social Action With Application to Conflict Within Nations." General Systems: Yearbook of the Society of General Systems 10.

——(1966a) "A Foreign Conflict Behavior Code Sheet." World Politics 18, 2 (January): 283-296.

——(1966b) "Some Dimensions in the Foreign Behavior of Nations." Journal of Peace Research 3: 201-224.

——(1968) "The Relationship Between National Attributes and Foreign Conflict Behavior." In J. D. Singer (ed.) *Quantitative International Politics.* New York: Free Press.

——(1969a) "Field and Attribute Theories of Nation Behavior: Some Mathematical Interrelationships." Paper presented at the First Far East Peace Research Conference (August). Tokyo, Japan.

——(1969b) "Field Theory and Indicators of International Behavior." Paper presented at the American Political Science Association Convention (September). New York.

——(1969c) "Indicators of Cross-National and International Patterns." American Political Science Review 68, 1 (March): 127-147.

——(1970a) *Applied Factor Analysis.* Evanston: Northwestern University Press.

——(1970b) "New Developments in Field Theory: The 1963 Behavior Space of Nations." Paper presented at the Seventh European Peace Research Society (International) Conference (August 30-31). Rome, Italy.

——(1970c) "Social Time and International Relations." Paper published for the Eighth World Congress, International Political Science Association (September 1-7). Munich, Germany.

——(1972) *Dimensions of Nations.* Beverly Hills, Calif.: Sage.

Russett, B. M. (1963a) *Community and Contention: Britain and America in the Twentieth Century.* Cambridge: MIT Press.

——(1963b) "The Calculus of Deterrence." Journal of Conflict Resolution 7, 2 (June): 97-109.

——et al. (1964) *World Handbook of Political and Social Indicators.* New Haven: Yale University Press.

——(1965) *Trends in World Politics.* New York: Macmillan.

——(1967a) *International Regions and the International System.* Chicago: Rand McNally.

——(1967b) "Pearl Harbor: Deterrence Theory and Decision Theory." Journal of Peace Research 2: 89-105.

——(1968a) "Components of an Operational Theory of Alliance Formulation." Journal of Conflict Resolution 12, 3 (September): 285-301.

——(1968b) " 'Regional' Trading Patterns, 1938-1963." International Studies Quarterly 12, 4 (December): 360-379.

——(1970) *What Price Vigilance?* New Haven: Yale University Press.

——(1971) "An Empirical Typology of International Military Alliances." Midwest Journal of Political Science.

Russett, B. M., and W. C. Lamb (1969) "Global Patterns of Diplomatic Exchange, 1963-64." Journal of Peace Research 3: 37-55.

Russett, B. M., J. D. Singer, and M. Small (1968) "National Political Units in the 20th Century: A Standardized List." American Political Science Review 62, 3: 932-951.

Schilling, W. (1965) "Surprise Attack, Death, and War." Journal of Conflict Resolution 9, 3 (September): 385-390.

Schwartzman, S. (1966) "International Development and International Feudalism: The Latin American Case." Proceedings of the IPRA Inaugural Conference. Assen, Netherlands: Van Gorcum.

Schwartzman, S. and M. M. Y Araujo (1966) "The Images of International Stratification in Latin America." Peace Research Journal 3: 225-243.

Schwarzenberger, G. (1951) *Power Politics.* New York: Frederick A. Praeger.

Scott, A. M. (1969) "The Department of State: Formal Organization and Informal Culture." International Studies Quarterly 13 (March): 1-18.

——(1970) "Environmental Change and Organizational Adaptation: The Problem of the State Department." International Studies Quarterly 14 (March): 85-94.

Scott, F. D. (1950) *The United States and Scandinavia.* Cambridge: Harvard University Press.

Seally, K. (1957) *The Geography of Air Transport.* London: Hutchinson.

Sears, R. R. (1951) "Social Behavior and Personality Development." In T. Parsons and E. A. Shils (eds.) *Toward a General Theory of Action.* New York: Harper and Row.

Segal, D. R. (1969) "Status Inconsistency, Cross Pressures, and American Political Behavior." American Sociological Review 34 (June): 352-359.

Shimbori, M., et al. (1963) "Measuring a Nation's Prestige." American Journal of Sociology 64: 63-68.

Shirer, W. L. (1955) *The Challenge of Scandinavia: Norway, Sweden, Denmark and Finland in Our Time*. Boston: Little, Brown.

Simmel, G. (1904) "The Sociology of Conflict." American Journal of Sociology 9 (January): 490-525.

Simon, H. A. (1953) "Causal Ordering and Identifiability." In W. C. Hood and T. C. Koopmans (eds.) *Studies in Econometric Method*. New York: John Wiley.

Singer, J. D. (1958) "Threat-Perception and the Armament-Tension Dilemma." Journal of Conflict Resolution 2, 1: 90-105.

———(1961) "The Level-of-Analysis Problem in International Relations." World Politics 14, 1 (October): 77-92.

———(1963) "Inter-Nation Influence: A Formal Model." American Political Science Review 57, 2 (June): 420-430.

———(1970) "Knowledge, Practice and the Social Sciences in International Politics." In N. Palmer (ed.) *A Design for International Relations Research*. Philadelphia: American Academy of Political and Social Science: 137-49.

Singer, J. D., and M. Small (1966a) "The Composition and Status Ordering of the International System, 1815-1940." World Politics 18, 2: 236-282.

———(1966b) "Formal Alliances, 1815-1939: A Quantitative Description." Journal of Peace Research 3, 1: 1-32.

———(1966c) "National Alliance Commitments and War Involvement, 1815-1945." Peace Research Society (International) Papers 5: 109-140.

———(1968) "Alliance Aggregation and the Onset of War, 1815-1945." In J. D. Singer (ed.) *Quantitative International Politics: Insights and Evidence*. New York: Free Press.

———(1972) *The Wages of War, 1816-1965: A Statistical Handbook*. New York: John Wiley.

———(1973) *The Strength of Nations: Comparative Capabilities since Waterloo*. (forthcoming)

Singer, J. D., and J. L. Ray (1972) "Measuring Distributions in Macro-Social Systems." Ann Arbor: Mental Health Research Institute.

Singer, J. D. and M. D. Wallace (1970) "Inter-Governmental Organization and the Preservation of Peace, 1816-1965: Some Bivariate Relationships." International Organization 24, 3 (Summer): 520-547.

Singer, J. D., M. D. Wallace, and S. Bremer (1973) *A Structural History of the International System, 1816-1965*. (forthcoming)

Singer, J. D., and P. Winston (1969) "Individual Values, National Interests and Political Development in the International System." Paper presented to the annual meeting of the American Political Science Association, Washington, D.C.

Skjelsbaek, Kjell (1971) "Shared Memberships in Intergovernmental Organizations and Dyadic War, 1865-1964." In E. H. Fedder (ed.) *The United Nations: Problems and Prospects*. St. Louis: Center for International Studies.

Small, M., and J. D. Singer (1969) "Formal Alliances, 1816-1965: An Extension of the Basic Data." Journal of Peace Research 3: 257-282.

——(1970) "Patterns in International Warfare, 1816-1965." Annals of American Academy of Political and Social Science (September): 145-155.

Sorokin, P. A. (1943) Sociocultural Causality, Space, Time. Durham: Duke University Press.

Sprout, H. and M. Sprout (1962) Foundations of International Politics. New York: D. Van Nostrand.

Stillman, E. O. (1970) "Civilian Sanctuary and Target Avoidance Policy in Thermonuclear War." Annals of the American Academy of Political and Social Science, 392 (November): 119.

Strausz-Hupé, R., and S. T. Possony (1954) International Relations in the Age of the Conflict Between Democracy and Dictatorship. New York: McGraw-Hill.

Sullivan, J. D. (1969) "National and International Sources of Alliance Maintenance." Ph.D. dissertation. Stanford University.

——(1970) "The Location of Social Science Research for the Foreign Policy Decision-maker." Paper prepared for the Conference on Social Science Research and Foreign Affairs. Arlie House, Virginia.

——(forthcoming) "Cooperation in International Politics: Quantitative Perspectives on Formal Alliances." In M. Haas (ed.) Behavioral International Relations. San Francisco: Chandler.

Sullivan, M. P. (1969) "International Conflict Systems: Two Models." Tucson: University of Arizona (September).

——(1970) "Commitment and the Escalation of Conflicts." Tucson: University of Arizona (February).

Tanter, R. (1966) "Dimensions of Conflict Behavior Within and Between Nations, 1958-1960." Journal of Conflict Resolution 10 (March): 41-64.

Teune, H., and S. Synnestredt (1965) "Measuring International Alignment." Orbis 9, 1 (Spring).

Thurstone, L. (1935) The Vectors of Mind. Chicago: University of Chicago Press.

Tolman, E. C. (1951) "A Psychological Model." In T. Parsons and E. A. Shils (eds.) Toward a General Theory of Action. New York: Harper and Row.

Turner, M. E. and C. D. Stevens (1959) "Regression Analysis of Causal Paths." Biometrics 15, 2: 236-258.

Vandenbosch, A. (1955) Dutch Foreign Policy Since 1815: A Study in Small Power Politics. The Hague: Mantinus Nijhoff.

Von den Berghe, P. L. (1960) "Distance Mechanisms of Stratification." Sociology and Social Research 44 (January-February): 155-164.

Voth, A. (1967) "Vietnam: Studying a Major Controversy." Journal of Conflict Resolution 9, 3 (December): 438.

Wall, C., and R. J. Rummel (1969) "Estimating Missing Data." Dimensionality of Nations Project Research Report No. 20. Honolulu: University of Hawaii.

Wallace, M. D. (1970) "Status Inconsistency, Vertical Mobility, and International War, 1825-64." Ph.D. dissertation. Ann Arbor: University of Michigan.

——(1971) "Power, Status and International War." Journal of Peace Research 1: 23-35.

Wallace, M. D., and J. D. Singer (1970) "Inter-Governmental Organization in the Global System, 1816-1964: A Quantitative Description." International Organization 24, 2 (Spring): 239-287.

Warner, L. G., and M. L. DeFleur (1969) "Attitude as an Interactional Concept: Social Constraint and Social Distance as Intervening Variables Between Attitudes and Action." American Sociological Review 34 (April).

Watanabe, S. (1969) Knowing and Guessing. New York: John Wiley.

Weinstein, F. (1969) "The Concept of Commitment in International Relations." Journal of Conflict Resolution 13 (March).

Wesolowski, W. (1966) "Some Notes on the Functional Theory of Stratification." In R. Bendix and S. M. Lipset Class, Status and Power (2nd edn.) New York: Free Press.

White, R. K. (1968) Nobody Wanted War: Misperception in Vietnam and Other Wars. Garden City, N.Y.: Doubleday.

Wicker, T. (1968) JFK and LBJ: The Influence of Personality on Politics. New York: William Morrow.

Wiener, N. (1948) Cybernetics; or Controlled Communication in the Animal and the Machine. Cambridge: MIT Press.

Wilkenfeld, J. (1968) "Domestic and Foreign Conflict Behavior of Nations." Journal of Peace Research 1: 56-69.

——(1969) "Some Further Findings Regarding the Domestic and Foreign Conflict Behavior of Nations." Journal of Peace Research 2: 147-156.

Williams, E. (1963) Holland Growing Greater. Amsterdam: Bezige Bij.

Williams, R. M., Jr. (1947) The Reduction of Intergroup Tensions. New York: Social Science Research Council.

Winch, R. and D. T. Campbell (1969) "Proof? No. Evidence? Yes. The Significance of Tests of Significance." American Sociologist 4, 2 (May): 140-143.

Wohlstetter, A. (1968a) "Illusions of Distance." Foreign Affairs 46 (January).

——(1968b) "Theory and Opposed-Systems Design." Journal of Conflict Resolution 12, 2 (September): 302-331.

Wold, H.O.A. (1960) "A Generalization of Causal Chain Models." Econometrica 28, 2 (April): 443-463.

Wold, H., in association with L. Jureen (1953) Demand Analysis. Baltimore: Johns Hopkins Press.

Woods, F. A., and A. Baltzly (1915) Is War Diminishing? Boston: Houghton Mifflin.

Wright, Q. (1955) The Study of International Relations. New York: Appleton-Century-Crofts.

——(1965a) *A Study of War* (2nd edn.) Chicago: University of Chicago Press.

——(1965b) "The Escalation of International Conflicts." Journal of Conflict Resolution 9: 434-449.

Wright, S. (1934) "The Method of Path Coefficients." Annals of Mathematical Statistics 5.

——(1960) "The Treatment of Reciprocal Interaction, with or without Lag, in Path Analysis." Biometrica 15, 3 (September): 423-445.

Wuorinen, J. H. (1965) *Scandinavia.* Englewood Cliffs, N.J.: Prentice-Hall.

Yakobson, S., and H. D. Lasswell (1949) "Trend: May Day Slogans in Soviet Russia, 1918-1943." In H. Lasswell, N. Leites, et al. *Language of Politics: Studies in Quantitative Semantics.* Cambridge: MIT Press.

Young, H. D. (1962) *Statistical Treatment of Experimental Data.* New York: McGraw-Hill.

Zinnes, D. A., and J. Wilkenfeld (1971) "An Analysis of Foreign Conflict Behavior of Nations." In W. F. Hanrieder (ed.) *Comparative Foreign Policy: Theoretical Essays.* New York: David McKay.

Zinnes, D. A., J. L. Zinnes, and R. D. McClure (1972) "Markovian Analyses of Hostile Communications in the 1914 Crisis." In C. F. Hermann (ed.) *Crisis in Foreign Policy Decision-Making.* New York: Free Press.

NAME INDEX

Adams, J. S., 53
Alcock, N., 171
Alexander, B., 139
Alker, H. R., Jr., 26, 239, 244
Almond, G. A., 310
Andersson, I., 247
Ando, A., 258, 260
Araujo, R., 82, 86, 109, 240

Baltzly, A., 246
Banks, A. S., 121, 123, 281
Bentley, A., 76, 78
Berkowtiz, L., 92
Berman, P., 139
Bernstein, G., 185
Berry, B.J.L., 84
Blalock, H. M., 34, 36, 52, 59, 67, 258
Bleicher, S., 47
Bobrow, D., 318
Boeke, J. H., 251
Bogardus, E. S., 81
Bolton, J., 139
Boudon, 59, 62
Boulding, K. E., 83, 172, 214
Brams, S., 26, 167
Bray, O., 213
Bremer, S., 12, 14, 20
Butterfield, H., 71

Campbell, D. T., 23
Caspary, W., 9, 244, 301, 310
Castro, F., 74, 167
Catton, W. R., Jr., 83
Chauvenet, 30

Chester, L., 186
Choucri, N., 11, 13, 15, 16, 59, 134, 241, 242, 244, 245, 250, 258, 275, 319
Christ, C. F., 259, 271
Chunk, C., 115
Claude, I., 54
Coleman, J., 188
Converse, P., 299
Coplin, W., 167
Corson, W. H., 221, 236
Coser, L., 89, 92, 183
Coltam, R., 167
Cutler, N. E., 318

Deber, R., 239
Denton, F. H., 276
DeRivera, J., 243
Deutsch, K. W., 19, 37, 75, 83, 93, 122, 246, 310
Deutsch, M., 188, 189
Dinerstein, H. S., 123
Dodd, S. C., 76
Dollard, J., 144
Donaldson, R., 167
Durbin-Watson, 265
Duroselle, J. B., 240

East, M. A., 21, 50
Easton, D., 77, 92
Edelman, M., 191
Ehrlich, A. M., 249
Ehrlich, P. R., 249
Eisenhower, D. D., 300, 315, 318

Etheredge, L., 139
Etzioni, A., 92, 109
Ezekiel, M., 37

Farrell, R. B., 276, 277
   Fisher, F. M., 258, 259, 260
Fisher, R., 74
Forbes, H. D., 67
Fossum, E., 50
Fox, D., 30, 37
Frankel, J., 277
Friedman, J., 167
Fucks, W., 25
Fulbright, J. W., 73, 299, 301

Galanter, E., 144
Galtung, J., 50, 52, 54, 63, 71, 82, 86,
   87, 109, 249, 314
Gamson, W. A., 123
German, F. C., 5, 57, 170
Gleditsch, N. P., 20, 82, 91, 109
Glenn, N., 308
Goldberger, A. S., 271
Goldman, R., 9
Gonzales Casanova, P., 277
Gregg, R., 121, 123, 167, 281
Gulick, E. V., 23, 54, 64, 92
Gurr, T. R., 190, 199, 201

Haar, J. E., 73
Haas, E. B., 76
Haas, M., 24, 45, 55, 122, 246, 276
Hanson, B., 139
Harrison, B., 185
Hastings, P. K., 299
Haviland, H. F., 73
Head, K., 301
Heintz, P., 109
Hero, A. O., 299, 301
Hitch, C. J., 170
Hitler, A., 74
Ho Chi Minh, 167
Hodgson, G., 186
Holsti, K. J., 187, 189
Holsti, O. R., 122

Homans, G. C., 82, 87, 144
Hopmann, P. T., 10, 11, 13, 16, 235
Howard, A., 144
Huang, M., 139
Hughes, B., 213
Hula, E., 74
Hull, C. L., 144
Huntington, S. P., 301, 309, 314

Iklé, F. C., 215, 216

Jacob, P., 83, 93
Jensen, L., 219, 222
Johnson, L. B., 185, 191-195, 203,
   204, 206-210, 312
Johnston, J., 67

Kadane, J. B., 139
Kahn, H., 172
Kant, E., 92
Kanter, A., 299
Kaplan, M., 76, 77, 79, 95
Katz, D., 188, 189, 191, 192
Kennedy, J. F., 210, 215, 236, 300
Khrushchev, N., 215
Kimberley, J. C., 53
Kirkwood, J., 139
Kissinger, H., 23, 73
Klingberg, F., 178, 318
Knorr, K., 25, 57, 171
Kraslow, D., 206

La Barr, D., 19
Lagerstrom, R. P., 244
Lagos, G., 53, 82, 86
Lamb, W. C., 122, 123, 124
Landis, J. R., 81
Langer, W., 23
Lasswell, H. D., 77, 95, 187, 191, 210
Lauring, P., 247
Lawrence, R., 185
Leiserson, M., 123
Leng, R., 20
Lenski, G., 82, 86, 87

Lerche, C. O., 88
Levi, W., 186, 206
Lewin, K., 76
Licklider, R. E., 115, 275
Lippmann, W., 300, 301
Liska, G., 54, 83, 116
Liu, T. C., 258
Loory, S. H., 206
Luft, R., 139
Luke, T., 207
Lussier, V. L., 275
Lustgarten, D., 139
Luterbacher, V., 20

McClelland, C., 10, 76
McClure, R. D., 286
McKean, D., 170
McNamara, Sec., 318
McNeil, E. B., 241
Mao tse-tung, 73, 74
Margenau, H., 76
Margolis, M., 167
Markov model, 275, 278, 284, 295
Marsh, R. M., 81
Marshall, D. B., 9, 115
Meister, 111
Merritt, R. L., 310
Merton, R. K., 82
Midlarsky, M., 9, 21, 50
Mikesell, R. F., 111
Miller, G. A., 144
Milstein, J. S., 12, 13, 14, 16, 115, 319
Mitchell, J. M., 188, 189
Mitchell, R. E., 87
Mitchell, W. C., 188, 189, 245
Moll, K., 245
Momferratos, P., 239
Morgenstern, O., 42
Morgenthau, H. J., 50, 53, 77, 83, 116, 169
Morris, A., 139
Morse, E. L., 88
Moses, L. E., 221
Moyer, H. W., 299
Mueller, J., 311, 312
Mulhall, M. G., 249, 251

Nadel, R., 115, 139
Newcombe, A., 171
Nixon, R. M., 73, 158
North, R. C., 59, 221, 241, 242, 244, 245, 250
Nye, J. S., 239, 246

Oakley, S., 247
Ogburn, C., Jr., 73
O'Leary, M., 167
Olsson, G., 81
Organski, A.F.K., 50, 53, 57, 71, 83, 92, 95, 170, 240
Owen, R., 167

Page, B., 186
Park, T. W., 84
Parkman, M. A., 81
Parsons, T., 76
Patel, J. J., 88
Pearson, F., 275
Phillips, W., 71, 84
Platig, E. R., 73
Poincaré, H., 76
Polk, 111
Popper, K. R., 24, 74
Possony, S. T., 77
Press, M., 139
Pribram, K. H., 144

Rapoport, A., 47, 144
Ray, J., 19, 26
Renouvin, P., 240
Richardson, L. F., 55, 74, 76, 178, 179, 214
Robinson, J. P., 301
Rogers, S., 73
Roosevelt, F. D., 300, 307
Rosecrance, R. N., 249, 276
Rosen, S., 10, 11, 12, 14, 15, 172, 179, 182
Rosenau, J. A., 15, 71, 81, 82, 85, 86, 100, 108, 188, 189, 190, 277
Rosenberg, M. J., 277

Rubin, T., 115
Rummel, R. J., 10, 12, 14, 15, 16, 74, 76, 77, 78, 80, 81, 84, 85, 90, 95, 96, 99, 105, 106, 111, 117, 119, 121, 165, 171, 249, 276, 278, 279
Rusk, J., 301
Russett, B., 9, 10, 13, 20, 21, 26, 37, 54, 57, 68, 69, 71, 75, 76, 78, 83, 92, 93, 105, 108, 109, 122, 123, 124, 134, 170, 171, 179, 214, 254, 269, 281, 300

Sawyer, J., 81
Schainblat, A., 115, 118
Schilling, W., 172
Schutz index, 26
Schwartzman, S., 82, 86, 109
Schwarz, J., 185
Schwarzenberger, G., 23
Scott, A. M., 73
Scott, F. D., 247
Scott, R. A., 144
Sears, R. R., 79
Segal, D. R., 87
Seymour, J., 139
Shimbori, M., 84
Shirer, W. L., 247
Simmel, G., 183
Simon, H. A., 59, 258, 260
Singer, J. D., 10-14, 20, 21, 25, 26, 34, 37, 48, 49, 51, 55-58, 66, 76, 87, 165, 174, 176, 178, 260
Skjelsbaek, K., 20
Sloan, T., 139
Small, M., 19, 20, 21, 25, 34, 51, 55-58, 87, 174, 176, 178, 260
Smith, K., 37, 317
Snyder, R., 74, 190
Sorokin, P. A., 76
Spearman, E. E., 76, 170, 176, 178
Sprout, H., 83
Sprout, M., 83
Stancliff, C., 115
Stegenga, J., 9, 207
Stevens, C. D., 62
Stillman, E. O., 172
Strausz-Hupé, R., 77

Stuckey, J., 12, 14
Sukarno, 74
Sullivan, J. D., 10, 12, 15, 16, 109, 122, 123, 135, 136
Sullivan, M. P., 11, 13, 16, 186, 191, 192, 210, 299

Tanter, R., 276, 278, 279
Teune, H., 83, 93
Textor, R. B., 281
Thorndike, E. L., 76
Thurmond, S., 317
Thurstone, L. L., 76
Tolman, E. C., 76
Truman, H. S., 312
Tufte, E. R., 67
Turner, M. E., 62
Tyler, J., 167

Uhler, R., 49

Van Atta, R. H., 275
Vandenbosch, A., 253
Veit, 111
Von den Berghe, P. L., 81
Voth, A., 172

Wagner, J. R., 185
Walcott, C. E., 213, 235
Wall, C., 111
Wallace, M. D., 10-15, 19, 20, 21, 50, 55, 57, 65, 69, 86, 110, 249, 319
Walters, R. S., 167
Weinstein, F., 189
Wesolowski, W., 56
Westerfield, H. B., 299
White, D., 167
White, R. K., 243
Whiting, A. S., 24, 276
Wicker, T., 207
Wiener, N., 144
Wilde, C., 185
Wilkenfeld, J., 10, 13, 15, 16, 276, 278, 279, 281, 282, 284, 290, 295

Williams, E., 251

Williams, E. J., 185

Williams, R. M., Jr., 86

Winston, P., 57

Wohlstetter, A., 83, 172

Wold, H.O.A., 51, 258

Woods, F. A., 246

Wright, Q., 71, 76, 77, 82, 89, 90, 92, 93, 95, 108, 109, 187, 189, 246, 247, 276

Wright, S., 51, 59

Wuorinen, J. H., 247, 249

Yacobson, S., 187

Young, H. D., 30

Zinnes, D. A., 286

Zinnes, J. A., 275, 276, 278, 281, 282, 286, 290, 295

SUBJECT INDEX

Aggregate perspective, 10, 11, 80, 109;
  vs. individual, 73-75, 78
Alignment, informal:
  defined, 116;
  and geographic distance, 15, 124, 127-132;
  and international organization membership, 15, 122, 127-135
  measures of, 117-120;
  and military alliances, 15, 116, 130-135;
  past and current patterns of, 15, 125-135;
  and socio-political similarity, 15, 120, 121, 127-135
  sources of, 116-138;
  and trade, 15, 124, 127-135
Alliance formation, 58, 64, 123;
  and arms levels, 54, 65, 67;
  and war, 12, 55, 64, 65
Alliances, military, 116, 120;
  predictive power for alignment, 16, 128, 129, 133, 135
Arms races, 214, 237, 319
Attribute distance, 12, 71-113
Attribute theory, defined, 85
Attributes:
  of dyads, 12, 15;
  of the international system, 20;
  national, and foreign behavior, 10, 13, 15, 16, 23, 72, 81, 240-251, 255

Balance of power, 23, 24, 54, 157-162, 165

Capabilities, economic:
  and foreign behavior, 15, 16, 72, 78, 81, 85-96, 106, 108;
  measures of, 78, 95, 124, 257, 261, 269;
  as a measure of war power, 170-172;
  and military expenditures, 15, 171, 243, 244, 249, 257, 266, 269-274
  as predictor to alignment, 16, 123, 127-135;
  as predictor to victory, 177-183

Capabilities, military, 14, 56, 157-162, 165, 243
Capabilities, national:
    assessment of, 14, 15, 54, 183, 243;
    changes in, 14, 53, 56, 64, 68, 160-161, 272-273;
    changes in distribution of, 14, 21, 23, 46, 82, 83;
    distribution of, 21, 23, 24, 35, 45-47, 82, 83, 157-162, 240, 241;
    measurement of, 25, 26, 78, 157-162, 169-172;
    measurement of changes in distribution of, 26-28;
    table of comparisons, 250
Characteristics of nations, see Attributes, national
Commitment, formal:
    vs. informal alignment, 116
Commitment, symbolic, 11, 186-212;
    defined, 187-189
Conflict, 140, 141, 157;
    effect on negotiation, 13, 217-219, 224-225;
    interaction, 12, 13, 16, 141, 142, 144-145, 152, 163-166;
    measurement of, 25, 220, 221, 279, 280;
    relation between foreign and domestic, 13, 15, 69, 276, 291, 294, 297, 298;
    relationship to cooperation, 16, 88, 89, 91, 99, 215, 216, 241;
    and symbolic usage, 190;
    systems, 241-245, 253, 255, 265, 267, 272, 273;
    types of, 276, 278;
    in U.S. foreign behavior, 71-110;
    see also War; Violence
Cooperation:
    against third parties, 12, 116-138;
    and economic similarity, 16, 86-89, 91, 93, 106-109, 123, 124, 127, 128;
    effect on negotiations, 217-219, 227, 233, 234;
    and geographic distance, 16, 83, 91, 94, 108, 124, 125;
    and socio-cultural similarity, 16, 83, 93, 108, 123, 135;
    measurement of, 117-125, 220-222;
    relationship to conflict, 16, 88, 89, 91, 99, 215, 216, 241;
    in U.S. foreign behavior, 71-110
Cost tolerance, 174;
    as an aspect of war power, 172, 173, 179, 182, 183;
    measurement of, 169, 173;
    as predictor to victory, 169, 173, 177, 183

Defense, see Military expenditures
Dyads, 12, 71-113, 117-138, 220, 221, 228-231;
    defined, 78, 117

Economic development, see Capabilities, economic
Escalation:
    patterns of, 13, 16, 17, 162-166, 203-206, 253;

and symbolic commitment, 16, 185-212;
theories of, 145, 152, 153

Field theory, 12, 84
  defined, 76, 77;
  as explanation for U.S. foreign behavior, 109
Foreign aid:
  American, 16, 98-100, 106, 108, 140, 141, 153-157, 165, 166;
  Soviet, 16, 140, 141, 153-157, 165-166
Foreign behavior:
  of centrist states, 290, 294, 297, 298;
  cooperation and conflict in U.S., 71-110;
  and the distribution of national capabilities, 21-24, 35, 45, 52, 53, 82, 86-88,
    92, 106, 109, 240;
  and domestic, 15, 276, 291, 294, 297, 298;
  effect of economic development on, 16, 86-89, 91, 93, 98, 106-109, 123-128,
    240-274;
  effect of socio-cultural similarity on, 16, 83, 93, 98, 108, 109, 123, 135;
  and geographic distance, 16, 83, 91, 94, 108, 124, 135;
  and national attributes, 10, 13, 15, 16, 23, 72, 81, 86, 106, 240-251, 255;
  of personalist states, 290, 291, 294, 298;
  and political structure, 15, 78, 93, 102, 106, 108, 121, 123, 135, 276, 277,
    297, 298;
  of polyarchic states, 290, 291, 294, 298;
  prior and subsequent levels of conflict in, 291, 294, 296, 298;
  and relative status, 15, 21, 22, 50-69, 82, 87, 109;
  six types of U.S., 98-106

Geographic distance:
  and alignment patterns, 16, 124, 127-132;
  and foreign behavior, 16, 83, 91, 94, 108, 124, 135;
  measurement of, 124

Homogeneity, see Socio-cultural similarity
Hostile reaction theory, 144, 145, 152, 165

Influence, of Superpowers over Arab-Israeli violence, 16, 140-142, 153-157,
    165-166;
  see also Power
Interactions of nations, 10, 12, 13, 116, 187;
  in negotiations, 219, 233, 235
International environment, 11, 17;
  effects on negotiation, 216

International organizations
    shared membership in as predictor to alignment, 15, 122, 127-133;
    and arms levels, 66;
    and status inconsistency, 55, 65
International system, 20, 50, 82, 120;
    structural characteristics of, 10, 11, 17, 47, 66
Involvement, see Commitment

Learning theory, 144, 145, 153

Macroscopic perspective, see Aggregate perspective
Military expenditures:
    and alliance aggregation, 12, 54, 65, 67;
    causes of increasing, 16, 241-245, 257, 265, 308;
    congressional attitudes towards, 315-317;
    effect of war on public attitudes towards, 311, 312;
    effects of population and technology on, 15, 243, 244, 249, 255, 257, 266,
        269-274;
    and international organizations, 55, 65, 66;
    as a measure of power, 26, 158-162, 171;
    measurement of increases in, 58;
    public opinion toward, 15, 300-319;
    and trade, 13, 257, 261, 266, 268-273;
    trends in, 273, 274, 313;
    and war, 13, 15, 55, 65, 66, 69, 158-162, 166, 245, 319

Negotiation:
    definition of, 215;
    process, 216, 219, 233
Negotiating behavior:
    effect of endogenous factors on, 217-219, 224-235;
    effect of positive attitudes on, 219, 233-235;
    symmetry of, 16, 216, 229-235

Parity-fluidity model, 35-46;
    see also Capabilities, national; Power parity
Peace, 9, 14, 207;
    and the distribution of power, 14, 19, 35, 43, 45;
    as a relationship between conflict and cooperation, 16, 88, 89;
    research, 10, 17, 48, 50;
    systems, 240-274
Pecking order, see, Status, distribution of
Population, as indicator of national power, 26, 78, 170

Population growth:
   and conflict, 15, 68, 240-243, 259;
   effect on military expenditures, 15, 243, 244, 249, 266, 272-274
Population loss, as predictor to victory, 175-182
Power:
   as a measure of achieved status, 15, 86-89, 102, 106;
   measures of, 25, 26, 78, 157-162, 169-172;
   parity, 12, 15, 19, 24, 25, 45, 46, 92, 102, 109;
   as predictor to victory, 14, 15, 167-183;
   preponderance, 12, 15, 19, 24, 25, 45, 46, 102, 109;
   vs. prestige, 21;
   as a relationship, 77;
   relative distribution of, 12, 14, 21-24, 35, 45-47, 82, 83, 92, 108, 240-241;
   vs. status, 109;
   see also Balance of power, Capabilities, War Power
Preponderance-Stability model, 35, 41, 43, 45, 46
Pre-theory of James Rosenau, 15, 71, 81, 100, 106
Prestige, national, 12, 15, 22, 86;
   vs. power, 21;
   see also Status
Public opinion:
   and symbolic usage, 209-210;
   and U.S. military expenditures, 300-319

Ranking, see Status

Socio-cultural similarity:
   and alignment, 16, 123, 127, 128, 131, 132, 135;
   and foreign behavior, 83, 93, 98, 108, 109, 123, 135;
   measurement of, 120, 121
Stability:
   of alignment patterns, 16, 137;
   of attitudes toward defense, 16, 300, 309;
   of cooperation and conflict patterns, 16;
   of international system, and distribution of power, 12, 23, 24, 43-47
Status, national:
   achieved vs. ascribed, 15, 50-53;
   distribution of, 12, 14, 21, 47, 58, 82;
   and foreign behavior, 50-53, 82, 86, 89-91, 102, 108, 109
Status inconsistency:
   and alliance formation, 54, 55, 64, 67;
   causes of, 52, 87;
   defined, 12, 50-53, 87;
   and international organizations, 55, 66;
   measurement of, 58;
   symbols and escalation, 190, 196-198, 202, 205;

and war, 12, 15, 50-53, 63-69, 87, 102
Structure:
    of international system, 11, 12, 66;
    of major power subsystem, 21
Subsystem:
    of major powers, 21, 22, 23;
    maintenance, 122, 123;
    Middle Eastern, 141, 142;
    Scandinavian, 246
Symbolic commitment, see Commitment, symbolic

Technological development, see Capabilities, economic
Tensions, international, 49, 69, 153, 214
Trade:
    effect on Arab-Israeli conflict of American and Soviet, 12, 16, 140, 141,
        153-157, 165, 166;
    as a measure of cooperation, 96-98, 122;
    and military expenditures, 13, 257, 261, 266, 268-273;
    predictive power for alignment, 15, 122, 127-135

Uncertainty, as a cause of war, 12, 23, 24, 26, 45-48, 183

Violence:
    action-reaction patterns of, 12, 163-165;
    and aggressive symbols, 190, 199;
    Arab-Israeli, 139-166;
    foreign and domestic, 13, 69, 276, 277, 291;
    sources of international, 10, 12, 14, 23, 24, 47, 165, 183, 186;
    theories of, 144-145, 152, 153, 163;
    see also Conflict; War

War:
    and military expenditures, 13, 15, 55, 65, 66, 69, 158-162, 166, 214, 237,
        245, 319;
    status inconsistency as a cause of 50, 53, 54, 87, 102;
    and the structural conditions of the international system, 48;
    in the twentieth vs. nineteenth centuries, 14, 48;
    uncertainty as a cause of, 23, 45-48;
    and alliance aggregation, 55, 64, 65;
    and assessment of national capabilities, 14, 15, 54, 183;
    and international tensions, 66, 69;
    and differential rates of national capability changes, 14, 52, 53, 160-162,
        273;
    and pressures of population and technology, 13, 243-246, 273, 274;

and the relative distribution of national capabilities, 14, 21-24, 34, 35, 45-58, 157-162, 165, 241;
see also, Conflict; Violence
War power:
    and cost tolerance, 167-183;
    measurement of, 25, 26, 169-172;
    theories of, 13, 167-172;
    see also Power; Capabilities, military; Capabilities, national
Wealth, national, see Capabilities, economic

CONTRIBUTORS

STUART BREMER is Assistant Professor of Political Science at the University of Michigan and a co-investigator in the Correlates of War Project. He completed his Ph.D. at Michigan State University in 1970, with a dissertation entitled "National and International Systems: A Computer Simulation."

NAZLI CHOUCRI received her Ph.D. from Stanford University in 1967, and is now Assistant Professor of Political Science at M.I.T. She has written several articles on international alignments and non-alignment, analyses of conflict, and on forecasting methodologies. She is co-author (with Robert C. North) of the forthcoming *Nations in Conflict: Prelude to World War I.* Her current research focuses on the political consequences of population dynamics, resource constraints, and technological development.

BETTY CRUMP HANSON received her Ph.D. in 1966 from Columbia University, writing on "American Diplomatic Representatives to the Soviet Union, 1933-1945: A Study of Political Reporting." She is now an Associate in Research with the World Data Analysis Program at Yale University.

P. TERRENCE HOPMANN is Assistant Professor of Political Science and Assistant Director of the Center of International Studies at the University of Minnesota. He received his B.A. from Princeton University in 1964 and his Ph.D. from Stanford University in 1969. He is co-author with Ole R. Holsti and John D. Sullivan of *International Alliances: Unity and Disintegration.*

JEFFREY S. MILSTEIN received his Ph.D. from Stanford University in 1970. He then taught at Michigan State University, and is now at Yale University. His interests include conflict and peace research in general, and the Vietnam War and Arab-Israeli conflict in particular. He has delivered more than a dozen papers on these topics, and his dissertation, "The Escalation of the Vietnam War, 1965-67: A Quantitative Analysis and Predictive Computer Simulation," will be published shortly by the Ohio State University Press.

STEVEN ROSEN received his Ph.D. in Political Science from Syracuse University in 1970. He then taught at the University of Pittsburgh, and is now at Brandeis University. He is co-editor of *Alliance in International Politics* and author of a number of articles on war and other aspects of international politics.

RUDOLPH J. RUMMEL received his Ph.D. from Northwestern University in 1963, and subsequently taught at Indiana University and Yale University. He is currently Professor of Political Science and Director of the Dimensionality of

Nations Project at the University of Hawaii. Chairman of the Interpolimetrics Section of the International Studies Association, he has written *Applied Factor Analysis*, the forthcoming *Dimensions of Nations*, and numerous articles.

BRUCE M. RUSSETT received his Ph.D. in 1961 from Yale University, where he is now Professor of Political Science and Director of the World Data Analysis Program. He has held appointments at M.I.T., Columbia, Michigan, and the University of Brussels. The most recent of his books on international politics are *What Price Vigilance? The Burdens of National Defense*, and *No Clear and Present Danger: A Skeptical View of the United States Entry Into World War II.*

J. DAVID SINGER, Professor of Political Science at the University of Michigan, has also been asociated with New York University, Vassar College, The Naval War College, and the Universities of Oslo and Geneva. Among his books are *Financing International Organization: The United Nations Budget Process; Deterrence, Arms Control and Disarmament; Human Behavior and International Politics: Contributions from the Social-Psychological Sciences; Quantitative International Politics: Insights and Evidence;* and *The Wages of War, 1816-1965: A Statistical Handbook.*

JOHN STUCKEY is a graduate student and teaching fellow in the Department of Political Science at the University of Michigan. He served in the Foreign Service of the United States Information Agency from 1964 to 1967 and has been associated with the Correlates of War research project since 1970.

JOHN D. SULLIVAN, Assistant Professor of Political Science, Yale University, received his Ph.D. from Stanford University in 1969. His research interests include formal alliances, informal alignments, and international cooperation concerning pollution and resource allocation. He is co-author, with Ole Holsti and P. Terrence Hopmann, of *International Alliances: Unity and Disintegration.*

MICHAEL P. SULLIVAN received his Ph.D. from the University of Oregon in 1968, and is currently Assistant Professor of Government at the University of Arizona.

MICHAEL DAVID WALLACE was born in 1943 in Montreal, Canada. He received his B.A. in 1964 and M.A. in 1965 at McGill University, and his Ph.D. at the University of Michigan in 1970. From 1967 to 1968 he was engaged in research at the United Nations in Geneva. He is at present Assistant Professor of Political Science at the University of British Columbia in Vancouver, Canada.

JONATHAN WILKENFELD received his Ph.D. in Political Science from Indiana University in 1969 and is now Assistant Professor of Government and Politics at the University of Maryland. His publications include *Conflict Behavior and Linkage Politics* (editor, forthcoming) and a number of articles.